Media Technologies

Inside Technology

edited by Wiebe E. Bijker, W. Bernard Carlson, and Trevor Pinch

Media Technologies

Essays on Communication, Materiality, and Society

edited by Tarleton Gillespie, Pablo J. Boczkowski, and Kirsten A. Foot

The MIT Press
Cambridge, Massachusetts
London, England

This book was set in Stone by the MIT Press. Printed and bound in the United States of America.

Library of Congress Cataloging-in-Publication Data

Media technologies : essays on communication, materiality, and society / edited by Tarleton Gillespie, Pablo J. Boczkowski, and Kirsten A. Foot.
    p.   cm. — (Inside technology)
Includes bibliographical references and index.
ISBN 978-0-262-52537-4 (pbk. : alk. paper)
1. Digital media. 2. Communication and technology. I. Gillespie, Tarleton, editor of compilation. II. Boczkowski, Pablo J., editor of compilation. III. Foot, Kirsten A., editor of compilation.
P96.T42M43   2014
302.23'1—dc23
2013014966

10 9 8 7 6 5 4 3 2

Contents

About the Contributors

Pablo J. Boczkowski is professor and director of the Program in Media, Technology and Society at Northwestern University. He is the author of *Digitizing the News: Innovation in Online Newspapers* (MIT Press, 2004), *News at Work: Imitation in an Age of Information Abundance* (University of Chicago Press, 2010), and, together with Eugenia Mitchelstein, *The News Gap: When the Information Preferences of the Media and the Public Diverge* (MIT Press, 2013), as well as over thirty journal articles and book chapters. His projects include a study of the demise of print newspapers as a window into understanding how institutions decay.

Geoffrey C. Bowker is professor at the School of Information and Computer Science, University of California at Irvine, where he directs the Evoke Laboratory (http://evoke.ics.uci.edu). Recent positions include professor of and senior scholar in cyberscholarship at the University of Pittsburgh iSchool and executive director, Center for Science, Technology and Society, Santa Clara University. Together with Leigh Star he wrote *Sorting Things Out: Classification and Its Consequences* (MIT Press, 1999); his most recent book is *Memory Practices in the Sciences: 1830–1990* (MIT Press, 2006).

Finn Brunton is an assistant professor of information in the Department of Media, Culture, and Communication at the Steinhardt School, NYU. He is the author of *Spam: A Shadow History of the Internet* (MIT Press, 2013). His other projects include a collaboration with an online/print-on-demand publishing venture, the Office of Net Assessments, and research for a book in progress on encrypted currencies.

Gabriella Coleman is the Wolfe Chair in Scientific and Technological Literacy in the Department of Art History and Communication Studies at McGill University. She is the author of *Coding Freedom: The Ethics and Aesthetics of Hacking* (Princeton University Press, 2013) and is working on a book for Verso on the politics of Anonymous and digital activism.

Gregory J. Downey is a professor in both the School of Journalism & Mass Communication and the School of Library & Information Studies at the University of Wisconsin-Madison. He is the author of *Closed Captioning: Subtitling, Stenography, and the Digital Convergence of Text with Television* (Johns Hopkins University Press, 2008) and *Telegraph Messenger Boys: Labor, Technology, and Geography, 1850–1950* (Routledge, 2002). His research attempts to uncover and analyze information labor over time and space.

Kirsten A. Foot is an associate professor of communication and adjunct faculty in the Information School at the University of Washington. She is the lead author of *Web Campaigning* (MIT Press, 2006) and coeditor of *The Internet and National Elections* (Routledge, 2007). She coedits the Acting with Technology series at MIT Press, and is writing a book on interorganizational and multisector collaboration in efforts to combat human trafficking.

Tarleton Gillespie is an associate professor in the Department of Communication and Department of Information Science at Cornell University. He is the author of *Wired Shut: Copyright and the Shape of Digital Culture* (MIT Press, 2007), and cofounder of the scholarly blog *Culture Digitally* (http://culturedigitally.org). His research is supported by the National Science Foundation and Intel Research. His forthcoming book (Yale University Press) examines the way social media platforms set and enforce rules about disreputable content, and how their approaches for private content governance impact the contours of public discourse online.

Steven J. Jackson is an associate professor in the Department of Information Science at Cornell University, with graduate field appointments in Communication, Science and Technology Studies, and Public Affairs. His research on technology maintenance and repair, collaboration, and science technology policy has been supported by the Ford Foundation, World Bank, Intel Research, the Social Science Research Council, and a U.S. National Science Foundation CAREER award. His work has appeared in *Science, Technology and Human Values, Technology and Culture, The Journal of the Association for Information Systems, Information and Organization, Computer-Human Interaction,* and *Computer-Supported Cooperative Work.*

Christopher M. Kelty is an associate professor at UCLA with appointments in the departments of Information Studies and Anthropology and the Institute for Society and Genetics. He is the author of *Two Bits: The Cultural Significance of Free Software* (Duke University Press, 2008), and articles on the culture, politics, and philosophy of software, nanotechnology, and biology.

Leah A. Lievrouw   is a professor in the Department of Information Studies at the University of California, Los Angeles. Her research and writing focus on social theories of new media and information technologies and social/cultural change. Her most recent book, *Alternative and Activist New Media* (Polity Press, 2011) explores the ways that artists and activists use new media technologies to challenge mainstream culture, politics, and society. With Sonia Livingstone, she is coeditor of the four-volume *Benchmarks in Communication: New Media* (Sage, 2009) and *The Handbook of New Media*, 2nd ed. (Sage, 2006). Her works in progress include *Media and Meaning: Communication Technology and Society* (Oxford University Press, forthcoming) and *Foundations of Media and Communication Theory: Communication and Technology* (Blackwell, forthcoming).

Sonia Livingstone   is a professor in the Department of Media and Communications at the London School of Economics and Political Science. She is author or editor of seventeen books, including *Audiences and Publics* (ed., Intellect, 2005), *The Handbook of New Media* (ed., with Leah Lievrouw, Sage, 2006), *Children and the Internet* (Polity, 2009), *Media Consumption and Public Engagement* (with Nick Couldry and Tim Markham, Palgrave, 2010), *Media Regulation* (with Peter Lunt, Sage, 2012), and *Meanings of Audiences* (ed., with Richard Butch, Routledge, 2013).

Ignacio Siles   is a PhD candidate in the Department of Communication Studies at Northwestern University. His doctoral dissertation examines issues pertaining to the stabilization and use of new media through an analysis of the historical development of blogs in the United States and France. He has authored articles in *Communication Theory, Journal of Computer-Mediated Communication, New Media & Society, Social Studies of Science*, and *The Information Society*.

Jonathan Sterne   teaches in the Department of Art History and Communication Studies and the History and Philosophy of Science Program at McGill University. He is author of *MP3: The Meaning of a Format* (2012, Duke University Press), *The Audible Past: Cultural Origins of Sound Reproduction* (2003, Duke University Press); and numerous articles on media, technologies and the politics of culture. He is also editor of *The Sound Studies Reader* (Routledge, 2012). Visit his website at http://sterneworks.org.

Lucy Suchman   is professor of anthropology of science and technology in the Department of Sociology at Lancaster University, and codirector of Lancaster's Centre for Science Studies. Before taking up her present post she spent twenty years as a researcher at Xerox's Palo Alto Research Center.

In 2010 she received the ACM Special Interest Group in Computer-Human Interaction Lifetime Research Award. Her writings include *Human-Machine Reconfigurations* (Cambridge University Press, 2007).

Fred Turner   is an associate professor in the Department of Communication and director of the Program in Science, Technology, and Society at Stanford University. He is the author of several books, including *From Counterculture to Cyberculture: Stewart Brand, the Whole Earth Network, and the Rise of Digital Utopianism* (University of Chicago Press, 2006) and most recently, *The Democratic Surround: Multimedia and American Liberalism from World War II to the Psychedelic Sixties* (University of Chicago Press, 2014).

Editors' Acknowledgments

We are indebted to Margy Avery at MIT Press for pitching the idea for this volume to us, and for her encouragement and advice throughout the process of developing it. Feedback from anonymous reviewers and from Trevor Pinch was invaluable at several stages of development, as was Nancy Bixler's outstanding copyediting. Finally, we are very grateful for the financial support provided for this volume by the departments in which we work at Cornell University, Northwestern University, and the University of Washington.

1 Introduction

Tarleton Gillespie, Pablo J. Boczkowski, and Kirsten A. Foot

Beyond the Plateau

This volume is both an invitation to those scholars who have undertaken the study of media technologies and a provocation to the broader fields and traditions in which they work. We believe a productive plateau has been reached, wherein distinct intellectual trajectories originating from disparate fields have gathered around a common purpose: to understand media technologies as complex, sociomaterial phenomena. In much of contemporary scholarship, media technologies are no longer treated as things that simply happen to society, but rather as the product of distinct human and institutional efforts. They are not seen as emissaries of revolution or harbingers of imminent disaster, but as constructs richly etched with the politics, presumptions, and worldviews of their designers. They are not necessarily fulcrums of change in people's lives, but protruding bits of material culture that incorporate into and sometimes press upon the lived practices of their users. They are not gleaming icons of the new, but have specific historical trajectories as individual objects and as the residue of societal ambitions.

Still, though social researchers[1] of media and of technology should, by now, be able to easily enjoy fruitful exchanges of ideas, efforts to engage in substantive conversation have too often been constrained by two impediments. First, in communication and media scholarship, the overwhelming focus has been on texts, the industry that produces them, and the viewers that consume them; the materiality of these devices and networks has been consistently overlooked. News, in the study of media, has been typically construed as paragraphs on a page, rather than the page itself; the headlines are examined, but not the newsboys who shout them, the teletypes that clatter them out, or the code that now renders them into clickable hyperlinks. This has made it difficult to examine media not merely as messages that affect minds, but as social relations by other means, an engagement of people through information and through things, that happens to use words, sounds, and images as social currency.

When media scholars have turned their attention to the technology involved, they have rarely attended to "the tightly-interwoven relationship between the material and the symbolic" (Boczkowski and Lievrouw 2008, 967). Instead, explicitly or by omission, they have tended to cling to the assertion that the technology is neutral with respect to the communication being undertaken—or have leapt to its opposite, to seductive and often naïve forms of technological determinism, proclaiming the things themselves as ushering in dramatic change.

The turn to digital, networked media technologies has begun to move this literature past this first impediment. But the field of communication and media studies has always been a distinctly heterogeneous intellectual space, stitched together as a loose patchwork rather than emerging as a family tree from common roots of inquiry. So when communication and media scholars' attention turned to the digital, it happened in many places and for many reasons, with an intellectual response that was far from cohesive.

Social psychologists interested in interpersonal communication and collaboration began exploring computer-mediated communication in the 1990s. While this research has made important advances in understanding the mediation of cognition, conversation, and group dynamics (see Kalman et al. 2006; Kraut et al. 1998; Parks and Floyd 1996; Walther 2011), it has been more interested in using the technology as a convenient opportunity for plumbing the complexity of human communication per se than in problematizing the technology. During the same period the study of mass media also shifted its attention to digital media and the Internet (Chaffee and Metzger 2001; Morris and Ogan 1996; Newhagen and Rafaeli 1996; see also Walther, Gay, and Hancock 2005). More often than not, this work borrowed conceptual and theoretical lenses developed in earlier studies of traditional print and broadcast media: media effects (Metzger 2009; Shah, McLeod, and Yoon 2001; Walther 2011), uses and gratifications theory (Althaus and Tewksbury 2000; Papacharissi 2012), and audience studies (Baym 2000; Silverstone and Hirsch 1992). Critical political economists, who cut their teeth on the highly concentrated media industries, posited the nascent digital industry as simply continuing or exacerbating this oligopolistic control (Bagdikian 2004; McChesney 2004). Media ecologists began to fasten the "information revolution" onto their histories of broad, media-driven social change (Kittler 1999; Levinson 1997); cultural studies scholars championed "cyberculture studies" as an emergent interdiscipline (Silver 2000; Silver and Massanari 2006).

So, while many scholars in the field of communication and media studies do now address information technologies, most have done so in ways that enact, either explicitly or by omission, a deterministic understanding of technology as one of the following: the intervening variable that explains a measurable change, the historical catalyst that explains a social shift, or the tool with which passive audiences can finally succumb to or resist the tyranny of mass culture.

There have been exceptions to this tendency. Raymond Williams, back in 1974, urged us to look beyond claims that media change our world, for "behind all such statements lie some of the most difficult and most unresolved historical and philosophical questions. The questions are not posed by the statements; indeed they are ordinarily masked by them" (9). Roger Silverstone (1994) later noted the "double articulation" of communication technologies as being at once a tool for conveying meaning, and a meaningful thing in its own right. Both of these analyses, though focused on television, proved influential for scholars of the digital technologies to follow. And all along, cultural historians were revealing communication technologies as the product of social forces and specific contexts, whether they be electricity (Marvin 1988), radio (Douglas 1987), the telephone (Fischer 1992), television (Williams 1974; Spigel 1992), computer systems (Edwards 1996), or the Internet (Abbate 1999) and the web (Turner 2006).

By the late 1990s, information technologies were becoming a more embedded part of social practice, and more and more central to the circulation of news, entertainment, and public discourse. Although social researchers were not always quick to respond, there were calls, from scholars and funders, to study Internet technologies and their social impact. For media scholars, it was the rapid technological change that seemed to most warrant explanation: the texts and genres of new media have been difficult to analyze, in part because they are so prolific and so evanescent. This helped to foreground the material technology over the symbolic content. And although both stakeholders and commenters too often wrapped these technologies in breathless hyperbole, their overstated proclamations themselves may have helped make it so apparent that more nuanced social, political, cultural, behavioral, and historical understandings were required. In response, some communication and media scholars—eager to get a handle on these new artifacts and practices, but troubled by the way the sociotechnical was so often bracketed, reified, or entirely overlooked—began to look for intellectual resources elsewhere.

A more nuanced debate about the impact and complexity of the material artifact had been going on in sociology, history, anthropology, and philosophy of technology, particularly under the rubric of science and technology studies (STS). This comparatively smaller but vibrant domain of inquiry was also in part a response to the very same notions (technology as neutral, technology as revolutionary) evident in communication and media studies, but focused on public and political understandings of technology. To counter these assumptions, STS scholars took as their central concern the ways that materiality, practice, and politics are necessarily entangled. In contrast to most work in communication and media studies, STS scholars debated the ramifications of the material without oversimplifying it, and posited these sociotechnical ensembles as situated historically and in specific social and political contexts.

However—and here we reach the second impediment that has hindered efforts to engage in substantive conversation—until recently, STS-based scholars have largely overlooked media technologies. Perhaps because they had to justify themselves to colleagues studying the "hard" sciences, and to scientists and engineers skeptical of their entire undertaking, STS scholars have preferred studying those technologies perceived to be important, serious, historic, substantial—particularly those involved in industry and engineering, knowledge production, the military, and transportation. There has been no STS-based analysis of the Internet or the World Wide Web on par with Latour's (1996) experimental French train systems, Winner's (1980) bridges, Vaughan's (1997) space shuttle disaster, or Pinch and Bijker's (1984) bicycles.

The attention STS scholars have paid to information technologies has tended to focus on the computerization of work practices and environments. Most prominent among this work, which many of the contributors to this volume see as formative intellectual predicates for their own scholarship, are the "social informatics" approach championed by Rob Kling (1996), the early work of Lucy Suchman (1987) within the field of Computer Supported Cooperative Work (CSCW), the attention paid to information practices and infrastructures by Geoffrey Bowker and Susan Leigh Star (1999), Steve Woolgar's (1991, 2002) "configured user" and "virtual society" projects, the use of activity theory by Bonnie Nardi and others (Nardi 1996; Kaptelinin and Nardi 2006) to examine systemic contradictions in the cultural-historical trajectories of technologies, and Andrew Feenberg's (1991, 1999) critical theory of technology.

Over the course of the last decade, this ideational meeting point, between communication and media studies on the one hand and science and technology studies on the other, is where fruitful intellectual exchanges have emerged. Theoretical perspectives originating in STS, particularly the social shaping of technology and actor network theory, have been taken up by communication and media studies scholars working on digital media. Some STS scholars studying information and computer technologies (ICTs) began tying their work to communication and media studies to better attend to the symbolic dimensions of these tools. In the annual international conference of the STS field, the Society for the Social Study of Science (4S), attention to new media has grown over the past decade from a panel here or there to multiple streams of presentations, preconference events, and even keynotes. In the communication and media studies journals and conferences that attended to new media, the theoretical vocabulary of STS began to take hold.

These are the routes through which social researchers of media technologies have reached the current plateau of an emergent community of scholars with some common insights and aims. They have fended off the slippery presumption of technological determinism and legitimated media technologies as a worthy object of scholarly analysis. They have made the case that the study of media technologies, to be compelling, must contextualize the technology historically, culturally, and systemically, and explicate the social, material, and temporal dimensions of how technologies are produced, deployed, configured, and used. They have grappled with the conceptual changes made salient by digital, networked media: decentralization of production, ubiquity of access, the disintegration of the mass/interpersonal distinction, the resurgence of the amateur, the modularity and opacity of software, the fluid shape of networked knowledge, and the laterally connected practices of social meaning. They have brought the intellectual tensions between structure and agency, control and resistance, and change and stasis—so fundamental to social and cultural theory of the last century—to the fluid technological landscape of this one. Leaders from this community, many now mid-career, have made inroads in convincing their home disciplines of both STS and communication and media studies that nuanced social research into media technologies is a relevant part of the broader disciplinary aims. As editors, our primary purpose for producing this volume was to provide some conceptual paths forward for future scholarship within this community and beyond.

Though terminology and angle of approach may differ, similar directions are being pursued in recent work in media and cultural studies (Bruns 2008; Gitelman 2006; Jenkins 2006; Varnelis 2008), in the ethnographies of digital cultural practices (Ito et al. 2009; boyd 2010; Gray 2009; Baym and Burnett 2009), in the materialist turn being explored in cultural theory (Berry 2011; Galloway 2004; Gane and Beer 2008; Packer and Crofts Wiley

2011; Parikka 2012), in game studies (Bogost 2012; Monfort and Bogost 2009; Taylor 2006), in debates in media theory and elsewhere on the concepts of "mediation" and "mediatization" (Couldry 2008; Lievrouw 2009; Mansell 2012; Silverstone 2005; Wajcman and Jones 2012), in the scholarship on information policy (Benkler 2007; Cohen 2012; Lessig 1999; Nissenbaum 2009; Zittrain 2008), and in critical information studies (Dourish 2004; Edwards 1996). This volume builds on and extends facets of the intellectual project of each of these works.

But what should come next? There have been some suggestions as to how to move forward from this plateau, how to most fruitfully extend contemporary inquiry into media, technology, and society. These fall into three categories. Some propose to identify key dynamics of new media, meso-level qualities sufficiently common to all media technologies that, extracted from their specific contexts, can be held up as defining characteristics, or at least distinctive ones. These conceptual vocabularies—numerical representation, automation, modularity, variability, transcoding (Manovich 2001); accessibility, peer-to-peer, value at the edges, aggregation (Ito 2008); network, information, interface, archive, interactivity, simulation (Gane and Beer 2008)—provide scholars ways to pin a social consequence to a dynamic, rather than to a particular tool or to "new media" in their entirety. At the same time, these terms can easily become unmoored and dizzying as they proliferate.

Others propose a more diligent attention to the complexity of new media technologies, shedding old analytical frameworks that prove too constrictive. Lievrouw and Livingstone (2006), for example, propose to replace a linear understanding of traditional media with a heuristic that has predictable components, but does not presume beforehand how those components are related in any given context:

We do not specify *a priori* any set relationship among the three component processes of infrastructure. Where the mass communication tradition has spent decades struggling with and, more recently, unpacking the linear relationship among production, text, and audience (i.e., production makes texts which have effects or impacts on audiences, consistent with the sender-message-receiver model of communication), in new media research no such linear assumption is necessary . . . it is precisely the dynamic links and interdependencies among artefacts, practices and social arrangements that should guide our analytic focus (3).

Tools designed to examine "mass media" or "mass society" will no longer suffice; the "multiple, shifting configurations" (5) of the network provide a more appropriate metaphor.

In his recent work, Sterne (2012) offers a different take on the complexity of media technologies, proposing that we "modulate the scale of our analysis of media somewhat differently. Mediality happens on multiple scales and time frames. Studying formats highlights smaller registers like software, operating standards, and codes, as well as larger registers like infrastructures, international corporate consortia, and whole technical systems" (11).

Finally, some social researchers of media and technology argue that it is not sufficient to merely acknowledge complexity, that scholarship has an obligation to work toward conceptual frameworks that enable more robust analyses. For example, Boczkowski and Lievrouw (2008) propose not just to recognize a perennial tension between determination and contingency, but also to note that the tension plays out differently in different contexts: "future work might address the particular conditions that may tilt the balance towards determination or contingency, or the specific mechanisms and processes that 'harden' sociotechnical configurations under certain conditions, or make them more malleable in others" (966).

In producing this volume, we do not seek to map all the intersecting scholarship on media technologies, or to merely showcase the new and exciting work happening at its cusp. Instead, we want to propose new questions and pathways, where scholars of media technologies might want to go next, given not only the theoretical exchange now occurring but also what the shifting media and information landscape now makes possible and, arguably, requires or even demands of us. We hope the volume can be a starting point for just that.

How This Collection Came to Be

This volume began with Margy Avery, a senior acquisitions editor at MIT Press. She sought us out as dialogue partners about the streams of work she had observed at recent STS and communication and media conferences, and suggested that we develop a scholarly collection that mapped the intersections of communication and media studies, and science and technology studies. One model she proposed was a collection she had helped develop a few years earlier, Pinch and Swedberg's 2008 volume, *Living in a Material World: Economic Sociology Meets Science and Technology Studies*. But soon after embarking on the project, we had to acknowledge that the approach taken by Pinch and Swedberg would not work with our own fields. While economic sociology is a specific domain of inquiry housed within the field of sociology, communication is a field unto itself, and one with sprawling subfields and somewhat porous boundaries. Were we to attempt to address *all* the ways in which ideas in STS intersect with the field of communication, much less all the ways it conceivably might, we would need to incorporate journalism studies, bibliometrics, sociolinguistics, political economy, management and organization, the rhetoric of science, education, and so on.

Instead, we wanted the collection to identify and enliven the key conceptual challenges for scholars devoted to the study of media and information technologies across the fields of communication and media studies and STS. Soon we latched on to a different model: Bijker, Hughes, and Pinch's landmark 1987 collection, *The Social Construction of Technological Systems*. More than representing the Venn diagram overlap of two fields, that collection articulated an emerging intellectual project that grew from those fields, and in some ways called that project into being. Since its publication, that collection has served as a benchmark for that intellectual project as it has moved forward. All three of us have found value in Bijker, Hughes, and Pinch's collection (often known as the "school bus" book because of its stark, two-toned cover) for how it opened up for us a new space of inquiry. We have sought to craft a collection of essays and commentaries, which, when read together, offer similarly provocative and agenda-guiding insights that may inspire others to break new conceptual ground in the social research of media and technology.

We began by inviting potential contributors whose scholarship we knew already spoke both to and about these fields and the intersections between them, who had made important empirical contributions in this arena, and who offered conceptual tools and insights that transcend their respective empirical cases and illuminate potential paths forward in the study of media technologies. Though we tried to err on the side of editorial restraint, to allow contributors to develop essays that sprang from their own thinking and that made the contribution they most wanted to make, we did make one stipulation: that each step back from the particulars of their work and methodological interests to reflect on underlying areas of conceptual concern that build from or speak to theorizing media technologies.

However, we did not want to enlist such accomplished scholars and then ask them to labor alone to produce essays that would merely share adjacent pages. One of the reasons the Bijker, Hughes, and Pinch volume is so strong is that it emerged from a face-to-face workshop designed to push the sociology and history of technology forward; the individual essays, though exploring quite different theoretical avenues, read like a coherent conversation when taken together. So it was extremely important to us that our collection develop a similar coherence. Toward that end we would need to engage in focused dialogue together, at each stage of the volume development process, about the ideas and gaps in the work we had read and the work we had produced.

This effort took a number of forms. First, contributors provided a short abstract of the essay they planned to develop. These abstracts were circulated with the entire group, and became objects of discussion between the contributor and one of the editors. The contributors then produced three-thousand-word sketches of their essays, which also were circulated, in anticipation of an intensive day-long workshop (preceded by a substantially less intensive dinner) that took place just before the 2011 4S conference in Cleveland. There, at the Great Lakes Science Center overlooking chilly Lake Erie, we worked in pairs to swap feedback on the essays we were preparing, then met in groups organized around commonalities among them to identify connections and oversights. As editors, we also provided the contributors with a concept map of eleven meso-level concepts we felt live in and across the fields of communication and STS, and asked them to draw where their essays were situated in relation to these concepts. These impromptu visualizations became another opportunity for discussion of what the entire collection had in common. We continued and expanded these discussions in a lively and well-attended roundtable at the 4S conference itself.

Following the Cleveland conference, the contributors developed drafts of their essays. We editors discussed how the essays might speak to each other, and decided on the two groups of four that form the two main parts of the collection. The contributors then peer-reviewed each of the other essays in their part. We saw this as important for two reasons: first, each author enjoyed the benefit of several sets of talented eyes during the writing process; second, seeing the other three essays helped contributors to sharpen their own. All of the drafts and the comments were made available to the entire group. A draft of this introduction was also posted to the group, where feedback and criticism were solicited.

In addition, it was important to us to tie these essays to a longer legacy of scholarship. We therefore invited four scholars who have had a deep impact on the social, cultural, and historical study of media technologies to each serve as discussants for one of the parts of essays we have assembled. We did not want these to be afterthoughts, pasted onto the volume. The discussants were urged to not only comment on each essay in their part but to also illuminate points of intersection among them, and to relate the problems probed in the essays to other veins of thought.

We asked a great deal of the participants in this volume, and we are deeply grateful not only for what they delivered but also for the willingness and good spirits they offered along the way. The overarching goal of all of this editorial orchestration, this great taxing of our colleagues and friends in which we engaged, was to produce a volume that would gather the scholarship under a single umbrella while giving back to that scholarship a set of dialogical provocations that might serve the field well by providing fertile starting points for the next wave of scholarship.

In our efforts to collect this work, articulate vexing problems, and find common threads in scholarship on media technologies, we have crafted two sets of essays and commentaries that we believe illuminate some useful paths forward. The first addresses materiality and the mediation that produces and embeds new forms of knowledge and expression; the second addresses the practices and meanings that maintain the sociomaterial formations that are media technologies by animating, building, translating, and repairing them. This is not to say that these are the only two possible directions. The volume reveals both some common assertions and some rich diversity and disagreement. But it does attempt to hold a focus on these two thorny sets of issues, showing how they are vital to understanding media technologies but also fundamental to the study of communication and society. Thus, what started as a mapping exercise about the past and present turned into a more programmatic attempt to chart future pathways in the study of this domain of inquiry. Revealing where we have been motivated reflections on where we might go next.

Part I: The Materiality of Mediated Knowledge and Expression

At the most fundamental level, media technologies are about the linkages between the symbolic and the material. That is, all technologies have a symbolic dimension, but media technologies have distinctive, material capabilities to embed, transform, and make accessible symbolic content such as news stories, novels, movies, and songs. How to best characterize the relationship between these two dimensions has been a longstanding concern of scholarship about media technologies. The four essays in part I offer different, yet related ways to account for those linkages at the intersection of communication and media studies and STS.

In chapter 2, Leah A. Lievrouw examines the causal connections between the symbolic and the material in the making and circulation of media technologies. Calling the scholarship thus far an "unfinished project," Lievrouw begins by unpacking the strong rejection of technologically deterministic views in both communication and media studies and STS, in order to question the persistence of causal accounts in social constructionist views. She calls for a renewed emphasis on "mediation" as a way to overcome the limitations tied to the lingering of social constructivism. Mediation, defined as "an ongoing, articulated, and mutually determining relationship among three components [artifacts, practices, and social arrangements] of communication technology infrastructure and three corresponding processes or modes of change [reconfiguration, remediation, and reformation, respectively]," affords an explanatory stance that better balances the material and the symbolic. In a formulation that echoes Latour's (1991) claim that "technology is society made durable," Lievrouw notes that "the real power of the intellectual connections between STS and media studies will ultimately be theory that moves beyond 'determinisms' to capture the multifaceted complexity of technology as *communication* made durable."

Chapter 3 by Pablo J. Boczkowski and Ignacio Siles complements Lievrouw's argument by noting that most of the existent scholarship on media technologies has exhibited a silo mentality, focusing on either the material or the content dimension, and on either the production or the consumption dimension, but rarely both, and almost never all four. Some studies look at the making of media content, but ignore issues of materiality and reception; some focus on the uptake of new artifacts, but pay scant attention to how this uptake might be shaped by the content they carry. Arguing that this silo mentality has presented significant limitations in accounting for the interpenetration of materiality and content, and production and consumption, in the "life cycle" of media technologies, Boczkowski and Siles call for a more cosmopolitan perspective. They argue that this perspective "seeks to create new opportunities for reimagining established approaches and for conceiving new modes of inquiry." To this end, the authors offer suggestions in the theoretical, methodological, pedagogical, and design domains of scholarly practice on media technologies.

In chapter 4, Finn Brunton and Gabriella Coleman provide a different entry point to some of the issues addressed by Lievrouw and Boczkowski and Siles in their attempt to "get close to the metal." Brunton and Coleman focus on infrastructural dynamics as a problem for media studies. Their emphasis on infrastructure, practices, and users echoes Lievrouw's call for mediation as the mechanism that brings these disparate elements together. By looking at these three elements, and the ties that bind them, Brunton and Coleman encounter "the multiple, sometimes contradictory and sometimes coexistent experiences that obtain on the network infrastructure." They propose ways to escape the "misplaced concretism" and the "collapse" of multiple perspectives into one. Those who can successfully navigate the networks using a technical expertise that permits them to reside closer to the material and farther from the purview of network operators—their examples include network sysops, Anonymous hackers, and spammers—have no such illusions about the hardness or inaccessibility of the material strata. Albeit different in intention and emphasis, Brunton and Coleman's position resonates with Boczkowski and Siles's proposal for a cosmopolitan sensibility in the study of media technologies, though Brunton and Coleman prefer to emphasize multiplicity.

Geoffrey Bowker starts in chapter 5 where Brunton and Coleman end by taking up the issue of multiplicity not only as a descriptor of what has been but also, most important, of what might be when we think about the future of our own modes of knowledge expression. Bowker focuses on the embodiment and circulation of (scientific) knowledge, and the implications for how this knowledge is generated and appropriated. Here he reflects on the limitations that the dominance of the single-authored journal article, as both a content genre and a material artifact of sorts, has had for knowledge practices in the contemporary context. By historicizing how this dominance came to be and remaining mindful of the manifold options ahead of us, Bowker calls for imagining alternative forms of scholarly publication that might better suit our networked, data-intensive knowledge landscape. By calling attention to "the dangers of the mass production of knowledge," Bowker believes that "the promise of this moment is that we can deliberatively produce ways of knowing and ways of expressing knowledge that open rich futures."

Part I closes with sharp and textured responses by Jonathan Sterne in chapter 6 and Lucy Suchman in chapter 7. Recounting the history of different causal formulations in the study of media technologies, Sterne interrogates the centrality of materiality in the chapters in part I and reminds us that, while we may clamor against social constructionism now as insufficiently material, it is instructive to remember that constructionism itself was clamoring at the excesses of positivism. He concludes with astute observations about how questions of causality continue to animate attempts to articulate the relationship between materiality and constructivism. Suchman draws on her own intellectual trajectory and recent research to reflect on the positions proposed in chapters 2 to 5, and contends that developing adequate frames for the ways in which media and technologies configure each other remains a necessary and worthwhile aim.

Part II: The People, Practices, and Promises of Information Networks

The story of stabilization is fundamental to the social constructivist understanding of technology, whereby once-contested technologies seem to settle into some comfortable frame of understanding. But this narrative arc is a matter of perspective. In contrast to stabilization processes, what may be remarkable about technology as a social achievement, and of media technologies in particular, is that they must be maintained, that their contested meanings persist and thrive, that they are the fragile residue of constant activity, and that they must be made and remade in every instance. Their seeming stability is itself a social accomplishment and an important myth to preserve in the face of a reality in which they require constant handling, ongoing repair, and regular upkeep of their public legitimacy.

Perhaps our stories about media technologies are a bit like our commonplace understanding of glass. Glass, as most understand it, can be shaped because it is malleable when it is first heated, before cooling into its familiar, solid, clear form. But from the benefit of a longer view, we just might be able to perceive that even cold, hard glass remains a liquid, constantly but slowly changing—its stillness in fact an illusion, its clarity in fact a trick. Each of the essays in this part tries on this phase shift in perspective, seeing technology as in motion, as maintained, as in process, as remaining contradictory, as held together time and time again through the minute, unobserved practices of the many.

For technologies that often appear to function instantly, automatically, even magically, it may be that the hardest and most important story to tell is about the real people who make them possible, narrate them into significance, repair them when they break, and tinker with them when they need to change. But this phase shift in perspective requires a concerted effort to look beneath the technology at the human underbelly of the sociotechnical system. The essays in part II each invite us to do so. Beneath the artifacts and within the networks are people attempting to construct, maintain, and ultimately disassemble material things. The way they make, remake, and unmake media technologies has lasting consequences for the artifacts and for their users.

Gregory J. Downey begins chapter 8 with a call to recognize all manner of "virtual workers" who help make information move in what feels like frictionless ways. We are seduced by the ease of Google search or the speed of our ATM to believe that these are simply networks of computers responding to our requests at lightning speed. When our query to the library database serves up a multitude of results, we too often forget the immense work required to classify, sort, arrange, and connect library resources—digital ones just as much as those on library shelves. Downey wants to draw our attention to the "informational labor" that allows information, situated in a particular time, space, and institution, to "jump context."

Using as historical examples librarians and archivists, telegraph delivery boys, and the real-time stenographers who caption media programs, transcribe court proceedings, and translate speeches, Downey highlights how each helps information move across space or time, from institution to institution, or from one semantic context to another. The flow of information is in fact a product of human labor, pushed forward by the hands of these invisible workers. An analysis of information networks that overlooks these kinds of labor fundamentally misunderstands how these systems work and further reifies the invisibility of their efforts. It also may miss the way that these laborers, working at key transactional points in the flow of information, have historically been aware of and politically active around key sociocultural tensions, tensions that matter for the users for whom the information is designed.

In chapter 9 Tarleton Gillespie focuses on a more contemporary moment of disappearance but raises a complementary set of questions to Downey's analysis. He calls for sustained attention to the place of algorithms in the public information landscape. These tools, from search engines to recommendation systems to the organization of social networking sites, render information unto users according to human, but now automated, criteria. He argues for unpacking these systems, not just as artifacts with politics, but also as new knowledge logics that are displacing more editorial modes of information legitimation. This is vital in the face of our embrace of these tools as sites for public discourse, the seductive calls for new insights through "big data," and the turn to using these systems to both curate and govern the contours of public speech.

Gillespie articulates six dimensions of the political valence of algorithms. Together, these are intended as a heuristic for how to consider the values behind what information is included in the database and what these systems attempt to know about their users; for how algorithms impose oblique but human-generated evaluative criteria and how they present their results under a rubric of objectivity that legitimates their intervention; and for how algorithms tangle with but may also shape users' information practices, sometimes providing a terrain for political contest, but also mirroring back to users calculated snapshots of themselves as members of taste publics or participatory communities. In these ways, the algorithm, presented as a cleanly mechanical offer of results simply returned in response to query, in fact shapes, curates, and legitimates knowledge and the publics who engage it.

In chapter 10, Christopher M. Kelty suggests we also must attend to the political ideologies that travel with these technologies. Computers and information networks were born amid strident debates about political freedom, and for many of their designers and public champions, they are icons of those ideals, so much so that our notions of freedom have developed and changed around them. To do justice to this tangle of the material and the inspirational, Kelty proposes that we tease out the complexities of these notions of freedom and liberty that swell unexamined in the ad campaigns of manufacturers and in the eager chatter of fans, journalists, and critics.

For Kelty, the way to do this is to return to the claims made by some of the Internet's founders, particularly in the "man-computer symbiosis" envisioned by J. C. R. Licklider and the "augmented intelligence" pursued by Douglas Engelbart. Here, in their visions for the future of computational technology, competing ideals of freedom were served up and negotiated. Revealing the contours of their beliefs, Kelty suggests, will inform modern political philosophy and add depth to the claims made by new media scholars about the political imaginaries that animate new media. But, Kelty warns, we must understand how information technology designers are thinking about political freedom, because thinking about freedom as something that can be delivered by a technology, or designed into it, changes the meaning of freedom itself.

In attempting to think about media technologies, social researchers tend to focus on their beginnings: the context in which they were developed, the moment they were released, their early adopters. Perhaps too much is made of the initial decisions, the early controversies, the first implementations as the most crucial constitutive choices (Starr 2004) defining the technology and the practices that will coalesce around it. This myopia is suspiciously aligned with both the marketing of technological novelty and the planned obsolescence of gadgets. Steven J. Jackson argues here, in chapter 11, that despite this "productivist bias," it may be just as important to unearth what it is that keeps a technology going, who makes its continued use possible, how it changes over many iterations, and how it ends. To look, as Downey also does in this volume, to the labor involved in the maintenance and the dismantling of things, reveals not only invisible work, but also another source of innovation and change happening well outside of the R&D department of the software giant or the garage of the amateur inventor. Change often comes in the moments of breakdown, and in the myriad responses to it.

But Jackson's aspirations here are greater. He posits an entirely different frame of mind around technology, what he calls "broken world thinking." If we were to see technologies not as dazzling sparks that shoot off into the lived world, but as fragile achievements constantly needing repair to survive, this might shift our focus from the politics of artifacts to a more sober attention to the wondrous and persistent attention and care people pay to things they hold quite dear.

In their commentaries, chapters 12 and 13 respectively, Sonia Livingstone and Fred Turner each engage in creative reflection, making intriguingly different arguments about what the essays in part II have in common and about the emerging scholarship around media technologies they signal. Both Livingstone and Turner tie insights from these essays to longstanding concerns that have animated the study of media more broadly. Livingstone reminds us that thinking about users and audiences remains critical to understanding our contemporary media environment. Each of the essays, she argues, is concerned about users, but implicitly frame them in different ways. Calling out these assumptions, and putting users politically front and center, even if they are not the analytical object, is a gesture vital to the examination of new media technologies as a part of public life. Turner considers whether the classic media studies concerns about representations, their commercial aims, and the worldviews they deliver still matter when scholarship seems more interested in the shape of networks and the politics of software. His closing reminder is that although networked culture may seem to have left behind the stodgy concerns for "mass society" that shaped twentieth-century scholarship about media, perhaps it has powerfully brought those fears to fruition, accelerating and normalizing them, and building its own worldviews not into the representations it constantly churns, but into the social and technical infrastructure itself.

* * *

There may be no way to comprehensively or exhaustively map all the intersecting work of social researchers of media and technology. We certainly do not accomplish it here. But the heterogeneity of the scholarship is its highest virtue. We hope that every one of the chapters in this volume, and the dialogue among them, will serve as foundational starting points for a new set of questions going forward. We hope that readers of this volume exploring issues around media technologies can light upon one of these chapters, and find in it a careful consideration of a thorny problem in the field, a breadth of understanding of the contours of that problem, and a provocative insight to chase. We also hope that this volume affords social researchers of media and technology the impetus to move their own inquiries beyond the obligatory rejection of technological determinism (and beyond an uncritical embrace of social constructionism)—and to begin reclaiming the centrality that understanding media technologies should have in the fields of communication and STS and beyond.

Note

1. We have chosen in this introduction to refer to "social researchers" of communication and media and of technology as a way to negotiate both whom we mean to refer to and whom we do not. The scholars we have in mind make their intellectual home in a number of fields, including sociology, communication, anthropology, science and technology studies, history, philosophy, cultural studies, and information science. Although we are joined by an interest in the way that media technologies emerge from and reshape social practices, meanings, and institutions, to aggregate us under the term "sociology" would exclude too many people. At the same time, those of us who intermingle with scholars with technical expertise, be they in computer science, engineering, or information systems, often use the tag "social," to distinguish ourselves from those who focus on the technical. So, rather than have to repeatedly say, "the social, cultural, historical, economic, and institutional" and "as opposed to technical" every time, we used the shorthand term "social research" to encompass this.

Part I The Materiality of Mediated Knowledge and Expression

2 Materiality and Media in Communication and Technology Studies: An Unfinished Project

Leah A. Lievrouw

Introduction: Communication Meets STS

"One paradox of media studies is that over the years scant attention has been paid to . . . the medium. . . . Media studies today is still devoted to content analysis, to the effects of these contents on social behavior, and to the analysis of ideological or institutional apparatuses."
—Paulo Carpignano, "The Shape of the Sphere" (1999), 178

It is fair to say that the specter of technological determinism no longer haunts the study of communication technologies, despite being an enduring theme in media research. Classical mass media studies from the 1920s onward analyzed the "effects" of print, broadcasting, and cinema on audiences' opinions, attitudes, values, and behavior; although this work focused mainly on media content, it also grew out of concerns that the channels themselves might have some inherent power to influence audiences. Later, studies of "new" information and communication technologies (ICTs) and information society in the 1970s and 80s investigated the "impacts" of computer conferencing, videotex, Usenet groups, and electronic mail technologies on occupational patterns, organizational structure, small group interaction, and individual "users."[1]

However, by the late 1980s a different perspective on media and ICTs had begun to reverse this familiar causal logic in studies of communication technology (Boczkowski and Lievrouw 2008). Concepts and critiques arising from studies of science, technology, and society (later recast as science and technology studies, or STS; Hackett et al. 2008) came to the forefront in studies of new media and communication technology. These included interpretative flexibility (Collins 1985; Pinch and Bijker 1987), notions of inscription and "technology as text" (Woolgar 1991), boundary objects (Star and Griesemer 1989), and in particular, the social construction of technology (SCOT) approach to the analysis of technology and society (Pinch and Bijker 1987; Bijker and Law 1992). These concepts and frameworks encouraged communication technology researchers to reject technological determinism in favor of a view of technology as socially constructed.

Moreover, this "user turn" was reinforced by critical and cultural media studies and its socialized, culture-driven approach to media analysis, including a central focus on media institutions and power (see the section to follow on Critical/Cultural Media Studies). Following the lead of Raymond Williams (1974), these writers cast people as engaged, critical, "active audiences" rather than passive receivers or consumers of mass media messages and content (Ang 1990; Jensen and Rosengren 1990; Livingstone 2004; Morley 1993)—a perspective that seemed to apply just as well to "active," and interactive, Internet users.

Consequently, to a great extent the classical "effects" or "impacts" viewpoint in new media research gave way to studies with a broadly social constructivist perspective and an emphasis on social shaping, the shared or negotiated meaning of technologies, user studies, and technological systems as products and representations of culture. The question was no longer what communication technologies or media do *to* people, but rather, how people appropriate, understand, make sense and continuously reconstruct them. Communication technologies—at once resources for and manifestations of communication, meaning, and culture—seemed to epitomize the articulation between the technical and the social. As the means for expression, interaction, and cultural production, and cultural expressions and productions in themselves, media and communication technologies could be seen as both "cultural material and material culture" (Boczkowski and Lievrouw 2008, 955)—but the socially constructed nature of technology took priority. Ultimately, the move from technological determinism to social constructivism was a pivotal development in communication and media research in the 1990s; by the 2000s a strong form of social/cultural determinism had "become the dominant perspective in new media studies" (Lievrouw and Livingstone 2006, 4).

STS, meanwhile, became widely associated with strong social constructivist views, especially among scholars outside the field (MacKenzie and Wajcman 1999; Sismondo 2008). Yet within STS itself, social constructivism was never a singular or unitary perspective, nor was it universally accepted. Sergio Sismondo (1993), for example, distinguished between "mild" and "radical" social constructivism; the former holds that science and technology involve social factors, while the latter contends that technologies are solely the product of socially negotiated meanings and constructs. Trevor

Pinch identified three varieties of radical constructivism in STS, including social construction of technology (SCOT), actor-network theory (ANT), and "the systems model" (Pinch 1996, 22), with SCOT "the most explicitly social constructivist of the three" (23).

In fact, over time, approaches within STS that privileged the social side of the sociotechnical framework faced important challenges from advocates of a more dialectical, mutual-shaping, or co-production perspective, where artifacts and social action are seen as mutually constitutive and determining. Some argued that the stabilization, embeddedness, and sheer material presence of technological artifacts influence and shape human action just as surely as action shapes artifacts: both directions of the relationship should be accounted for (Jasanoff 2004; Wyatt 2008). In stronger formulations of this viewpoint (for example, actor-network theory) the claim that artifacts might have power, and even agency, comparable to that of human actors is controversial to say the least. On the whole, however, over the last two decades mutual-shaping and co-production approaches have encouraged STS scholars to take the material nature of technology as seriously as they do its social construction.

To varying degrees, new media and communication technology researchers, especially those familiar with the debates within STS and social historians of media technologies, have embraced the mutual-shaping approach. Several writers have explicitly adopted the language of sociotechnical articulation and co-production (Boczkowski 2004; Gillespie 2007; Haddon 2006; Hartmann 2005; Lyon 2003; Sterne 2003; van Zoonen 2002). The materiality of media technologies has been invoked and even celebrated in various post-browser cultural studies of the Internet and digital media since the early 1990s (for example, see Bolter and Grusin 1999; Druckrey 1996; Liestøl, Morrison, and Rasmussen 2003; Porter 1997; Stone 1995).

Others have highlighted the material *affordances* of communication technologies, that is, the physical properties or features of objects and settings that "invite" actors to use them in particular ways (Hutchby 2001b), a perspective that is discussed at more length later in this chapter. Sonia Livingstone and I have proposed a definition of new media that unites communication artifacts, practices, and social arrangements and formations as inseparable and mutually determining (Lievrouw and Livingstone 2006). There is also a new and growing interest among communication scholars, especially in the Anglophone world, in emerging fields like media archeology (Huhtamo 1997; Parikka 2012) and media archives (Spigel 2010); the "new materialisms" of the digital humanities (Coole and Frost 2010; Gitelman 2006); and the radical and even frankly deterministic materiality of so-called "German" media studies exemplified by the work of Friedrich Kittler, Vilém Flusser, and Peter Sloterdijk, among others (Lovink 2008; Peters 2010; Winthrop-Young 2011).

Nonetheless, as I hope to show in this chapter, most technology scholarship in the communication field, informed by classic streams of media research, continues to follow a broadly constructivist, culturalist line, privileging the technologies' social and cultural meanings and appropriations and framing technology primarily as an outcome or expression of culture. As a result, the shift toward conceptualizing the intrinsic social *and* material character of communication technology as equally definitive and co-determining remains something of an unfinished project in communication and media research. By and large, communication scholarship remains "tilted" (Jackson, Poole, and Kuhn 2002) toward the social/cultural side of the sociotechnical duality (or, per Lievrouw and Livingstone [2006], toward practices and social arrangements rather than artifacts; or toward social behavior and institutional apparatuses per Carpignano 1999). As Trevor Pinch (1996) has observed, communication researchers (like others outside STS) have often seemed drawn mainly to the critical and emancipatory politics associated with social constructivist views.

Thus the main purpose of the following discussion is to explore how the material nature of communication and media technologies has been conceptualized at the intersection of STS and communication studies. On one hand, two decades of debates have encouraged STS researchers to theorize technology as simultaneously and inextricably social and material, to see both aspects as co-determining, and to attend as closely to the physical design and configuration of objects as to the beliefs and social circumstances of their creators and users. Among communication scholars, on the other hand, the physical, material features of technology are still more likely to be explained as outcomes or *products* of abstract social forces, cultural discourses, or economic logics—or as all of these together. Only secondarily, if at all, are material artifacts and devices themselves considered to have anything like a parallel power to influence human action, society, and culture, or do scholars insist as strongly on the influence or "agency" of material objects and artifacts as that of human actors and institutions. Even where devices themselves are the main focus, as in some social histories of media technologies, they are often analyzed from interpretive points of view that privilege the signifying or discursive aspects of technological artifacts over the concrete, embodied quality of crafting and using them.

The chapter is addressed to readers with interests in both STS and communication and media studies. Key theoretical approaches from both fields are reviewed, including (from STS) autonomous technology, technological momentum, actor networks, and sociotechnical co-production, and (from communication) media effects research, the communication network perspective, critical/cultural media studies, and medium theory grounded in the Toronto School tradition. These are by no means the only frameworks or theories in either field relevant to the study of communication technology, but they are featured here because each of them has generated a major literature in its own right, and has been elaborated by some of the most influential theorists in their respective fields. The overviews are brief and retrospective, and may seem elementary for expert readers. However, the aim is to provide introductions and framing to concepts in one field for readers in the other, in order to situate the rise of STS-inflected studies of ICTs and new media, including their treatments of materiality, within a broad cross-disciplinary perspective.

Materiality itself is a complex, multidimensional idea, and open to a variety of interpretations, emphases, and disciplinary assumptions. It has been invoked to describe phenomena as diverse as the economic and institutional power of media industries and markets, cultural practices like art making and religious rituals, and the microscale utterances and turn taking of speech and interpersonal interaction. Obviously all these levels and shades of meaning cannot be adequately addressed in a single chapter. Therefore, for the purposes of the present discussion I use a much narrower conception based on the three-part definition noted previously, where communication technology is conceived as the articulation of artifacts, practices, and social arrangements (Lievrouw and Livingstone 2006). All three elements are interwoven and mutually determining, but here I focus on the first element, to define materiality as the physical character and existence of objects and artifacts that makes them useful and usable for certain purposes under particular conditions.

Such a definition foregrounds the materiality of *artifacts*, of things, not to deny the materiality of practices or social or institutional forms, but to consider how communication technology studies might also engage more fully with the materiality of the devices themselves without necessarily opening itself to charges of simple technological determinism. A more evenhanded or congruent approach to the materiality of objects as well as practices and social arrangements and institutions might, for example, open the way to reconceptualizations of core communication phenomena, like channel, interaction, message, organizing, and group communication, or effects. It would require communication scholars to adapt established ideas and look across enduring divides in the communication field, such as those that cast interpersonal interaction and media as fundamentally different modes of human communication, or administrative and critical research as essentially incompatible perspectives. It could also suggest new approaches to pedagogy that could help overcome the conventional division of communication curricula into rigid and largely incommensurate silos, such as interpersonal communication, media production, social-psychological media effects, or cultural-historical criticism, for example.

Following the discussion of materiality in STS and communication and media studies, I close the chapter by considering the factors that have discouraged a more materialist approach to artifacts in communication studies, particularly the field's longstanding intellectual tendency toward idealist ontologies (Peters 1999; Rogers 1998). I conclude by sketching some suggestions for new media theorizing that bring the materiality of artifacts back in, specifically an analytical framework for *mediation* that examines the reconfiguration of artifacts, the remediation of expression and interaction, and the reformation of patterned social and institutional arrangements.

Artifacts and Materiality in STS

If there is a single concept that has epitomized STS to scholars outside the field, it is the social constructivist approach to studies of scientific knowledge and technological systems. It originated among historians of science, where it was seen as a counterintuitive and controversial account of scientific practice, and was later adopted in more sociologically oriented studies of technology and society (Pinch 1996). The view of scientific knowledge as socially determined provoked outrage among many scientists, and generated a backlash that culminated with the "science wars" of the 1990s and the infamous "Sokal hoax" (Gross and Levitt 1998; Ross 1996; Sokal and Bricmont 1999).

Engineers and technologists, however, have not been so quick to dismiss the constructivist viewpoint, or as insistent on the exceptional status of their knowledge, perhaps because they are necessarily more aware of and sensitive to the collaborative, contingent, and contested process of technology design, manufacture, and implementation. "Successful practicing engineers have always known that their work is as much economic, organizational, and even political, as it is 'technical'. . . [and that] real-world engineering . . . [is] the engineering of social relations as well as of physical things" (MacKenzie and Wajcman 1999, xv).

This linking of the social and the material may be one of the most important distinctions between social studies of technology and social studies of science. Bruno Latour has captured the idea in a single apt phrase: "technology is society made durable" (Latour 1991). The need to account for the presence and durability of material artifacts, and to approach artifacts, social, political, and economic conditions, and cultural practices alike as part of a "seamless web" (Bijker, Hughes, and Pinch 1987) has produced a lively debate in technology studies about what might be called technological determinism 2.0: how to recognize and account for the materiality of technology without losing sight of the specific conditions, actions, and understandings that generate and sustain it. As Sally Wyatt has observed, "Our guilty secret in STS is that really we are all technological determinists. If we were not, we would have no object of analysis; our *raison d'etre* would disappear" (Wyatt 2008, 175).

Autonomous Technology

Langdon Winner is among the most notable critics of strong social constructivism in STS, and his concept of *autonomous technology* is one of the most widely disputed concepts in technology studies (Winner 1977, 1980, 2001). One of Winner's important influences, the French philosopher and avowed technological determinist Jacques Ellul, argued that technology, suffused with modern rationality, logic, and efficiency, becomes an irresistible and autonomous force that drives social action, relationships, and knowledge (Ellul 1964, 1980). Winner takes this a step further, to propose that technological artifacts are the embodiment of the political, economic, social, and cultural conditions of their development and creation. Once built, they are the physical manifestation of those conditions, and have both intended and unintended consequences to which users and society must adapt. Winner's autonomous technology is "technology that has grown so big and so complex that it is no longer amenable to social control" (Wyatt 2008, 175).

As Sally Wyatt (2008) has noted, Winner's perspective has propelled a series of "skirmishes" within STS. Constructivist critics (see Joerges 1999) charge that Winner's most famous case study—Robert Moses' plan to build bridge overpasses between New York and Long Island that were too low for buses to pass under them, creating a not-so-subtle barrier to poor and working class visitors to the city (Winner 1980)—misrepresents Moses' project, and overstates the power of artifacts to exert and enforce political values and power. Others decry Winner's avowedly political commitments and his reliance on "old safe dichotomies of critical theory and Marxism [which oppose] society, social interests, and politics, on the one side, and technology, artefacts, and machines, on the other" (Pinch

1996, 34). Ultimately, they argue, there is no fixed or stable interpretation of what technologies represent or what they are for (Joerges 1999; Woolgar and Cooper 1999).

For his part, Winner criticizes strong social constructivists for being more interested in the abstract conceptual origins of technologies than in their pragmatic consequences, for focusing on the seemingly endless contingency of negotiations among "relevant social groups" and their agnosticism about those groups' contending and competing interests, and for neglecting entrenched technologies' concrete, enduring effects (Winner 2001). The proper study of technology, he says, requires a rigorously critical perspective and normative commitments that enable analysts to identify not only the social processes that negotiate and shape technology, but also, first, which technological choices are actually made and implemented, and second, how members of democratic societies can participate and intervene in those choices. The answers depend on a view of materiality in which physical artifacts and practices manifest and perpetuate the designer's values, beliefs, assumptions, privileges, and preferences, and once in place, are relatively closed to continued reframing or reinterpretation.

Technological Momentum

Technological momentum has been advanced by Thomas Hughes (1983, 1987, 1994) to account for the dual social and material nature of technology. Based on historical studies of electrical power systems and other large technical systems, Hughes rejects both technological and social determinism: "both approaches suffer from a failure to encompass the complexity of technological change" (Hughes 1994, 102). Instead, he suggests a cycle of mutual shaping in which social and material components are joined into complex, networked relationships. "Cultures of technology" grow up around certain technological systems and create momentum, "the propensity of technologies to develop along previously defined trajectories unless and until deflected by some powerful external force or hobbled by some internal inconsistency" (Constant 1987, 229).

Technological momentum is not singular or unidirectional, but diversified and open to contingency. It encompasses "acquired skill and knowledge, special-purpose machines and processes, enormous physical structures, and organizational bureaucracy" (Hughes 1994, 108). Successful engineers like Thomas Edison are "heterogeneous," working not only with "inanimate physical materials, but on and through people, texts, devices, city councils, architectures, economics and all the rest" (Law 1991, 9).

Hughes disagrees with Winner's concept of autonomous technology. "Technological systems, even after prolonged growth and consolidation, do not become autonomous; they acquire momentum. . . . Momentum does not contradict the doctrine of social construction of technology, and it does not support the erroneous belief in technological determinism" (Hughes 1987, 76, 80). Nonetheless, once technological systems become stabilized and acquire momentum, the artifacts generated by and enmeshed in those systems can exert influence, just as social action influences them. Remarking on the Muscle Shoals (later Wilson) Dam project built as part of the Tennessee Valley Authority, Hughes notes, "This durable artifact acted over time like a magnetic field, attracting plans and projects suited to its characteristics. Systems of artifacts are not neutral forces; they tend to shape the environment in particular ways" (Hughes 1994, 111).

Some committed social constructivists see Hughes's account of technological change as a potential stalking horse for technological determinism (Bijker and Law 1992). Nonetheless, Hughes's framework (or "pattern"; Hughes 1987, 56), and the related study of large technical systems (LTSs), have been particularly important for scholars investigating extensive, complex, dynamic systems such as energy, military technology, computing, and telecommunications (see, for example, Galambos 1988; MacKenzie 1991; Mayntz and Schneider 1988; Schneider 1991). To recap, we might say that in Hughes's view, not only are engineers heterogeneous; so is technological materiality itself.

Actor Networks

Perhaps the best-known approach to technology studies among researchers outside STS is associated with Michel Callon, Bruno Latour, John Law, and their colleagues (Latour 2005; Law and Hassard 1999). *Actor-network theory* (ANT) maps relationships among material entities and artifacts, human actors, and the ideas or symbols associated with them as "heterogeneous" and open sociotechnical networks. Human actors and material artifacts or *actants* are nodes in interlinked webs of relations, with the ability to exert multiplex influence on other relationships and nodes in the network. The actor-network perspective resists the "purification" of issues or practices into singular categories like nature, science, politics, culture, or even place: all these categories, and more, are necessarily and simultaneously implicated in a given network (Latour 1993). The insistence on heterogeneity, especially the idea that material artifacts and objects can be agents within networks of relations among humans and knowledge, is perhaps the most controversial aspect of ANT, and most firmly places the materiality of things at the center of the theory.

As with social networks among people, relationships among nodes within actor networks are continuously reconstituted by the agents themselves. These dynamic relationships enable technological systems to evolve, stabilize, break down, or reorganize in new and unexpected ways. Taking their cue from Hughes, ANT scholars have examined large or intricate technical systems (see Callon 1986, 1999; Latour 1996; Law 1987; Mol 2002), and count heterogeneity, networks, and the systems perspective as important influences (Law 1987).

Some ANT theorists depart from Hughes, however, with respect to the role of conflict in sociotechnical networks: where trajectories and momentum seem to suggest that successful technological systems must overcome or smooth out conflict in the process of organizing and stabilizing around a particular technological solution, certain ANT researchers hold that conflict is an ongoing, inevitable, and vital part of the evolution of networks and the technological systems they generate. In sum, in terms of materiality, ANT shares Hughes's emphasis on heterogeneity, but also recognizes that technological forms and artifacts can develop in highly contingent and situation-dependent ways, according to the changing configurations and reconfigurations of sociotechnical networks, rather than in relatively straightforward trajectories.

Co-Production

A fourth concept not only suggests that science and technology are simultaneously material and social, but also aims to elaborate the dynamics of the relationship, especially as a means for confronting authority and intervening in technological controversies and policy. According to Sheila Jasanoff, its most notable proponent, *co-production* is the simultaneous creation of knowledge and artifacts/practices, which actually constitutes social life: "the ways in which we know and represent the world (both nature and society) are inseparable from the ways in which we choose to live in it. Knowledge and its material embodiments are at once products of social work and constitutive of forms of social life" (Jasanoff 2004, 2).

In co-production, knowledge is fundamentally material: "Knowledge . . . crystalliz[es] in certain ontological states—organizational, material, embodied—that become objects of study in their own right" (Jasanoff 2004, 3). In some ways, co-production echoes Winner's contention that artifacts manifest the values and assumptions (that is, knowledge) of their creators, but extends this insight to social practices and organizational forms. And like autonomous technology, co-production is concerned with the practical governance of science and technology (Irwin 2008). It rematerializes power, so that it is no longer an abstract "force" or institutional "structure," but is actually instantiated and observable in the physical forms of social practices, relations, and material objects and artifacts. Co-production encourages a move away from strong social determinism, and the assumption that "social controversies around science are 'really' all about politics or that complex areas of innovation can be reduced to 'social' construction" (Irwin 2008, 589).

However, unlike autonomous technology, and like technological momentum and actor networks, co-production regards science and technology as heterogeneous by definition: "scientific knowledge, in particular . . . both embeds and is embedded in social practices, identities, norms, conventions, discourses, instruments, and institutions . . . the same can be said even more forcefully of technology" (Jasanoff 2004, 3).

Jasanoff suggests that co-production can be found in four "sites" or processes: making identities, making institutions, making discourses, and making representations. In the social sciences, cultural studies, and the humanities, these phenomena are often treated as abstract concepts that are independent of their particular manifestations or physical forms. Jasanoff, however, insists that such material forms actually constitute identity, institutions, discourses, and representations. Identity, for example, is manifested in modes of dress, speech, food, kinship relationships, and so on. Discourses are articulated in political campaigns, architecture, publishing, conversation, stock prices, or monthly bills for Internet services. Institutions exist in the form of legal codes, educational practices, configurations of space, or social roles. Representations convert concepts into concrete form, as when terrorism is equated with an image of a hooded street fighter, or genetically modified crops are labeled "Frankenfood." In each case the physical forms and objects *constitute* the ideas in question; such manifestations can be parsed and analyzed, and new ones crafted as needed.

* * *

These four sketches allow us to consider how materiality, particularly with respect to technology artifacts, figures across them all. First, and most obviously, all four frameworks attempt to theorize the physical character, presence, or durability of technological devices and objects as a factor on par with social, cultural, or political negotiation and construction. They do not deny or downplay social construction, but attempt to join the material and the social as essential, and essentially co-determining, elements in technological change. Second, all the frameworks, to varying degrees, emphasize the heterogeneity of technology, that is, as a multifaceted and dynamic phenomenon that entails and imbricates not just artifacts, social practices and relationships, and knowledge, but a *variety* of all these elements. If, as Latour and his colleagues say, analysts must "follow the actors," this means dealing with a host of interconnected artifacts and social formations as well as people (Latour 1987).

Third, all four frameworks address the stabilization or standardization of material objects as a key mechanism for explaining their influence. Social studies of technology often highlight technological innovation and the origins of particular devices or systems; these early stages, after all, are more likely to be dominated by social construction processes, negotiations, and contingent, contested meanings and understandings. However, the frameworks presented here pay as much attention to technological stabilization and routinization processes in which the artifacts themselves (whether due to habit, physical inertia or scale, sunk costs, network effects, or reliability) acquire the capacity to shape social practices and organize action.

Perhaps the best commentary on materiality in technology studies is provided by John Law (1991), who (with just a bit of tongue in cheek) accuses his fellow sociologists of "speciesism" for their reluctance to take machines and artifacts seriously as agents of technological change. Ultimately, "Structures do not simply reside in the actions of people, or in memory traces. They exist in a network of heterogeneous material arrangements. The genius of STS is to have stumbled on this" (Law 1991, 16).

Artifacts and Materiality in Communication and Media Studies

Media systems have preoccupied communication researchers since the early twentieth century, when broadcasting and cinema began to take their place alongside publishing as powerful institutions and shapers of popular culture and politics. The power of newspapers to influence public opinion and elections had long been part of political culture in the Europe, North America, and elsewhere. However, the introduction of commercial radio and cinema in the 1920s and 30s, and their use by revolutionary and fascist movements and regimes during this period, aroused fears that these new media technologies, and not just the messages they carried, might have some inherent and irresistible power to move mass audiences to disruptive action, to influence the morals and behavior of marginal or susceptible groups like children, immigrants, women, workers, or the poor, or to enhance the persuasive power of charismatic but dangerous or anti-authoritarian leaders.

After World War II, television became the main focus of similar concerns and research investigations into media "effects" on audience psychology, values and mores, decency, economic expectations, cultural practices, and political opinions. In the 1990s and 2000s, the explosive growth of personal computing and Internet access and use among the general public, fostered by the introduction of web browsers, search engines, and the conversion of the Internet from a nonprofit infrastructure for research and education to a privately operated platform and distribution system for commerce, consumption, and entertainment, would provide yet another media stage upon which the same types of social and cultural anxieties would be replayed.

Given the importance of media in communication study over the last century, it may seem surprising that the technologies themselves, as built systems and devices, have played a fairly limited part in most mainstream communication research. Apart from a few specialized subfields (media/ telecommunications law, economics and regulation; development communication; organizational communication), studies of media devices and platforms per se have been largely overshadowed by studies of message production and consumption, the generation and contestation of cultural discourses, and the institutional/political power of media industries and regulators. The following discussion examines four major streams of communication and media research and the extent to which the materiality of technological devices and artifacts is a consideration in their conceptions of the communication process.

Media Effects

The study of media "effects" is one of the oldest and most foundational areas within the communication discipline, dating back to classic studies of newspapers and public opinion (Lippmann 1922), propaganda in wartime and domestic political discourse (Bernays 1928; Lasswell 1927), the Payne Fund studies of the influence of motion pictures on children's attitudes and behavior (Blumer 1933; Peterson and Thurstone 1933), the role of mass media in elections (Lazarsfeld, Berelson, and Gaudet 1944) and in the reinforcement of popular taste and culture (Lazarsfeld and Merton 1948). After World War II, effects research (and indeed, the discipline as a whole) expanded along with the dramatic rise of television and "information-processing" perspectives on audience perception and cognitive change influenced by the information theory of Claude Shannon and Warren Weaver, originally formulated for telecommunications (Shannon and Weaver [1949] 1963).

In this context, Harold Lasswell formulated the basically linear view of the communication process that prevailed at the time as "who says what in which channel to whom with what effects" (Lasswell 1948). Paul Berlo (1960) adapted Shannon and Weaver's "communication theory" to elaborate a new, but also linear, model in which discrete, "encoded" messages are transmitted from senders, through channels, to receivers who "decode" them, with the possibility of feedback (a model now enshrined in most introductory communication textbooks as "SMCR," for sender-message-channel-receiver).[2] Although widely criticized, linear models and the concept of *channel* as an intervening element in "real" human communication have proven to be remarkably resilient, at least in introductory textbooks.

The full scope of effects research over the last ninety-plus years cannot be covered comprehensively in a single chapter. However, major "through-lines" include controversies over whether media content and representations exert powerful, direct effects on audience knowledge, opinions, and behavior, or only indirect effects that are attenuated and mediated by people's interactions with others (Katz and Lazarsfeld [1955] 2006; see also Park and Pooley 2008); whether messages can actually change people's minds or simply set the agenda for what issues are important (Shaw and McCombs 1977); and whether audiences should be seen as passive receivers of content or engaged, and subversive, "active audiences" that use media according to their particular interests or to gratify certain needs (Ang 1990; Morley 1993; Livingstone 2004). Broadly speaking, media effects research explores the ways that media may influence or even determine cognitive, attitudinal, and behavioral change; which types of media have which effects; and whether people choose and use different media for different purposes. It is important to note, however, that although "channel" is often used as a variable in classical effects research, in practice channel and content are frequently conflated, as in studies of "radio plays," "television soap operas," or "newspaper political reporting."

These basic questions (and the conflation of channel and content) have carried over into the Internet era in *computer-mediated communication* research (CMC), which examines the effects of various computer-based communication technologies on interpersonal interaction, group processes, and organizing rather than on mass "audiences" (Thurlow, Lengel, and Tomic 2004; Walther, Gay, and Hancock 2005). It asks how effective, meaningful human interaction can occur via technologies that span time and space, that is, without being face to face and simultaneous. Early CMC studies in the 1970s and 1980s were often conducted in private firms or academic research labs, which were the first adopters of experimental systems for group meetings, electronic mail, teleconferencing, and so on. Research questions focused on organizational processes and change (for example, the quality and speed of decision making, superior-subordinate relations, teamwork, and substituting systems for travel) rather than mass-media-style audience effects.

Today, CMC research continues the effects tradition, ranging from microscale studies of language, identity, and relationships online, to analyses of computer-supported teamwork and collaboration, to studies of online communities and cultures. Continuing major themes include technological features of systems (that is, sound, still or moving images, immediacy or lag time, text only), which features are used for which purposes, whether users employ them effectively, and what difference various features make for different communicative purposes or outcomes. But like classical mass-media effects research, CMC studies often blur the relationship among the technological devices and the messages and meanings they convey, such as email, Facebook, web pages, or blogs.

Communication Networks

A second technology-oriented tradition in communication research takes a broadly sociological view, emphasizing the role of social structures, networks, and relations in the communication process (Burt 1982; Rogers and Kincaid 1981; Wellman and Berkowitz 1988). Interpersonal relationships are conceived as communication networks through which people share information, seek and share advice, form affiliations and loyalties, build communities and trust, and so on; and these networks are often supported and sustained by communication technologies. In early network studies, social influence was often framed as a kind of "contagion" process in which new ideas and practices spread from person to person.

One of the most important concepts in this stream is *diffusion of innovations* (Rogers 2003), which theorizes the communication and adoption of novel ideas and practices within social systems. Since the 1950s, the elements of diffusion theory have been refined and applied to a diverse range of social settings and policy problems across a number of disciplines, but a major area of research has been the spread (adoption and use) of information and communication technologies. For example, in development communication research, investigators have sought to understand the social factors affecting people's adoption and uses of radio, telephones, and direct broadcast satellites, as well as the economic and cultural consequences of these innovations once communities adopt them. Likewise, a substantial body of diffusion research examines the dynamics of IT adoption in organizations and the consequences of diffusion for organizational structure, workplace relations, productivity, and so on. Diffusion studies have also highlighted the role of adopters in the diffusion process as well as change agents, the reinvention of innovations as they diffuse, how critical masses of adopters develop, and the threshold or degree of adoption that any new idea or practice must achieve in order to be successful.

Materiality is a complex quality of communication networks. First, the social relations that comprise networks are conceived as fundamentally material, constituted in actions, interactions, and contacts that can be directly observed and reported. Of course, network members may perceive or understand their relationships in divergent ways, but from the network viewpoint it is crucial that network links are not just perceived, but *acted*. Second, the consequences of communication and relationships—particularly the recommendation and adoption of a new activity or device—are material practices. Residents of a remote village may or may not boil their drinking water or plant new kinds of crops after outsiders urge them to do so. An American parent may not immunize her child if a trusted friend convinces her that vaccination causes autism. "Adoption" is a multifaceted, but ultimately material, action that is undertaken within networks of social ties.

Third, again in the context of diffusion theory, the innovation itself is frequently material, a device, system, or practice with which a given network member was previously unacquainted or inexperienced, but once introduced to it, readily adopts. Fourth, and contrary to most social science theorizing, the material links among network members (network structures) are considered to have at least as much or more influence on members' actions than their personal traits or ascribed roles. Together, these commitments make communication network studies somewhat more focused on the multilayered materiality of communication, including the physical character of technological devices, social practices, and relations, than some other traditions of communication research.

Critical/Cultural Media Studies

Another stream of research takes a critical or cultural approach to the study of communication and technology. Here, two traditions have been particularly influential. One, sometimes referred to as "British media studies" or the Birmingham School of cultural studies, is grounded in the work of Raymond Williams (1974), Stuart Hall (1980, 1997), Richard Hoggart, and their colleagues at the Centre for Contemporary Cultural Studies at the University of Birmingham between the 1960s and its closure in 2002. Informed by neo-Marxist Frankfurt School critical theory, political economy of media industries and institutions as producers of systems and content, and a phenomenological, interpretive approach to the consumption and reception of media forms and content (typically construed as "readings" of media "texts"), Birmingham School scholarship seeks to reveal and challenge established media institutions and power by demonstrating how existing media products (systems and content) and industries shape popular understandings of culture and politics; how media support or undermine social and cultural values such as social and economic access, diversity, fairness, and equity; and how people may reinterpret, redefine, and ultimately reform media culture for themselves. An important feature of "British" critical/cultural media studies is the critique of "administrative" research, that is, research that claims scientific objectivity or policy neutrality, but that serves to reinforce the status quo or the biases and interests of established institutions, markets, or states (Lazarsfeld 1941; Melody and Mansell 1983).

A key development in the Birmingham School tradition related to new media technologies has been *domestication theory*, developed by the late Roger Silverstone and his colleagues at the University of Sussex and the London School of Economics (Haddon 2006; Hartmann 2005; Silverstone 2005, 2006). Domestication research examines how people consume and appropriate media and communication technologies in their everyday lives, particularly in the home. Taking a page from STS as well as Raymond Williams's critique of strong social/cultural determinism (Williams 1974, 13), domestication research rejects both technological determinism and strong social constructivism in favor of a heterogeneous view of households as sociotechnical networks in which technology and action are mutually shaped. Analysts employ qualitative and ethnographic methods to discover how people appropriate, use, and negotiate the meanings of technologies, particularly how such meanings "move" across the boundary between the home and the world, that is, between the private and public spheres. Silverstone argues that ICTs are "doubly articulated," at once commodities in themselves, appropriated into the home from the world beyond and consumed like other goods, and carrying content that promotes and reinforces further consumption.

A second tradition of critical/cultural media scholarship is more humanistic and historical. Some of this work is associated with the late media theorist James Carey and his students and colleagues at the Institute for Communication Research at the University of Illinois, and the traditional emphasis on media history, literature, criticism, and connoisseurship in schools of media performance and production (theater, film, television).

Media history also plays an increasingly prominent role in emerging "digital humanities" programs.

While these scholars may share the general social outlook and emancipatory political orientations of British media studies, like the Toronto School media theorists (see next section), they take a more explicitly literary and philosophical perspective on communication technologies. Classically, they argue that cultural contexts, models, or narratives "produce" given technological systems, or they emphasize the role of technologies as cultural representations or texts (see Gitelman 1999). However, some recent works are moving toward more of a mutual shaping perspective in their analyses, suspending material objects, human practices, cultural representations, and institutional formations in ongoing historical relations of tension, contingency, or indeterminacy, and with a much sharper focus on the design, engineering, and implementation of the technological artifacts themselves (see Sterne 2012; see also Gitelman 2006).

Social and cultural histories of media and communication technologies are the hallmark of this tradition; notable contributions include Carolyn Marvin's *When Old Technologies Were New* (1988), Carey's *Communication as Culture* (1989), John Durham Peters's *Speaking into the Air* (1999), Lisa Gitelman's *Scripts, Grooves and Writing Machines* (1999), and more recently, Jonathan Sterne's *The Audible Past* (2003). The views of Carey and Peters regarding the idealist character of communication studies are considered later in this chapter, but in terms of theory Carey's distinction between technology-driven *transmission* versus face-to-face, communitarian, *ritual* views of the communication process and his observations about the conflation of time and space brought about by nineteenth-century electrical media like the telegraph and telephone, are cornerstones of this intellectual tradition.

Medium Theory

A fourth major stream of research dealing with communication technologies dates to the work of Harold Innis, Marshall McLuhan, and their colleagues at the University of Toronto in the 1950s and 1960s, dubbed the "Toronto School" of communication research. These scholars, and their contemporary intellectual successors, are perhaps unique in communication and media studies for their unapologetic focus on the material features or "biases" of media and communication technologies, and the consequences of that materiality for societies and civilizations over the long historical term. Joshua Meyrowitz has characterized this stream as "medium theory," to "differentiate it from most other 'media theory' . . . medium theorists ask: What are the relatively fixed features of each means of communicating and how do these features make the medium physically, psychologically, and socially different from other media and from face-to-face interaction?" (Meyrowitz 1994, 50).

Often characterized as marginal, Canadian "outsiders" to mainstream (that is, American) communication research (Flayhan 2005; Katz 2007) as well as British and U.S. cultural studies (Grosswiler 2005), many of the most renowned Toronto School scholars, including McLuhan, Eric Havelock, Northrop Frye, and Walter Ong, were humanists—historians and literary/cultural critics—rather than social scientists. (Notable exceptions included Innis himself, who was a political economist, although his work focused on economic history; and Edmund Carpenter, who was a cultural anthropologist and media producer.) Their concern, like that of medium theorists today, was to document and critique the influence of key communication technologies per se, especially as extensions of human communicative faculties, apart from the effects of content, representation, and meaning that preoccupy effects researchers or the institutional, economic, and power questions that animate critical/cultural theorists.

The materiality of technological devices and artifacts, then, lies at the core of medium theory: "we [medium theorists] must always be true to the central insight that media are physical and that their physical features frame the social relations they engender" (Wasser and Breslow 2005, 261). Innis's characterization of communication systems from ancient empires to the present day as either time- or space-biased (that is, either durable and maintained over time, or less permanent and more transportable over distance; Innis 1951) is perhaps the paradigmatic example, and laid the foundation for channel-focused "orality-literacy studies" undertaken by other Toronto School scholars like Jack Goody, Eric Havelock, and Walter Ong, among others (Strate 2004). Innis hypothesized that a culture's dominant systems could produce "monopolies of knowledge" that "block the emergence of alternatives, and ultimately enhance the effects of the monopolistic medium and skills on society and on its political, social and cultural profile" (Blondheim 2007, 57). Such monopolies can only be broken, and dominant institutions overturned, "by the development of new media" (Flayhan 2005, 239).

If Innis was the original intellectual force behind medium theory, McLuhan became its most prominent and controversial champion. He acknowledged Innis's crucial influence on his own turn from more conventional literary criticism to a new kind of critique emphasizing the materiality of communication technologies (Flayhan 2005; McLuhan 1962). "[McLuhan] had to get the literary types to stop talking about content" (Wasser and Breslow 2005, 261).

However, the two thinkers diverged in important ways. Innis was principally interested in macrolevel consequences of communication technology for long-term historical processes and social change. McLuhan, in contrast, became more concerned with the influence of technology on human perception and cognition, and how technologies extend the human "sensorium." For example, his distinctions between the effects of "cool" and "hot" media on perception and behavior, and the maxim that the "medium is the message," became some of his most famous observations. Many contemporary cultural critics cite his notion of the "global village" generated by broadcasting and satellites as the key ancestor of today's digital culture.

* * *

Clearly, the different streams of media research sketched here vary in terms of their views of the materiality of technological artifacts. All acknowledge— if implicitly—that the use of technological systems makes a difference in the manner and consequences/effects of communication. Nonetheless, their relation to materiality can seem uneasy. Effects and CMC research continue to emphasize the relatively short-term influence of messages and content on individuals' attitudes, cognition, and behavior, although CMC has directed more attention to channel effects.

Network studies, grounded in interactionism, Chicago School sociology, and the European structural sociology of Georg Simmel and Ferdinand Tönnies, considers the diffusion of new ideas and practices, as well as interpersonal relations and interactions, as fundamentally material entities. But adoption depends as much on cognitive and attitude change among network members as their interaction per se. Network research is frequently criticized for being administrative (advancing the interests of technology industries or hegemonic political viewpoints) and technologically deterministic (that is, assuming that the spread of new devices or practices will have predictable social outcomes), and for its presumed pro-innovation bias (promoting innovations and privileging the interests and entities that introduce them). To critics, the network emphasis on relations, links, and structures is also problematic because it treats social structures as though they are "real," material phenomena with greater influence on action than content, representations, and appropriated meanings.

Critical/cultural media studies takes a much longer-term view of the social, cultural, and economic implications of media technologies, but the

Birmingham School tradition still often relies on a binary, economic-style model of the communication process, focused on the power and influence of content and institutions (on the production side) and audiences' "appropriation" and reception of media content (on the consumption side). While many cultural and media historians have begun to embrace a broad, mutual-shaping or contingency view of the technology-culture relationship, and to feature the material qualities of particular devices and systems, some analyses continue to foreground culture as the driving force or "origin" of technology, to treat material artifacts primarily as cultural expressions or representations, and to distance themselves from any suggestion of technological agency or determinism. For example, Jonathan Sterne (2012, 12) adopts a complex and nuanced mutual-shaping view of the development of the MP3 audio format that extends back to the early days of psychoacoustics at AT&T's Bell Labs. However, he also suggests the priority of culture in that process: "we don't have to subscribe to a single model of historical causality or historical change in order to appreciate that a change in format may mark a significant cultural shift."

Of all the traditions, and despite criticisms from other quarters in communication research, medium theorists seem to be the least ambivalent about materiality, and remarkably unconcerned with the charge of technological determinism. From Innis and McLuhan to the present day, medium theorists have put the materiality of media systems and artifacts at the center of their analyses, on the assumption that media "effects" are principally due to their physical features and those features' influence on individual behavior as well as the whole society's existence within the material constraints of space and time. For the medium theorists, content and messages are secondary to the physical character and existence of the artifacts themselves. (The influence of Innis and McLuhan, and a similar disregard for allegations of technological determinism, are also seen in "German" [more accurately, northern European] media theory since the 1980s, as noted previously; see Peters 2010; Winthrop-Young 2011).

One theme arising across different traditions is a tendency to blur the lines between channel and content, so that the production and consumption of material formats or renderings (books, software, Facebook postings, texting) are tied up with the meanings or messages they carry or represent (such as mystery stories, financial spreadsheets, self-representation, or affection). Channels are generally conceived as tools for rendering messages and meanings into various channel-shaped formats, styles, or genres of content. Although the renderings (forms) themselves would seem to influence the ways people receive, use, understand, appropriate, or consume them, it often seems difficult to sort out how much, or what sorts, of consequences can be attributed to either form or content independently.

Resisting Materiality

Certain communication scholars have suggested some intriguing reasons for the field's ambivalent stance toward the material character of communication technologies. For example, John Durham Peters (1999, 9) argues that the communication discipline is characterized by entrenched idealism and a belief in the possibility and promise of "wordless contact": the undistorted, immediate, and even transcendent understanding among persons, and the perfectibility of knowledge about others, uncorrupted by the physical constraints and breakdowns of the medium of communication—including live, personal interaction. The "improvement" or optimization of shared human understanding has been a theme throughout the field's history, generating a broadly "therapeutic" discourse and faith in the socially and culturally corrective, healing power of communication.

Peters associates the introduction of electrical media (telegraph, telephone, and especially radio broadcasting) with the rise of idealist concepts of knowledge, understanding and "presence" that featured in late nineteenth and early twentieth century culture in the United States, including the popular fascination with psychic phenomena, telepathic contact, and spiritualism. He notes that many influential thinkers during the period—Ludwig Wittgenstein, John Dewey, Sigmund Freud, Martin Heidegger, Martin Buber—were concerned with the limits and barriers to human communication. Cultural critics and social scientists alike worried that "mass society" (and "mass communication") were producing dislocated, alienated individuals, anonymous and isolated in "the crowd" and beset by anomie. After World War II, similar worries drove the rise of development communication, "information theory," information-processing views of communication, and cybernetics. Engineers' attempts to quantify and control the likelihood and ratios of systematic patterns of desirable "information" versus random interference and "noise" in technological communication channels were transmuted by social psychologists and communication researchers into models of social and interpersonal interaction.

Along the same lines, and perhaps with a touch of hyperbole, Gary Gumpert attributes what he calls the "disappearance" of Marshall McLuhan's work from communication syllabi in the 1980s and 1990s to the fact that "the field of communication has had an antitechnology bias built into its historical structure—particularly in the United States . . . the deterministic aspect of McLuhan's ideas are particularly appalling and threatening to communication traditionalists who maintain that the creation of thought is either divinely inspired or the result of complete self-will" (Gumpert 2005, 233).[3]

James Carey observes that the telegraph and other early electrical media were greeted with a kind of religious or millennialist fervor. Building on Leo Marx's notion of the "technological sublime" (Marx 1964; see also Nye 1994), Carey proposed an "electrical sublime" that incorporates fundamentally idealist conceptions of mediated communication: "electricity—a force of great potency and yet invisible . . . made electricity and the telegraph powerful impetuses to idealist thought . . . [and] located vital energy in the realm of the mind, in the non-material world" (Carey [1983] 1989, 206).

The observations of Carey, Gumpert, and Peters certainly reflect their engagement with cultural history and the medium theory tradition; they seem to be more sensitive than most to the idealism and "missing materiality" of media research. But idealism has been critiqued in other domains of communication studies as well. In organizational communication, for example, Leonardi and Barley (2008) point out that "because scholars have spent nearly 30 years battling the tenants [sic] of technological determinism, the role of materiality in organizational change remains understudied . . . they have wittingly or unwittingly conflated determinism with the material and voluntarism with the social" (171).

Similarly, Richard Rogers critiques the "socially constitutive" (that is, constructivist) view of discourse that pervaded rhetoric and speech communication studies in the 1990s. He concedes that strong constructivist stances provide critical scholars with the "obvious political benefit" of being able to "refute claims about the 'essential nature' of sexual, racial and other differences that are used to legitimize oppressive social systems" (Rogers 1998, 244). Nonetheless, "constructionism is anthropocentric" (260) because it presumes humans' ability to make the entire world virtually *ex nihilo*. The idealism underpinning constitutive theories actually serves to sustain and entrench the ideal/material division that, on one hand, privileges language and discourse as transcendent, and on the other, mystifies, essentializes, and even erases the natural, the material, and the feminine. Although he agrees with colleagues who hold that rhetoric is fundamentally material as a practice and artifact (that is, speech), and in terms of its pragmatic effects in the world, he contends that such views do not go far enough: they simply shift the analytic focus to the material side of the binary. Rather, Rogers calls for ending "the tyranny of the symbol" (267) by formulating materialist theories of discourse that reject the nature/culture dualism and embrace a "transhuman" perspective.

Ways Ahead: Materiality and the Study of Communication Technology

This chapter has reviewed key research traditions in STS and communication technology research to show how each field has theorized and situated materiality, especially the materiality of technological devices and artifacts. Both fields have shown some degree of ambivalence on the subject; as Richard Rogers points out, paraphrasing Derrida, "To participate within the bounds, even expanding ones, of academic and other 'literate' discourses is to participate in the idealist heritage" (Rogers 1998, 264). On balance, however, communication research seems to be slower to adopt explicitly materialist accounts of technology, an idealist tendency that has been reinforced by the embrace of social constructivism from STS and critical/cultural media studies.

So, at the intersection of media/communication technology research and STS, how might researchers engage more fully with the materiality of things, of media devices and artifacts?

At a general level, communication technology scholars could adopt frameworks that more explicitly account for the interplay and mutual shaping of technological tools, human action, and social/cultural formations. This move is already underway in some areas of cultural studies and media history, as well as among STS researchers with interests in media technologies; notable examples include Pablo Boczkowski's (2004) study of newspapers' halting adoption of Internet technologies, and Tarleton Gillespie's (2007) incisive critique of digital rights management (DRM) technologies.

Lincoln Dahlberg (2004) urges investigators to avoid what he sees as three "reductionist" views of communication technology associated with different strands of new media research. Studies that focus on "uses" of technology, he argues, risk falling into simplistic instrumentalism. Those that focus primarily on "technology" (built systems) tend toward technological determinism, while an exclusive focus on "social context" can lead to social determinism. Ultimately, Dahlberg offers a discursive, "texts-readings-readers" analytic strategy, which perhaps unintentionally underplays the materiality of technological devices. Calling technological devices and features a "small aspect" of the complex relations among uses, technology, and context, he suggests that frameworks combining critical political economy and cultural theory, or established theories like Anthony Giddens's *structuration* (bridging human agency and social structure) (Giddens 1986), or Jürgen Habermas's distinction between system and lifeworld (Habermas [1981] 1987), may be sufficient to account for the mutually constituted nature of communication technologies.

Technology and Mediation

The problem of bringing "things" in, then, remains a challenge in communication technology studies. Elsewhere, I have proposed *mediation* as a framework for understanding the mutually constitutive elements of new media technology (Lievrouw 2009, 2011, 2012). Here, I expand on this approach to suggest how it might help resituate the materiality of devices and objects in studies of media and communication technology.

Mediation[4] can be understood as an ongoing, articulated, and mutually determining relationship among three components of communication technology infrastructure and three corresponding processes or modes of change (see figure 2.1). *Artifacts*—material devices and objects—enable, extend, or constrain people's abilities to communicate, and develop through a process of *reconfiguration*. People engage in communicative *practices* or action, some of which may employ those devices; practices change in an ongoing process of *remediation* of interaction, expression, and cultural works. *Social arrangements*—patterns of relations, organizing, and institutional structure—form and develop in concert with the artifacts and practices through a process of *reformation*. Reconfiguration, remediation, and reformation reflect several common meanings of "mediation" in English, specifically, the insertion of technological channels in the human communication process; interpersonal intercession, intervention, or negotiation in interaction; and the reflexive, continuous self-organization (and reorganization) of society and institutions which define, classify, circulate, and regulate power and knowledge.

This tripartite scheme aligns broadly with Dahlberg's three areas of new media studies (technology, uses, and social context). It also echoes the analytic trio of text, production and audience that is central to critical/cultural media studies. However, the triad of artifacts, practices, and arrangements is more inclusive, and more explicitly oriented toward the material, observable character of technology, than these other frameworks. For example, *arrangements* denotes the pragmatic, observable process of making and remaking social relations, and includes a wider range of patterned formations, from interpersonal networks and roles to whole-society institutional forms and structures, than is suggested by either "social context" or "audience." *Artifacts* foregrounds the material, made nature of communication technologies, which is nearly missing in the notion of "texts," and to some degree obscured by the blanket term "technology," which from a mutual-shaping perspective would include all the elements of infrastructure comprised in mediation. *Practices* is a concrete way to describe communicative action, especially compared with "production" (which implies a distant

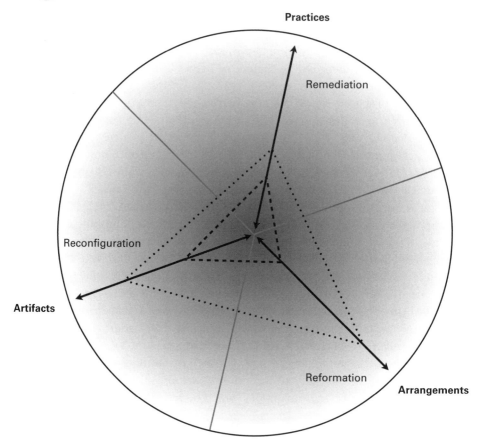

- Circle segments represent three elements of infrastructure (labels outside the circle) and corresponding modes of change (labels and arrows inside the circle)

- Change processes are **more stable toward the center** of the figure, and **more dynamic toward the periphery**

- Example cases graphed as "profiles" across three sectors:

  - Twitter feeds (adaptable devices, limited choice of action, open regulatory climate) · · · · ·

  - Broadcast/cable television (stable devices, routinized practices, restricted regulatory and institutional environment) ▪ ▪ ▪ ▪ ▪

Figure 2.1
Materiality and communication technology: mediation framework.

industrial or institutional process) or interpretive, discursive ideas of "reading" or "reception." It also encompasses a wider repertoire of communicative action than the narrowly instrumental concept of "uses."

All three elements and their corresponding processes articulate and influence one another. Artifacts are made, implemented, and remade (that is, *reconfigured*) according to people's purposes and actions, as well as the social structures and institutional sanctions that enable or constrain them. For example, people want, and may themselves craft, software applications and devices that are easy to use, reliable, secure, and safe. Institutional authorities demand that systems comply with (or even automatically enforce) an expanding range of privacy laws, intellectual property claims, national security and law enforcement directives, competitive rivalries among firms and trade blocs, and cultural/ethical norms.

Similarly, devices and systems that exist in a given time and place shape users' practices and larger social expectations about what the artifacts can do, what they are for, and what people might actually do with them (that is, practices are *remediated*). For example, the Internet has become a venue for interpersonal interaction and personal expression as well as straightforward information seeking or the consumption of media products. Facebook members, Twitter users, or subscribers to location-based services like foursquare may worry about how the services gather, aggregate, and share data about them. But many of those same individuals may also readily offer real-time information about their location, or surrender other detailed personal information, if they consider it a fair exchange for the conveniences a service provides, or if authorities assure them that the collection of such information is a necessary and appropriate means to control terrorism, fraud, and so on.

Social and institutional formations also respond and adapt to available systems and devices and to communication practices and norms; that is, they are open to *reformation*. For example, technology platforms and media products are often designed to be incompatible with those of competitors (the Kindle, Nook, and iPad e-readers; European vs. North American mobile telephone standards). Digital rights-management technologies physically restrict access to and certain uses of various types of media content. The size, responsibilities, and political power of state and private security and law enforcement agencies have vastly expanded in parallel with the proliferation of systems for surveillance, data capture, storage, and analysis, and sharply increased citizen demands for public safety and shelter from risk.

In sum, the articulations among artifacts/reconfiguration, practices/remediation, and social arrangements/reformation are dynamic. Each builds on and reinforces the others; a shift in one aspect can generate corresponding shifts in the other two. This may or may not be a welcome prospect: from the progressive-left or libertarian perspective, preoccupations with risk, safety, control, reliability, and security, and resulting moves toward increasingly monitored, standardized, filtered, regulated, and exclusionary communication systems, actions, and patterns of social and institutional organizing, may look like a vicious circle or regressive feedback loop. On the other hand, articulations also create gaps, spaces of alternative action, or opportunities for pushback, and help ensure that communication technologies remain open to new or unanticipated uses, forms, and understandings.

Mediation and Affordances

How might the mediation framework be applied to the study of media and communication technology? The theory of *affordances* of communication technology, particularly as elaborated by Ian Hutchby, provides one possible model (Hutchby 2001a, 2001b, 2003).

The concept of affordances was developed by the perceptual psychologist James Gibson (1979, 1982), who characterized them as "what [things] furnish, for good or ill, that is, what they *afford* the observer" (1982, 403). All kinds of objects, substances, artifacts, locations and places, other creatures, and events, have perceivable affordances. They "are not simply phenomenal qualities of subjective experience . . . [nor are they] simply the physical properties of things . . . Instead, they are *ecological*, in the sense that they are properties of the environment *relative to* an animal" (404). An object's affordances do not change as the actor's needs or perceptions change; and not all of an object's affordances may be immediately obvious to the observer.

Affordances, in short, are opportunities for or invitations to action that things present to actors. Bruno Latour has paraphrased Gibson's idea of affordance as "at once [the] permission and promise" of a thing (Latour and Venn 2002, 250). Affordances can be seen as the "potential uses" of an object (Hjarvard 2008, 121). Designer Donald Norman, who popularized Gibson's idea in a series of insightful books and his own design practice, has proposed that affordances, and Gibson's ecological, relational approach to understanding them, should be at the center of the study and practice of design (Norman 1988).

Hutchby, however, argues that a focus on affordances in studies of communication technology "offers a reconciliation between the opposing poles of constructivism and realism" that avoids both technological essentialism/determinism, and strong social constructivism/voluntarism" (Hutchby

2001a, 444). It also offers a method for investigating "the empirical question of embodied human practices in real time situated interaction involving technologies" (Hutchby 2003, 582) and for establishing "a sustained and analytically rigorous program based on investigation of the nature of ordinary actions in the context of such material enablements and constraints" (583).

Hutchby rejects both the technology-as-text approach, and linear, information-processing concepts of communication. Instead, drawing on Gibson's theory and the interactionist conversation analysis tradition in sociology and communication research, he takes communication to be an observable practice that pervades social interaction at every level, including the use of communication technologies. He draws parallels between technology affordances and features of conversation: "In ordinary conversation, an action hearable as an 'invitation' is something that delimits the range of possible rational actions to be produced 'next' by a co-participant in the sequence of talk. Put slightly differently, an invitation *affords* the production of a turn . . . you may choose to respond or not, but whatever you do can be heard as an action in response to the affordances offered by the prior action" (Hutchby 2001a, 450, emphasis in the original).

Affordances have three key qualities: they are *functional* (enable and constrain action), *relational* (link actors with the world of objects), and *learned* (repertoires of uses and relations with objects gained through experience according to culturally and socially sanctioned concepts and values). These qualities align with the three elements and processes of mediation: An affordance's functionality is the result of an object's configuration and how actors may reconfigure it; the relation of actors and objects provided by affordances is manifested in technological and communicative practices, including remediation; and what people may learn about and through affordances is shaped by the patterns of relations and institutional formations (and re-formations) that create and regulate social knowledge and power.

Hutchby's critics (see Rappert 2003) contend that he overstates the dominance of strong social constructivism in STS and the stability of technological artifacts, and neglects more nuanced concepts like social shaping or boundary objects. They also charge that he neglects the different ways that the concept of affordances itself has been used by others who see it as the product of discourse and interpretation (Pfaffenberger 1992). Rappert suggests that everyday communicative practices may be less important for social studies of technology than the implications of technology or "big issues" like the negotiation of policy, power, cultural shifts, and so on.

Nonetheless, Hutchby's approach has the merit of reframing the study of communication technology with a clear emphasis on material objects and action, particularly how actors engage with one another, and employ and adapt various technological devices to do so. He does not deny the influence of institutions or representations in the communication process, but calls for an approach to analyzing technology and society that keeps all the relevant and co-constitutive factors—things, action, social structures and arrangements—in play.

To conclude, the way ahead for communication technology studies at the intersection of media and technology will be enriched by analytic frameworks and theoretical concepts that attend to the material, tangible features of technological devices and artifacts, as well as their cultural significance and meaning, the values and power they represent, the institutional interests that advance them, and the attitudes and motivations of their users. Mediation may be one useful way to frame these relations. But the real power of the intellectual connections between STS and media studies will ultimately be theory that moves beyond "determinisms" to capture the multifaceted complexity of technology as *communication* made durable.

Acknowledgments

I thank the editors and commentators of this volume for their feedback on earlier drafts of this chapter. I would also like to acknowledge the lively discussion and invaluable suggestions of participants of a symposium on STS and social media, "The Co-Production of Knowledge," at the University of York in July 2012, where I presented the main points of this chapter as a keynote talk.

Notes

1. For an insightful critique of such "impact talk" about new media and the Internet, see Wouters et al. 2008; see also Hutchby 2001a.

2. Media theorist Stuart Hall, whose work is foundational for British media studies, takes a thoroughly cultural approach to the analysis of media production and consumption; nonetheless, he also uses the "encoding/decoding" binary to characterize relations between producers and consumers (Hall 1980).

3. In more recent years McLuhan's work has enjoyed something of a revival in both communication courses and related fields ranging from sociology to design to information science.

4. In prior work I have defined "mediation" as the interplay between reconfiguration and remediation, each of which is described in this section. However, for this discussion, I have expanded the concept to incorporate the interaction of those two processes with a third, reformation. A complete review of the literature and debates surrounding mediation and a variety of alternative terms (mediatization, mediazation, the mediatic turn, and so on) is outside the scope of this chapter. Interested readers will find more complete discussions in Couldry (2008, 2012), Livingstone (2009), Lievrouw (2009, 2011), and Lundby (2009).

3   Steps Toward Cosmopolitanism in the Study of Media Technologies: Integrating Scholarship on Production, Consumption, Materiality, and Content

Pablo J. Boczkowski and Ignacio Siles

The Story Behind the Story

In the mid-1990s, one of us (Pablo J. Boczkowski) became interested in the development of alternatives to newspaper news that went beyond ink on paper. Following on previous work on computer-mediated communication (Boczkowski 1999), he began a dissertation on the emergence and evolution of online newspapers in the United States, treating them as both technology and media. To this end, the study combined literatures on the sociology and history of technology that focused on the making of artifacts with sociological studies of media about how the news is made. Consistent with the analytical foci of these two literatures, the study looked at the making of an object, rather than on the uptake of that object, concentrating in particular on how material culture and work practices are combined to bring particular journalistic artifacts into being. The result of this study was *Digitizing the News: Innovation in Online Newspapers* (Boczkowski 2004). It was also his realization that the intersection of the fields of science and technology studies (STS) and communication studies was a space both relatively under-explored and potentially generative.

Shortly after the publication of that book, Boczkowski embarked on a new research project that five years later would become his second book, *News at Work: Imitation in an Age of Information Abundance* (2010). Two events that took place in these five years are critical for the difference in approaches between these two books and, most important, for the raison d'être of this chapter.

News at Work was a study of the growth of imitation in news production and the homogenization of the resulting products. Building on scholarship on imitation in work practices and homogenization in the news, during the initial phases of the research Boczkowski gradually developed a tentative explanation that focused on what could be called the supply side of the issue: journalists, pressed for time and with so much content readily at their fingertips, would often chase the tails of their competitors. But at a 2006 presentation of preliminary findings to the Buenos Aires and Santiago de Chile offices of the Boston Consulting Group, one of the associates asked Boczkowski how he could tell that the homogenization of news products was not, in fact, the result of a convergence in consumer taste. Given that news media are market-driven organizations, were these organizations perhaps reacting to perceived alterations in the nature of demand? Steeped as he was in a tradition of inquiry that focused on production while leaving consumption aside, Boczkowski realized that he did not have any evidence to answer this question. To remedy this, he began to examine the extent to which the news choices of consumers converged and to assess their experience of consuming fairly homogenized news content. It turned out that consumer taste for news was far less homogenized than stories supplied by the media, and that consumers in general disliked the lack of diversity in the stories that the media publish. In this case, Boczkowski felt confident in his explanation of the rise of imitative activity and the resulting homogenization of news products as a supply-side issue. But this would not have been possible to ascertain without an examination of the demand side of the equation.

Technology was a critical component of that emerging explanation. The constant publication of stories in the online space and the ease with which they could be replicated and retold greatly exacerbated monitoring and imitative tendencies that had long existed in newsrooms. However, as research progressed, it became evident that this explanation only applied to those devoted to production of hard news, but not to the work of journalists specialized in the production of soft news and commentary. Here the homogeneity of content was much less than that for hard news. Thus, similar technological capabilities were put to use very differently by journalists in the same newsroom, depending on the kind of content they were asked to produce. Had Boczkowski kept the approach used in *Digitizing the News*—which focused on materiality and left content in the back seat—he would have missed this central component of the imitative phenomenon that was critical in *News at Work*.

When the research was complete and it was time to write *News at Work*, Boczkowski looked for examples in the literature that had examined the triad of production, product, and consumption within a single study, as well as those that had analyzed the interplay of technology and content that is so distinctive of media artifacts. He not only found very little but, most important, he also realized that most of the scholarship was divided into traditional intellectual silos: those who studied production matters rarely focused also on their reception (and vice versa), and those who looked at the technological dimension of media artifacts seldom also examined their content dynamics (and vice versa). As the research findings showed, the limitations of these silos were not purely aesthetic; only by operating at the intersection of production and consumption, and technology and content, did it become possible to offer an explanation that accounted for the growth of imitation in the production of hard news—but not other content—despite the dislike for homogenized content among the consumers of the resulting stories. *News at Work* attempted to develop a conceptual framework that broke down the barriers across these various intellectual silos.

Because the problem transcended a singular research project, he also created a graduate seminar for students in the Program in Media, Technology and Society at Northwestern University, which aimed to foster alternatives ways of conducting research on media technologies. Ignacio Siles, the coauthor of this chapter, was one of the students who took this class the first time it was offered. Drawing on the conceptual framework developed through the process described earlier, Siles sought to take advantage of this seminar to rethink the development of a key artifact in the contemporary media landscape: blogs.

Siles designed a project for the class—which later became his dissertation research—that analyzed the co-construction of "blogs" and "bloggers" from the mid-1990s to the present day, so as to examine the evolution of the web as a media technology of self-expression. Applying a more "traditional" approach that retained the intellectual silos in order to make sense of this process would have likely assessed the emergence and evolution of the identities of both blogs and bloggers by examining only how these users appropriated websites through the creation of specific content configurations and certain linking patterns. Instead, the project brought together the worlds of production, consumption, technology, and content—a shared foundation making it possible to analyze and theorize about this process in novel ways.

In particular, this research project benefited from the integrative approach explored during the seminar in two main ways. First, it supplemented the traditional focus on users by directly examining the work of software developers and, consequently, the processes that led to the production of specific blogging software applications and the values and practices inscribed in these processes. This approach helped overcome the assumption that websites and software applications function as a neutral background against which users enact their identities (Siles 2011, 2012b).

Second, it enabled an investigation of how both the materiality and the content of blogs are part of online self-expression practices, and how the intersections of these dimensions matter for understanding the sociotechnical trajectory of the web itself as a media technology. Thus, it could reveal how users and developers established various linkages between artifacts and content through which the identities of both websites and their producers were performed (Siles 2011, 2012a).

Together, these two insights created fruitful grounds for rethinking a fundamental notion of Western thought: the public/private distinction. All of these different dimensions—production, consumption, materiality, and content—mattered when it came to studying self-presentation practices on the web. Any look at how individuals enact visibility on the web must take into account the production and use of websites and software applications, as well as the content written and consumed by users. By bringing these dimensions together, it became possible to understand how the web has functioned as a means for enacting varying degrees of publicness.

In light of how generative the approach that we developed through our recent respective projects has been for us, what we here call a "cosmopolitan perspective," we decided to use our contribution to this volume to articulate its rationale and explore its potential beyond our own work. To this end, the sections that follow explicate the cosmopolitan label; situate its distinctive character within the existent literature; and probe its theoretical, methodological, pedagogical, and design implications further.

Steps Toward Cosmopolitanism in the Study of Media Technologies

As we have noted, two of the main conceptual organizers in the social and cultural study of media technologies have been the coexisting tendencies to focus on either the production or consumption of these technologies, and on either their content or material dimensions. Production, in this context, refers primarily to the process and relations through which media technologies, that is, assemblages of both content and artifacts, are created and acquire particular forms (Abbate 1999; Flichy 2007; Gans 1979; Gitlin 2000; Mosco 2009). Scholars interested in consumption have examined instead the practices and dynamics by which users actively appropriate objects (including media technologies) in various contexts (Bourdieu 1984; Cowan 1987; de Certeau 1984; Fischer 1992; Oudshoorn and Pinch 2003). By content, scholars have often designated the particular texts, images, and representations that meaning-making practices take in communication processes (Hall 1980; Jensen 2008; Krippendorff 2004; Radway 1988;

Silverstone 1994). Finally, "materiality" is a term increasingly employed in many fields to refer to a spectrum of artifacts, objects, and technologies through which cultural products are conveyed (Gitelman 2006; McLuhan 1968; Miller 2005; Packer and Wiley 2011; Suchman 2006).

If these tendencies were arrayed on a two-dimensional map of the field of inquiry, they would produce four quadrants of relatively distinct spaces of scholarship: production/content, consumption/content, production/ materiality, and consumption/materiality. This division of intellectual labor has arisen from the evolution of linkages across the different traditions of inquiry that inform the social study of media technologies, and it has long been taken for granted.[1] It has produced major insights about the construction of media technologies, their appropriation by users, the interpretation and generation of meanings associated with media technologies, and the cultural and political consequences tied to their broad social circulation. However, this situation has also led to systematic shortcomings in scholarship, due to the imposing of a stronger separation between the two elements of each pair than is common in the life cycle of these technologies. The interpenetration of production and consumption is often such that it is difficult to make sense of one without also paying attention to the other. In addition, the material and content dimensions are usually so intertwined that one cannot be properly understood without reference to the other.

As suggested earlier, our goal in this chapter is to denaturalize these taken-for-granted epistemic assumptions. We also imagine what kind of alternative intellectual trajectories might emerge from reevaluating them from a cosmopolitan perspective. Cosmopolitanism has a rich intellectual history that can be traced back to ancient Greece. In natural law theory, Kant (1957) wrote of the "cosmopolitan condition" as a means to achieve peace among nations and a space where the capacities of people could develop. More recently, scholars have relied on the idea of cosmopolitanism to argue for a more universalistic concept of society, and to challenge political and methodological nationalism in social theory (Beck 2000, 2002; Beck and Sznaider 2006; Fine 2007; Fine and Boon 2007). Beck, for instance, maintains that a cosmopolitan vision centers on the "recognition of difference beyond the misunderstandings of territoriality and homogenization" (Beck 2006, 30). He advocates for renewed efforts toward a "dialogical imagination," that is, the capacity to "explore and exploit the creative contradictions of cultures within and between the imagined communities of nations" (Beck 2002, 35). Dialogical imaginations thus "compare, reflect, criticize, understand, combine contradictory certainties" (18).

Our use of the notion of cosmopolitanism is inspired by social theorists such as Beck who have argued for transcending forms of analysis anchored in a given set of assumptions and certainties through the exploitation of work done in other territories. We employ cosmopolitanism as a meta-phor to emphasize the need for constantly problematizing the certainties and assumptions that have prevailed within particular fields of inquiry by exploring the opportunities that arise when these certainties and assump-tions are reconceived through dialogical imaginations. Used in this way, a cosmopolitan perspective stands in contrast to a sort of intellectual insu-larity (or provincialism) that privileges a certain inward-looking commit-ment to a particular paradigm, set of ideas, or mode of inquiry without considering work done in others fields that might significantly enrich or transform it.

A cosmopolitan sensibility promotes the crossing of territorial scholarly quadrants in the study of media technologies to rethink assumptions and normalized processes. Building on this bridge-crossing exercise, cosmo-politanism seeks to create new opportunities for reimagining established approaches and for conceiving new modes of inquiry. It considers work done in other territories and uses this knowledge to illuminate common concerns across these territories, to explore new analytic forms that emerge when their intersections are investigated (rather than assumed), and to shed new light on the various intellectual spaces at stake. A major outcome of a cosmopolitan perspective should thus be fertile conceptual and empiri-cal grounds that potentiate transdisciplinary exploration of the life cycle of media technologies.

A Four-Quadrant Map

In this section we consider the advantages and limitations of conducting research situated within each one of the four quadrants we have mentioned: the production of content, the consumption of content, the production of materiality, and the consumption of materiality.[2]

Scholarship that focuses on the production of content has often been the purview of studies of media industries and institutions, and the politi-cal economy of communication (Gans 1979; Gitlin 2000; Mosco and McK-ercher 2008; Schiller 1984, 1989; Schudson 1978; Wasko 2001). Research in this tradition has helped to illuminate the social, cultural, political, and orga-nizational dimensions involved in the construction of information that is subsequently disseminated through media artifacts. In the parlance of Shan-non and Weaver's ([1949] 1963) mathematical theory of communication, scholarship in this quadrant has concentrated on the significance of the work of "senders" for the communication process. Gans's (1979) study of editorial work illustrates scholarship in this quadrant. Combining content analysis of the news and ethnography of journalistic practice, Gans examined important social, commercial, and political forces involved in the production of news. In this way, he showed how "objectivity" was constructed and reinforced as a value in news organizations through singular means, and how this affected the content of news. Another illustration of work in this quadrant is Gitlin's (2000) analysis of how prime time shows in the United States are shaped by three sets of dynamics: the decisions of executives, usually informed by statistics derived from ratings, tests, and shares, and scheduling theories and established formulas; the industrial complex, regulated through rules and structures (such as an oligopolistic structure, back-end deals, and commitments with suppliers and agents); and a particular context, informed by political, commercial, and religious forces. By opening the black box of prime time shows production, Gitlin shed new light on factors such as roles, norms, traditions, rituals, power, and symbols at play in the making of media content.

Research on the consumption of content has typically been the domain of scholarship on media audiences (Bird 2003; Liebes and Katz 1993; Livingstone 1998; Morley 1980; Radway 1984). The scholarship within this quadrant has made visible the practices whereby audiences appropriate media artifacts and the interpretive strategies they deploy to make sense of the content conveyed through them. Standing against a view of media consumption as a passive activity through which media users are largely controlled and dominated, this body of work has envisioned audiences as agentic interpreters of media texts. Morley (1980) noted that the result of negotiations between readers and media texts is largely shaped by the readers' position in singular social formations. These positions thus "structure [users'] range of access to various discourses and ideological codes, and correspondingly different readings of programmes will be made by subjects 'inhabiting' these different discourses" (158). In their analysis of the reception of *Dallas* in various ethnic communities, Liebes and Katz (1993) demonstrated that the meaning of the show was a product of the interactions between the media text and the emotional and cognitive investment of culturally situated decoders. The consumption of content, they concluded, "implies an active reader—selecting, negotiating, interpreting, discussing, or, in short, being involved" (19). They showed how the meaning-making strategies of these ethnic groups varied in significant ways. Whereas some of them tended to assume the reality of the media text, others tended to highlight its constructed nature. On the basis of this exploration of "audiencing" dynamics (Fiske 1992), researchers in this quadrant have also analyzed the political significance of "reception" as an agentic process (Livingstone 2005). Conceptualizing them as *publics*, scholars have characterized media users as reflexive groups of individuals who are capable of self-organizing, debating, and transforming their media preferences into singular demands (Dayan 2001).

Scholarship on the production of media artifacts has often been the province of STS-inspired analyses of the construction of media technologies and some work in the political economy of communication (Abbate 1999; Bijker, Hughes, and Pinch 1987; Mosco 1982; Sterne 2003; Suchman 2006; Wasko 1982). Scholars have conceptualized these technologies as cultural artifacts that are shaped by practices and relations among diverse groups of actors. According to Law (2010), "In STS materiality cannot be prised apart from the enactment of relations or, more generally, the practices that *do* these relations. . . . To understand mattering of the material, you need to go and look at practices, and to see *how* they do whatever reals [sic] that those practices are doing, relationally" (173–174). For example, in *Inventing the Internet*, Abbate (1999) traced the variety of relations and negotiations among various actors that resulted in the triumph of the Internet (and its defining set of protocols) in what is commonly referred to as the "standards battle" (155). Rather than attributing to it an intrinsic technical superiority, the author traced how the Internet entered into a myriad of relations among actors of different nature in order to explain how it was able to defeat alternative solutions to networking problems.

Finally, some scholarship in both communication studies and STS has focused on the consumption of media technologies and their wider circulation in society (Katz and Rice 2002; Marvin 1988; Meyrowitz 1985; Rogers [1962] 2003; Sproull and Kiesler 1991). Although the focus on materiality in communication and media studies is relatively recent as part of a wider turn in the social sciences and humanities (Coole and Frost 2010; Miller 2005; Packer and Wiley 2011), work in this field has long been devoted to understanding the significance of artifacts and technological features—or what the mathematical theory of communication refers to as the "channel"—for communication processes. For scholars associated with medium theory and the media ecology traditions, media create specific environments through singular material and technological features that largely shape the actions, responses, and identities of their users (Innis 1972; McLuhan 1968; Meyrowitz 1985; Postman 1985). Adopting a different perspective, scholars in the diffusion of innovations framework have analyzed how users adopt a variety of objects and technologies (Johnson and Rice 1984; Rice and Rogers 1980; Rogers [1962] 2003; Valente and Rogers 1995). In Rogers's ([1962] 2003) classic framework, innovations such as media technologies have five intrinsic features that shape their consumption process: relative advantage over previous innovations, compatibility with the adopter's context, the simplicity or complexity that characterizes the innovation, how easily the innovation can be tried or tested before adoption, and the degree to which an innovation can be observed by others. Consumption is also shaped by the social system or context in which the adoption process takes place and the communication means used to make the innovation known. Scholars in both STS and communication and media research have explored the relationships between the consumption and the materiality of media technologies through the lens of the theory of affordances (Gibson 1977, 1979; Jensen 2010). Researchers who adopt this perspective tend to investigate "the functional and relational aspects [of media technologies] which frame, while not determining, the possibilities for agentic action [of users] in relation to an object" (Hutchby 2001, 444).

An alternative way of thinking about the contributions and shortcomings of research in each quadrant is to divide the territory of inquiry differently: rather than thinking of it in terms of quadrants, one could look at it in terms of cardinal points (see figure 3.1). Doing so would show that the scholarship situated "north of the equator," regardless of whether the focus is on either production or consumption, is marked by a disregard for the role of materiality in shaping—and being shaped by—content configurations. Although materiality does not always affect content, and vice versa, there is enough scholarly evidence suggesting that it *can,* and sometimes does in powerful ways. Conversely, the accounts located "south of the equator," be they about production or consumption, share the reverse problem, namely a disregard for the role of content configurations in influencing—and being influenced by—technology design and use practices of various sorts. Again, given the available literature on how content can variously matter for material formations, ignoring its potential role unnecessarily limits the inquiry.

There are, of course, some outstanding studies in which both materiality and content configurations are deeply interconnected in either the production or the consumption of media technologies (see Hayles 2005; Pinch and Trocco 2002; Silverstone 1994; Thompson 2002; Williams 1974). In this body of work, media technologies are envisioned as what we have called "texto-material assemblages," that is, bundles of content and materiality (Siles and Boczkowski 2012). For example, Silverstone (1994)

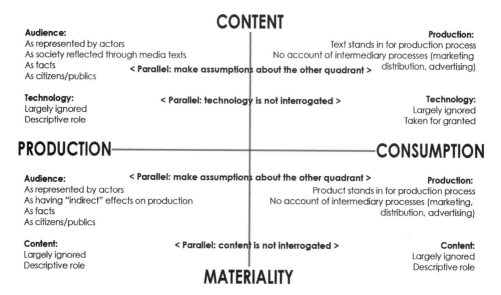

Figure 3.1
A four-quadrant map of the field of inquiry.

conceptualized these assemblages as "doubly articulated," that is, both cultural artifacts and media. Considering the case of television, Silverstone argued that, "As object[s], [media technologies are] bought and incorporated into the culture of the household for [their] aesthetic and functional characteristics . . . As [media], through the structure and content of [their] programming as well through the mediation of public and private spheres more broadly, [they draw] the members of the household into a world of public and shared meanings" (183). Silverstone thereby articulated very well the argument that both dimensions are required to understand the place that media technologies such as television occupy in the daily life of a household. In a similar manner, Pinch and Trocco (2002) analyzed the historical development of the analog synthesizer by examining its evolution as a technological artifact and considering a set of major records and songs produced with this artifact. In this way, they showed that technology and cultural forms (that is, particular types of music content) are mutually constitutive. From their perspective, "Technology—so important as a carrier of global culture—gets reworked and appropriated in new local contexts, sometimes generating new cultural forms that in turn push technology forward" (106). Likewise, as Thompson's (2002) account of the entanglements of jazz as a music genre and the material conditions of urban life suggests, technological and sound production can be co-constructed in powerful ways. Thus, for example, key in the history of sound technologies are the music and audio genres that have developed in response to the availability of formats, and that in turn might have triggered changes in the technology.

These studies suggest that the production and consumption of both materiality and content *can* be and often *are* shaped by the other dimension. Thus, for instance, the previously mentioned studies by Gans and Gitlin leave unanswered the question about whether content production dynamics were affected by issues such as the material conditions in the workplace, the broad infrastructure of media production, the technologies deployed to find information about the audience, and so on. By separating materiality and content, work that explores either one dimension without paying attention to the other has typically overlooked how these two dimensions intersect and why that matters.

As with the equatorial hemispheres of figure 3.1, the studies in the eastern and western regions, regardless of whether they focus on content or materiality, have tended to view their respective domains of inquiry as relatively self-contained in terms of the questions asked and the answers offered. That is, scholarship within the western region has tended to rely on indirect evidence of user appropriation dynamics and to give these dynamics a secondary role in shaping production patterns. Conversely, on the eastern side the research has often considered the media texts or artifacts under analysis as stand-ins for the processes of production. Going back to the examples provided earlier, the often complex and contingent nature of the production processes that yield the content of a TV program such as *Dallas* or the features of an innovation (such as its relative advantage, compatibility, simplicity or complexity, trialability, and observability) are usually overlooked, or taken to be stand-ins for the intentions of their developers—which, in turn, are neither indirectly problematized nor directly interrogated. We argue that whether or not these proxies are defensible in a specific case should be a finding of the inquiry process rather than an assumption.

A few exceptional studies have shown how the production and consumption of media technologies are more interconnected in practice than in the dominant scholarly analyses of these processes (see Douglas 1987; Du Gay et al. 1997; Fischer 1992; Gamson 1994; Yates 2005). By conducting empirical research of both production and consumption dynamics—rather than relying on indirect accounts—these scholars show why consumption matters when production is investigated, and why production is key to making sense of consumption. Grindstaff (2002), for example, analyzed the production process of various daytime TV talk shows. Like others in the production of content quadrant, she observed the strategies and dynamics involved in producing a specific type of TV content that she referred to as "the money shot," that is, "the precise moment of letting go, of losing control, of surrendering to the body and its 'animal' emotions. It is the loss of the 'civilized' self that occurs when the body transcends social and cultural control, revealing human behavior in its 'raw' rather than its 'cooked' form" (20). Yet, unlike several scholars in this tradition, Grindstaff examined a variety of ways in which these shows' audiences played a major part in producing the money shot. By so doing, Grindstaff demonstrated the extent to which a depiction of the production of talk shows would have been incomplete without a major recognition of the role of audiences as producers in their own ways. Her account also showed that interactions between producers and audiences were crucial for better understanding "long-standing hierarchies between 'high' and 'low' culture" (Grindstaff 2002, 20).

Adopting this kind of perspective to the reading of *Dallas* suggests that the different audience forms of decoding might not only be shaped by conditions of reception but also by the social, political, and technological factors that affect the production of content in the first place. Similarly, the trajectory of an innovation is not only a function of the dynamics of diffusion but also of the values and practices embedded in their design. Studies in this integrative vein have also demonstrated the significance of intermediary processes such as marketing, distribution, regulation, and circulation in variously shaping both the production and the consumption of media technologies (Kline 2000; Pinch and Trocco 2002; Wasko 1982). As this body of work reveals, these processes can be of crucial importance in defining a "network of interactions" (Kline 2000, 6) among actors such as producers, consumers, and intermediaries through which users, media technologies, and the contexts of their interactions are shaped.

Thus far, we have discussed the benefits and limitations of doing research confined to particular quadrants and regions in the map of scholarship on media technologies. But what would enable the development of an intellectual program at the center of these quadrants? To go back to the organizing metaphor introduced at the beginning of this chapter, what would adopting a cosmopolitan perspective—one that integrates the study of both content *and* materiality, and both production *and* consumption— make possible, and how can it be done?

A Cosmopolitan Perspective for Scholarship on Media Technologies

In what follows, we begin answering these questions by developing the main contours of a cosmopolitan perspective on the four major components of intellectual labor about media technologies: theory development, methodological strategies, pedagogical opportunities, and design dynamics.

Theoretical Implications

Conducting research on individual quadrants has somewhat limited the possibilities for conceptual advancement due to the presence of intellectual tendencies of a rather provincial type, in the sense that questions and explanations developed outside of one particular quadrant that might be relevant to account for processes across the quadrants have remained largely unexplored. For example, debates as to what the social implications of media technologies are—particularly in the media-effects research tradition—have largely focused on the assessment of media texts and production institutions rather than the practices that tie production, consumption, materiality, and content together (Couldry 2004). Similarly, analyses of how technologies gain meaning have typically examined either the values inscribed in artifacts or the cultural frameworks that shape interactions between users and media technologies, without fully considering the meaning that arises from interactions between users and media texts. A crucial expression of this provincial attitude has been the disciplinarization of research on media technologies. As Messer-Davidow, Shumway, and Sylvan put it, disciplinarity is "the means by which ensembles of diverse parts [objects of study, methods of analysis, scholars, students, journals, and grants] are brought into particular types of knowledge relations with each other" (1993, 3). In this sense, they argue, disciplinarity brings coherence to what is disparate.

Returning to our cartographic metaphor, ideas and approaches that account for the social and cultural life cycle of media technologies have remained confined within the borders of disciplinary territories. For instance, whereas many STS scholars have specialized in the study of production and consumption of artifacts, communication and media researchers have often focused on the reception and the political economy of media texts (Boczkowski and Lievrouw 2007; Siles and Boczkowski 2012). This is not to suggest that scholars have not examined work done in other quadrants, but rather that when they have done so, they have incorporated insights from them mostly to supplement their approaches rather than taking advantage of this incorporation to engage in a broader reconstruction of their theoretical apparatuses. Borrowing from Beck's (2006) vocabulary, this has led to *multiculturalism* between the quadrants rather than *cosmopolitanism*. In other words, the disciplinary "'home-land' is [still] regarded as a closed, self-sufficient and sacrosanct unity" (36–37). A multiculturalist undertaking considers a plurality of approaches to analyze a given topic. However, these approaches are largely used in a "subordination-service mode," that is, they are "organized in a relation of subordination or service to other component disciplines" (Barry, Born, and Weszkalnys 2008, 28). In contrast, a cosmopolitan perspective not only recognizes work done in other fields and attempts to integrate them, but also uses this work as an opportunity to rethink established notions within disciplinary fields and expand the conceptual tools as a whole.

By limiting the type of engagement with work done outside any quadrant to a "subordination-service mode," provincialism and disciplinarization have come at the price of heuristic power and theoretical innovation. A cosmopolitan perspective in the study of media technologies seeks to shed light on research problems that cut across the concerns of scholars in different territories and to help rethink work that is done in the space of inquiry. A significant *result* of this perspective would be an inter- or transdisciplinary orientation toward inquiry on the life cycle of media technologies. To be sure, the problems of disciplinarization have been the subject of much previous discussion and debate. Thus, by proposing a cosmopolitan lens we seek to highlight its potential as a partial solution to a longstanding shortcoming in scholarship rather than point to its novelty.

Crossing the borders of established quadrants and exploring their intersections would require building on existing theoretical frameworks and traditions to investigate processes and outcomes that are usually taken for granted in other territories. For example, as noted previously, research in both STS and communication and media studies has yielded theoretical frameworks for understanding how users shape media technologies. In keeping with the disciplinary loyalties that we have discussed, whereas some scholars in STS have tended to conceptualize users as a "relevant social group" (Pinch and Bijker 1987) that shares a common interpretation of the meaning of an artifact, various researchers in communication studies have envisioned them as groupings that express social, political, and cultural interests through shared interpretations of media texts, that is, as "interpretive communities" (Jensen 1990). In his study of blogs previously mentioned, Siles (2012a) bridged these two concepts and showed that early blog users were both a relevant social group *and* an interpretive community in the sense that their material appropriation practices and interpretive strategies were mutually constitutive. In other words, how users attributed meaning to the blog (as a relevant social group) was tied to how they created content (as an interpretive community) that crystallized in a specific type of website. To tie together these two distinct but related practices, Siles (2011) relied on the notion of articulation, a central idea in cultural studies. Articulation helped to theorize how linking the materiality and the content of these websites was fundamental in the co-construction of blogs and their users. Thus, the creation of early blogs involved both interpreting them as artifacts and expressing certain interests through the creation of their content.

This brief example shows that a cosmopolitan perspective for the study of media technologies requires going beyond the "subordination-service" mode that has characterized much interdisciplinary research. It demands an attitude toward theory development that includes an open mind in terms of using existing notions from different traditions of inquiry; an awareness of their advantages and limitations; and a willingness to combine these notions in an innovative manner, in the sense of deploying them in ways that have not been tried before. The next subsection shows that this attitude is also resonant with strategies for conducting the empirical research that provides the material for such theoretical work.

Methodological Implications

The constitution of bodies of knowledge in each of the four quadrants has usually involved the deployment of specific research methods. Ethnography, for instance, has been typically used for studying production dynamics (Hess 2001). Although some work in both STS and communication studies has employed ethnography when examining consumption, most scholarship in the eastern region of our map has relied on surveys and interviews as the methods of choice (Dillman 2007). Moreover, scholars interested in the study of technology have made artifacts and technological systems their privileged units of analysis (Bijker 2010). In contrast, media researchers have typically examined symbolic formations using different kinds of content analysis techniques to interrogate media texts (Krippendorff 2004).

A cosmopolitan perspective on empirical research in media technologies would require combining methods of different capabilities in order to generate data that enables examination of the relevant issues at stake across quadrants. Beck refers to such strategies as "methodological cosmopolitanism" (Beck 2006; Beck and Sznaider 2006). This approach, he argues, "rejects the either-or principle and assembles the this-as-well-as-that principle" (Beck 2002, 19). In the context of media technologies, methodological cosmopolitanism may be defined as an empirical sensibility toward the use of multiple methods on the links between production and consumption, and materiality and content in the life cycle of media technologies. Thus, the goal of cosmopolitanism is not to simply to *add* methods with different strengths within a single study but to *combine* them into an empirical apparatus that can capture the interpenetration of the relevant dimensions of media technologies within a given project.

A key means of implementing this empirical orientation are research projects designed to interrogate, rather than to assume, the processes and issues that have been the province of one quadrant in particular or that lie at their intersection. For instance, a study of consumption practices through surveys could be articulated with artifact and content analyses of the technologies taken up by users and the texts they produce. This would help the understanding of how users appropriate artifacts to communicate in meaningful ways but would also provide close readings of the texts and artifacts they create and interpret. In a similar manner, the ethnographic study of how technologies and content are produced could be complemented with an examination of how they are distributed, commercialized, and regulated (through network analysis, archival research, or interviews), and how users appropriate them (through surveys, participant observation, or interviews). This type of project would illuminate the intersections and articulations that link issues of production, consumption, materiality, and content.

An example of methodological cosmopolitanism is Boczkowski's (2010) research design for his study of homogenization in the news. As mentioned before, to get at the life cycle of imitation, he combined ethnographic accounts of how journalists make news, quantitative content analysis of the actual news stories, server data on the levels of popularity of different kinds of these stories, and interviews with the consumers of these stories to assess how a homogenized news supply gets interpreted by members of the public. Thus, his research design blended qualitative and quantitative techniques, as well as ethnography, content analysis, and server logs, in an attempt to capture the many relevant dimensions that shape this life cycle, from production to consumption, and from content to materiality. By doing this, Boczkowski was able to show not only the mutual shaping of production and consumption but also how content and materiality affect each other. As previewed in the introductory section to this chapter, one of the findings from the study is that the increase of imitation in journalistic work affects disproportionally more hard news than other types of content, such as soft news, editorials, and various forms of commentary. The ethnography of news production revealed that this was a combination of new technological possibilities that make it easier for journalists to monitor and replicate the work of competitors and divergent organizational and cultural dynamics that shape the production of various types of content. However, because of its organizational focus, the ethnography could not yield conclusive knowledge about whether it affected this organization in particular or the wider journalistic field more generally. Therefore, Boczkowski combined this ethnographic account with a content analysis of the evolution of news stories across the main print and online news outlets in the Argentine journalistic field. This content analysis corroborated the overall conclusion that imitation in journalistic work is far more prevalent for the production of hard news than other type of content. It also added indispensable information about its field-level effects for homogenization in the resulting news stories and a nuanced portrait of how this homogenization plays out in the selection, presentation, and narration of news.

As this example suggests, a cosmopolitan sensibility creates the grounds for triangulation as a methodological principle by illuminating areas and issues that need to be investigated when the intersections of traditionally separated research territories are explored.

Pedagogical Implications

The classroom setting has been a critical locale for the transmission, legitimation, and development of scholarship within and across intellectual fields. Consistent with the theoretical and methodological preferences espoused by scholars in accounting for the dynamics of production, consumption, materiality, and content, teaching in academic institutions has tended to reproduce the quadrants described in this chapter. But since teaching also plays a crucial role in helping to generate new intellectual agendas, envisioning novel pedagogical approaches to the study of media technologies is an important means to further develop a cosmopolitan sensibility in this domain of inquiry.

A typical graduate curriculum in STS usually involves courses on key theories to analyze the technology-society relationship, such as actor-network theory and the social construction of technology framework. It also includes courses on the history, sociology, and politics of science and technology. More recently, courses have also incorporated more systematic training on how to investigate the role of users in shaping technological change in various contexts, such as daily life and organizational settings. From a methodological perspective, STS students usually learn how to carry out case studies through qualitative methods such as ethnography and archival research. In contrast, a representative curriculum for graduate training in communication and media studies generally incorporates extensive preparation on both the production and consumption dynamics of media texts. Moreover, training in this field often centers on theories of cultural production, political economy, and audience and reception analysis. Regarding methods, quantitative and qualitative techniques are normally taught, with the former often receiving more weight in graduate training. Furthermore, methodology courses that combine quantitative and qualitative techniques, or that are even built around mixed methods approaches, are far less common than comparable classes centered on a particular technique like survey design, content analysis, or ethnography.

A cosmopolitan perspective to graduate training about media technologies would entail extending these current practices in both fields at the curricular and course-specific levels. Regarding the former, the study of media technologies through the four quadrants discussed, as well as courses specifically designed to integrate cross-quadrant developments, should be incorporated into the curriculum. In addition, methodological training should be provided not only in a plurality of techniques, but also in particular with a sensibility that integrates the possibilities offered by various methods into multifaceted research designs. This would require the development and provision of courses that, rather than keeping the quadrants segregated or simply juxtaposing them, could help students establish dialogues across them and imagine how their links matter for making sense of the production and consumption, and materiality and content, of media technologies.

At the course-specific level, it would be critical to develop classes that bring together scholarship in at least two, if not all four, of the quadrants, and that problematize the benefits and limitations of the respective scholarships with an eye to exploring the possible articulations across them. Boczkowski's seminar at Northwestern University mentioned in the beginning of this chapter illustrates the potential of this sort of experience. This graduate seminar, called Media Meets Technology, began with four sessions that addressed the scholarship within each quadrant individually. This was essential to distill the advantages and disadvantages of conducting research that segregates production from consumption and materiality from content. In the following weeks, the course moved on to explore studies that bridged either the production/consumption or the materiality/content divide, or both. As the seminar unfolded, students were required to think about potential research projects at the center of the four research quadrants. These projects crystallized in a research design that was part of the required activities that the students had to produce for the class. Projects were in turn collectively discussed and further developed in the final weeks of the seminar.

The cosmopolitan perspective enacted in this seminar inspired students to imagine and, in some cases, implement a variety of new research initiatives. For instance, one participant proposed an investigation of the early history of the remote control through a combination of archival research and interviews with both producers and early users (Plotnick 2012a, 2012b, 2013). Another student proposed a study—which subsequently evolved into her dissertation research—of the ways that political campaigns understand and use digital technologies by looking at the interactions between materiality and content configurations (Baldwin-Philippi 2011a, 2011b). Together with the examples from Siles's research discussed previously, these brief illustrations show the generative capacity of a cosmopolitan sensibility in graduate student training, within the space of a class taught just a couple of times. They also reveal the multiplicity of ways in which cosmopolitanism in the study of media technologies can be enacted.

Design Implications

Scholars and developers have increasingly acknowledged the role of users in designing media technologies (Akrich 1992, 1995; Bardini 2000; Oudshoorn and Pinch 2003; Pinch and Trocco 2002). Research on "participatory design," for instance, has helped to illuminate how a multiplicity of users and communities can shape technological design dynamics (Schuler and Namioka 1993). Despite these valuable contributions, most work in this tradition has concentrated on issues of the consumption of materiality and failed to fully address the significance of production and content for design matters.

Regarding production dynamics, work in STS and the political economy of communication shows that organizational processes in the production and distribution of media technologies significantly shape their use. From this perspective, designers and developers would benefit from a better understanding of how both artifacts and texts are produced, distributed, and commercialized. A cosmopolitan perspective envisions design as a process shaped by the dynamics that variously connect the production and the consumption of media technologies, rather than as an isolated moment or phase. Thus, this approach seeks to understand the design of media technologies by looking at how production is structured and organized, how media technologies circulate, and how they reach user groups through different means and at different moments of development. From this perspective, considering how media technologies are displayed, regulated, and distributed might provide key elements toward understanding design as a dynamic of cultural mediation through which artifacts gain meaning and identities (Du Gay et al. 1997).

Researchers in STS have also emphasized how following the "biography" or the "journey" of an artifact might help identify loci for influencing its development (Hyysalo 2010; Rip and Schot 2002). Considering these processes can contribute to identify crucial moments, sites, and dynamics that mark the life cycle of media technologies. In a similar vein, scholars have stressed the relevance of investigating the "mediation junctions" between production and consumption as a means to understanding how "consumers, mediators, and producers meet to negotiate, articulate, and align specific technical choices and user needs" (Schot and de la Bruhèze 2003, 234). Overall, the cosmopolitan sensibility we advocate should help to illuminate how the design of media technologies is a multi-situated process shaped by the distribution of agency among designers, bundles of artifacts and texts, users, and intermediaries.

Concerning the content of media technologies, this dimension is often considered epiphenomenal to issues of materiality in discussions of design practices. For example, reflecting on the value of actor-network theory for participatory design, Callon (2004) noted that, "Intellectual achievements, ideas, projects, plans, production of information [in design], are through and through material processes. Technologies shape their content" (7). An expression of this tendency has often surfaced in treatments of the notion of affordances, one of the most generative ideas in scholarship on design (Norman 1988, 1999). This notion has commonly been applied to examine the material possibilities and constraints of new technologies. But analyses of how users take advantage of a media artifact's affordances to create and interpret content, and how these practices might shape design processes, have been rather scarce. Thus, while acknowledging that technologies shape their content, as Callon suggests, a cosmopolitan sensibility to design would also seek to understand how content shapes its technologies. As scholarship in communication and media studies has shown, content *can* greatly affect the use and stabilization of technology. That is, whether or not it *does* matter should be an empirical outcome rather than an epistemic assumption. Therefore, content dynamics should be considered a constitutive dimension of the process of design, rather being implicitly treated as a supplement to materiality.

For instance, the use of "personas," fictional characters created by designers as a representation of putative users, has become a popular interactional design technique (Cooper 1999; Grudin 2006; Pruitt and Adlin 2006). According to Grudin and Pruitt (2002), "Personas create a strong focus on users and work contexts through the fictionalized setting . . . [They] generate . . . a momentum that increase[s] general user focus and awareness [among designers]" (6). Although researchers have used media texts such as movies and television programs as a model for developing complex, realistic, and engaging personas, how users deal with these types of content has seldom been explored. Thus, while aspects such as "computer skills" and "technology attributes and attitudes" are considered central features of personas, no major reflection is devoted to their main content creation and interpretation practices (Ibid.). In a related vein, "user experience" approaches contend that design decisions must be "dictated by the psychology and behavior of the users themselves" (Garrett 2002, 8). However, how users appropriate different content options of media technologies is barely considered a significant part of this definition of experience, despite the reliance on media for helping people make sense of the world. As Bird has shown, "We cannot really isolate the role of media in culture, because the media are firmly anchored into the web of culture, although articulated by individuals in different ways. . . . The 'audience' is everywhere and nowhere" (Bird 2003, 3). A better understanding of content interpretation practices might thus lead to more nuanced definitions of personas and user experiences and, therefore, to different design pathways.

In sum, a cosmopolitan perspective sensitizes us to look at technological design as a process that is linked with the dynamics traditionally studied across the quadrants, rather than a phenomenon that belongs to a single one. Such perspective will not only lead to a better understanding of the factors that inform technological design but could also contribute to a more thorough assessment of the dynamics that shape the life cycle of media technologies.

Concluding Remarks

The pursuit of a cosmopolitan perspective entails returning to the epistemic inclinations that led to the development of STS and communication and media research. Both fields emerged from vibrant conversations that crossed established disciplinary formations. A curiosity toward new research objects triggered a variety of questions that cut across disciplinary territories and stimulated new theoretical approaches. Over recent decades, however, these initial outward-focused dynamics turned inward within each of these fields. This has led to work that is based on a significant degree of tacit knowledge and taken-for-grantedness about what constitutes adequate theoretical lenses, suitable methodological strategies, relevant pedagogical practices, and desirable design approaches. This, in turn, has enabled concentrated efforts on particular topics and a high level of field-wide disciplinarization of specific modes of inquiry. These efforts have generated many valuable insights. But, as shown in this chapter, they have also come at a price in terms of reduced descriptive fit and diminished explanatory power. Thus, moving forward might require, in a paradoxical fashion, also going backward by revisiting the cosmopolitan sensibility that animated prior phases in the development of both fields.

The cosmopolitan sensibility that informed the early phase of development of both fields was intertwined with a central attitude of curiosity about the object of inquiry. Over time, these objects became fetishized (ends in themselves, rather than means toward a goal of empirical enlightenment and theoretical development) as the dialogue became reified into self-contained intellectual quadrants, and the overall tone became one of provincialism rather than cosmopolitanism. In the past couple of decades, digital media technologies have come to play an increasingly ubiquitous role in our experience of the world, being present in almost every arena of social life, from finance and medicine to travel and sports. This new role affords a renewed curiosity about media technologies as objects of inquiry, which, in turn, should contribute toward a cosmopolitan perspective. Studying the work of scientists, Knorr Cetina (1999) wrote about the "object-centered" management approach that characterizes molecular biology laboratories. By this, she referred to "the sense of the continuous, daily interactions with material things, . . . the need to establish close relationships with the materials, and . . . the experience bench scientists can gain from them" (86). Inspired by Knorr Cetina's depiction of object-oriented management in scientific pursuits, cosmopolitanism in the study of media technologies conceives research objects as means of bringing about innovative combinations of scholars and ideas from various fields. Cosmopolitanism, we suggest, envisions media technologies not as the destination but as a point of departure for exploring the multiple dimensions that constitute them and the significance of how these dimensions intersect.

A cosmopolitan perspective for the study of media technologies should result in the creation of fertile grounds for examining relevant matters across the broader landscape of the social sciences and the humanities. Despite the centrality of media technologies in almost every aspect of contemporary social, political, cultural, and economic life, scholarship about them has not only self-segregated into the four research quadrants, but also been somewhat isolated from larger debates in social, cultural, and behavioral theory. In other words, work on media technologies has been the concern of a set of distinct intellectual provinces, rather than also a contributor to theoretical discourses cutting across multiple objects of inquiry. But because media technologies have become, as Appadurai puts it, crucial in "rebuilding the fabric of reality itself" (from an interview in Morley 2011, 45), their study presents an opportunity for broader intellectual engagement in the social sciences and the humanities. Using the renewed interest in media technologies as a point of departure, because of its dialogical orientation, a cosmopolitan sensibility affords an opportunity to move in this direction. We hope this chapter provides some initial steps in this journey.

Acknowledgments

We thank Geof Bowker, Finn Brunton, Gabriella Coleman, Kirsten Foot, Tarleton Gillespie, Leah Lievrouw, Gina Neff, Trevor Pinch, Jonathan Sterne, Lucy Suchman, and the students at Northwestern University who took the "Media Meets Technology" seminar with the first author in the spring 2009 and winter 2010 quarters.

Notes

1. Although we are aware that science and technology studies and media and communication research vary in their levels of institutionalization and disciplinarization, throughout this chapter we refer to both as intellectual fields characterized by somewhat coherent sets of theories, methods, and objects of study (Bijker, Hughes, and Pinch 1987; Craig 1999; Law 2008; Rogers 1997; Schramm 1997; Woolgar 2004).

2. We use this two-dimensional map as a heuristic device to discuss major approaches and concerns in STS and communication studies. As a tool, this map allows us to identify key ideas by discussing important works in both fields. Yet we are aware of the limitations that constructing such a tool has and the difficulties of situating particular studies within the confines of specific quadrants. The cosmopolitan sensibility we advocate is precisely a means to signal these limitations and to explore the possibilities illustrated by those studies that are difficult to classify.

4   Closer to the Metal

Finn Brunton and Gabriella Coleman

Introduction

Our project in this chapter is to reflexively break down the analysis of information and media infrastructure that we have developed, in our work as scholars, into its component parts. We do this to better understand the strengths and flaws of our approaches to working on subjects like Anonymous (the online activist group) and spam (nuisance messages and unwanted advertising online), and what these approaches might offer scholarship more generally. We assert the value of getting closer to the metal, and understanding in depth the technical architectures and processes that underlie online phenomena, but also assert that this dive into hardware is not a simple revelation of some true, foundational reality. When we peel back that deepest layer of materiality, we find people and practices underneath: populations of users, and the "superusers" who operate close to the metal in their work, including system and net administrators (sys/net admins), hackers, and spammers in complex, contingent, ambiguous relationships. The layers of hardware, users, and maintainers that make up many Internet phenomena are, in turn, fashioned into stories, theories, and concepts by which many others—from scholars to journalists to designers to politicians—take them up and turn them to various purposes, a fashioning which often dangerously and damagingly oversimplifies what is actually happening.

Consider, as a parallel, Lisa Gitelman's *Always Already New,* in which she seeks to "bedevil the strict dichotomy of production and consumption" (2006, 60) that characterize much of the received history and conceptions of media technology. To put it most crudely: a brilliant lone inventor, or a group in a garage, invents the technology. Masses of people consume it, and have their experiences mediated by it—and soon they inhabit a different world as a consequence. The producers create, and from their labs and workshops come tools, formats, and systems that make publics as a thresher makes grain from a field of wheat. Bedeviling this inaccurate and oversimplified story, Gitelman brings in the users—"diverse, dynamic, and disaggregate" (61) groups who are actively involved in shaping the features, the values, and the future of the systems they use. Her multilayered understanding of media systems is built on the historical example of how phonography comes about. This chapter concerns itself with the contemporary Internet, and two very different phenomena that happen there, but Gitelman's structure provides an excellent introduction to our argument, in goal as well as in structure. Gitelman asks, "Who made the phonograph?" and the answer turns out be much more extensive than the roll call of Edison and workers at Bell and Berliner. In our work, we ask "Who makes spam?" and "What makes Anonymous possible?" and find answers of technical and social complexity that suggest consequences and a model for how we study current and future media technologies.

Let us unfold these simple questions, first, into their component parts. Our initial answer opens into three distinct but overlapping frames, each implying the next, and each with relevance for studying media.

Materiality: The Hardware Story
To answer the questions, "Who *makes* spam?" or "What makes Anonymous possible?" you must start with the making, with the computers, servers, switches, cables, filters and algorithms, the protocols and mail standards. The infrastructure must be accounted for, alongside the screens, software, and users. To discuss the infrastructure also entails discussing the groups (and their labor) along with institutions that produce, regulate, and maintain it: the sys/net admins and IT and telecom professionals. These imply a second frame.

Users and Superusers: The Social Story
The obvious answer to "*Who* makes spam?" is that it is made by many orders and assemblies of users. Discussing the infrastructure in detail reveals that there are differences of access to and capability with the hardware, starting with those system administrators. There are the diverse families of users discussed by Gitelman (2006) who make various contributions to what the technology becomes, and to this array we would like to add the "superusers," a concept we will discuss in detail. "Superuser" is a term from computing for a special account meant for administrative functions (different operating systems use different designations, such as root, admin, baron, or supervisor). Computers and computer networks offer many more degrees of

control than a phonograph or a magazine, and while all users play a significant role in the adoption and meaning of a technology, some can disproportionately produce functionality or wreak havoc. This includes the invention of new forms of social organization and labor that can take advantage of the material properties of the hardware, as we will see with Anonymous.

Concretion: The Facile Story

Finally, our final frame entertains more conceptual issues about categories and conceptual stabilization. Spam and Anonymous are spoken of as though they were single, self-consistent blocks of stuff, and made into stable, concrete objects that can be addressed with one name, in an act of misplaced concretism.[1] These stabilizations, too, are central to the making process and there are multiple sources with different agendas: academics, journalists, and law enforcement come most to mind as they distinctly represent and make Anonymous and spam. This making, whether in the form of law or journalistic rhetoric, must be borne in mind because it can interfere with how we answer the question of the ways these phenomena are produced.

In other words, hardware always entails institutional, structural, and designed potentials and constraints. Users and superusers take material objects up for many purposes and with many levels of agency. The things that happen then get rhetorically and discursively packaged, especially by the mass media, in the case of Anonymous, for still other groups to interact with and exploit. None of these frames alone provides a satisfactory entry point in itself to the questions of "Who makes spam?" or "What makes Anonymous possible?" Materialism is necessary, getting down to assembler language and undersea cables to produce an accurate sense of the substratum of a complex event—necessary, and often overlooked or marginalized, but not sufficient. The users and superusers have to be brought in, with their plethora of means, motives, and opportunities; no phenomenon would exist without them.

They, too, are necessary but not sufficient for a complete picture. The complete picture includes its own blind spots, occlusions, and range of focus, in the practices by which we as scholars research, document, and conceptualize our subjects. We need to close the loop by describing how the story of the phenomenon is made and told by others and by us, sometimes too easily and too simply. This awareness of how we make our model and construct our history—what gets included and why—feeds back into our analysis of hardware and our study of users. We need to reexamine where we place significance, where we set our starting point. (Someone from a sociological background can see in these three frames a modified and particular form of the natural, social, and discursive answers to the question of agency, linked together into a loop.)

The three parts that follow address each of these frames and help answer our initial questions about spam and Anonymous. The first takes the issue of hardware analysis and materiality, and demonstrates both the importance and the limitations of such an approach by itself—that we get down to the deepest, abiding bedrock layer of the material, peel it back, and find people, societies, and discourses at work. The second concentrates on Anonymous and the role of the technologists (user and superuser communities, sysadmins, discussants on an IRC [Internet Relay Chat] channel) in constituting the movement and its strategies, building on their technical fluency and varying control over the hardware, and on the role of secrecy and legal pressure in their practices. Finally, the third section takes up spam to explore how we build oversimplified conceptual models of complex and multifaceted technical events, and how those models can be productively bedeviled (to take Gitelman's [2006] term). To be clear, even as each section emphasizes its respective question, it also addresses the other two. Each frame—of hardware, of users, of stories—implies and affects the others. "Getting close to the metal" means getting close to the narratives and the people who tell them. Only with all three frames of reference in mind can we start to work at the breadth and detail appropriate to the polyphonic, massively multiuser, and materially intricate phenomena occurring on networked computers now.

Hardware, or the Concurrent Realities of Infrastructure

Where does infrastructure stop? For a start, keeping the system up, and keeping up with the system, requires power of at least three kinds. First, of course, is electrical: coal, diesel, sometimes nuclear, sometimes renewables. The clean, disembodied, virtual cyberworld produces a lot of coal smoke.[2] Second, it requires the production and maintenance of systems and software, which implies the third—a massive, often hidden, quantity of labor conducted by armies of net, system, and database administrators. A typical day for a system or net administrator might entail verifying backups, monitoring performance and connectivity, account provisioning, escalated support requests, and monitoring script output. Some days will be dominated by fixing problems and troubleshooting, trying to figure out why a server went down. Others are spent working proactively by, for instance, devising a backup scheme to time when backups happen, when old ones should be deleted, and then to automate the process. The infrastructure itself runs from that CAT-5 Ethernet cable plugged into the computer or the router through the jack in the wall over many different kinds of cables and lines provided by a proliferation of services in different countries, some monopolistic, some happily complying with governmental warrantless information requests, some filtering and blocking access, some public-private partnerships going through neoliberal convulsions. By occupational necessity, the system administrator is often conscious of the politics that run through the cable, undergird the co-location facility, and lay behind retaining (or not) server logs.

The cables likely pass through a co-location center, which houses noisy servers, where trunks of wiring run through the racks overhead or under the floor, and massive diesel generators sit on standby to assure redundant power. The co-location center is a site of many intricate stakeholder agreements and alliances. It may well be an "Internet Exchange Point," where the enormous Internet Service Providers (ISPs) and telecommunications carriers exchange data across their borders of proprietary ownership in the "Meet Me Room." (The Meet Me Room in the massive Southern California co-location center One Wilshire in Los Angeles is, in inches or centimeters, the most expensive real estate on Earth.[3]) From there, the request for a page may very likely go to one of the massive server farms—many of their locations kept top secret—with ranks and ranks of immaculate machines mounted into their racks in anonymous windowless buildings, blue LEDs glowing, in the permanent roar of the air conditioning, carefully laid out to ensure the flow patterns of cool and hot air. The cost of cooling a big server farm has led to the initiative to site them in locations like Iceland, where the ambient temperature suits them, or to the idea of "data furnaces," where those same racks, mounted in the basements of apartment buildings, vent waste heat by flue (Liu et al. 2011).

Depending on what you request, or to whom you're sending email, your packets may well pass through one of the major fiber optic "backbone" lines on the world's sea floors, and make landfall in Ajigaura, Porthcurno, Mombasa, Chongming, or span the Suez Canal (where they can be knocked out by a stray anchor), each with their own border-crossing issues of political context. System administrators install and tweak filtering software so that when your email arrives in your inbox, it does so only with only a trickle of spam instead of the torrent being sent every day, and your government may engage in filtering on a far, far larger scale.

We can go further, getting more material, beneath all the labor hours and BTUs, into the chips themselves. "Getting close to the metal" is a phrase with a rich connotative history. It means getting "deep" or "close," in the spatial language of programming, below the mediating layers of higher-level languages (much less the distracting, iconographic candy of the graphical user interface, the glossy streamlined chassis for computing-as-appliance). It means the work one does speaks as directly as possible to the underlying structure of the hardware and the labor directed at working with it. For instance, the memory management properties of the programming language C make it possible to get to grips with an approximation of what's actually happening inside the RAM chips in the computer, rather than pushing all that behind the curtain of mediating layers of management code. Using C can bring you closer to the metal, in that sense—to a version of interaction with the aluminum or gold and silicon in the thing itself. There are practical reasons for seeking this closeness or depth, mostly to do with exerting very fine-grained control over resources and functionality, with the corresponding danger of being able to make much riskier mistakes.

However, there is also a kind of crudely Platonic satisfaction to the idea of getting beneath the "fake" scrim of the graphics and the fussy abstractions of the higher-level languages. (It's a satisfaction generally not shared by actual working programmers and software engineers, who have to make pragmatic production decisions.) One can get down to the ultimate, unitary material reality of hard drive sectors and the queuing of instructions on chips, down to the wires, transistors, and "vias" where two layers of a chip connect and transact—into the realm of the Johnson-Nyquist noise, the thermal agitation of the electrons in a conductor at equilibrium inside the chip. It's hard to get more ontologically fundamental than physics, the drift and diffusion, heat, and electrostatic fields in the diode: no more language games, no more yarn-spinning in the agora. Bedrock at last! And what do we find there?

We encounter the multiple, sometimes contradictory, and sometimes coexistent experiences that obtain on the network infrastructure. Some of these realities—different kinds of subjectivities, publics, societies, and modes of living on the hardware—may be entirely distinct but nonetheless thrive together, like commensal bacteria in which the byproducts of one happen to create a suitable environment for the population of another. Others exist in tension or mutual ignorance and then, at the first moment of encounter, struggle to exterminate one another. There is a sysadmin experience, various hacker experiences (open source, black vs. white hat vs. grey hat), an Anonymous experience for many different values of "Anonymous," and likewise for spammers; an experience for "civilian" users who just need to get by, an experience for telecom executives, one for law-enforcement personnel and cryptanalysts and eavesdroppers and so on. These many distinct social realities are at every point mutable, some more so than others. They change with time and scale, and go through flip-flops where the content, shaped by the infrastructural context, becomes the context in which the content is designed and altered.

Writing in lower-level languages and tracing the hops across the network, observing the material at work, is vitally important. It helps us see more and in more detail about network activities. However, this necessary access does not provide a unitary much less single truth pertaining across the board to every last action, interaction, and place online. These demand awareness of the diversity of perspectives and uses available, sometimes gracefully coexisting, sometimes in conflict. It might also mean tactically emphasizing one perspective over others, especially in the event of its historical marginalization, as was the case, until quite recently, with the labor involved in the Internet's infrastructure (which we will address in the following section). When we get closer to the metal, we enter a domain of many potential forms, capacities, and uses, and must be conscious that our trace of the material is one path among many coexisting virtual paths. Getting into the chip and the switch is merely the first step on this journey.

Anonymous, or Sysadmins and Superusers

Unless otherwise noted, descriptions of Anonymous in the upcoming section are drawn from Gabriella Coleman's (2012, 2013) previous research.

Moving onto the study of users plunges us into the deep end of these diverse social relationships and cultures of users and superusers installing, maintaining, configuring, and using hardware. How do they constitute and understand themselves? What is necessary to stage a successful event online? As we will discuss, Anonymous touches on the importance of infrastructure (and differing degrees of access to and control of that infrastructure), on the complex agency of various users and stakeholders, and on the conceptual and narrative problems around how to define what we mean by "Anonymous." In the following sections we will discuss technical dimensions that contribute to the visibility and stability of Anonymous, and then trouble this perspective by briefly turning to its obverse—the maintenance of secrecy and invisibility.

Weapons of the Geek: Anonymous and Popular Misrepresentations

Anonymous is one example of a burgeoning arena of political life: interventions staged by geeks and hackers. These individuals not only understand how the Internet works but also culturally constitute themselves by spending copious time online with each other as they make, tinker with, and argue about technology. As Chris Kelty has shown, many care deeply about keeping the technical architecture of the Internet open so that it can be modified, extended, and altered (2008). A good portion of these geeks, from Bangalore to Sydney, will rise up, especially when the Internet and the values associated with it like privacy and free speech seem to be in peril; a smaller class can actually subvert the Internet's routers and protocols. The short history of geek and hacker politics has already shown that there are many ways to defend the Internet, from writing open source software, to joining the Pirate Party and donating to the Electronic Frontier Foundation (EFF) and activity like this only seems to be increasing.

Anonymous is part of this wider political constellation and distinctive for being scalable, irreverent, and hard to comprehend. Indeed, the very name used by the online activists *Anonymous* bears the difficulty in profiling this entity and those that make up its ranks. Though rather opaque in its constitution, it has achieved thunderous media notoriety due to the blizzard of activist interventions between 2008 and 2012 enacted in its name, from humiliating hacking assaults against security firms to orchestrating nonviolent street demonstrations, from opposing any bill that whiffs of censorship, to allying itself with local groups, as it did with the nonprofit Food not Bombs in Orlando, Florida, after members of the charity were arrested by police.

In contrast to open source software, let's say, which is straightforward to define and easy to study, Anonymous is resistant to the kinds of stable categories that we commonly insist on for description and analysis. Not only is impossible to gather basic—much less extensive—statistical data about users, but also some Anons seed misinformation as a counter-espionage tactic. Taking stock of their unexpected metamorphosis from Internet trolling to insurgent activism, the numerous regional and international nodes that compose this network, and the string of operations they delivered in the last three years, one certainly fumbles to bundle it all up into the linear and straightforward narrative so valued by academic analysis.

Yet this sense that they are at root *amorphous* (one of the most common descriptors hung onto them in the news and academic pieces) rests on woefully ignoring the most basic of technical and material realities about them. By painting Anonymous as, foremost, nebulous, we empirically misrepresent them. While this poses a problem for academics, this omission troubles us more for its broader implications. As researchers who work on a topic of great interest to law enforcement, it is difficult not to directly broach the broader ethical implications of leaving the "metal" out of this picture; to only highlight their spectral dimensions, we inevitably drift into hyperbole, exaggerating the extent to which people find them threatening, adding to the air of mystery surrounding hackers who fly under that banner, feeding into the hysteria that law enforcement (and the defense contractors selling security and "anti-hacker solutions") self-consciously seek to cultivate.

To be sure, Anonymous is not a singularity, but is comprised of multiple, loosely organized nodes with various regional networks in existence. No one group or individual can control the name and iconography, much less claim legal ownership over them, and as such their next steps are difficult to predict. Although many individual participants therein do resist institutionalization or even defining their norms, there are logics at play and stable places for interaction. Operations don't simply spring out of the ether and can be easily linked to a particular network, such as AnonOps, Anonset, or VoxAnon (to take three of the most important ones today). At minimum these networks usually will lay claim to, or deny, being the source of an operation. Anons are also not completely or always as veiled, as they are often portrayed: there are regular participants, cloaked under pseudonymity rather than anonymity, and often they are available on stable Internet Relay Chat servers where one can interact with them every day.

Having a firm grasp of basic sociological dynamics and the technological components of operations goes a long way to help us understand what they have done, what they are capable of doing, and what they will likely not (or simply can't) do. Take, for instance, the following common mantra: Anonymous is so unstable and incoherent that any individual can take its name for good and for evil. "They are chaotic good like Robin Hood, and there is chaotic evil as well . . . There are some people that just want to see the world burn," notes Josh Corman who has written extensively (and often quite insightfully) about their actions.[4] While there have been a handful of incidents we can describe as uncharacteristically un-Anonymous or as led by one individual (as was the case with the lone anti-abortion hacker who targeted Britain's largest abortion clinic), this doom-and-gloom prediction of chaos unleashed by evil hackers remains largely unfulfilled, though it looms in the public anxieties of Anonymous as excessively dangerous, in need of a Tora Bora spelunking mission to destroy them before they crack the earth in half.

However, in the astonishing number of Anonymous-led operations of the last three years, there has never been a single large-scale diabolical operation, nor has any existing network ever expressed the desire to do something as rash and problematic as taking down the power grid, as the

National Security Agency purported in February 2012.[5] The absurdity of this claim was put into (comic) relief by one participant who quipped: "That's right, we're definitely taking down the power grid, we'll know we've succeeded when all the equipment we use to mount our campaign is rendered completely useless."

Surface technical knowledge about their operations is imperative to assess their political tactics, but these basic technological facts rarely make their way into public and academic debate. Take for instance one common tactic deployed by AnonOps, the distributed denial of service (DDoS) attack; it is often incorrectly likened to a hack that *destroys* or *damages* servers or data. This digital protest tactic, when successful, essentially squats and blocks access to some of the Internet's biggest domains, but only their Internet-facing websites. By design, if companies are following basic security best practices, core infrastructure such as financial payment processing and trading networks is not sitting wide open on the Internet waiting to be attacked. If it were, any security professional would describe such a setup as reckless malfeasance, and those sites, where downtime spells financial hemorrhage, would have been attacked to shreds long before Anonymous came on the scene. Their DDoS tactics are a political stunt; the sites that are more vulnerable to DDoS tend not to be actual important infrastructure, just symbolic of that infrastructure.

Most accounts make Anonymous out to be more mysterious than it is, distort the nature and effect of many of their digital interventions, and also overlook the ways in which Anonymous is also quite accessible, knowable, and predictable. If we were to use most writings on Anonymous as guide, one would think they would be impossible to find. It is for this reason that nearly every time Coleman has been interviewed by journalists about Anonymous, she is asked, quite sincerely: "And just how do you find Anonymous?" Her reply (usually given while staring at Anonymous participants on her screen): "I talk to them for too long every day, on Internet Relay Chat."

IRC and Sysadmin Ethics

Anonymous, like so many domains of geek and hacker political action, is partly made possible by what we might think of as surplus technical capacity, such as the labor of system or net administrators. Many of these individuals gain, develop, and refine skills at work, which are then mobilized politically by a much smaller cohort; some of these even do activist work at their day job since many employers cannot distinguish between organizing sales backups and configuring an IRC server. To the untrained eye this technical language—it might be source code, or configuration files, or scripts—just looks like extremely complicated text, and many sys/net admins take advantage of this gap in digital literacy to accomplish activist work on their employers' dime.

In the case of Anonymous, system and net administrators, among other tasks, install, configure, and maintain Internet Relay Chat servers, one of the main platforms used by distinct Anonymous networks. Once they install an IRC server, their work is not over. Often aided by a small team of individuals with similar skills, these individuals act as part plumber, part groundskeeper, and part ninja, fixing problems, maintaining the system, and fending off endless attacks. For instance, in the last year a number of the largest and most stable IRC networks—AnonOps and VoxAnon—were routinely taken down by DDoS attacks; operations came to a screeching halt. Many of these individuals also deploy their extensive and intimate knowledge of servers, networks, botnets, security, and vulnerabilities to take part in a distributed denial of service attack or hacking attack, two common tactics used by Anonymous (not all of the net or system administrators contribute to illegal actions and some Anonymous network vehemently oppose any and all illegal tactics).

Even if much within Anonymous feels and is impenetrable, these individuals and the teams tasked with doing the work of maintenance and upkeep on IRC servers are some of the more active players on these networks. Some of the networks even erect web pages proudly announcing the "staff," and these individuals are usually "operators" of important channels; as on all IRC networks, operators can ban users, grant other users operator status, and set or change the channel topic. It is simply no mystery who these people are, for their nicknames are marked by some symbol such a star or flag designating such status.

Those who install an IRC server in some respects play a godlike role, having literal superuser access to the server and thus direct control over this dominion. They can scan the traffic coming in and out of the server, they can decide to log (or not) incoming IP addresses and whether or how to cloak the addresses, all of which have serious implications for law enforcement (this is not unique to Anonymous). They can even snoop on all private conversations, although certain encryption tools can make it a more difficult endeavor.

Indeed, *all* system and net administrators who tender and tend to servers housing web content, email, and databases have access to some of the most intimate (or most boring) details of our lives as recorded in email and chats. It should come as no surprise, then, that the profession of system administration has chartered a code: "The System Administrators' Code of Ethics."[6] Among other topics, including law and policy, this document prominently features privacy: "I will access private information on computer systems only when it is necessary in the course of my technical duties. I will maintain and protect the confidentiality of any information to which I may have access regardless of the method by which I came into knowledge of it" (League of Professional System Administrators 2006). On the other hand, Anonymous's technical elite are keenly aware of ethical implications of their technical power, though their thoughts and opinions tend to emerge only under certain conditions, usually strife. Take for instance this scathing critique culled from a web page, since taken down, which takes issue with the admins who run AnonOps, one of the most populated and popular Anonymous IRC networks in recent years:

• If there are no leaders, then who is there to wrest control from?
• If there's [sic] no leaders, why couldn't [sic] everyone read PMs [private messages] in realtime?
• If there's no leaders, why couldn't everyone set the target for the LOIC hivemind?
• If there's no leaders, why do opers [operators] have to be respected, and why can I be kicked/banned for mentioning [name deleted in original posting] too many times? Why can I be banned for making a joke that [name deleted in original posting] doesn't like?

As the list indicates, most accusations are directed at the system and net administrators who manage and own resources. Misgivings over AnonOps ran deep, owing to numerous security breaches that put participants at risk for using a piece of DDoS software (LOIC), and because an irascible administrator was regarded by many as particularly power hungry and erratic. By this time, hacking, which once occurred less frequently and certainly covertly had become an overt activity led by small groups bearing distinct names, like Antisec. They hacked for political purposes, largely to expose security vulnerabilities or search for evidence of corporate malfeasance (Coleman 2013).

By the fall of 2011, in response to these AnonOps shortcomings and to the small, necessarily clandestine Antisec crew that was behind a string of hacks, some disaffected Anons—many with significant technical skills and capacities—conceived of and built an alternative network called VoxAnon. Officially launched on February 12, 2012, VoxAnon did something new in the short history of Anonymous: its founders released a constitution explicitly outlining the purpose of the network and the role that technical guardians should (and should not) play. It is worth quoting it at length, for it gives a clear window not only into how VoxAnon's creators strive toward a moral commonweal but, more relevant to this chapter, how close they are to the machine—they hold a keen awareness of the ways technological capacities, affordances, realities, and skills impinge on the ethical realities they seek to engender.

Constitution of VoxAnon

1. This network upholds a policy of unconditional free speech, unless that speech poses a direct threat to the network. Such a threat must be proven.

2. Network administrators must not/are not allowed to interfere in channel management unless required to do so in order to prevent a direct threat to the network, or if the channel owner explicitly requests for a network administrator to do so.

3. You have the right to privacy in private channels. No oper may join a private channel unless invited, or to prevent a direct threat to the existence of the network.

4. Network business, channel business, and organization of operations must be kept completely separated at all times.

5. In channel/operation business, a network administrator is neither more nor less important than the user.

6. Network business and discussion by administrators is to be discussed in a publicly viewable channel, unless there is a specific well-argued reason to discuss it in private.

7. Except for situations that pose an immediate threat to the network, all network-related decisions have to be made by the administrator team as a whole, and not by individual network administrators.

8. Under no circumstances should network administrators be able to view, intercept, or manipulate personal messages sent over the network.

9. Network administrators are forbidden from giving out personal information of any user for any reason, even legal. (VoxAnon 2012)

Does the existence of this constitution mean that VoxAnon lives up to the leaderless ideal of Anonymous while AnonOps fails to do so? It is rather more complicated than this binary formulation. It is too early to tell whether the constitution will act as a guide for action or whether it merely expressed frustration at a given historical moment over existing power dynamics; we suspect the latter given how Anonymous resists institutionalization. The significance of the critique and constitution lies in how they reveal certain native understandings about the close relationship between political authority and technical labor and structures; but technical affordances also contribute toward the fragmentation of power, so that even in AnonOps, where technical elites hold more power and authority, power gets dispersed as well.

On IRC, where many operations are coordinated and discussed, users are generally afforded the freedom to initiate their own operations and channels. While the network founders and staff can and do ban individuals or a channel, or discourage an operation from flourishing, most IRC networks have a long tradition—and this is no different with Anonymous—of a laissez faire, hands off approach to the creation of channels. While those who manage and control technical resources do wield extra power, there is no one group with the authority to control and command the dozens of operations, much less control other networks in existence.

Still, when it comes to single operations, there usually are, as one Anon put it, ad hoc leaders who, if they stick around and continue to work, become prominent and trusted figures. Every operation has its own history and organizational culture, and of course the technologically naive rely on participants with technical skills. Individuals with fewer technical skills become prominent operators and ad hoc leaders, especially those who pour significant time into the network and who are adept rhetoricians (Coleman 2012).

Finally, while technical operations—hacking, launching DDoS—are crucial to Anonymous, so too are nontechnical ops: this entity is just as much a well-oiled populist and distributed PR machine as is any other more traditional organization. It is made possible by the labor of geeks, hackers, and activists of all stripes who at the drop of a hat can configure servers and provide each other with infrastructure—but who also create stirring press releases and propaganda posters, edit videos to promote their cause, and deface web servers and steal sensitive content from corporations and governments, or failing that, momentarily bring websites down entirely using denial of service attacks. While these skills may be essential to carry out an Anonymous operation (as I have discussed earlier) there are still no particular abilities required of participants to join the political carnival; one must merely desire to self-identify as "Anonymous"—one of the core reasons it has so easily spread across the globe, from Japan to Brazil.

Fascination with Secrecy

If there is a certain degree of clarity one gains by paying attention to system and net administrators and the technical power they wield, for much of the time and in many other contexts the waters within Anonymous are still murky. To veer toward laborers and their machines will yield sociological dividends, but only to a degree; scholars can grasp the sociology of Anonymous but it is rather partial and incomplete, largely because Anonymous is also built on a foundation of mystery.

To research Anonymous is to descend into a rabbit hole and find oneself in a maze, difficult to navigate, always under construction, and permeated with secrets: Who is who? Who talks to whom? Who does what? This mystery is partly hinged to the very technical affordance of IRC, which is built with the flexibility for someone to log on as multiple individuals; you can also watch people talking to each other on public channels, but there are multiple hidden discussions as well. Rumors of infiltration abound; such rumors proved real in early March 2012 after news broke that Sabu, one of the most notorious hackers of the Antisec crew, had been working since at least fall 2011 as an FBI informant. You never know whether the person who has befriended you on Internet Relay Chat has done so because that is part of their infiltration. And when someone tells you something you never know whether it is the truth or strategic disinformation they are counting on you to disseminate.

Part of the allure of participating in Anonymous is intimately bound with what sociologist Georg Simmel describes as the "fascination of secrecy" and the closely related desire for disclosure and at times betrayal it engenders (Simmel 1906). Over time the researcher comes to hold and bear secrets and have secrets disclosed to them. Although many operations are open to all to participate, there are many necessarily clandestine elements to Anonymous, especially the hacking operations, making parts of it feel somewhat like a secret society. And yet, despite knowing some secrets are in fact true— or they get verified over time—there is so much we don't know or can't verify; this too is also the state of affairs many active and long-time participants find themselves in, even those with significant technical power. Venting frustration over this situation to participants (many of whom are part of the technical elite) gets the earnest, consolatory reply that they feel the same way. That is to say that Anonymous is also built on a foundation of duplicity, in the sense that what we know, see, and feel is false or ineffable or unverifiable, a confused gossamer of deceptions, indirections, stretched truths, and blatant lies, mixed with facts and earnestness.

What the preceding discussion verifies is that Anonymous is anything but Cartesian. In fact, its nature is liminal, "betwixt and between," neither one thing nor the other. Its actions and sympathies straddle the lines between logical and illogical, principled and irreverent, unpredictable and predictable, and visible and invisible.

Spam, or the Problem of Concretism

Earlier in this chapter, we raised the problem we call "misplaced concretism": assuming that something multiplex, mutable, and richly concurrent is simple, coherent, and unified. Because something has the same name over time or for many manifestations, it is thought to be the same thing regardless of elapsed events and different forms, and that consistency becomes part of how the narrative of that thing is created. This process of making a complex phenomenon into a simple object is distinct from blackboxing in the sciences, in which we deliberately bracket some intricate process while concentrating on the inputs and outputs. Rather than blackboxing with the understanding that we aren't clear on what's going on in the box, misplaced concretism assumes that we know what this event is when we make a single, simple noun of it. It makes a claim for comprehensiveness and stability and therein lies the problem. Phenomena like Anonymous and spam are not the kind of complex, difficult, but inert objects we're used to, but rather are protean sociotechnical tangles running on politically laden infrastructure and updating in real time. Having gotten close to the hardware and its users, we must finally get close to the operation of the words and concepts we use to capture, describe, and change technologies and users.

Let us take, as a practical matter toward a theoretical end, the question of how one begins researching spam's history, that is, how spam got made, and who and what made it. We could begin by gathering traces of network history, building chronologies, and collecting instances, which sidesteps the first, obvious problem: professional spammers are not voluble or forthcoming about their work (for obvious reasons). Before the field had become almost wholly criminal, and driven by malware, there were many interviews with "Internet marketers," but some of the most significant people in the business are in hiding, in jail, or operating behind layers of technical secrecy. They are visible and traceable only through the work of police and security services who monitor and occasionally capture them—much as we now know about early Gnostics through the documentation of their heresy by the Christians in the process of their eradication. Along with journalistic work (most notably that of McWilliams 2005) and a few ethnographies of unusual cases like the low-level 419 spammers in Nigeria and Ghana (Burrell 2008; Smith 2007), the best sources came from anti-spam projects—like a spammer's computer hacked by a vengeful, pseudonymous sysadmin in 2000, with the contents posted online.[7] And one must also collect spam itself, which seems trivial: what other research materials arrive unbidden at our inbox and screen, in ceaseless waves, every day?

What becomes immediately clear in doing such a survey is that the meaning of "spam" is wildly varied, and its many genres and values have shifted dramatically over time. Nobody can settle on what spam is, as we can settle (to some degree) on the meaning of "kilogram" or "cirrus cloud," and the working definitions we do have change as fast as does the network itself. This is not to say that the word "spam" as used was meaningless, but rather that there was some generally agreed-upon body of things that were considered spam—spam mail, Twitter spam, spam web pages, and spam blogs ("splogs"), and so on—and in this agreement lay three issues. First, the whole continuum of things considered "spam" covered enormously different technical infrastructures and social offenses, from simple mass-mailing scripts to enormously sophisticated global botnets with military applications; while there are common elements among them, their behavior and mechanisms are as different as a hot air balloon is from a Predator drone. Second, while it would be easy to find a reasonable, canonical example of "spam" for each format, there was enormous trouble with the edge cases, things that were spam for some and not others, creating a space for negotiation that rendered most of the silver-bullet solutions for spam (legal, political, technological) ineffective. Third, the meaning had changed dramatically over time and on different computer networks; the semantic drift, and the changes in the practices described by the word, had rendered conversations only a few years apart completely incommensurate.

Was spam commercial? Not at first, no. In fact, it was a virtually meaningless term, pure noise: a chorus adopted from a *Monty Python* sketch by early online users to flood chat channels with repetitive language—SPAM SPAM SPAM SPAM SPAM SPAM, like an air horn blown in the midst of a conversation. From there, "spam" came to mean making duplicate copies of messages or text across the network, and taking an unfair share of the scarce bandwidth. (Indeed, there are early documents concerned with appropriate behavior on Usenet—shades of the VoxAnon constitution!—which explicitly distinguish spam from commercial messages [Pfaffenberger 1996].) It could be targeted or indiscriminate, about pills or mortgages or politics—or pornography, another category of human activity with grave definitional problems. Speaking purely semantically, it was all too flexible: a noun, both collective and singular ("spam" in general versus "this spam I got this morning"), a verb, and an adjective. Spam was both a word for bandwidth-hogging garbage and the garbage itself, and this ambiguity stays with it as it is applied to a steadily expanding range of sociotechnical problems online.

Indeed, many of the problems dogging early developers of spam-filtering technology revolved around that range of problems, and the variant understandings different users had of spam. No one had a "representative" corpus with which to train the filter, both for procedural reasons (you need a mix of representative, authentic non-spam messages, many of which will be personal and potentially embarrassing) and because it proved quite difficult to draw those lines. One of the first major anti-spam corpora was constructed from the internal email of Enron Corporation, gathered during the investigation into the company's criminal business practices. (It was the equivalent to an archeologist's midden, enabling researchers to work with everything that would normally be valueless and discarded, providing insights by virtue of its accidental nature.) Figuring out which stock tips and mass-mailed Christian homilies were spam, and which part of Enron's internal culture, became a stumbling block for evaluating the filters.

Let us set this aside, though, and select an example of a spam message that everyone can agree on, a classic, instantly recognizable come-on for Viagra, say, that arrived in our in boxes this morning. We can bracket all the definitional and terminological uncertainty. What made this message, and what gave it its distinctive technical and linguistic properties? Here, again, we encounter the problem of concretism. Obviously the spammer made the message—and yet so many additional elements did, as well. It was almost certainly sent from an innocent user's compromised computer, taken over by a malware attack, and surreptitiously added to a large network of remotely controlled computers called a botnet. It was sent as part of a campaign shaped by economic and legal forces, using software that has evolved in the culture of malware programmers. We could break out some of the factors as follows:

• covert discussions and Command and Control instructions sent over Internet Relay Chat, to coordinate the machines sending messages as part of the botnet
• botnet architecture, which is built in ways that rip off, compete with, and defend against other botnets
• the semi-secret markets for selling and exploiting stolen credit cards, whose dynamics affect the choice of types of messages (if the message is the pretext for credit card theft), or
• the evolving relationships between banks willing to transact certain kinds of online purchases, and gray market and black market pharmaceutical providers (if the message is, in fact, trying to sell pharmaceuticals)
• black markets for stolen identity information
• markets for renting capacity on botnets for messages for third-party clients, and, in turn:
• third-party spam clients, and their economics—whether or not certain pharmaceuticals are promising a return on investment at a particular time, for instance
• the larger ecosystem of insecure and ubiquitous Windows boxes, which can be commandeered to act as spam-sending machines—which touches on developed and developing world economics and software cultures
• malware engineers and programmers, and their culture
• the coevolution of spam filters and the polymorphic messages made to beat them

And so on. Every element has its role to play in the constitution of this particular instance of spam. There are underlying economic, technological, social, and legal developments which are factored in—and the shifts in power, influence, and access on the part of various of groups of users and superusers, from spammers themselves to developers of unethical software, illicit Internet Service Providers, and customers and those exploited to make the whole business worthwhile. Spam manages to be at once casually common—everyone receives it—and systemically rare, in that producing a comprehensive overview (that critical mass within which explanation emerges) is laden with snags and preliminary questions whose answers, in the manner of Hofstadter's strange loops, must be given before the question can be properly proposed.

The most useful starting point when one faces this question—"Who makes *spam?*"—is to address the question itself. Latour speaks of the task of "how to assemble, in a single, visually coherent space, all the entities necessary for a thing to become an object" (2007, 142). He is using these two terms in a particular way. *Thing* is a thickly described, contextually embedded matter, in the way the phrase is used by Heidegger—the thing, whether a pair of boots or an urn, folds in the material history and the ontological domain in which it exists, speaking of a way of life and a relationship to many other entities, and so on. *Object*, meanwhile, is thinly describable and idealized, almost invisible, a ready-to-hand hunk of something whose larger existence and construction is of no concern to us. We can address it, we can move it around, we can accomplish what we need to with it. The literally Earth-changing history of the globalized, thick thing that is the automobile becomes the car-object that we drive to the store.

Consider spam in this light. We can start from a single question ("Who sent me this spam?" as Gitelman asks, looking at the context of cultural data in new media systems) and turn it on its head (2006, 155). How did the profoundly weird phenomenon of spam become as banal as it is? Which is to say: what parts have we allowed to become obscure, and what complexities are we ignoring, blackboxing, or consolidating whose particular operations would illuminate the whole of the event?

Conclusions

Hardware, the underlying material stuff, turns out to be full of politics and negotiations rather than crisp ontological certainty. Anonymous, the mysterious storm cloud of geek ire, has had nuanced and vibrant internal cultures of debate whose users and superusers are articulate about even the nature of technical power and of the secrets they keep and selectively reveal. Spam, the noun, verb, and adjective which everyone recognizes without being able to precisely and entirely define, is a moving space. It draws a line around certain overlaps, where law, common online practice, technological and financial innovation and international politics meet, an intersection of hardware, users, and concepts feeding back and forth. The work of studying these events lies partially in our patience with their complexity, ambiguity, and layered character.

In working on phenomena like Anonymous and spam, we are careful to put off what in the lexicon of quantum mechanics is called "collapse"— when several possible states condense down at observation into one. The work we have described here implies both a methodological and a theoretical approach to forestalling this collapse, keeping the superposition of simultaneous meanings, values, and implications in play. We do this to compensate for the difficulties in getting a complete picture—with the secrecy, the simultaneity, the obscurity—but also because it is more accurate. There is no Anonymous, no spam, no Internet; there are, rather, many of each, simultaneous, all true at once and all tangled up together. Is the Internet making us stupid or making us smart? Is it empowering dictators or liberating populations? Is it destroying privacy or encouraging a proliferation of new identities and personae? Is it the domain of bullies and trolls or the framework for new, global, voluntary communities? Yes, all of the above, and more. The loop of hardware–users–theories makes it easier to sustain this collapse-resistant inquiry.

This raises the issue of time, an overlapping element in our master question of "who makes," and the smaller questions of hardware, users, and stories that it breaks out into. Both our subjects and our approach entail thinking in a distinctive temporality with two different properties. First, there is simultaneity: for many network events, including those described here, much of consequence is happening all at once, on an enormous scale, with nested feedback and overlapping interdependencies. This is particularly salient with Anonymous, which bears a singular name but is simultaneously composed of multiple nodes. Hardware, users, and the stories users and observers tell are all affecting each other, up and down the stack. Taking questions like "Who makes spam?" or "What makes Anonymous possible?" as loops of related answers, whose circulation doesn't stop, helps us create better descriptions. This brings up the second temporal issue in our work: the answers remain fundamentally provisional. While we should strive to reach a stable point of analysis which can accommodate different perspectives—material, social, historical—we will only remain there as temporary visitors. Prompted and provoked by a different set of concerns, or an unpredictable series of events that can dramatically shift possibilities (such as happened with Wikileaks and the technological politics of leaking [Brunton 2011] or when Anonymous unexpectedly took on the project of leaking [Coleman 2013]), our objects of analysis will move forward and force us to catch up. We may get closer to the dynamics of the machine and closer to the fact of the metal, but our work is asymptotic: we will never quite arrive.

Notes

1. Thanks to Geof Bowker for "misplaced concretism," an excellent turn of phrase.

2. Greenpeace International, "Make IT green: Cloud computing and its contribution to climate change." Paper presented at Greenpeace International Conference, Amsterdam, 2010. http://www.greenpeace.org/international/Global/international/planet-2/report/2010/3/make-it-green-cloud-computing.pdf, accessed May 16, 2012.

3. Triple8 Networking, "Data centers." http://www.triple8.net/about_datacenter.htm, accessed April 12, 2012.

4. Robert Lemos, "Anonymous must evolve or break down, say researchers," 2012. http://www.darkreading.com/advanced-threats/167901091/security/vulnerabilities/232900561/anonymous-must-evolve-or-break-down-say-researchers.html, accessed June 3, 2012.

5. National Cybersecurity and Communications Integration Center, "Assessment of anonymous threat to control systems." Bulletin A-0020-NCCIC / ICS-CERT –120020110916, September 16, 2011. As released by Public Intelligence, http://publicintelligence.net/ufouo-dhs-bulletin-anonymous-hacktivist-threat-to-industrial-control-systems-ics/. Accessed November 22, 2011.

6. "The System Administrators' Code of Ethics." League of Professional System Administrators, 2006. https://lopsa.org/CodeOfEthics, accessed May 10, 2012.

7. Elías Halldór Ágústsson's website, Beyond Enemy Lines. http://elias.rhi.hi.is/beyond_enemy_lines.html, accessed December 5, 2011.

5 Emerging Configurations of Knowledge Expression

Geoffrey C. Bowker

By Way of Introduction

Struggling with the definition of the novel form, E. M. Forster came down reluctantly to the finding that "Yes—oh, dear, yes—the novel tells a story" (Forster 1927, 25). There's really no way around that, even though folks like Joyce have done their darnedest. I feel the same nebulous dismay when I try to define what an academic product is. Here's a form that articles take in the field of computer-supported cooperative work: wide-ranging introduction; literature review section which covers far more reading than you will use in the text; truncated methods section which doesn't allow you to interrogate the text easily; objective findings, which generally seem otherwise and would often be known anyway by the average citizen without doing any research; discussion, which is too short; and (*pace* Paul Dourish [2006]), implications for design. If I'm asked what it is that most academics write most of the time, I'd have to say: "Yes—oh, dear, yes—the canonical academic product is the well-formed paper."

Who gets to read the unparalleled output that comes off the knowledge assembly line? Well, that's a more difficult question. In the nineteenth century, when what we call the archival literature was first developed by Poggendorff and others with eternal titles such as "Annals of . . ." or "Archives of . . . ," there was a sense of an academic field in most areas being at most several hundred.[1] I can read that sort of output—and still do, though it tends to be from my 700 closest friends. Today, most average academic articles are read by few and cited by fewer. And yet we persist in the venture. We adhere, especially in the human and social sciences, to the myth of the single author. Indeed our whole PhD system is very good at creating individual workers, who frequently get lost when they have to work in a fully collaborative environment. You can partly say the collaboration was always already so, and yet that's not the way we think, and not the way that we get PhDs or promotions. In a world where the preprint can be the true archival literature (the canonical example is http://arxiv.org/), we have a broken system that can neither recruit enough readers nor reflect our actual modes of knowledge production.

How did we get into this sorry mess? It is certainly a situation that was accompanied by the development of printing technology. Increasingly with this development, the concept of the single author gelled. Also, the nature of the reading may have changed definitively at the same time. We learned to read ideographically, rather than phonetically, when we had large amounts of text to look over (the distinction here being that we stopped having to imagine the words being spoken and began to rely on the shape of the words—Liu brilliantly discusses *Finnegan's Wake* as the ultimate ideographic novel; she points out that large parts of it are unpronounceable [Liu 2010, 113]).

At this point, a methodological point (which refreshes). It can be argued that there were origins of both ideographic reading and the concept of the author before this time. Thus, one could say that silent reading was *ab ovo* ideographic (though of course we have no way of knowing the degree to which it was still phonetic): however, scanning vast quantities of print text as part of normal daily practice for a scientist flourishes with the printing press. Equally, though the concept of the single author indeed precedes the printing press, it was technology that allowed it to flourish. The "which came first" question is generally a red herring with respect to information technology. Thus prior organizational changes in the insurance and railroad industries prefigured and made possible the development of information processing technology; however, the resultant artifact (the computer) clearly allows for the fixing of these prior forms.

Reading knowledge works and producing knowledge have tended, over the years and in an unfortunate sequence of path dependencies, to become ever more constrained. We now know the "natural" armature of the chapter heading, the footnote, and the index, for example, despite the fact that these were just as much creations as hot lead presses (though, as Drucker [2003] points out, not coeval with these). Unfortunately, at the outset of a new era of information infrastructure, we are still in general marching backward into the future (McLuhan and Fiori [1967] 1996). We have a great production machine—why not produce a million articles where once we had a thousand? This is the only, natural way to produce knowledge, after all. The new information technology will help with this: where once my personal filing system could hold a few hundred files and folders, I now command a virtual office where these number in the hundreds of thousands.

It is extremely hard to think beyond the current confines of our conceptual structures. Take the otherwise exciting project of Chronozoom,[2] which endeavors to map any set of events onto an ever-growing universal timeline. The architecture of the site is shown in figure 5.1, below. It's one darned thing after another . . . it precisely reproduces the linearity of the book in a medium flexible enough to represent a multiplicity of times. Yet everything will be given a unique, universal date. Book time in this vision becomes interface time. And yet, historical time is interesting for its nonlinearity. Things happen in cycles (women historically enter then leave the workforce to the beat of wars and plagues), in spurts, in rhythms (the Annalists [Braudel 1973] classify historical time in three rhythmic sequences). They are experienced phenomenologically along different dimensions of duration. Equally, scientific time is interesting enfolded. A central theme of evolutionary biology is heterochrony, different rates of development for different parts of an organism (Vrba 1994). String theory works best with time having a shape and dimensionality (Yau and Nadis 2010). Tying things down to single timelines and then hoping to deal with nonlinear reality is an interesting casuistic exercise, but it certainly ain't knowledge production. What appears to us as nonintuitive is often only so because our perception of it is mediated by the architecture of our underlying information infrastructure. This point resonates with Piaget's rich insight that quantum theory only feels strange after you have had Euclidean geometry (Piaget 1969) and linear time (Piaget and Inhelder 1967) beaten into you in the classroom. For preschool children, he argued, the theory is intuitive.

There was a period during the 1960s and 1970s when computer programmers were paid for the number of lines of code they wrote on a given day. As soon as this is enunciated, it's clear how silly it is: the best code does in two lines what others labor to do in a thousand (compare Euclid's two-line proof that there are an infinite number of prime numbers). However, it remains generally true that knowledge producers in our society are rewarded for the number of lines of text that they produce on a given day. "Oh, I intone to my graduate students, you need to be producing two to three peer-reviewed papers a year, work on your monograph—and then the kingdom of heaven shall be thine." This is really silly. Peer review broke down as a system about forty or fifty years ago; we have so many texts, and so little time to do free labor, that *in any field, in any journal,* you can find glaring errors. *Science, Technology and Human Values* carried a paper about a project which sent the same paper out to 146 journals in or related to social work. The paper was about (oh horrible word) "parentectomy" in the case

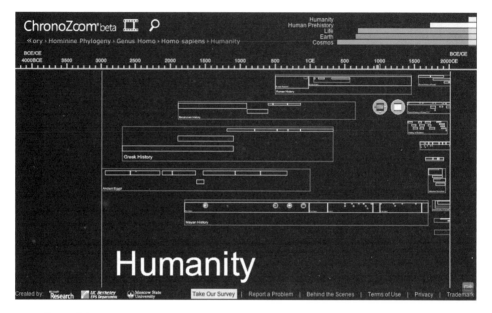

Figure 5.1
"One Million Years Past" (Schaffner et al. 1998).

of an asthma patient. The piece was modeled on and used large passages verbatim from a well-cited paper published in an Australian social work journal from 1969. Half of the "resubmissions" contained dubious statistics and a mangled version of the experimental protocol. Acceptance rate as is or with minor changes was high for both the mangled (25 percent) and unmangled (30 percent) versions. Only two journals picked out the plagiary (Epstein 1990).

If we want to produce scalable knowledge for planetary management (which is what most science is about today [Bowker 2006]), then we need to get away from the academic article. We certainly do not want text to trump resonance, since complexity can never be represented in linear form. Nor, more controversially, perhaps, do we want text to trump database. Since the Enlightenment, we have lived in the epoch of the database (Foucault 1991; Manovich 2001): it is in and through databases that our knowledge is represented, grown, and propagated. Let's call an end to the epiphenomenon of the text as central mediator of knowledge. Those fields (increasingly underfunded) not involved in planetary management also inhabit this epoch (witness the rise of "digital humanities"); indeed dominant cultural forms know little of putative divides between social sciences, natural sciences, and the humanities.

How Did We Get Here?

What is academic knowledge, that it should be expressed? A European or American epochal history might go as follows. We can start with Raymond Lull. He developed an *ars combinatoria* in order to "master" the burgeoning knowledge production machine. The basic idea was that all knowledge could be memorized through its imagined representation in tree form. The universe was divided into nine sections, each corresponding to one of the nine letters of his alphabet (Rossi 2000, 34). This device had a double impulsion, variably deployed over the next several centuries. First was that it could be part of a mnemotechnic practice to remember all of knowledge. You could add mental images to branches and leaves in such a way as to aid memory. The logical structure of the trees guaranteed that you covered all of knowledge; the images enabled you to remember appropriately. As Rossi and Yates (Yates 1966) have pointed out, memory and imagination (in this sense, the decoration with images) fused. Further, the tree itself could be used to generate new knowledge—the Lullian alphabet could generate a universal, pure, and logical language.

The quest for a universal language continued apace for several centuries (Slaughter 1982). There were, broadly, two strands: seeing original language as pure and our own languages as debased forms with adjectives, adverbs, qualifiers and other signs of decadence; or seeing the original language as giving rise to the more complex and refined, the present day permitting greater richness of expression (as Descartes would have seen it). We will cleave for the nonce to the former strand. Leibnitz in the eighteenth century, influenced by Lull, conceived a universal language in which each syllable would express a true proposition and each well-formed sentence would produce truths about the world. The search for the perfect language continued through Boole and indeed up to the present day. Latterly it takes the form of searching for a definitive ontology of the world (as Cycorp attempts to do[3] or the one and only amazing Large Knowledge Collider http://www.larkc.eu/): if we can name the objects in the world correctly and define their relationships, the reasoning goes, we can produce new kinds of truth automatically. (Thus, Swanson [Swanson 1986] talked about "undiscovered public knowledge," that is, separate truths masked by disciplinary silos which can be mixed and matched by algorithm in order to generate new facts about the world.)

A second strand of knowing everything about the world has been classification practices. Again, there is a strong link with memory. Linnaeus created the number of genuses that he did in order to facilitate memorizing by field biologists. In the eighteenth century, with the development of the Encyclopédie, all knowledge was conjured into divisions of reason, memory, and imagination (reason having the most subparts, imagination the fewest). Comte ([1830–1845] 1975) in the 1830s classified all sciences into the positivist tree that seems almost intuitive to many today: mathematics over physics, then chemistry, biology, and sociology. Each science was broken down into statics and dynamics. No one science related laterally with another—it was either higher up and dominating or the inverse. Each branch of knowledge was referenced by its evolutionary stage (the fixed pattern was theological, then metaphysical, then positive) (ibid.). During the nineteenth century, our universities came to reflect through their core disciplines some version of this classification. Today, that quest for a stable ordering of knowledge has passed its prime—indeed since the 1940s we have had a wild proliferation of disciplines and a concomitant recognition by many that the real work of science is interdisciplinary. Helga Nowotny and colleagues' vision of Mode 2 science is the apotheosis of this move because it sees science today as solving complex problems in the world by bringing together whichever batch of techniques are most appropriate (Gibbons et al. 1994)—how could one understand and solve biodiversity issues within a single silo or climate change dilemmas without a raft of specialties spanning the social and natural sciences?

Weaving these two strands together, we can say broadly that the purpose of the academic exercise of the past several centuries has been to know everything about the world, to develop languages to express that knowledge simply and powerfully, and to classify the knowledge so that it could be easily retrievable by any needing access to it.

In order to do this, you need to have a knowledge production system. And the history of mass production plays a significant part. Francis Bacon in 1620 argued for a systematization of the collection of knowledge. Inveighing against old forms of knowledge production, he suggested something new:

There remains but one course for the recovery of a sound and healthy condition—namely, that the entire work of the understanding be commenced afresh, and the mind itself be from the very outset not left to take its own course, but guided at every step; and the business be done as if by machinery. Certainly if in things mechanical men had set to work with their naked hands, without help or force of instruments, just as in things intellectual they have set to work with little else than the naked forces of the understanding, very small would the matters have been which, even with their best efforts applied in conjunction, they could have attempted or accomplished. (Bacon [1620] 1902)

In a brilliant paper, Siskin and Warner argue that the Enlightenment was a realization of the vision in Bacon's "Novum Organum." Breakthroughs in information technology on the one hand (the complex nonlinear information handling tools of the encyclopedists and Linnaeus) and institutionalization (the x-ologies of the early nineteenth century) permitted this vision to be realized (Siskin and Warner 2010).

There is a whole narrative of the scientific revolution which discusses this system in terms of infinities. This may be the infinitely small, as in the infinitesimal calculus discovered by Leibnitz and Newton, or the infinitely large, as in the size of the universe and the nature of time. However, this has always been tightly coupled with a discourse on finitude. Before Fukayama, Marx predicted an end to history with the withering away of the state and the final solution to the contradictions of capitalism. Trapped between infinities, knowledge workers prefigured an end to knowledge.

Indeed, it was generally assumed in the post-Enlightenment era that the universe of knowledge was finite and tractable. Newton's physics was perfect—there was no more to learn about the laws of motion, which were exquisitely expressed through mathematics. Now we learn in school that this was not the case. Lyell in the 1830s wrote both that the earth was effectively infinitely old and that we are approaching the end of geology (Lyell 1832). For the latter, he adapted Hutton's phrase of the "revolutions" of the earth's surface, where it goes through the cauldron of subsurface magma to be born anew. Today geologists tell stories which reconstruct the story of a given rock through several such cycles (similarly, cosmologists now tell stories of what happened before the "big bang"). Comte, for his part, was sure that we now knew all we could ever know about the solar system and the world beyond. Buffon in the late eighteenth century prefigured a number of prognoses that the era of scientific geniuses was in the past, echoing here a catastrophist geology, which saw the young earth as being more tempestuous than the current more stable one (Buffon 1770). Charles Babbage was so sure of this that he saw the role of scientific publication as opening a conversation between the good and great of all ages—never imagining that there might be too many at the table (Babbage 1837). Comte constructed a positivist calendar replacing the names of saints (theology) with those of scientists (positive) who were few enough to fit into the new year's thirteenth month, being eternal in their glory. The calendar parses oddly today; many of the immortals have proven transient, as shown in figure 5.2. Bookending the nineteenth century, Lord Kelvin opined: "There is nothing new to be discovered in physics now. All that remains is more and more precise measurement" (British Association for the Advancement

FINAL		
Treiziemè mois. Consacré à la science moderne		
BICHAT		
1	Lundi	Copernic *Tycho-Brahé*
2	Mardi	Kepler
3	Mercredi	Huyghens *Varignon*
4	Jeudi	Jacques Bernouilli *Jean Bernouilli*
5	Vendredi	Bradley *Halley*
6	Samedi	Volta *Ampère*
7	Dimanche	**GALILEE**
8	Lundi	Viète *Harriott*
9	Mardi	Wallis *Fermat*
10	Mercredi	Clairaut *Maupertuis*
11	Jeudi	Euler *Monge*
12	Vendredi	D'Alembert *Daniel Bernouilli*
13	Samedi	Lagrange *Joseph Fourier*
14	Dimanche	**NEWTON**
15	Lundi	Bergmann *Scheele*
16	Mardi	Priestley *Dary*
17	Mercredi	Cavendish
18	Jeudi	Guyton Morveau
19	Vendredi	Berthollet
20	Samedi	Berzélius *Ritter*
21	Dimanche	**LAVOISIER**
22	Lundi	Harvey *Ch. Bell.*
23	Mardi	Boërhaave *Sthal.*
24	Mercredi	Linné *Bern. De Jussieu*
25	Jeudi	Haller *Vicq d'Azyr*
26	Vendredi	Lamarck *Oken*
27	Samedi	Broussais *Morgagni*
28	Dimanche	**GALL**

Figure 5.2

Excerpt from Comte's Positivist Calendar, http://www.louisg.net/calendrier_positiviste
.htm.

of Science Address, 1900). Poincaré felt much the same (Poincaré 1908). Gabrielle Tarde prefigured the end of science as a cultural form, akin to the end of religion:

When modern science will have reached its conclusion, by which I mean the period of the definitive fixation of its principles and methods, there will be, in all minds, the same hierarchy of knowledges, a concatenation of systematized problems that will have been answered by a certain number of crucial books, and answered so perfectly that the majority of new books . . . will be rejected by this recognized supremacy of elders. Dissident books will be put on the social index. Only orthodox books will be read, ones that conform to the principles and prolong them, and, it must be said, the latter will be, for a more or less extended stretch of time, both instructive and beautiful. (Candea 2010, 624)

We have a knowledge production machine which could fill in infinite bricks in the wall of a known, structured edifice. Throughout the nineteenth century (a span of time known for visions of unbridled growth and infinite resources), there was a strong current of belief in the end of science. The dream of the structured canvas has continued in various ways to the present, one recent version being Tykociner's science of zetetics, which would hold all knowledge in a structured classification with knowledge gaps being apparent from the resultant chart (Tykociner 1971). A trope of stasis always accompanies one of progress (Bowker 2006); it is just that the latter tends to both clamor for and receive the most attention.

Along the way, particularly during the nineteenth century, we developed the standard form of the academic article—with beginnings, middles, and ends—and a professional, disciplinary readership for said work. When the field of science was restricted largely to the "center" (MacLeod 1980) and to gentlemen, then there certainly were few enough in any one field that they could all know each other and read each other's work. Further, since there were a restricted number of sciences and each science was approaching its end, you could imagine reading all the basic works in a field.

The Database as a Knowledge Product

At first blush, nothing seems more naturally so than that knowledge should be encapsulated in text. For we seem to think in text, we have been trained using textbooks, and the quintessential knowledge product seems to be the written text. However, there are many things which cannot be described verbally (Crompton 2008); and if we suppress for the nonce our textual urges, we can see that knowledge is always already expressed in a veritable ferment of forms. As it is so often, "always already" is a key term here: as

Latour's *We Have Never Been Modern* (1993) can be led to suggest, new forms do not emerge fully blown from the dictates of new technologies (for that indeed would be determinism); rather the latter afford the possibility for creative rethinking and remix.

Movement is one "new" form which is afforded. There is a lovely passage in Gargantua and Pantagruel describing a mime duel between two great philosophers, with a thunderous fart capping the triumphant argument (Rabelais [1532] 1964). More mundanely, people gain much of their knowledge about the world through observation—sometimes this is mediated through words, often not. Jaana Parviainen cites Sheets-Johnstone: "Precisely in the way we intuitively knew as infants on the basis of our tactile-kinesthetic experiences, and knew without the aid of scare quotes, of qualitative happenings and vitality affects. Such knowing is a manner or perhaps better, a style—of cognition that may be difficult for some adults to acknowledge since it is nonlinguistic and nonpropositional and, just as significantly, has no solid object on which it fastens" (Parviainen 2002, 14).

Adrian Cussins has come at this same insight along another path when he develops the notion of "non-conceptual thinking" (Cussins 1992). The concept of visual thinking is another. Though I might have learned how to reproduce the calculus as a series of symbols, my knowledge of it was earned through diagrams. Similarly, as Reviel Netz argues, much early mathematics (he writes largely about Euclid and Archimedes) can be understood in terms of visual reasoning (1999). Text can be a straitjacket. In the mid to late twentieth century, a number of theorists experimented with topological renderings of reasoning. Claude Lévi-Strauss read widely in topology and indeed used origami as a tool for thinking.[4] His analysis in the *Mythologies* sequence could be rendered within a multidimensional frame, where one could visualize the sets of topological transformations he envisages and potentially deepen his analysis through this more felicitous representational form. Jacques Lacan studied the theory of knots, and his later highly symbolic work can best be expressed visually. Movement and visual reasoning cannot be expressed simply in text; however, they can be housed in multimedia databases. This is the real beauty of our brave new information infrastructure: the ability to express knowledge using a wider range of our senses. This is not just about representation (though that in itself is a lot). Haptic interfaces being developed will allow us to bring in touch. Technology such as Leap[5] will enable us to think gesturally.

A plethora of new forms of 'rendering public' (a term we often reduce to the textually linked term of "publication") will not in itself render possible a reduction in the current cacophony of knowledge production. Transitional possibilities are marked by Johanna Drucker, who argues that with current agglomerative forms of writing, "We become authorettes, components of an authorial stream, bits of the larger code tide" (2012, 9). Already being demonstrated are two possibilities which take seriously Manovich's (2001) claim that the database is the central symbol for our time.

In contradistinction to traditional academic writing, databases can be built and shaped by a large collective. Thus the Protein Data Bank[6] is a collective exercise on the part of the proteomics community that gathers together all protein sequences. At present, this sequence work is still ultimately expressed in papers (for they are the coin of the realm), but with creative interfaces, they can become the site of knowledge repository and indeed generation. So "data" are in many ways the knowledge product. Much as many papers in the field of computer science are really just pointers to programs where the knowledge work is actually done, many scientific papers today are pointers to databases. The Protein Data Bank is a successful scientific database which scientists must publish in if they want their papers to come out.[7] Similarly, the Ecological Society of America mandates publishing databases alongside papers in its journals.[8] It is a slow process, but techniques for citing databases are gaining ground.[9]

One project which points the way here is Ruth West's *Atlas in Silico*, which provides tools for exploring metadata in very large genomics databases (in her initial case, microbial ocean life).[10] These tools take three forms: the invention of a visual script for describing metadata configurations; the generation of music reflecting one's position in the database and providing aural cues to its configuration there; and direct numerical manipulation of database fields. A database and its interface can be the outcome of sustained creative endeavor—one where output is significantly slowed down from the frenzy of ever-shorter scientific papers we are now experiencing. The journal *Vectors* is a fine example of this possibility.

Where Are We Going?

Where the nineteenth century was one of progress and finite science, we have since its apogee been gradually losing progress from our collective vocabulary and we see each of our disciplines and interdisciplines as being in their relative infancy. (A Google Ngram—bracketed here because it's such a problematic tool—shows "progress" in constant decline since the "age of certainty" [Briggs 1965] peaking in the 1850s).[11]

It is difficult to see beyond the creation of a dominant form, to sense how it might have been otherwise. For reading, Mary Douglas provides a wonderful example (Douglas 2007). She argues that we used to be able to read other than linearly. She grounds her work in the Book of Numbers, frequently described as the most difficult-to-read part of the Bible. It alternates in apparent narrative chaos between sets of laws and adventure narratives. In the context of our acquired way of reading (the linear form of print discussed by Eisenstein [1979]), it just makes no sense. However, if you arrange the episodes on the perimeter of a circle, there is a perfect symmetry. The cardinal points of the circle represent major transitions in the story. Taking the book to start at north, south reproduces and refines the initial message. North, south, east, and west are all marked by textual cues; and each circle diameter matches like with like (adventure with adventure). Douglas does not develop this for many works, however, her brilliant analysis of *Tristram Shandy* (a book often considered very hard to follow) as a circular form brings us right back to the time of the Enlightenment. Ironically, that same novel is seen by some as heralding hypertext. The question of how cultures "forget" skills they had is a rich one (it's akin to the English "forgetting" the purpose of Stonehenge despite continuous habitation of that locale). It is not that expressive forms were better in some prior golden age; it is just that there was a different available ecology, which has been ineluctably altered by the book and the journal.

One way into emergent forms is to consider the nature of data collection. Much of the recent history of science has been about the collection of data and its classification. Linnaeus and the Encyclopedists in the eighteenth century used complex information technologies in their efforts, such as strips of paper strung together to allow sorting of new information and its random access in a "ficelle" (the origin of the word "file") (Blair and Stallybrass 2010). In the early nineteenth century, with the rise of modern empires and burgeoning populations, information collection gathered steam through the power of steam. Statistics (information about the state) grew up as a discipline of governmentality (Foucault 1991); huge geological and natural history surveys developed. Today, this massive work of data collection is increasing exponentially—we have terabytes of data from sensors of all sorts chronicling the natural world, and a dizzying array of devices monitoring the human world. (The overlap in technologies and techniques justifies the actor-network ontology that a distinction between these two worlds is at least performatively moot).

A great myth of the scientific article was that, largely through the power of classification systems to define kinds rather than detail incidents, the paper itself contained all and only the information to replicate an experiment or finding—in Poincaré's terms, scientists were all laborers constructing the edifice of science through laying these permanent bricks. But it has been a commonplace in science studies (Collins 1985) that papers never provide enough information for replication; they are but part of a larger ecology (including, for example, the circulation of tacit knowledge through the circulation of graduate students [Ravetz 1971]). The scientific paper acted as a screen which through its linear narrative protected the reader from the data. Where data was referred to, it was as represented in other texts.

The very difficulty of the process recalls the invention of the concept of the single author which followed close on the heels of the printing press. All scientific papers can be described as collaboratively written: colleagues comment on drafts; journal reviewers help you strengthen your arguments and together with editors help you tailor your arguments for that journal. As a matter of convention, all these coauthors tend to get relegated to Acknowledgments, so that a single citable, responsible author is created. Even the single author is breaking down: papers in high-energy physics frequently have hundreds of authors, all of whom collaborated on the epistemic object (Knorr Cetina 1999) that collided their particles. With databases, there should be ways to credit database designers, producers of particular modules which mine the database, contributors of specific datasets, and those who produced the metadata (without which the database itself would be unreadable).

However, if the database is a knowledge product, it is hard to parse. There are two emergent approaches here. One is to incorporate the database into the narrative text in captivating ways. The article "Blue Velvet" by David Theo Goldberg and Stefka Hristova (2008) shows text falling from the sky into the database, which reveals itself as a set of videos, images, census tables, and so forth. However, for complex databases one needs to go further. We need as a society to learn both how to read databases and how to design databases which can be read. The field of virtual archeology has proven interesting here. In traditional archeology, a site would be dug, it would be assembled according to a best guess, and conclusions would be drawn from studying the recreated site. In one noted nineteenth-century case, an additional story was added to a building, but this was a difficult and expensive hypothesis to demolish. There has developed the possibility of circumventing the building as hypothesis and indeed leaving a site subsoil and mapping with scanning technology. With or without this virtualization, the best-guess hypothesis can be used to generate a manipulable model through which theories can be tested. In this case, knowledge is expressed directly in the database without passing through the mediation of text. Papers can be written, but they become one of a suite of expressive forms.

The centrality of data in knowledge expression is wonderfully described by Walter Benjamin's observation, which Ellen Gruber Garvey and Markus Krajewski cite: "And even today, as the current scientific method teaches us, the book is an archaic intermediate between two different card index systems. For everything substantial is found in the slip box of the researcher who wrote it and the scholar who studies in it, assimilated into its own card index" (Gitelman 2013).

We typically conceive of knowledge as passing from knowledge worker to knowledge worker via the intermediary of the datum. However, as Marx displayed so brilliantly with his M-C-M (money-commodity-money) cycle, we can achieve analytic purchase by looking at C-M-C (which in our era, felicitously, may refer to computer-mediated communication).

We can start perhaps by refining the terms of the cycle. Much of our "knowledge" today surpasseth human understanding. Stephen Hawking (1980), in his inaugural lecture for the Lucasian Chair of Physics at Cambridge—once held by Newton, who had all those giants standing on his shoulders—pointed to the day when physicists would not understand the products of their own work. With the world of string theory upon us, it is clear that we cannot "think" linguistically in the necessary 10+1 dimensions and the complex geometries they entail. Fields such as climate science or any others which deploy agent-based modeling systems are much the same. The intelligent citizen cannot read the programs which run our datasets; they can be "groundtruthed" to some extent, though increasingly scientific models are compared primarily against other models (Edwards 2010). So let's take the unnecessary human out of the equation and talk about the program-data-program or data-program-data cycles. If we turn the database into an expressive form, this kind of reading—essential today for understanding science, economics, and politics—can become part of regular educational content.

If the prestige of the scientific paper is blinding us to new sites of knowledge expression, it is also presenting full consideration of emergent forms. Within the fields of musicology and anthropology examples abound of dancing as the performance of knowledge and wisdom. (*Science* magazine's annual "Dance your PhD" competition is an amusing shadow.)[12] Dance is a rich modality for knowledge expression. Eevi Beck's "Thundering Silence" performance, for example, involves a text narrator, an automated Prezi presentation, and herself dancing. Just like the motif in Wagnerian opera, the dancer provides a rich subtext to the text and images. The knowledge experience for the witness resonates in all registers (Lévi-Strauss 1969) simultaneously.

I was at a workshop recently where someone posed a difficult question to the speaker (a computer scientist). He gave an embarrassed chuckle and said: "I could give you a good answer to that question, but unfortunately I don't have the slideware to hand" (slideware, the third dimension to software and hardware). Slideware is PowerPoint slides which are bartered, in a curious gift economy (Hénaff 2002), extensively in scientific work. Many of my colleagues—including myself as my own best colleague—have many PowerPoint presentations that we've not yet had the time to put into text. And yet you can see the problem with the latter predicate: why insist on a PowerPoint to text to PowerPoint knowledge expression machine, when the work of "text" can be truly counterproductive—it drains multi-dimensionality. *Pace* Tufte (2006), who only seems to have seen bad presentations, PowerPoint can be seen as a new art form. It does, however, have its own problems with linearity. More flexible forms like Prezi, with its infinite canvas, present new forms of trail making (resonant with the phenomenology of trails in Ingold's work on lines [2007]).

Hans Rösling's TED talks[13] are good examples of performed knowledge. I disagree with almost all his findings, but they are impressive for his use of his body, together with artifacts and his Gapminder[14] application for dynamically representing statistical arguments. The very movement of the bubbles in Gapminder expresses his findings much better than could any static text. This dynamic form of expression is not new, as Rembrandt's 1632 painting, *Anatomy Lesson*, reminds us; indeed many scientists during the nineteenth century performed theatrically as well as wrote. The difference today is that the performance of knowledge is frequently captured and preserved: it is a mechanism for transmitting knowledge in multidimensional ways.

Getting There

As figure 5.3 shows,[15] there is a hoary divide in informatics among data, information, and knowledge. One parsing of this is that data is "raw" numbers; information is those numbers arranged in a database; knowledge is reasoning with information. Or again, we gather data in the field, and arrange it in such a way that it can inform our knowledge products. We are now at a juncture where the fundamental architecture of our knowledge production machine can be changed. However, the timing is important: just as with the printing press, or analogously the computer (trapped now in von Neumann architecture), decisions made early on in the processes of epochal shift are hard to undo.

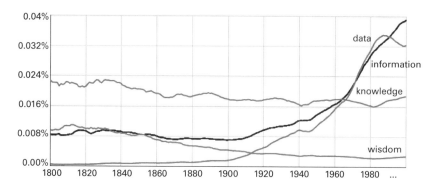

Figure 5.3

Truth and wisdom in historic decline, data and information doing well (Google Ngram).

However, this does not mean that the judicious path forward is clear. New forms do not simply supersede old ones: the old ones tend to survive in a redefined ecology. Thus, as Chartier explores, manuscript culture throve during the latter part of the eighteenth century (2005). Books which might be severely censored, for instance, de Bergerac's wonderful *Voyages to the Moon*, which includes a pope transmogrifying into a hedgehog ([1657] 1995), would circulate in restricted print and fully florid manuscript form. When speed was of the essence, for example, in reporting on the stock exchange in London, manuscript news sheets (much quicker to produce than setting hot lead type) would be deployed.

Speed is a useful concept here, since a generalized speeding up of all productive activity, including knowledge, is a central feature of the past several hundred years. Communication technologies have been key. Thus, to continue the example, stock exchanges have been great mediators of communicative changes which have enabled the development of new experiences of time and space. In the nineteenth century, the invention of the telegraph led to the flattening of geographical space and cyclical time through the creation of futures markets (Cronon 1991) and to new forms of time discipline (Preda 2006). In the twenty-first century, some stock traders are moving closer physically to the exchange because light doesn't quite go fast enough to ensure trading at the desired interval (Hecht 2011). (There are only two sets of people on earth who find lightspeed annoyingly slow: cosmologists and stock traders). More broadly, the rise of the railroad and steamships and the telegraph (heralded multiply in the early nineteenth century as annihilating space and time—a language still resonant today) allowed the rapid transit of people and goods, and the rapid acquisition of knowledge: this was the epoch of great natural history, and geomagnetic and geological surveys, for example. Along the way, it allowed the creation of large-scale nation states (see Richard John [1995] on the role of the post office in America, mediated by national newspapers) and large-scale scientific enterprises.

The question of how to make the academic exercise more reasonable tends to stutter into a set of usual suspects: reward structures which maximize word count and along the way discourage experimentation; the behemoths of academic publishing which are reluctant to change since their profit margins are so high; relentless pressure to finish doctorates faster; and so forth. We misunderstand the academic exercise if we see it as exceptional because it is about knowledge, which is said to be purer, more timeless than our other productions. The locus of change will not be the university per se, nor any other single social driver. You cannot just create a new cultural space and time as a free enclave within social space and time—the two are coeval; just as you cannot have, as Trotsky reminded us, socialism in one country.

However, it is possible to parse this more positively. Academics can create new production modes for knowledge; it is just that they will be evanescent unless they ramify across a set of institutions outside of the university. Equally, we can be sensitive to emergent forms elsewhere and seek to apply them: "crowdsourcing" has recently made the move into core parts of the academy, such as for classifying galaxies and folding proteins. Although in this process we lose the putative sway of knowledge work over all others, we gain multiple new sources of innovation in our own enterprise. This is always already so to some extent: the phenomenon of classification swept the economic, social, cultural, and scientific "worlds" in the nineteenth century as if blind to the difference between them (Melvyl Dewey even created a system for the classification of factory stock). However, if we had been sensitized to just this sort of phenomenon, we could have facilitated and shaped it through creating a knowledge base concerned with classification in all its forms, whereas today many disciplines are still rediscovering their own classificatory wheels—effectively in the end, but haphazardly (Tort 1989).

Since the late eighteenth century, the system of mass production has taken the world by storm. Millions of acres of crops and countless cows have been processed into Big Macs. Yet just because a system is massively successful does not make it right. We are living in a period when we as a species have commandeered vast percentages of the available incoming and stored energy in the planet, have affected every major waterway, are changing the climate, and are destroying species at a great rate. A natural question (but whom do we ask?) is whether we are producing knowledge of an appropriate kind at an appropriate rate in order to forge a positive future.

No one "discipline" can answer that question: we have lost the power of generality that philosophy used to have (before the field was progressively stripped of all the sciences). The fields of science studies and communication (both inherently anti-disciplines) cannot step into the breach. However, through their insights into information infrastructure, they can both speak to the issue of what kinds of things we know and how we know them. We are clearly not creating a species of knowledge-power appropriate to the issues that we face. We are producing knowledge that is predicated on and replicates mass production and mass consumption. Our information infrastructure, willy-nilly, is the fold in the Moebius strip that permits the world to seem as society writ large.

The beauty of the two fields is that they don't take an information infrastructure to be just a bundle of wires: it is a "dispositif technique," as Foucault would call it—a bundle of technologies, techniques, administrative procedures, and cultural forms. When our gaze is not trapped by the shiny machines, we can see the world we inhabit and the world we make as being lived in and produced through these bundles. Only when we get beyond the terrifying claims that science knows the answers (a task that the first Enlightenment had with respect to the church) can we reflexively build a society and a world in new ways. (Science studies scholars may believe we won the "science wars" in this respect, but a glance at the rhetoric of certainty in climate science, for example, shows that we have not: climate change believers are as dogmatic as Jehovah's Witnesses—though, as a "modest witness" (Haraway 1997), I have to say that both may be right). The thread of this chapter has been the dangers of the mass production of knowledge; the promise of this moment is that we can deliberatively produce ways of knowing and ways of expressing knowledge that open rich futures.

Envoi

A Portrait of the Artist as a Young Man (Joyce 1917) is a classic case of a text that exemplifies itself. Stephen Daedalus undertakes a quest for a new form of novel and the resultant novel is written in the new form which he discovers. Before James Joyce wrote this book he completed his first novel (published posthumously) *Stephen Hero* (1963), in which the protagonist undertakes a quest for a new form of novel, but the novel itself does not instantiate the temporality and materiality proposed therein. Joyce viewed the fact that the representational style in his first novel did not match the complexities it described as an acute dissonance. So it feels slightly odd to be producing a chapter in a book about new forms of expression when many of the arguments here are better expressed at the Emerging Configurations website (http://econfigs.ics.uci.edu).

Acknowledgments

I thank the editors and fellow contributors to this volume, Judith Gregory, and Cory Knobel for their insights, help, and patience. Johanna Drucker provided invaluable comments.

Notes

1. The academic journal article goes back further in time, to the gearing up of the Enlightenment machine described further on. However, the sense of the archive comes to the fore in the nineteenth century.

2. ChronoZoom, University of California, Berkeley, http://eps.berkeley.edu/~saekow /chronozoom/, accessed April 22, 2013.

3. Cycorp, http://www.cyc.com/, accessed April 22, 2013.

4. From a personal communication from Bernard Dionysius Geoghagen.

5. LeapMotion, Inc., https://www.leapmotion.com/, accessed April 22, 2013.

6. Protein Data Bank, Research Collaboratory for Structural Bioinformatics, http:// www.rcsb.org/pdb/home/home.do, accessed April 22, 2013. It is interesting that "banks" for data and "vaults" for preserving biodiversity are now standard terms: the circulation or not of capital underlies the metaphors.

7. Protein Data Bank, Research Collaboratory for Structural Bioinformatics (RCSB), http://www.rcsb.org/pdb/home/home.do, accessed April 22, 2013.

8. Ecological Archives, Ecological Society of America, http://esapubs.org/archive/, accessed April 22, 2013.

9. See, for example, work by the Global Biodiversity Information Facility on data citing—currently an enormously unwieldy structure. http://www.gbif.org, accessed April 22, 2013.

10. Center for Research in Computing and the Arts, University of California, San Diego, http://www.atlasinsilico.net/, accessed April 22, 2013.

11. Google Books, http://books.google.com/ngrams/graph?content=progress&year_ start=1800&year_end=2010&corpus=0&smoothing=3, accessed April 22, 2013.

12. J. Bohannon, "'Dance Your PhD' Winner Announced," *ScienceNOW*, October 20, 2011. http://news.sciencemag.org/sciencenow/2011/10/dance-your-phd-winner -announced.html, accessed April 22, 2013.

13. Hans Rösling video talk, *TED* (June 2006). http://www.ted.com/talks/hans_ rosling_shows_the_best_stats_you_ve_ever_seen.html, accessed April 22, 2013.

14. GapMinder, http://www.gapminder.org/, accessed April 22, 2013.

15. Google Ngram, http://books.google.com/ngrams/graph?content=truth%2C+wis dom%2C+knowledge%2C+data&year_start=1800&year_end=2000&corpus=0&smo othing=3, accessed April 22, 2013.

6 "What Do We Want?" "Materiality!" "When Do We Want It?" "Now!"

Jonathan Sterne

Starting around the turn of the last century, a generation of Chicago School sociologists went off in search of the community they found missing from their own world. Today, many of us constructivists go off in pursuit of an ever-receding horizon of materiality, one we are equally sure will fill a void we feel around us. As Finn Brunton and Gabriella Coleman put it in chapter 4, the quest for materiality is asymptotic: "we will never quite arrive." If there has been a collective call to emanate from the many different kinds of constructivists in the humanities and social sciences, it has been a cry for materiality. The desire is especially strong in the various human sciences that converge on the study of technology. I imagine throngs of professors and graduate students in various strains of media studies and science and technology studies taking to the streets, signs in hand, chanting their demands.

There are many sources for this longing. The writers in this collection have their own conception of materiality to which they attach it. Leah Lievrouw tells the story like a pendulum swing, where the constructivists have so thoroughly won in the battle against technological determinism and various behaviorisms that our attentions have swung too far in the other direction. Geoff Bowker argues that it is in part a reaction to our current condition of information overload. As journal articles proliferate to the point of cacophony, the project of "knowing everything about the world" (as Bowker puts it, in chapter 5) runs aground. Pablo Boczkowski and Ignacio Siles suggest the issue is that we've become too bounded up in intellectual silos, tied to objects in one or another corner of the study of media technology—production, consumption, content, materiality (which seems to function as "form" in their scheme)—when the real action happens in the middle. All of the authors, but most forcefully Brunton and Coleman, acknowledge the challenge is not to arrive at firm ground, an end point that also serves as a beginning, but rather to find some new kind of middle: "Each frame—of hardware, of users, of stories—implies and affects the others. . . . Only with all three frames of reference in mind can we start to work at the breadth and detail appropriate to the polyphonic, massively multiuser, and materially intricate phenomena occurring on networked computers now" (chapter 4). Today, many constructivists are like Brunton and Coleman's geeks. We want to get "closer to the metal." We are exhausted by "the text-centered, social constructivist paradigm" (Packer and Wiley 2012, 7; referring to Coole and Frost 2010).

But what is this quality called *materiality*? Reading around in the humanities and social sciences, we can find dozens of calls for materiality, but often little agreement over what the term entails. For instance, Jeremy Packer and Stephen B. Crofts Wiley suggest that the material turn encompasses materialist approaches not only to technology, but also to economies, bodies, spaces, and even discourse itself. One finds different materialisms in the traditions of German media theory and what Bernard Siegert more recently calls "cultural technics" (Gumbrecht and Pfeiffer 1994; Kittler 1999, 2010; Siegert 2011); science and technology studies (Bowker 1993, 1994; Canales 2009; Galison 1994, 2003; Pinch and Trocco 2002); the turn to object-oriented ontology (Bogost 2012; Harman 2002); the new feminist materialisms (Grosz 2011; Bennett 2010; Hayles 1999); as well as other extensions of philosophical programs found in the writings of Foucault and Deleuze and Guattari (Foucault 1991; Deleuze and Guattari 1987; see also Massumi 2002).[1] This is to say nothing of the rising fashion for neuroscience in philosophy and some of the humanities like art history, film studies, and music; and the enduring interest in various intellectual descendants of Western Marxism (Hardt and Negri 2000; Terranova 2000; Lazzarato 1996; Grossberg 2010; Berland 2009). The various permutations of the term "material" signal the shape and affordances of the physical world we make and move through, as well as the constitutive social relations that compose our lived reality. But there are major disagreements over how to talk about the various relationships among the things that constitute our thoroughly technical *and* human realm: physical and social processes, consciousness and subjectivity, power and justice.

There is also a growing literature that suggestively argues against equating constructivism with relativism. Rather than assuming that there are multiple constructions of a single material reality, these authors argue, we should instead base our analyses on *multiple realities,* each of which is treated as an empirical fact, and each of which has its own materiality (Viveiros de Castro 1992, 1998; Hage 2011, 2012). This is a particularly challenging conception of materiality, and in an alternate reality to this one, it would be the subject of my response to this collection.

I am entirely sympathetic to the call for more attention to materiality (Sterne 2003, 2012), so long as materiality refers to both physical things and the irreducibly relational character of reality: a phonautograph made partly from human ears, a telephone made partly out of cats; the bandwidth in a transmission channel, the wear on a record or tape; the configuration of people at either end of a sound-reproduction event, whether a broadcast, phone call, or disparate and distributed moments of recording and playback; the institutions that condition "the technological imagination" (Balsamo 2011) as their inhabitants build devices and research their users; the signal-processing routines that operate and direct activity at the most basic and banal levels of infrastructure and consumer electronics; the political, economic, and regulatory apparatuses that motivate so much movement of communication technologies in capitalist societies. All of these things aren't simply material, but they have irreducibly material dimensions. To claims that data are immaterial, there is Matthew Kirschenbaum's (2008) rejoinder about the physicality of hard drives. If data took up no space, there would be no limit to the number of songs on your MP3 player or mobile phone. I conceive of technologies as repeatable social, cultural, and physical processes crystallized into mechanisms. But, of course, defining *technology* is one of the messiest operations in philosophy, history, and the humanities at large (no doubt because it also entails a definition of "humanity" as either technological or nontechnological, no small issue). At worst, "technology" is an amorphous term for an amorphous field. At best, when we get beyond immediate appearances of gadgetry, the term has tremendous breadth and capaciousness, from Mumford's (1934) *technics* to Heidegger's (1977) four causes, to Foucault's (1977) diagrammatics.

* * *

But before we go too far down the path of affirming our fatigue with constructivism and seek refreshment in the garden of materiality, it is worth pausing for a few pages to remember why scholars pursued constructivism in the first place. For as strongly as we may feel the call of materiality, it was not so long ago people felt the same way—and more strongly—about constructivism.[2] A brief detour through intellectual history begins with an earlier generation of writers who turned to constructivism to solve epistemological problems caused by excessive commitments to positivism. They wrote what they wrote because they felt certain concepts—the ones in most dire need of critique—were beyond reproach in the available discourse. Scholars like Berger and Luckmann (1966), James Carey (1989), and David Bloor (1976) challenged correspondence theories of language and instrumental understandings of representation, in part because both positions were increasingly incompatible with philosophical and political aspects of the liberal, reformist projects they championed. Berger and Luckmann radically extended the sociology of knowledge by assuming that knowledge of the world was itself a social fact, which in turn had effects: "How is it possible that human activity should produce a world of things? In other words, an adequate understanding of the 'reality *sui* generis' of society requires an inquiry into the manner in which this reality is constructed" (Berger and Luckmann 1966, 18). Bloor extended their approach into the sociology of science, arguing for an initial impartiality around truth and falsity so that the construction of scientific facts can be studied (Bloor 1976, 7). By resisting the correspondence theories of language, both writers sought to show how facts about the world came into being and had real (we might say material) effects. As Carey reflected on his own critiques of positivism in the 1960s and 1970s, "it was necessary to write such things at that time to try and clear some space in the academy so other things could be done" (Carey and Grossberg 2006, 199).

If we widen our scope, there is a whole wide range of Western intellectual traditions that have nourished one or another strain of constructivism and to which we can point back. Even the most mild constructivist owes debts to writers like Marx (Marx and Engels [1932] 1970), who argued that the ruling ideas were inextricably tied to power relations; Nietzsche, who asked after the obvious taken-for-granted opposition of terms like "good" and "bad" ([1887] 1967); Peirce, James, and the American pragmatists, who pursued ideas for what they could do, rather than searching for immortal truths (James 1970; Peirce 1955); and Canguilhem and writers in the French history of science tradition (Canguilhem 1978), who challenged the disinterestedness and normalism of scientific reasoning. But something special happened in the 1960s and 1970s. As Carey suggested, this work cleared a space for the wave of constructivists who would follow.

Over the last quarter century, much constructivist work on communication technology has carried all these influences (in varying combinations). But in this more recent period it is also marked by an often quite explicit reaction to the broader, commercial, technological culture that surrounded middle-class academics. From the 1980s on, scholars confronted a world full of grand claims for each new wave of digital technology, a world full of institutionally sanctioned, commercially amplified, technological imperatives and initiatives, ornately decorated with millennial rhetorics of inevitability, revolution, transformation, and the transcendence of materiality. To write about technology in this moment was to guide a sailboat against this gust of common sense that came from a hurricane of industrial and institutional initiatives. Writers confronted a particularly virulent form of digital utopianism, and they encountered it personally in their own lives, their own institutions, among their colleagues and their students. Fighting back against this mass of ideas often meant directly confronting the proposition that technology was a causal agent in historical change. We might say that certain institutional imperatives in digital cultures and economies were the cause, and (constructivist) critiques of digital utopianism and technological determinism were the reactions. Fred Turner (2006) has given a particularly compelling account of the rise of digital utopianism. Besides his *From Counterculture to Cyberculture,* dozens of articles and books in this period built their accounts of communication technology on critiques of utopianism—whether historical or contemporary, and regardless of the specific technology. They started pouring out in the 1980s, and intensified in the 1990s (see in order of publication, Czitrom 1982; Slack 1984; Douglas 1987; Marvin 1988; Robins and Webster 1989; Spigel 1992; Stabile 1994; Brook and Boal 1995; Robins and Webster 1996; Balsamo 1996; Edwards 1996; Gitelman 1999; Jones 1999; Peters 1999; Swiss and Herman 2000; Sconce 2000; Abbate 1999. Another set of works of media history also dealt with technology in a constructivist fashion, but were more broadly cultural historical in orientation (Barnhurst and Nerone 2001; John 1995; Hilmes 1997; Ohmann 1996; Thompson 2002). These bodies of work mark a fairly significant shift from the earlier constructivists: the work on technology was often less epistemologically motivated or preoccupied. It was not fighting against positivism for the purpose of liberal social critique. It was debating about what it was fighting: some authors labeled it as capitalism, others as an institutional problem, and still others saw it as a technological problem.

By the twenty-first century, the critique of technological utopianism was so well made that I can't think of a single text (I am including my own writing here) that offers an argument about it that wasn't already available in the 1990s or before. And yet, the critiques of technological utopianism kept coming because cultural and commercial forces—beyond the content of scholarship—also shaped the conversation. To use Pierre Bourdieu's phrase, we struggled with the "pregiven" (Bourdieu, in Bourdieu and Wacquant 1992, 251). Even today, dissertations on communication technology still commonly take a moment to rehearse the terms of debate between determinism and constructivism as they were laid out in this period and before, and then take a position somewhere in between. It's a hard habit to break.

By the turn of the twenty-first century, constructivist work on communication technology routinely combined careful analysis of how the technologies themselves worked as physical and social mechanisms (in order of publication, Zielinski 1996; Hillis 1999; Terranova 2004; Fuller 2005; Gitelman 2006; Slack and Wise 2006; Goggin and Newell 2006; Cartwright and Goldfarb 2006; Gillespie 2007; Helmreich 2007; Bijsterveld 2008; Kelty 2008; Zielinski 2008; Striphas 2009; Hildebrand 2009; Parikka 2010; Balsamo 2011; Mills 2011; Huhtamo and Parikka 2011; Gates 2011). These newer works combined constructivism and materialist analysis in various configurations. Depending on the author, their interest in materiality came from history, anthropology, political theory, philosophy, or science and technology studies, even though the basic premise behind looking at artifacts as themselves having some substance is quite old. It also came from the conflicted intellectual legacies of historical materialism, including some of its most heretical incarnations, like cultural studies. Increasingly, these approaches to materiality were supplemented by the range of conflicting materialisms I listed at the top of this chapter. But we couldn't fully escape the terms of the argument just by turning them around, and even today, scholars of communication technologies sometime still collapse their objects into *technology as such* (another rhetorical habit of digital promoters), begging the question of how and under what conditions communication technologies might be special cases of the more general category, *technology*, as well as whether things we attribute to communication technologies are in fact more broadly technological problems.

If a critique of consumerism and millennialism lay beneath one version of constructivism, another comes from the social construction of reality, and not just the construction of technology. This was constructivism's more discursive and less materialist guise, especially in the Anglophone world. Academic responses to movements like feminism, decolonization, civil rights of all kinds, AIDS activism, disability rights, and a host of other political movements all took up a specifically discursive version of constructivism. They did so in part because of the moments in which they emerged, where various poststructuralisms came into vogue as the university faculties started to diversify, allowing more people to occupy the position of professor and author, and putatively, bring with them more perspectives. A turn to a particularly discursive constructivism made it quite easy to argue that, for instance, there was no essential content to a category like "woman"— while still acknowledging the existence of differential power relations that would bear unequally on people as they were classed by gender. Indeed, classic work like Donna Haraway's mid-career writings, ranging from her work on cybernetics to her more famous "A Cyborg Manifesto" (in *Simians, Cyborgs, and Women,* 1991) attacked essentialisms and determinisms around gender, species, and technology as part of the project of imagining other possible ways of being in the world and alternatives to male domination. This body of work engaged with science and technology, but it was not solely confined to it.

The discursive approach was a barricade against the weighty tendencies that collapsed descriptions of people into descriptions of their bodies, an issue still widely unresolved, especially in newer fields like disability studies (Butler 1993; Gilroy 1994; Kleege 2005; Siebers 2008).[3] This work is in one sense a direct heir of the earlier epistemological constructivists. But politically, they deliberately broke with the liberalism that animated Berger and Luckmann, Carey, and Bloor, borrowing instead from the various radical social movements by which they were inspired (even if there was not always a direct link between activists and scholars). It is difficult to overstate the importance of this move, not only for contemporary scholarship, but also for contemporary politics.

To oversimplify in the hope of making my point clearly, the difference between constructivism in fields like feminist theory, postcolonial studies, disability studies, and cultural studies, and the constructivism in science and technology studies (STS) and actor-network theory, is a matter of kind and strategy. Both are politically minded and assume the political character of knowledge, but they differ on what politics is and where scholarship is to be situated with respect to it. The former group methodologically presupposes the irreducibly political character of the constructive operation, they assume that power relations preexist the constructivist scenario, and they assume that any analysis is always situated and positioned (which is not to say that ideas are simply reducible to biography). They begin from the presumption that differential power relations animate any context before they arrive on the scene to analyze it, and they are motivated (often implicitly) by a normative framework that challenges those axes of difference at their very base. In STS, the motivations are similar but the working assumptions are different. Wiebe Bijker, for instance, wrote that his own interest in constructivism was rooted in Dutch peace activism, especially against nuclear weapons (Bijker 2001). But the employment of the "Strong Programme" and various other strategies of epistemological agnosticism insist on a strategic neutrality for the purposes of analysis. This affirms the traditional rhetorical position of the liberal social critic, at arm's distance from the fray. Latour, meanwhile, attends to politics but from a largely managerial point of view, where the scholar may care about politics, but does not take an oppositional stance (Latour 2004). Again, we find care and interest, but also the assertion of distance.

Yet today, many feel that constructivism itself, along with the critique of technological determinism, has overreached and run aground. This argument is also older than it feels, since some of the parameters are already apparent in Ian Hacking's (1999) *The Social Construction of What?* More specifically in relation to communication technology, writers like Geoffrey Winthrop-Young (2011) and John Durham Peters (forthcoming) have taken on the epithet "technological determinism." As Peters points out, the accusation of technological determinism is a conversation stopper. It often begs the question of what the term "technology" includes. For many writers tarred with the brush of determinist, "technology" is actually a much bigger term than "gadgetry."

It seems that we are tired of having this argument over and over. But why are we so compelled to have it and what are we to do about it? Geoff Bowker's materialist and somewhat scary analysis of our own situation in the production of knowledge is quite telling. As he surveys the ever-growing glut of journal articles, each of which has a smaller and smaller audience, he sees: "We are clearly not creating a species of knowledge-power appropriate to the issues that we face. We are producing knowledge that is predicated on and replicates mass production and mass consumption. Our information infrastructure, willy-nilly, is the fold in the Moebius strip that permits the world to seem as society writ large" (chapter 5, this book). The declining relevance of the journal article as the materialization of scholarly knowledge, and the uncertain struggle to find alternatives, demands a certain patience, since if there is a new form of knowledge coming, it hasn't yet arrived. Bowker finds some hope in massive collaborations and new database logics. For my part, I retain some confidence in the resiliency of both the essay form and the codex, which have thrived for hundreds of years. Meanwhile, the journal article seems to undergo transformations every two or three decades.

Boczkowski and Siles turn more hopefully to pedagogy as a solution, getting students to work across disciplinary categories. If I still believe in the book and the essay, I still believe in the seminar even more. I am experimenting with disallowing rehearsals of "technological vs. cultural determinism" arguments in my classes and exams. It's harder than it sounds, especially when the rhetoric of techno-utopianism is alive and well in the commercial world and still operates in the truth spaces of journalism and online discussion. It's also difficult given how much this comes up in cultural analyses of technology of whatever stripe. But if we want to get beyond the argument, our students stand a better chance of succeeding than we do, so it's up to us to stop trying to reproduce it, even as a historical curiosity. At the graduate level, my seminar on the historiography of new media in winter 2013 takes Boczkowski's approach to the extreme, though my model is less the social scientific diagram (with its quadrants) than the record collection with its eclecticism. Students will select the topic of their semester's research at the beginning of the term and each week retrieve a primary source relevant to it. Each week, they will also read a distinctive work of media historiography (mostly books, since that is still the core traffic in the field). They will then write about their artifact in the style of the author, which requires them to determine what the important stylistic aspects of the work really are. At the end of the term, the students can then revise these short papers into something longer, synthesized into something approaching their own authorial style. The approach is meant to encourage openness to other ways of writing and thinking, to free students of the pressure to take positions as their own against the positions of others, and to challenge them to reverse-engineer the work of other scholars so that they get a better sense of what's actually involved in the interface between writing and thought. The pedagogy imposes some strict limits and demands for imitation (at first) to encourage creativity by freeing students of the demand for creativity in the places we usually look for it (choice of object, originality of voice, etc). It is drawn from how musicians learn their instruments: when I wanted to learn to play a good bass line, my teachers had me learn to imitate what the best bassists did. I either succeeded and incorporated their techniques with my own, or failed and came up with something original-sounding in the process.

Of course, coming up with something original is harder than coming up with something original-sounding. This leads us to Bowker's most serious provocation, which is to ask: what if we no longer want for knowledge of the world, but have too much? As with the other rehearsed arguments mentioned earlier, the information overload proposition is an old one, and it demands the repetition of an old answer. While collaboration is becoming more common in the humanities, and it should, the humanities and social sciences also must continue their projects of interpretation, analysis, system building, and generalization, even as we are forced to confront the partiality and mortality of all knowledge. Our job is still to produce synthetic, meaningful accounts of the world, to answer big how and why questions, even if the job of "knowing everything about it" is really too much to impose on a single person. Transcendence, after all, is situated transcendence. All universalisms start from somewhere. Constructivists showed this to be true for the sciences; it is equally true for the humanities and social sciences. When we look beneath the debates about technological determinism and constructivism, we find a mess of arguments about causality, and causality is where the action is. The desire for materiality is a desire for firm foundations. The excess of positivism was to assume it could be satisfied once and for all. The excess of technological utopianism was to co-opt it into an intellectualized consumerism. The excess of constructivism was to denigrate the desire altogether.

Acknowledgments

Thanks to Carrie Rentschler, Emily Raine, and the editors.

Notes

1. Throughout this essay I refer to long lists of works. The point is to be suggestive, not exhaustive. In most cases, I'm only referencing a very small segment of work that would exemplify what I'm describing. "Materiality" is such a central term for so many people that it's hard to stop the lists. Certainly, *copia* seems like a fitting rhetorical strategy.

2. Though we must remember this is only true in some places—take a look at how your school's strategic plan talks about technology and you're likely to see that a very simplistic notion of causality is alive and well among some academics.

3. To see how deep this goes, do a text search of your favorite humanities scholars for disparaging references to blindness and deafness. The blind and Deaf never seem to fare too well in the ableist critical imagination.

7   Mediations and Their Others

Lucy Suchman

The essays collected in this volume explore the many ways in which media and technology, both conceptually and materially, are deeply implicated in one another's existence. This includes naming (and questioning) persistent disciplinary divides between media studies and technology studies, and articulating the evident empirical and analytic relations that join their research objects together. The digital enters the scene as well, as a third party that simultaneously complicates and reinforces these relations. The digital complicates insofar as its textuality underscores the inseparability of medium and message, and also further undoes professional boundaries historically drawn between making and using, themselves reinforced through the materialities of broadcasting and publishing. At the same time, the digital reinforces historical divides insofar as it's often mistaken for the immaterial, or treated as simply a new channel for the delivery of independently existing information and communication content.

I came to technology studies myself through an anthropology committed to "studying up," and with an orientation to practice based in ethnomethodology (Suchman 2011). My research objects weren't conceptualized at the time as "media technologies," but rather in terms of my colleagues' efforts to write humanlike capacities into machines. Nor were my colleagues oriented to media as such, but rather to human–machine interaction as a site of research and development. At the same time, it was the specific materialities and capacities of the machines in question (DIY personal computers then under construction at Xerox Palo Alto Research Center [PARC], programmed in LISP) that defined the imaginaries on both sides of the interface. This led me to an interest in what in media studies might be classified as "content," in this case in the form of assumptions regarding cognition, communication, and action that animated both cognitive scientists and their cognate machines.

Our subsequent work at Xerox PARC unfolded as projects in practice-based co-design, enacted across what could be classified as sites of production and consumption, or design and use. Our method of case-based prototyping was quite explicitly founded on the argument that content and media are inseparable for practitioners: that the efficacy of a digital document technology can't be judged unless it incorporates actual work materials, and is incorporated into working practices. We came to see our prototypes as an alternative to formal requirements specifications—as things that embodied, rather than represented, emergent desiderata for technologies in the making (Suchman, Trigg, and Blomberg 2002).

Coming to this volume as an anthropologist and STS researcher, then, I'm perhaps already convinced by arguments aimed at those who are more invested in traditional modes of scholarship within media and communications studies. At the same time I recognize that, however much engineers and technologists may now embrace "the social" as an inherent aspect of their professional practice (see Lievrouw, chapter 2 in this book), dominant discourses still imply that this is a category separable from—even secondary to—the technical artifacts that are their work's objects. In this sense I would agree that refiguring the social/technical divide continues to be what Lievrouw calls here an "unfinished project." One particular preoccupation of these contributions is the technical-as-material side of that dichotomy: a realm of articulation that the authors generally agree has been neglected within studies of media. A tension appears here, between commitment to a conceptual frame that places relationality at its center, and the ways in which calling out the material as an object of study inescapably also works to reenact its separateness. The relationality that is needed to resolve this is not between two preexisting entities, but rather the relational materiality of actor-network theory and its aftermath (where rather than preexisting relations, entities are themselves relational effects), or that of feminist theory (where entities are effects of what Barad [2007] has named the "agential cuts" [140] of making difference).[1] In both of these conceptualizations, matter and meaning are always already entangled.

Lievrouw helpfully points out (chapter 2) that, like engineering, technological materiality is intrinsically heterogeneous. Technology, Jasanoff reminds us, "both embeds and is embedded in social practices, identities, norms, conventions, discourses, instruments, and institutions" (2004, 3). A turn to materiality, it follows, does not mean a return to a mode of materialism that takes sense and significance as epiphenomenal. So Brunton and Coleman's call for "getting close to the metal" is not, they emphasize, about a foundational return to hardware and that which lies beneath, but an attention to new modes of production/use in the sociomaterial practices of geeks, hacktivists, sysadmins, and other practitioners, deeply engaged in all of the multilayered infrastructures of digital media. Taken together (rather than considered through their differences), Geoffrey Bowker suggests with respect to media studies and STS that "the beauty of the two fields is that they don't take an information infrastructure to be just a bundle of wires: it is a 'dispositif technique,' as Foucault would call it—a bundle of technologies, techniques, administrative procedures, and cultural forms" (chapter 5, this book).

In a similar spirit, in chapter 3 Boczkowski and Siles urge us to study the mutual constitution of production and consumption, content and artifact. Media technologies, by their definition, are always already assemblages of these. And yet I wonder about the discursive technologies that the authors themselves deploy in their call for integration, based in their concern that contemporary media studies and STS are caught in the divisions of a quadrant (a classification that by the authors' own account resists their efforts at neat sorting). Perhaps we might invert that concern and ask, given the evident fluidity of the distinctions that order the quadrant, what are the stakes in making differences between production and consumption, or content and materiality, when, and for whom? This is an empirical question, which leads us to the "cosmopolitan sensibility" that Boczkowski and Siles recommend as the remedy for the divisions that their quadrant reiterates. I'm less convinced that we need a new name for inventive, mixed methods-based research, which they identify as the historical basis for both media studies and STS, and as the way forward. It is notable that Boczkowski and Siles themselves have each done research that undoes the divisions that they delineate. So why not start from there? Might we not abandon the matrix altogether, as a device that inescapably reproduces the kinds of categorical sorting that Boczkowski and Siles call on us to transcend? The most compelling, and instructive, refutation of the divisions is the studies themselves, particularly insofar as they exemplify generative theorizing brought into relationship with careful empirical research and thoughtful analysis.

Bowker's contribution to this collection addresses the possibilities for reinventing scholarship, by questioning a genre that runs across the disciplines (and interdisciplinarity)—namely, that of the single-authored academic paper. He builds on the premise that the success of a text lies in the extent of its distribution, how widely it gets read. But what are the genealogies of this faith in the virtue of large numbers? Is it inherently obvious that the value of any writing lies in the quantity of its readers? I take to heart as well Bowker's reminder of the myth of single authorship: that all that we say is a remix, and remixing can be generative of things never expressed or heard before. At the same time, confirming the death of the single author, I would argue, requires intensified forms of careful citation, of recognition that we have always been part of an authorial stream rather than its source, and that everything we write presupposes its (re)animation through a lively and specifically situated reader. My own scholarship is devoted in large part to becoming more conscious of, and more adequately acknowledging, the genealogies of my own assumptions. Put another way, the time that I spend reading and writing alone is always at the same time an intensive engagement with others. I have no question that everything that I write is a refraction of a long and multivocal discursive history of which I'm more and less (largely less) cognizant. At the same time, the labors of scholarship for me also represent a form of resistance to the imperative of collaboration that characterizes certain forms of contemporary life—the always public "sharing" ethos of Facebook, the normative subtexts of group work and of good citizenship. The danger seems at least as great to me that, as well as finding themselves inadequately equipped to work together, our students may find themselves lost when called on to work alone.

Through his own labors of scholarship, Bowker traces the form of the academic article to its formation within the Enlightenment crucible of a belief in authoritative truth telling. And insofar as we accept that genre and content are inseparable, the traditional form must indeed in significant ways tether us to its onto-epistemic assumptions. But does that necessarily imply that the form of the academic article is fixed? What modes of experimental writing and publication might there be that work to dismantle the premises of authority and truth that underpin the form, while also expanding our ability to acknowledge the sources that enable our own capacities for expression? Might we work against the privileging of text, while also preserving the distinctive and generative capacities that it offers as a medium? The Protein Data Bank may be powerful, but it's not a form that works for all modes of knowledge transaction; the journal *Vectors* is inspirational, and works, inter alia, through text inventively remediated. Along with literacy in the (critical) reading of databases, I would also gladly join a campaign for the slow reading of texts.

Perhaps my relative tolerance for the academy and my love of text is due in part to my twenty years in industry, with its privileging of the take-away message over the nuanced argument, the diagrammatic (or at least the bullet pointed) over the discursive, and of corporate teamwork over contemplative scholarship. While I strongly support reform of academic assessment from its overvaluation of individual performance, I see the problem equally as one of the undervaluation of alternative ways of being a productive academic—as a teacher most obviously, and as a contributor to the overall well-being of one's colleagues and students through administration and what is named "professional service." As we all know, however much assessment may be organized along multiple dimensions, publication (narrowly defined) remains the "one right way" to academic success.

It may be that the sense of what we mean by "media technologies" requires some expansion as well. My own current project focuses on what der Derian (2009) has named the "military-industrial-media-entertainment network" (MIME-NET) (xxvii). Media technologies here infuse unmanned aerial vehicles (UAVs) piloted by distant operators relying on a distributed network of real-time satellite imaging, video feeds, instant messaging, radio communications, and remote controls. These configurations shift our focus from consumer technologies (though not from the presence of industry vendors), to extended historical, political, and economic infrastructures of information and communications technologies and their associated body/machine "dispositif techniques." Der Derian traces the latest developments to British experimentation with networked warfare between 1927 and 1931, in the adoption of wireless radio communications to coordinate ground troops. By 1928, "150 wireless sets were used for a strategic maneuver that left an assembled group of brass and members of Parliament highly impressed" (der Derian 2009, 25). From the first Iraq War forward, media scholars have traced the elaborating conjunction of weapon systems and sign systems (xxi). What der Derian names the contemporary MIME-NET "runs on video-game imagery, twenty-four-hour news cycles, multiple modes of military, corporate, university, and media power, and microchips, embedded in everything but human flesh (so far)" (125).

As a model of "virtuous war," der Derian argues, the current U.S. military strategy "projects a technological and ethical superiority in which computer simulation, media dissimulation, global surveillance, and networked warfare combine to deter, discipline, and if need be, destroy the enemy" (2009, xx). The final term of this sentence indexes the "kill list," a medium that translates persons into "the enemy" and joins American technologies of terror to their targets. The regime under President Obama reportedly operates on a premise of guilty until proven innocent, in effect counting all "military-age males" in a strike zone as combatants unless there is explicit intelligence—posthumously—proving them innocent.[2]

However much the photographic image has been denaturalized in contemporary media studies, it is what Caplan (2012) names its "testimonial validity" that underwrites the promise of precision in the case of the targeting that mediates drone warfare. Military analysts agree, however, that despite their promise of illumination, information and communications technologies have intensified rather than dissipated what nineteenth-century military theorist Carl von Clausewitz famously described as the "fog of war," remaking it into a matrix of ever faster and noisier channels of transmission. The enduring problem of "situational awareness," defined by military commentators as "the ability to maintain a constant, clear mental picture of relevant information and the tactical situation including friendly and threat situations" (Dostal 2001) is the tether by which I connect my own previous research to the indigenous preoccupations of contemporary warfare (Suchman forthcoming). This definition by Major Dostal continues: "RSTA [Reconnaissance, Surveillance, and Target Acquisition] elements must provide situational understanding of the operational environment in all of its dimensions—political, cultural, economic, demographic, as well as military factors." In its ambiguous reference to RSTA "elements" as the source of situational understanding, this articulation of the military apparatus implicitly references the latter's hybrid composition, enfolding humans and media(ting) technologies into a sensing/acting machinery. The scope of the latter's perceptual field expands, moreover, to encompass not only the battlefield (no longer existent as such), but also an indefinitely bounded "operational environment," to be parsed into its discretely identifiable "dimensions" and "factors." Through these terms, the sites/sights of war are positioned within a familiar frame of reasoning and action, but the actual reports from the field indicate (as they always have) that something quite different is happening.

The incidents abound. To take just one recent example, in September of this year, Reuters reported that a U.S. drone had killed "five suspected militants" in Yemen. Variously referred to as being "linked to al Qaeda" and as "Islamists," the story goes on to report that the strike was carried out on a vehicle "which was believed to be carrying militants. . . . Five were killed and eight injured and we are still investigating who these men are and in what way they were linked to al Qaeda," one official said.[3] A story two days later, in CNN's International edition, reported the same incident as "A U.S. drone strike targeting al Qaeda suspects in Yemen killed thirteen civilians, including three women," and a senior Yemeni Defense Ministry official confirmed that, "It was a mistake," adding, "we hope it will not hurt our anti-terror efforts in the region."[4] Residents in the area, however, explained that while they did not deny the existence of al Qaeda operatives in their area, incidents such as this assist the latter greatly in their recruiting. And Faisal Shahzad, the Pakistani American who tried to set off a car bomb in Times Square in 2010, justified targeting civilians by telling the judge, "When the drones hit, they don't see children."[5]

Rachel Plotnick (2012) argues that while scholars in the humanities and social sciences have written extensively on media reporting on war, and on military technologies, too little attention has been paid to their intersection. In an exemplary demonstration of the "cosmopolitan sensibility" encouraged by Boczkowski and Siles (chapter 3), Plotnick echoes the concerns of this volume by addressing that gap, with particular attention to media representations of the future of automation in warfare, both "real and imagined." "Making sense of journalists' framing of 'push-button warfare,'" Plotnick argues, "requires first understanding how button interfaces achieved salience as technical and social objects" (Plotnick 2012, 656). She traces this figuration to a 1942 *Los Angeles Times* editorial cartoon, "featuring an image of Uncle Sam caught in a tangle of wires and push-buttons that signified the United States' messy control system," with the caption, "Our push button war"(657).[6] Singularized during the Cold War as "the button," control systems were progressively blackboxed by the media. If, as Plotnick suggests, the "reification of push-buttons offered a powerful sign for making sense of paranoia and anxiety surrounding nuclear war," it is the configuration of the drone operator in the Nevada desert and the "militant" in Afghanistan and its neighboring territories that animates American anxieties over terrorist attacks today. In an era of proliferating forms of push-button devices, as Plotnick observes, remote control achieves wider rhetorical agency. And with the advent of the first Gulf War, the disillusionment with earlier rhetorics of remote-controlled war was replaced with new optimism: Writers for *Newsweek* in 1991 admitted that, despite earlier realizations that "push-button, remote-control war won without casualties" was an unrealistic prospect, in fact "the promise of high-tech warfare still beckons: to move men farther and farther from the killing fields."[7] Plotnick concludes:

By the late twentieth century, when push-button war no longer referred to a future fantasy or fear, participants and observers were forced to cope with the messiness of predictions-turned-realities. That anxiety has continued to proliferate in a post-9/11 context, with journalistic frames trying to sort out perceived binaries of human/machine, manual/automatic, sacrifice/cowardice, etc. By recycling these binaries, media accounts have never fully begun to process the rich and complex dimensions of long-distance, technological warfare. . . . While news sources and world leaders try to collectively reevaluate and "reprogram" what push-buttons mean in the twenty-first century, it becomes that much more important to understand why symbolic objects take hold—and how they help/hinder discussions of socially and politically charged issues that persist over time. (2012, 668)

In this extended quote Plotnick flags for us the continued importance of thinking together the material and discursive, the symbolic and technical. As we move through successive waves of response and correction regarding the conceptualizations that prevail in media and technology studies at any given moment (from technological determinism to interpretive flexibility, from social constructionism to material semiotics, and so forth), our aim might be (or at least this seems apt for this moment) a frame that allows us to come to grips with the ways in which media and technologies configure each other.[8]

Restoring the conceptual and material unity of making and using, and of medium and message, has its parallel in our own research methods in the social sciences, historically rendered as independent of their specific objects. As we acknowledge the performativity of our methods, our investigations and the stories they generate are themselves crucial media for remaking technology (Haraway 1997; Law 2004). The most generative projects, in my view, are those that work to recover the lived experience and the embodied, situated interactions of those immediately implicated in particular assemblages, the material practices and cultural imaginaries that create and articulate those arrangements, and the political/economic investments that sustain them. This might lead us in turn to engage in modes of analysis that, in their detailed articulation of the sociomaterial arrangements in which we are implicated, help to illuminate how our imaginaries and material practices variously work to reiterate or transform, or both, the worlds that we collectively enact.

Notes

1. For a full explication of agential realism see Barad 2007. On relational materiality see Law 2002, and for a recent case of its mobilization in an illuminating study see Burrell 2012.

2. Joe Becker and Scott Shane, "Secret 'Kill List' Proves a Test of Obama's Principles and Will." *New York Times*, May 29, 2012.

3. Reuters, "U.S. drone kills five suspected militants in Yemen." September 2, 2012. Online edition, http://www.reuters.com/article/2012/09/02/us-yemen-violence-idUSBRE88106S20120902, accessed September 12, 2012.

4. Hakim Almasmari, "Suspected U.S. drone strike kills civilians in Yemen, officials say." CNN online edition, September 4, 2012. http://edition.cnn.com/2012/09/03/world/meast/yemen-drone-strike/, accessed September 12, 2012.

5. Becker and Shane, note 2.

6. The results of Plotnick's quantitative analysis of mentions of "push-button warfare" between 1945 and 2010 show the largest spike by far in the years immediately after World War II.

7. Evan Thomas and John Barry, "War's new science." *Newsweek*, February 18, 1991. http://www.thedailybeast.com/newsweek/1991/02/17/war-s-new-science.html, accessed September 1, 2012. See Suchman (forthcoming) on the unmarked identification of "men," or more broadly "humans," with our side in references to the life-saving capabilities of remote weapon systems.

8. For further reflections on configuration see Suchman 2012.

Part II The People, Practices, and Promises of Information Networks

8   Making Media Work: Time, Space, Identity, and Labor in the Analysis of Information and Communication Infrastructures

Gregory J. Downey

Making Media Technology Work

I work with media all day, every day, as both a researcher and a teacher in a public university, wrestling with questions about our relationship to information and communication technology, both past and present. As a researcher, I proudly identify as a historian and geographer of technology, and my own most detailed case studies so far—in telegraphy, librarianship, and stenography—all have roots in the nineteenth century. But each of those topics also extends tendrils into the twenty-first century: urban bicycle messengers using smartphones recall the telegraph messenger boys of decades past; library catalogers retool their standards and practices to produce metadata for digital libraries accessible over the web; and live closed captioning on cable television is often created through computer-aided stenography. As a teacher, the pattern is reversed; my specialty is addressing the "new media" concerns of the current day, with syllabi on The Information Society, Digital Divides and Differences, and Media Fluency for the Digital Age littering my website, my Facebook page, and my Twitter feed. But each of these new media courses holds at its core a set of historical examples and arguments drawn from old media. This chapter presents my humble attempt to distill and defend the main insight that I've drawn from these productive contradictions over the last fifteen years or so: that a wide range of human "information labor," enabling and constraining the constant circulation of information across a wide range of technological and social contexts, remains crucial to making media technologies work.

That idea of "work" lurks within our relationship to present-day media technologies in a variety of ways. Ask my current undergraduates on the first day of the semester about the "work" they do to find information today, and they will reply that finding information is no work at all. The answer to any brief question of fact is just a Google search away, as likely (in their minds) to lead to an amateur blog post as to a professional piece of journalism. The explanation for any named but unfamiliar event or idea is as close as the next Wikipedia page, a source they know was shunned by their former high school teachers, but which they suspect is secretly employed by their time-pressed college professors. Questions of a vaguer nature might be posed to their vast social network of friends, relations, and acquaintances through Facebook, as a public "wall" or "status" post inviting the crowd to reply. And any informational product which eludes these three strategies, somehow not available to them instantly as a web-based link to a downloadable digital file, can certainly be delivered in physical form—they still remember "books"—in twenty-four hours or less, if one is willing and able to pay, from the mega-retailer Amazon.com. Often sounding a bit too much like advertising copy, my students regularly inform me that these new tools "free" them from the pesky work of having to travel to the library, having to read through long and turgid books, and having to remember facts and definitions that are only a click away.

Press them further, of course, and they will agree that there is much "work" still to be done once any given bit of information has been supplied by the network. There are exams to study for, papers to write, presentations to compose. This kind of creative labor is easy for them to see, and easy for them to see themselves performing. It is written into the university curriculum as "complex communication" and "critical thinking" (Bok 2007; Booth, Colomb, and Williams 2008). It is the kind of high-status, high-value labor that they are paying to practice and master with their college tuition dollars in the first place. Such labor experiences will provide them with entry into those elite areas of the "space of flows" of the information society (Castells 1996)—what decades of scholars have called the postindustrial bourgeoisie, the symbolic analysts, or the creative class (Bell 1976; Reich 1991; Florida 2002, respectively). With the raw materials of information, gathered from their vast and always-on data, content, and knowledge networks, these students trust that they will end up on the correct side of the digital divide (Eubanks 2011; Norris 2001; Warschauer 2003).

In this trust, many of my students display a narrow understanding of history and geography, which underpins their narrow understanding of their own position and privilege. Media history for them is a textbook teleology of technological advances (from print culture to radio culture to television culture to digital culture) and market redefinitions (from elite audience to mass audience to individual audience), which result in their own ultimate emergence at the top of an information food chain as both target market and content originator (Baughman 1992; Downey 2011;

John 2010; Starr 2004). Structures of media consolidation and content personalization have made it all too easy for them to live within a self-reinforcing informational geography of safe and satisfying answers, an "echo chamber" whether on the political right, the political left, or the political apathetic (Bagdikian 2004; Kovach and Rosenstiel 2010; Jamieson and Cappella 2008; McChesney 2008; Pariser 2011). And their own amateur media activity—whether uploading photos to their social network profile or downloading the latest cultural content outside of intellectual property paywalls—reinforces the fiction that information circulation is driven simply by "play" and that information content is simply available for "free" (Gillespie 2007; Jenkins 2006; Kline, Dyer-Witheford, and de Peuter 2003; Lessig 2010; Vaidhyanathan 2001). No wonder they are unable to see much of the actual work that underpins this media.

How might we as teachers break through this narrow, instrumental, and rather triumphalist understanding of new media infrastructures? The standard strategy of "media literacy" is to demonstrate to students that none of these admittedly extraordinary technologies, Google or Wikipedia or Facebook or Amazon, are able to deliver an information experience that entirely frees the user from further work, especially when one approaches these services with anything more than a trivial question (Fallows 2011; Gillmor 2008; Jenkins 2006; Levinson 2009; Lievrouw and Livingstone 2006; Martens 2010; Manovich 2001). It is easy to Google the name of a well-known corporation, access the Wikipedia biography of a well-known historical figure, discover a Facebook friend of similar interests, or find plenty of competing purchase options on Amazon for a mainstream, bestselling book. But pose a more complicated question on Google, and the search transforms from an "I feel lucky!" first hit success to an information overload of pages and pages of dubious result candidates, computed not simply from the original "PageRank" algorithm whereby sites with lots of links, from sites with lots of links, recursively float higher in the search rankings, but from an increasingly complicated set of contextual variables including the searcher's own geographic location, query history, and "psychographic" marketing profile (Battelle 2005; Kink and Hess 2008; Morozov 2011). Seek a more contextual summary from Wikipedia of a broad time period in which a historical figure lived, and the "encyclopedia that anyone can edit" reaches the limits of its "no original research" restriction and its lack of professional historian contributors (Hansen, Berente, and Lyytinen 2009; Mangu-Ward 2007; Pentzold 2010; Poe 2006; Rosenzweig 2006). Attempt to define yourself on Facebook using markers other than "Likes" of purchase choices and pop-culture affiliations, and the social network application programming interface (API) is unable to parse your descriptors (Papacharissi 2009; Watkins 2009).[1] And ask for Amazon user suggestions about a more obscure, out of print text and you may very well fall prey to the "review spam" of paid advertising disguised as customer satisfaction, or the petty squabbling of zealots who give zero stars to any work that suggests a difference of opinion with their immovable, ideological world-view (Auletta 2010; Robinson 2010; Roychoudhuri 2010). Media literacy exercises can be an eye-opening demonstration of the limits of automation in many of these seemingly laborless systems, revealing both the need for users to learn and apply sophisticated query strategies, and the influence of layers of algorithms which combine to produce complex and sometimes contradictory results (Gillespie, chapter 9, this volume).

However, teaching media literacy skills, no matter how effective, still keeps the focus of work on the students themselves. The greater challenge is to convince them that even when tools like Google and Wikipedia and Facebook and Amazon work as intended at the moment they are invoked, behind the scenes and before the fact there actually occurred great amounts of design, organization, production, reproduction, and "repair" labor on the part of many, many others besides themselves (Jackson, chapter 11, this volume). A cursory understanding of the battles between Google engineers and the outside "search engine optimization" (SEO) vendors reveals an ongoing arms race through which the search algorithm is constantly repaired from the inside and then reverse-engineered from the outside, in an environment where dropping off of the first page of a Google search can mean significant and unexpected revenue loss for online retailers (Basen 2011). Similarly, the briefest exploration into Wikipedia article production reveals the power-law division of labor represented by the small number of users who actually write substantive original articles for the site, versus the larger number who merely tweak and reorganize and spell-check and, yes, sometimes vandalize those articles—not to mention the work of algorithms known as "bots" to flag and queue articles for quality and revision (Niederer and van Dijck 2010). For the first time, journalists and scholars are beginning to reveal that social networking sites like Facebook demand constant human content moderation and censorship of photos, videos, and even text speech that violate legal terms of service, zones of personal privacy, and community norms of propriety.[2] And once one peeks behind the virtual facade of Amazon, it is easy to see the material realities of logistics and fulfillment and customer service, with (high-paid) technology workers keeping server farms running in one region, (low-paid) warehouse workers packing product in another region, and an Internetwork of both public and private delivery services shuttling boxes back and forth from suppliers and customers in between.[3] The best outcome for me as a teacher is when students realize that the media literacy skills that they employ in order to effectively use and critically evaluate such web tools are useless without an understanding of the deeper context of how those tools deliver what they promise. In other words, the sporadic information labor of my students as Google, Wikipedia, Facebook, and Amazon users is intimately connected to the ongoing information labor of the many, many behind-the-scenes designers, builders, operators, and maintainers of Google, Wikipedia, Facebook, and Amazon themselves.

As these present-day examples suggest, what I am loosely calling "information labor" here represents a broad diversity. Certainly some information labor reflects the same expectations of my students for their own successful futures: expensive, individual, high-status, high-value labor (or "knowledge work"), as predicted by the post-industrialists, produced by the elite universities, and circulated among the leading transnational corporations (Deuze 2007; Levy and Murnane 2004). Other information labor is collectively organized work outside of a formal organization, aggregated over a network into the so-called "wisdom of crowds" (Kreiss, Finn, and Turner 2011; Shirky 2008; van Dijck and Nieborg 2009). When such labor occurs outside of a formal wage or salary relation, it goes by various names: some have called such labor "gift exchange," such as in the case of advice provided within online communities; others have termed it "produsage," if it comes as a consequence of a formal user or customer relationship; or it may be termed "playbor," if it is considered to have both entertainment value and exchange value (Bermejo 2009; Elk 2011; Kollock 1999). Still more information labor is only a little more expensive than free: contingent labor assembled by the temporary agencies and independent contracting arrangements of digital distributed work online, or emplaced in the sprawling factories of free trade zones, for a wage hopefully considered livable in its local context, but likely considered subminimum in its employing context (Rogers 2000; Benner 2002; Christensen and Barker 1998). And a growing portion of information labor is almost entirely abstracted from human minds and hands, existing as automated, algorithmic labor forever capturing some previous human expertise, judgment, pattern, or intention as replicable and executable code (Gillespie, chapter 9, this volume).

All of these forms of information labor share a crucial aspect, however: users tend not to see it. For one thing, this labor is obscured by the perpetual marketing claims of both the technologies that surround it and the content that flows through it—after all, customers are motivated to buy iPhones

and apps, not the aggregated and morselized labor power of factory workers and developers. Whether through user-friendly interfaces, supply-chain
intermediaries, cultural myths of smart technology, or plain old "commodity fetishism" (where a single-minded focus on the price of a good or service
distracts us from considering the conditions of production for that good
or service), information laborers of all sorts are likely to be hidden, out of
sight and out of mind, from those who encounter their products and processes on a daily basis (Downey 2001, 2004b). The clickstream engineers of
Google, the volunteer editors of Wikipedia, the outsourced moderators for
Facebook, and the logistics army behind Amazon—all must be revealed,
situated, and explored in order for us to reveal, situate, and explore our own
daily labor with these systems.

Conceptualizing and Exploring Information Labor

What kinds of research interventions, from science and technology studies on one hand, and communication and media studies on the other, can
help us with this task of "uncovering information labor" in the classroom?
It is helpful to start by putting the concepts of "information" and "technology" in context. After all, the very purpose of information and communication technology is to make information—whether conceptualized
as data, content, or knowledge—accessible across space and across time,
from one context to another, from one community of practice to the next.
But all information and communication technologies also depend, both for
their daily functioning and for their overall meaning, on different forms of
human labor, each with its own temporal and spatial characteristics as well.

Tools from both history and geography can be brought to bear on the
question. All of the contexts and all of the communities in which we might
look for information, technology, and labor are necessarily situated geo-
graphically and temporally, a condition we can analyze in terms of place,
space, and scale. Individual places support or constrain certain kinds of
informational activities, which are structured by their users and inhabitants, their natural and built environments, and the social meanings ascribed
to them. Places connect through relationships of all sorts—technological,
social, political, and economic—into broader conceptual spaces for action,
be it the state space of government and military control, the market space
linking raw material extraction to component assembly to consumer retail,
the cyberspace interface of bodies and technologies exchanging encoded
electronic communication, or the imagined space of a cultural or diasporic
or aspirational community fragmented across other national, economic,

and technological boundaries. And finally, these spaces are assembled, reassembled and, sometimes, disassembled at both small and large scales simultaneously, with complicated arrangements of power and uneven possibilities for making change (Downey 2007b, 2009).

Information and communication technologies, and the larger media infrastructures within which they are situated, developed, used, and understood, by their very nature exist to transcend history and geography, storing ideas across time and moving ideas across space in an organized and productive manner (Edwards 2003; Star and Bowker 2006; Wright 2007). This work of making information accessible is really about (a) making information useful (or what we might call "realizing its use value") and (b) bringing that information into motion (or what we might call "putting information into circulation"). Especially in our current, overwhelmingly capitalist, global political economy, these two issues—how a society values information, and how information circulates through a society—are not just connected. In what we might call a dialectical relationship, each concept helps to define the other: to be useful, information must circulate through many minds (and eventually through yours); and to circulate, many minds must judge some piece of information to be (at least potentially) useful. All the agency that we bring to information along the way—whether producing information as a part of work or play, appropriating information as private property, commodifying information for market exchange, offering information up in a creative commons, or claiming the right to information in the public interest—must be understood within this basic structure of value and circulation (Dyer-Witheford 1999; Harvey 2001, 2010; Schiller 1999).

Setting up the parameters of structure and agency in this way gives us a framework for understanding media infrastructures as sites for the performance of information labor, but it doesn't give us any clues as to what to look for when investigating the laborers themselves. Fortunately, recent scholars of technology have established quite clearly that spatial, temporal, and technological circumstances are inevitably part and parcel of social relations and cultural meanings (Nakamura 2002; Smith and Kollock 1999; Turner 2009). Within information infrastructures, for example, the evolving and overlapping categories of computer engineers, scientists, entrepreneurs, and enthusiasts over the last several decades have been revealed to involve profound meanings in terms of lots of "identity" categories—age, gender, class, race/ethnicity, political philosophy, and nationality, for example—especially as the labor practice of computer programming has been professionalized in the capitalist workplace, institutionalized in the college curriculum, implicated in interdisciplinary science, and globalized in the network economy (Aneesh 2006; Ensmenger 2010; Light 1999; Nelson, Tu, and Hines 2001; Turner 2005).

Thus what starts out as a simple classroom question about "how do you find out what you need to know?" turns out to be a rich and complicated set of related research questions about one's place in a whole set of extended relationships of information circulation—in other words, a question about "who does what kind of information work, when and where and why?" To explain to our students what is necessary to "make media work," I believe we must study both information and labor, in both spatial and temporal context, with attention to social relations: (1) how human labor applied to information always takes place in, and depends on, a particular spatial/temporal and political-economic context; (2) how that human labor, and the social relations and cultural meanings attached to it, both enable and constrain the ability of information itself to move from one context to another; and (3) how that circulation of information from one context to another comes full circle to affect the subsequent spatial/temporal patterns, political-economic conditions, social relations, and cultural meanings for further labor.

That can be a lot to juggle in a single research project. But attention to this basic dialectical relationship of change—where labor of a particular sort is mobilized to circulate information, and the circulation of that information helps to alter the parameters of that labor—brings a useful insight. In order to productively categorize, historicize, analyze, and, yes, teach about any "new" media infrastructure (be it the "lightning lines" of the telegraph in the 1840s, the "electronic brain" of the digital computer in the 1940s, the "electronic hearth" of the television in the 1970s, or the "information superhighway" represented by the World Wide Web today) *we must continue to pay attention to the space, time, and social relations of the human laborers who are bound up in that infrastructure as well.*

Jumping Context with Informational Labor

Time, space, and social relations are big categories; demonstrating how to operationalize them in the study of information labor, and why operationalizing them matters to scholarship and teaching, requires some specific examples. In fact, I argue that the very concept of information itself is meaningless without some sort of context—an organizational location, a community of practice, an end-user market, a shared public purpose—within which to construct that information as "data" to be manipulated, "content" to be enjoyed, or "knowledge" to be utilized.

Whether constructed at the scale of data, content, or knowledge, the value of information can only continue to be realized to the degree that the information circulates from one context to the next. This is where labor of some sort is always required—to set information in context, to move information across context, and to reset that information in a new context. I've used the term "jumping context" as a metaphor for these transformations, especially in the case where that shift in context provides a surprising, productive, or contradictory moment for consideration through research and teaching (Downey 2004a).

Let me describe three variations on this theme of jumping context that are drawn from my own research: (1) the case of urban messenger boys in their early twentieth-century encounter with not just electromagnetic telegraph signaling, but also gasoline-powered postal services and voice-carrying telephone services (Downey 2000, 2002, 2003); (2) the case of library technical workers in their mid-twentieth-century encounter with general purpose digital computers for both electronic indexing of materials and online searching for materials (Downey 2007c, 2010a; Eschenfelder, Desai, and Downey, 2011); and (3) the case of real-time stenographers in their late-twentieth-century encounter with minicomputers, microcomputers and laptops in courtroom service, broadcast captioning, and computer-assisted transcription, respectively (Downey 2006, 2007a, 2008, 2010b).

Telegraph Messenger Boys (Early Twentieth Century)

Studying the history of the telegraph from the point of view of its teen-aged messenger labor force might seem, at first, to be a contradiction in terms. The telegraph network was an information infrastructure of wires and repeaters, of sounders and printers, of skilled operator labor and craft lineman labor. As most previous historians understood the telegraph—and as the telegraph firms themselves often tried to maintain—messenger boys were literally outside of the network, unworthy of attention and unable to tarnish the reputation of the "lightning lines" for speed, efficiency, and modernity. And with our focus today on World Wide Web-based networks of news, reference, and sociability that seem to remove all human labor from our Google, Wikipedia, Facebook, and Amazon searches, it is no wonder that we recast the telegraph as a "Victorian Internet" of similar automation and virtuality (Gabler 1988; Standage 1998).

But of course, that contradiction is just the point: this high-tech electromagnetic communication system of its age, existing as a viable business for roughly a century from the 1850s to the 1950s, was actually entirely dependent on human labor for funneling information—data, content, knowledge—into and out of its material network. That basic insight, and basic contradiction, sits at the heart of any historical work on information labor: look for such labor precisely where system builders, promoters, and proponents assert it isn't to be found, where it isn't supposed to matter, where it isn't supposed to count as part of the "new media" that they are selling (Hughes 1989; Chandler and Cortada 2000).

So this first step of uncovering the information labor of the telegraph messengers is one of situating them within a larger system that stretches over time and space: where and when are they to be found? This question is a fundamentally geographical one, and suggests the first way of understanding the value of information labor: it enables *the jumping of context from one sociotechnical infrastructure to another*, involving changes in technology, environment, or institution. Messenger boys did this in at least three ways:

1. *Jumping context from the virtual to the physical.* While present-day understandings of cyberspace and networked communications might lead us to conceptualize the telegraph merely as a system of virtual communications and connections—enabled through the trinary dot, dash, and delay code, first of trained (mostly male) telegraph operators and later untrained (mostly female) teletypists—the messengers remind us of the transcoding interface between scrawled messages and forms on the input side and printed yellow-tape telegrams on the output side. A materiality of message delivery was necessary on both the front and back ends of this virtual system, with telegraph companies paying regular sums of money for boots and bicycles to outfit their messenger forces for trudging the town and city streets.

2. *Jumping context from the intra-urban to the inter-urban.* This boundary between virtual and physical was not just technological; it was institutional and spatial as well. The telegraph industry as a whole evolved from the gradual merger of regional telegraph firms exchanging intelligence between cities combined with local alarm call box and messenger services that handled subscriber security and delivery services as well as telegram connections within cities. It is impossible to understand this relationship between national and local business partnerships without considering that boundary as one crossed daily by the telegram messengers.

3. *Jumping context from the telegraph to the post office and the telephone.* Through most of the telegraph's history, it was by no means the single consumer choice for message delivery, either within cities or between cities. The government-subsidized postal system was always a competitor, increasingly so with greater frequency of delivery and due to sorting

mechanization and gasoline-powered distribution. And from the late nineteenth century the telephone network both competed and cooperated with the telegraph (sometimes owning it outright), first in local traffic, but eventually in long-distance service. Yet through the long period of technological and process innovation in these various industries, messengers provided a ubiquitous link for calls made to people without telephones, telegrams sent to people through the mails, or postal deliveries sent to someone without a fixed address.

Telegraph messenger boys carried the forms and rules for translating spoken messages into price-per-word telegrams; they parsed the hidden signals on an envelope to determine whether a telegram contained a birthday greeting or a death notice; and they contained the practical street address information necessary to pin telegraph, telephone, and post office networks together. In this way they performed a sort of *protocol labor* within these information, communication, and transportation infrastructures.

The key point linking all of these varied activities of jumping context between virtual and physical systems, across urban and national scales, among public and private institutions—which we might call *transcoding processes*—is that the need for messengers did not decrease with increasing technological sophistication; rather, it increased until the crash of the telegraph post-World War II. The telegraph industry did not merely depend on capital investments in the spaces of offices, wires, and railroad rights-of-way; they also had to invest in messenger employment offices and locker rooms, messenger equipment warehouses and uniform laundries, messenger assembly halls and classrooms. Both within their own buildings, and throughout the wider city as well, creating a physical space to ground the virtual space of the telegraph meant creating physical spaces for the messenger boys.

Library Technical Workers (Mid-Twentieth Century)

Studying library technical workers—particularly those involved in such processes as acquiring, cataloging, classifying, indexing, and retrieving works held by the libraries—might seem less surprising than studying telegraph messenger boys. After all, without human care and expertise, libraries are merely warehouses of books and periodicals. Throughout most of the history of the modern library, the very ability of materials to circulate from authors to readers through the library depended on the continuous and visible work of librarians, whether in school, public, university, or corporate settings (Battles 2003; Buschman and Leckie 2007; Cmiel 2009).

As with the telegraph messengers, these workers are engaged in the sort of "transcoding processes" necessary to move information from one socio-technical system to another, especially in the daily flow of patron information requests that must be encoded to query languages in library database systems, or in the interpretation of results lists that must be explained to library patrons. In this way they too deal in "protocol labor," applying the codes and fields of particular cataloging and classification schemes to both storage and search processes. But their role carries with it more of an intellectual production quality than the telegraph messengers; they are not merely shepherding information back and forth across a virtual and material divide, but are actively adding contextual information along the way, in order to make that transition even possible (Bowker and Star 1999).

However, recent attention to the new media of the "digital library" serves to hide this activity. It is now possible to conduct reference searches through a virtual catalog interface, to query library holdings remotely through networked databases, and even to receive materials in fully electronic form, such as a "born digital" journal article or a scanned book from the Google Print project (Borgman 2000; Darnton 2009; Gorman 2003; Marcum 2001). Again, our present-day notions of how a library functions may blind us to the historical case, where the long and tense introduction of computers to libraries through the 1960s, 1970s, and 1980s is now cast as an inevitable series of progressions from bulky, slow, and expensive-to-update card catalogs to networked, user friendly Online Public Access Catalogs (OPACs); from the expense of original and isolated catalog production work to the shared and distributed labor possible through the Online Computer Library Center (OCLC); and from librarians as guardians of reading and culture to librarians as information analysts and consultants.

So the question for this case of information laborers is not so much uncovering that they exist, or uncovering that they matter, as it is uncovering their historical and ongoing value over a long period of technological and economic transformation. The answer is also a fundamentally geographical one (although dealing with time as much as space), and suggests a second way of understanding the value of information labor: as *providing a way for information—cast as data, content, or knowledge—to jump context from one temporal, organizational, or cultural milieu to another.* Library technical services workers enable this in at least three ways:

1. *Jumping context from the past to the future.* Whether library cataloging and classification is done in a centralized or distributed division of labor, with or without the aid of networked technology, the basic contradiction of

the practice is a temporal one: to take an informational product produced in the past (say, a nonfiction book), and describe and define it using the tools and terminology of the present, all in a way that will presumably make sense to a potential reader seeking it in the future. All such decisions must be made imperfectly: there is never enough time or money or even shelf space to perfectly catalog and safely keep every possible item available today for every possible audience of tomorrow.

2. *Jumping context from one kind of knowledge institution to another.* Besides mediating jumps across time, librarians must prepare materials for sensible leaps across institutional (and intellectual) domains. Again, considering the basic nonfiction book, the institution which sponsors its production might be a university, government office, or knowledge business, with public-service or market-success goals for its product; the institution that sponsors its collection would likely be a public or quasi-public library with some sort of overt public service mission (and likely collective public funding) meant to expand the reach of that book beyond its original constituency or market; and with increasing networked cooperation between libraries, what one organization collects is made available for another organization's users, meaning the institution that spurs a book's eventual wide-ranging circulation may be yet another university, government office, or knowledge business. Especially as intellectual and professional domains of knowledge have grown and fractured and specialized over the twentieth century, the need for books produced for one thought community to be accessible and understandable to other transdisciplinary thought communities has only increased.

3. *Jumping context from one set of cultural meanings and expectations to another.* Even if librarians could reliably predict the future needs and intellectual scaffolding of their most likely eventual users—a task in which they succeed surprisingly well, all things considered—there remain two problems. First, books circulate across global cultures where not just language and jargon, but also meaning and category may differ substantially (and often normatively). And second, even within a single cultural community, social attitudes and values change over time; categories like "Third World" in one decade shift to "Developing Nations" in the next, gaining and losing approbation and scorn. If libraries are to remain relevant as tools of knowledge production and circulation, they must not only do their best to produce intelligible cataloging at the entry point of a collected item, but they must also continue to reproduce and repair that cataloging through the life of an item—in fact, the life of an item in the library actually depends on the

effectiveness of its cataloging, because no matter how theoretically valuable it may be, it is only actually valuable if it circulates.

All this labor of moving data, content, or knowledge from one context to another—be it from past to future, from discipline to discipline, or culture to culture—depends on understanding, manipulating, producing, and reproducing further descriptive, contextual information about that data, content, or knowledge. We might call such contextual information "metadata," or "metacontent," or "metaknowledge," but at any of these scales, the production and reproduction of metainformation for information storage, as well as the effective use of that metainformation at the point of retrieval, are both necessary for preserving not only the sense but also the value of the information from the old context to the new. Thus librarians engage in a particular form of *metainformation labor* that is unique from that of the messenger boys.

This metainformation labor of preparing and preserving books for such leaps of context across time, space, and intellectual community—what we might call *transposing processes*—is fraught with contradiction. Library catalogers are expected to make rapid and hard-to-change decisions about how to organize texts in a way that is meant to serve future populations and needs that cannot reliably be known, balancing the intellectual depth and detail of their work (with greater-quality cataloging thought to bring greater long-term usability) with the very real economic and time cost of that work (with lower-quality cataloging thought to bring greater short-term savings). Lower-quality cataloging might save money in the short term, allowing the purchase of more books out of limited budgets, further pressuring libraries to spend less time (and money) on cataloging. And every new information infrastructure developed to automate or assist these processes—whether print or mechanical or digital—reproduces in a different way these same dilemmas.

Real-time Stenographers (Late Twentieth Century)

My third case involves a more diffuse set of information workers: a group I am calling real-time stenographers. This category grows out of at least four different streams of information labor: (1) office stenography, or the skilled, machine-aided transcription of speech to some encoded and recorded format that can be reconstituted into English text later; (2) courtroom stenography, which further casts that reconstituted English transcription as the official record for civic and criminal legal proceedings, demanding verbatim accuracy; (3) media captioning, which involves the production of a time-matched textual representation of speech and sound to be displayed along with a movie, video, or audio recording, sometimes even in a different language than the original; and (4) simultaneous language translation, or the ability to listen to speech in one language and simultaneously recast it for a different language audience as a live performance. Real-time stenographers combine the skills and machines of stenographic practice in the office and the courtroom with the outputs and audiences of media captioning and language translation (Robson 2000).

Like the telegraph messengers, real-time stenographers sit at the interface of different sociotechnical systems, and could be said to perform transcoding processes in a very direct way, turning variable, analog, ephemeral human speech into fixed, digital, permanent typed transcript. Theirs could certainly be seen as "protocol labor" in the sense of knowing the fixed terminology and parameters for constructing legal documents. Similarly, the shepherding of a transcript from the initial moment of courtroom production to the eventual moment of use in an appeals process years later, or the one-time live encoding of a television captioning track on a program that might be replayed or repurposed years later for either public rebroadcast or private digital access, can be thought of as a transposing process across time and space. If an audio or video stream is considered the "information," then producing the text-captioning track associated with it would certainly qualify as "metainformation labor." But there are also some new categories of information labor that the case of the real-time stenographers suggests.

First of all, real-time stenography represents a case of labor that was "born digital"—it could not have been pinned together from its antecedents without the application of the digital minicomputer to the mechanical stenotype keyboard, starting in the 1960s, in a human–machine symbiosis. What uncovering information labor means in this case is asking: *how has this new form of work been adjusted and adapted to jump context into a variety of different social purposes and economic markets?* Real-time stenography offers a unique example of a set of information laborers being constituted anew out of a number of historical technological and organizational changes, but then jumping context time and time again from one audience of consumers and clients, and one set of political-economic and social relations, to another. In one realm, that of the legal transcript, the audience demands verbatim accuracy between the original speech and its translated, written equivalent, and is willing to allow for delays in delivery in order to ensure perfect reproduction; in another realm, as in media captioning, the audience requires an immediate interpreted translation, and is willing to accept flaws in reproduction for an informational product that is able to "keep up" with live events. In between are a network of brokers and officials and employers interested mainly in keeping costs and complaints down while maintaining high throughput and, sometimes, profits (a similar set of pressures as the library catalogers face). Real-time stenographers learned to negotiate this complicated set of contexts, audiences, purposes, and demands over a series of particular historical changes:

1. *Jumping context from the defense industry to the legal industry.* The tools of real-time stenography originated in the Department of Defense and its "Machine Translation" projects of the 1960s, in an experiment to use stenographic keyboards and computer dictionaries of words and phonemes to enable instant language translation from Russian to English. Entrepreneurs brought the technology into the courtroom and promised to make "computer-compatible" every new professional court reporter they trained. In this way, the perceived authority of the computer, in an environment where the official courtroom transcript had to be both perfectly accurate and affordable to shrinking public budgets, lent ammunition to courtroom stenographers who were fending off challenges to have their jobs replaced by automated videotape systems. Thus a new labor category whose development was funded by federal research dollars for Cold War security projects spun off as a set of privately owned tools and training opportunities, to be marketed back to the public courts at the local, state, and federal scales.

2. *Jumping context from the administrative realm to the media realm.* Once the real-time stenography equipment moved to the microcomputer, a new audience opened up: television captioning, which got its start in the early 1980s through a much-heralded public-private partnership between the "big three" broadcast networks and a federally funded National Captioning Institute, intended to help Deaf and hard-of-hearing individuals fully participate in the cultural life of the society. As this partnership quickly began to unravel, however, the ability to live caption one of the most sought-after television programs—the evening news—was considered crucial to captioning's ultimate success. This category of programming straddled the public-private divide as well: seen as the ultimate public-service obligation for broadcast stations by the FCC, news was at this time being reconceptualized by station managers from a "loss leader" to a "profit center" since production costs were so low in comparison to local advertising rates. It was also a new arena for real-time stenographers to claim expertise and utility, quickly expanding from news programs to talk and entertainment programs as well, as new federal laws and growing numbers of cable channels demanded the rapid and inexpensive captioning of more and more

content, whether live or prerecorded, through stenographic means. As a result, this labor shifted from delivering a tangible product to the state (a printed courtroom transcript) through a per-page piecework fee paid for by public tax dollars, to delivering an intangible product to a private broadcaster (a captioning track to be recorded on videotape), through a per-program cost underwritten by advertising. The public-service claims of the profession, however, were renewed and rearticulated in this new context.

3. *Jumping context from the mass entertainment imperative to the individual communication imperative.*   The success of real-time stenography with the media captioning audience, its growing reputation as an assistive technology, and the new portability offered by laptop computers allowed the real-time stenographers to jump context yet again, into a new market for direct captioning for Deaf and hard-of-hearing individuals, live and on site, at schools, churches, and conferences. These markets grew rapidly after the passage of the Americans with Disabilities Act in 1990. However, this shift from the courtroom to the classroom rendered the informational object of the real-time stenographer in an entirely different way. Rather than producing the legally binding, verbatim transcript of highly technical but relatively narrow spoken proceedings, these information laborers now had to use much the same skills and equipment in service of an entirely different goal: producing a "good enough" just-in-time transcript of highly variable spoken proceedings, often even summarizing, paraphrasing, and interpreting along the way for reading level, subject knowledge, and language familiarity. Once again, its practitioners and proponents reestablished the public-service claims of the field; however, in this context, captioning was a per-hour personal service, once again often paid for through public tax dollars.

In each of these cases, the real-time stenographers overtly claimed to be serving the public interest by making an important aspect of an audiovisual performance—its textual representation—available in a new way, which increased the accessibility of that performance to a target community. These information workers were trained to understand the protocols necessary to transcode meaning from English speech to phonetic stenoforms to English text. They were also charged with producing a metainformation resource that was attached to that speech (on a magnetic computer disk or videotape) in a way that would be storable, indexable, and searchable so that the speech might be transcoded to different contexts. And in doing so, no matter what the actual political-economic relationships that enabled their training, equipment, and wages, they cast themselves as defenders of the public record, making courtroom proceedings accessible to future claims of appeal; or as defenders of media justice, making entertainment products accessible to disadvantaged audiences; or as defenders of social justice, making personal education and political participation in a hearing world possible for nonhearing citizens. We might call this *accessibility labor.*

All three of these realms are examples of what we might call *translation processes* in a broad sense, because in each case they involve not just moving information unaltered from one set of technical codes to another (like in telegraphy), nor just creating the contextual environment for information to circulate from one institutional or intellectual context to another (like in librarianship), but a sort of recasting of the very meaning of the information content in the first place. Real-time stenographers in the courtroom must reflect pause and nuance in the official record, but they must also take care to strike portions of the record deemed inadmissible, and to "clean up" the slang or shorthand of a lawyer or judge, all the while preserving the words of witnesses for possible future appeal. Real-time stenographers on television must adapt written scripts and speedy verbal delivery to the very limited time and space of the television screen, taking care to judiciously drop words, phrases, and even sentences when the flow becomes too fast (and when the commercial break looms). And real-time stenographers in the classroom or conference hall, often serving Deaf or hard-of-hearing individuals directly, must balance all those same needs with those of clarity and understanding—which might require not just transcription, but also editorial intervention and personal knowledge of the client's needs and wants.

The Difference That Labor Makes to Information Infrastructures

As I hope my brief description of these three historical research cases shows, when we study media infrastructures from the point of view of the information laborers, we can begin to identify and analyze different kinds of context-jumping categories: the protocol labor that allows transcoding across sociotechnical infrastructures, the metainformation labor that allows transposing across decades and institutional contexts, and the accessibility labor that results in translating from a majority community of meaning to a marginalized one. These categories are certainly not the only ways to understand the work that these information laborers do, but I think they provide a nice place to start—one that privileges the spatial metaphors of movement and circulation which are necessary to any conception of informational value.

These same kinds of context jumping are important to seek out in our modern media infrastructure. Google survives on the collaborative production of metainformation by the anonymous millions of weblinkers and clickstreamers; Wikipedia thrives only as long as legions of volunteer editors practice protocol labor as they learn and share conventions for structuring different kinds of pages and writing encyclopedic forms of prose; our every entry, selection, and deletion on Facebook involves decisions that make our personal media either more or less accessible to friends, family, coworkers, and advertisers; and the work necessary to keep Amazon.com profitable can be understood as involving all the many protocols, metainformation, and accessibility practices necessary to bridge the both the digital and the physical divide.

There's a final reason for wanting to focus on the information laborer throughout media technology history, however. Just like with any category of work, a combination of historical circumstance, social expectation, political-economic power, and demographic difference all come together to make some groups more likely than others to be found as laborers in any particular information infrastructure. At the same time, often the meanings we ascribe to information technologies themselves are circulated back and forth with the meanings that we ascribe to the information laborers who work within these technologies. Tracing those individuals whose work lives (and recreation lives and home lives and citizen lives) get bound up with our technological infrastructures shows us both something about how we value those technologies and something about how we value those individuals. And especially in information infrastructures, with their intrinsic value wrapped up in movement across space and time, *uncovering the spatial and temporal relations of labor helps us to simultaneously uncover these social relations of labor* (Dear and Flusty 2002; Giddens 1990; Graham and Marvin 1996; Harvey 1982; Orr 1996; Peck 1996; Wheeler, Aoyama, and Warf 2000;).

Again, consider the telegraph messengers. What's most striking about these workers is not necessarily their ubiquity within this technological infrastructure, or their longevity over a century of infrastructure change and evolution. The most striking thing about them is that they remained young, school-aged boys and teenagers throughout most of this period. Their demographic age, coupled with the contemporary cultural meanings of childhood and adulthood, combine to create an important analytical category of *maturity* that was bound up with this group's information labors in a number of important ways. In the early twentieth century, messengers became a symbol of both the worst excesses of child labor exploitation and the greatest hopes for vocational education, particularly in the site of their greatest concentration, New York City. The telegraph industry was obliged to perpetuate a myth of messenger advancement, rationalizing the employment of school-age children by claiming that such work provided the skills and connections that would bring a young boy into the world of national commerce. Eventually both the city and the industry reached a material compromise in order to continue to legitimize this fiction, creating a part-time public school on the Western Union premises for its messenger boy labor force. Such educational activities only ended once the figure of the telegraph messenger made a decisive move along the maturity scale from child to adult, in taking on a public identity of labor union participation that was soon followed by work rules limiting the job to those eighteen years old and over. While other social constructions of class, gender, and ethnicity were certainly at play as well in this story of the messenger's movement from "boy" to "man," the opportunity to view this particular information laborer through the lens of maturity helps connect the messenger to similarly positioned youth cultures in the early twentieth-century information revolution, from newsboys to ham radio operators to nickelodeon patrons.

Or consider the library technical workers. Here, although questions of class and education and ethnicity also loom large, it is the analytical category of *gender* that moves to the forefront. Librarianship has long been "feminized" in four senses of the word: its demographic overrepresentation of women, its managerial overrepresentation of men, its relative lack of high status and salary, and its stereotyping as "women's work." But starting in the late 1960s, library workers of both sexes began to question and critique such conditions, as the ideas of a new national women's movement took hold within professional librarianship. What's striking from the perspective of information labor is that this period also represented the entrance of computer-based automation and networking systems into U.S. libraries, especially the first computer-readable catalog format (MARC) and the first cooperative cataloging network (OCLC), both of which drastically altered the spatiality and temporality of library catalog production. The new "push-button library" demanded a new attention to the kind of metainformation discussed earlier, and it was largely women library workers who produced, reproduced, and used that metainformation on behalf of both authors and readers. In this case, what was most striking from the historical record was the disconnect between librarians' own extensive professional discussions of two intensely argued topics—sexual discrimination and information automation—which were almost never considered at the same time. A century-old legacy of librarianship seen as a gendered combination of behind-the-scenes "housekeeping" work and before-the-public "nurturing" work continues to affect these discussions today.

Finally, let's revisit the real-time stenographers. Here, too, gender issues are a long thread in the history of stenographic work, as are issues of professional versus clerical identity construction in the twentieth-century office. However, the analytical category that ends up being the most interesting as this information labor jumps context is that of *disability*, which we should remember is less an absolute medical condition and more a socially constructed condition of resources and expectations (for example, in a society with fewer demands on personal mobility or a greater commitment to public transportation, would a person who uses a wheelchair to get around be considered "disabled"?). The real-time stenographers had made a series of movements toward professionalization during their decades-long history. From their first association with the minicomputer in the 1970s, the claim was that becoming "computer-compatible" was the route to respect, status, and job security in the face of videotape automation threats. Then in their movement to the world of entertainment captioning, speed and accuracy under the time and space demands of the broadcast were valued, and a notion of public service for Deaf and hard-of-hearing viewers (as well as English language learners) appeared. Finally, with the movement of these laborers into the meeting rooms and lecture halls of direct service provision to individual Deaf and hard-of-hearing clients, real-time stenographers found themselves lobbying Congress on behalf of disability communities for media justice accommodations—a professional role wholly different than the one they claimed just two decades earlier. Today, with the very real possibility that personal, mobile, and automated audio transcription and translation devices (such as Google Translate or Apple's "Siri" voice-operated search tool) might provide a new round of technological fixes for Deaf and hard-of-hearing users, real-time captioners may have to pivot once again, away from the space and time of disability accommodations.

How might our understandings of contemporary media infrastructures change if we were able to reveal not just the forms of information labor that support them, but also the spatialities and temporalities within which they work, in connection with the positionality and power relations of the information laborers themselves? Might we think differently about our first screen of Google results if we conceptualized all of our own searches as little bits of useful labor helping to produce the metainformation behind the Google PageRank algorithm itself—and its personalized search and advertising results based on whether it knows (or guesses) that we are young or old, White or Black, struggling or affluent, urban or rural, employed or unwaged? Or might we evaluate that Wikipedia article differently if we knew that statistically, it was likely to have been written by someone from a strikingly similar (or dissimilar) social class, educational background, ethnic experience, and political orientation as our own? How might it matter if we find that the demographic and economic groups most using Facebook are culturally and professionally quite distinct from the behind-the-scenes content monitors and persuasion experts that mold their experience? And does it matter that the low prices of my Amazon Kindle e-book are subsidized, in part, by the low wages of contingent warehouse workers during the holiday season, shipping printed versions of the same book to more traditional customers? We'll never know unless we can get behind the human–machine interface of all of these systems, unless we can really explore the labor conditions of the online infrastructure, unless we can seek out and enter the spaces of work performed by others that enable the nonspaces of nonwork performed by ourselves.

Less a Conclusion Than a Call to Action

I'm convinced that the historical examples of the telegraph messengers, the library technicians, the real-time stenographers, and many, many others still have much to teach us about the information labor embedded within our latest new media infrastructures today. Thinking about the way information labor helps put data, content, and knowledge into circulation—enabling owners, consumers, and publics to realize value from that information—opens up a rich metaphor of informational context, and the labor required to "jump" information productively from one context to the next. Sometimes information demands transcoding across different sociotechnical systems by mastering the protocols of both—programmers porting video games to new hardware systems or clerical workers reentering data for new software systems come to mind today. Sometimes information requires transposition from one intellectual community or audience market to the next, with the metainformation linking and tagging—and both the work of amateur bloggers in recirculating news items, and the work of LinkedIn members recommending each others' resumes qualify here. And many times, information requires a more complete translation, across not only differing technological protocols and differing metadata contexts, but also differing sites of meaning and expectation, for the purposes of accessibility in the public interest. The work of professional science journalists in reinterpreting complicated research findings for the nightly news audience, as well as the work of partisan political activists spinning the latest government figures for the voting public, are contemporary examples.

But the historical exploration of information labor offers us more than a set of rich case studies; it offers us a connecting thread for tracking change and constancy across time. The "long twentieth century" has brought a seemingly perpetual effort to render greater amounts of data, content, and knowledge into automated systems in order to replace the communication function of individuals who are seen as merely manipulating data in a scripted way, and thus adding more cost than value—a "scientific management" strategy that scholars have tied to the early twentieth-century "control revolution" where new information technologies became such a powerful tool of management's "visible hand" over the market (and over labor) (Beniger 1986; Braverman 1974; Chandler 1977). Such automation efforts were clear in the case of the telegraph messengers (installing teletype units directly in corporate offices), the library technicians (schemes to catalog and index books directly from computer analysis of the text), and the real-time stenographers (continuing attempts to perfect voice recognition software in all environments and with all speakers). Today such efforts to automate away the need for information labor are increasingly complemented by efforts to outsource that information labor, whether to globally distant contingent subcontractees, or to web-dispersed volunteer crowds.

At the same time, our period has been one of utopian schemes to valorize and uplift labor through information and communication technology, at least for some. Such projects strive to make both available and intelligible greater amounts of data, content, and knowledge to those precious individuals who are seen as developing analytical content in a creative way, and thus adding more value than cost to the circulation of information—the postindustrial knowledge worker or "creative class" strategy. Such hopes only ever existed as myth for the messenger boys, a sort of "uplift by osmosis" claim that walking the halls of business would open one's door to an industrial career. But for the library technicians, the digital database tools of the 1980s were supposed to transform them into "information analysts." And for the real-time stenographers, becoming "computer compatible" during that same period promised a shift from merely producing the courtroom transcript to managing the flow of legal information. Such promises are still made today, where smartphones and Twitter feeds are now advertised as generic business intelligence and marketing tools that can give every knowledge worker a competitive edge.

History teaches that both deskilling and uplift are imperfect, contingent, and contradictory processes, at best. And geography teaches that the landscape resulting from these imperfect, contingent, and contradictory processes is both vast and uneven. Certain aspects of human communication at both low levels and high remain uncomputable or unstandardizable; and each new round of technological achievement to automate or augment intellectual work simply shifts the problem to a different scale (up or down). As a result, workers formally or informally engaged in complex information labors—transcoding, transposing, and translating, helping to keep both information and metainformation circulating productively across multiple contexts for multiple purposes—are continually re-embedded in each new round of the knowledge infrastructure.

After engaging in this work for a little over a decade, I think it's more important than ever before to keep "uncovering" this information labor. After all, in our present-day political-economic environment, we've seen the culmination of a decades-long strategy not just to ignore the contribution of labor, but also to cast labor as a drag on the economy, rather than as the economy's creative engine. Neoliberal strategies of regulatory rollback and privatization rollout have shredded what was once a functioning safety net for all workers (all the more necessary in times of rapid technological change), and eliminated many of the keystone public jobs for public workers (along with the high-quality benefits, pensions, and wage floors with which all businesses were obliged to compete). Yet these very same neoliberalization proponents preen as they declare themselves to be the true "job creators."

Such contradictions are not new. Promotional advertisements for young, male telegraph messengers in the 1920s cast the telegraph monopoly as a progressive welfare capitalism organization. Promotional advertisements for female library workers in the 1960s and 1970s juxtaposed them with the same digital technology meant to eliminate their jobs. And business press images of home teleworkers in the 1980s (often with women shown unproblematically managing a small child in the background) fed directly into the construction of a remote real-time stenography labor force for captioning a booming universe of twenty-four-hour cable television channels. The frustration comes when these same laborers are demonized for any organized efforts across space and time to address their working conditions, improve their career prospects, or bring public attention to the value of their work.

As teachers and researchers within knowledge-producing institutions, I think this all points to an ongoing, scholarly imperative. We need to keep uncovering, analyzing, and explaining the intertwined spatial, temporal, social, and technological contexts of information labor, as we continue to attempt to both train our students and to understand for ourselves how media infrastructures emerge and evolve, persist and perish, from their birth as "new media" to their obsolescence as "old." It's an easy trick to simply ask "Where is the labor?" to get such a conversation going—and that's a trick I've employed myself many times in both the classroom and the conference hall when I didn't yet have a roadmap to understanding a particular new media phenomenon. But asking the question is only the first step.

As for me, I find hope in the fact that many of the workers implicated in today's world of digital information labor, as both professionals and amateurs, are drawing on the examples of the past to mobilize in service of a new, collective goal: uncovering labor's place in society as a whole. In this widespread, decentralized, and raucous effort—involving Facebook-organized occupations of both Wall Street and Main Street, Twitter-fed and YouTube-broadcast sit-ins at public campuses and state capitols, and social and economic justice blogs on the web—activists both seasoned and new are demonstrating well that the same information/communication technologies that allow for greater fragmentation, casualization, control, and devaluation of labor can themselves be used to calculate and reveal the presence, importance, and impact of labor in new ways (Nichols 2012; Sagrans 2011; Yates 2012).

Notes

1. See also Jose Antonio Vargas, "The face of Facebook." *The New Yorker*, September 20, 2010.

2. Brad Stone, "Concern for those who screen the Web for barbarity." *The New York Times*, July 18, 2010.

3. David Streitfeld, "Inside Amazon's very hot warehouse." *The New York Times*, September 19, 2011.

9   The Relevance of Algorithms

Tarleton Gillespie

Algorithms play an increasingly important role in selecting what information is considered most relevant to us, a crucial feature of our participation in public life. Search engines help us navigate massive databases of information, or the entire web. Recommendation algorithms map our preferences against others, suggesting new or forgotten bits of culture for us to encounter. Algorithms manage our interactions on social networking sites, highlighting the news of one friend while excluding another's. Algorithms designed to calculate what is "hot" or "trending" or "most discussed" skim the cream from the seemingly boundless chatter that's on offer. Together, these algorithms not only help us find information, they also provide a means to know what there is to know and how to know it, to participate in social and political discourse, and to familiarize ourselves with the publics in which we participate. They are now a key logic governing the flows of information on which we depend, with the "power to enable and assign meaningfulness, managing how information is perceived by users, the 'distribution of the sensible.'" (Langlois 2013)

Algorithms need not be software: in the broadest sense, they are encoded procedures for transforming input data into a desired output, based on specified calculations. The procedures name both a problem and the steps by which it should be solved. Instructions for navigation may be considered an algorithm, or the mathematical formulas required to predict the movement of a celestial body across the sky. "Algorithms do things, and their syntax embodies a command structure to enable this to happen" (Goffey 2008, 17). We might think of computers, then, fundamentally as algorithm machines—designed to store and read data, apply mathematical procedures to it in a controlled fashion, and offer new information as the output. But these are procedures that could conceivably be done by hand—and in fact were (Light 1999).

But as we have embraced computational tools as our primary media of expression, and have made not just mathematics but *all* information digital, we are subjecting human discourse and knowledge to these procedural logics that undergird all computation. And there are specific implications when we use algorithms to select what is most relevant from a corpus of data composed of traces of our activities, preferences, and expressions.

These algorithms, which I'll call *public relevance algorithms*, are—by the very same mathematical procedures—producing and certifying knowledge. The algorithmic assessment of information, then, represents a particular *knowledge logic*, one built on specific presumptions about what knowledge is and how one should identify its most relevant components. That we are now turning to algorithms to identify what we need to know is as momentous as having relied on credentialed experts, the scientific method, common sense, or the word of God.

What we need is an interrogation of algorithms as a key feature of our information ecosystem (Anderson 2011), and of the cultural forms emerging in their shadows (Striphas 2010), with a close attention to where and in what ways the introduction of algorithms into human knowledge practices may have political ramifications. This essay is a conceptual map to do just that. I will highlight six dimensions of public relevance algorithms that have political valence:

1. *Patterns of inclusion*: the choices behind what makes it into an index in the first place, what is excluded, and how data is made *algorithm ready*.
2. *Cycles of anticipation*: the implications of algorithm providers' attempts to thoroughly know and predict their users, and how the conclusions they draw can matter.
3. *The evaluation of relevance*: the criteria by which algorithms determine what is relevant, how those criteria are obscured from us, and how they enact political choices about appropriate and legitimate knowledge.
4. *The promise of algorithmic objectivity*: the way the technical character of the algorithm is positioned as an assurance of impartiality, and how that claim is maintained in the face of controversy.
5. *Entanglement with practice*: how users reshape their practices to suit the algorithms they depend on, and how they can turn algorithms into terrains for political contest, sometimes even to interrogate the politics of the algorithm itself.
6. *The production of calculated publics*: how the algorithmic presentation of publics back to themselves shape a public's sense of itself, and who is best positioned to benefit from that knowledge.

Considering how fast these technologies and the uses to which they are put are changing, this list must be taken as provisional, not exhaustive. But as I see it, these are the most important lines of inquiry into understanding algorithms as emerging tools of public knowledge and discourse.

It would also be seductively easy to get this wrong. In attempting to say something of substance about the way algorithms are shifting public discourse, we must firmly resist putting the technology in the explanatory driver's seat. While recent sociological study of the Internet has labored to undo the simplistic technological determinism that plagued earlier work, that determinism remains an alluring analytical stance. A sociological analysis must not conceive of algorithms as abstract, technical achievements, but must unpack the warm human and institutional choices that lie behind these cold mechanisms. I suspect that a more fruitful approach will turn as much to the sociology of knowledge as to the sociology of technology—to see how these tools are called into being by, enlisted as part of, and negotiated around collective efforts to know and be known. This might help reveal that the seemingly solid algorithm is in fact a fragile accomplishment. It also should remind us that algorithms are now a communication technology; like broadcasting and publishing technologies, they are now "the scientific instruments of a society at large," (Gitelman 2006, 5) and are caught up in and are influencing the ways in which we ratify knowledge for civic life, but in ways that are more "protocological" (Galloway 2004), in other words, organized computationally, than any medium before.

Patterns of Inclusion

Algorithms are inert, meaningless machines until paired with databases on which to function. A sociological inquiry into an algorithm must always grapple with the databases to which it is wedded; failing to do so would be akin to studying what was said at a public protest, while failing to notice that some speakers had been stopped at the park gates.

For users, algorithms and databases are conceptually conjoined: users typically treat them as a single, working apparatus. And in the eyes of the market, the creators of the database and the providers of the algorithm are often one and the same, or are working in economic and often ideological concert. "Together, data structures and algorithms are two halves of the ontology of the world according to a computer" (Manovich 1999, 84). Nevertheless, we can treat the two as analytically distinct: before results can be algorithmically provided, information must be collected, readied for the algorithm, and sometimes excluded or demoted.

Collection

We live in a historical moment in which, more than ever before, nearly all public activity includes keeping copious records, cataloging activity, and archiving documents—and we do more and more of it on a communication network designed such that every login, every page view, and every click leaves a digital trace. Turning such traces into databases involves a complex array of information practices (Stalder and Mayer 2009): Google, for example, crawls the web indexing websites and their metadata. It digitizes real-world information, from library collections to satellite images to comprehensive photo records of city streets. It invites users to provide personal and social details as part of their Google+ profile. It keeps exhaustive logs of every search query entered and every result clicked. It adds local information based on each user's location. It stores the traces of web surfing practices gathered through their massive advertising networks.

Understanding what is included in such databases requires an attention to the collection policies of information services, but should also extend beyond to the actual practices involved. This is not just to spot cases of malfeasance, though there are some, but to understand how an information provider thinks about the data collection it undertakes. The political resistance to Google's StreetView project in Germany and India reminds us that the answer to the question, "What does this street corner look like?" has different implications for those who want to go there, those who live there, and those who believe that the answer should not be available in such a public way. But it also reveals what Google thinks of as "public," an interpretation that is being widely deployed across their service.

Readied for the Algorithm

"Raw data is an oxymoron" (Gitelman and Jackson 2013). Data is both already desiccated and persistently messy. Nevertheless, there is a premeditated order necessary for algorithms to even work. More than anything, algorithms are designed to be—and prized for being—functionally *automatic*, to act when triggered without any regular human intervention or oversight (Winner 1977). This means that the information included in the database must be rendered into data, formalized so that algorithms can act on it automatically. Data must be "imagined and enunciated against the seamlessness of phenomena" (Gitelman and Jackson 2013). Recognizing the ways in which data must be "cleaned up" is an important counter to the seeming automaticity of algorithms. Just as one can know something about sculptures from studying their inverted molds, algorithms can be understood by looking closely at how information must be oriented to face them, how it is made *algorithm ready*.

In the earliest database architectures, information was organized in strict and, as it turned out, inflexible hierarchies. Since the development of relational and object-oriented database architectures, information can be organized in more flexible ways, where bits of data can have multiple associations with other bits of data, categories can change over time, and data can be explored without having to navigate or even understand the hierarchical structure by which it is archived. The sociological implications of database design has largely been overlooked; the genres of databases themselves have inscribed politics, as well as making algorithms essential information tools. As Rieder (2012) notes, with the widespread uptake of relational databases comes a "relational ontology" that understands data as atomized, "regular, uniform, and only loosely connected objects that can be ordered in a potentially unlimited number of ways at the time of retrieval," thereby shifting expressive power from the structural design of the database to the query.

Even with these more flexible forms of databases, categorization remains vitally important to database design and management. Categorization is a powerful semantic and political intervention: what the categories are, what belongs in a category, and who decides how to implement these categories in practice, are all powerful assertions about how things are and are supposed to be (Bowker and Star 2000). Once instituted, a category draws a demarcation that will be treated with reverence by an approaching algorithm. A useful example here is the #amazonfail incident. In 2009, more than fifty-seven thousand gay-friendly books disappeared in an instant from Amazon's sales lists, because they had been accidentally categorized as "adult." Naturally, complex information systems are prone to error. But this particular error also revealed that Amazon's algorithm calculating "sales rank" is instructed to ignore books designated as adult. Even when mistakes are not made, whatever criteria Amazon uses to determine adult-ness are being applied and reified—apparent only in the unexplained absence of some books and the presence of others.

Exclusion and Demotion

Though all database producers share an appetite for gathering information, they are made distinctive more by what they choose to exclude. "The archive, by remembering all and only a certain set of facts / discoveries / observations, consistently and actively engages in the forgetting of other sets. . . . The archive's jussive force, then, operates through being invisibly exclusionary. The invisibility is an important feature here: the archive presents itself as being the set of all possible statements, rather than the law of what can be said." (Bowker 2006, 12–14). Even in the current conditions of digital abundance (Keane 1999), in which it is cheaper and easier to err on the side of keeping information rather than not, there is always a remainder.

Sites can, themselves, refuse to allow data collectors (like search engines) to index their sites. Elmer (2009) reveals that robot.txt, a bit of code that prevents search engines from indexing a page or site, though designed initially as a tool for preserving the privacy of individual creators, has since been used by government institutions to "redact" otherwise public documents from public scrutiny. But beyond self-exclusion, some information initially collected is subsequently removed before an algorithm ever gets to it. Though large-scale information services pride themselves on being comprehensive, these sites are and always must be censors as well. Indexes are culled of spam and viruses, patrolled for copyright infringement and pornography, and scrubbed of the obscene, the objectionable, or the politically contentious (Gillespie forthcoming).

Offending content can simply be removed from the index, or an account suspended, before it ever reaches another user. But, in tandem with an algorithm, problematic content can be handled in more subtle ways. YouTube "algorithmically demotes" suggestive videos, so they do not appear on lists of the most watched, or on the home page generated for new users. Twitter does not censor profanity from public tweets, but it does remove it from their algorithmic evaluation of which terms are "Trending."

The particular patterns whereby information is either excluded from a database, or included and then managed in particular ways, are reminiscent of twentieth-century debates (Tushnet 2008) about the ways choices made by commercial media about who is systematically left out and what categories of speech simply don't qualify can shape the diversity and character of public discourse. Whether enacted by a newspaper editor or by a search engine's indexing tools, these choices help establish and confirm standards of viable debate, legitimacy, and decorum. But here, the algorithms can be touted as automatic, while it is the patterns of inclusion that predetermine what will or will not appear among their results.

Cycles of Anticipation

Search algorithms determine what to serve up based on input from the user. But most platforms now make it their business to know much, much more about the user than the query she just entered. Sites hope to anticipate the user at the moment the algorithm is called on, which requires knowledge of that user gleaned at that instant, knowledge of that user already gathered, and knowledge of users estimated to be statistically and demographically like them (Beer 2009)—drawing together what Stalder and Mayer (2009) call the "second index." If broadcasters were providing not just content to audiences but also audiences to advertisers (Smythe 2001), digital providers are not just providing information to users but also users to their algorithms. And algorithms are made and remade in every instance of their use because every click, every query, changes the tool incrementally.

Much of the scholarship about the data collection and tracking practices of contemporary information providers has focused on the significant privacy concerns they provoke. Zimmer (2008) argues that search engines now not only aspire to relentlessly index the web but also to develop "perfect recall" of all of their users. To do this, information providers must not just track their users, they must also build technical infrastructures and business models that link individual sites into a suite of services (like Google's many tools and services) or an even broader ecosystem (as with Facebook's "social graph" and its "like" buttons scattered across the web), and then create incentives for users to remain within it. This allows the provider to be "passive-aggressive" (Berry 2012) in how it assembles information gathered across many sites into a coherent and increasingly comprehensive profile. Providers also take advantage of the increasingly participatory ethos of the web, where users are powerfully encouraged to volunteer all sorts of information about themselves, and encouraged to feel powerful doing so. As our micropractices migrate more and more to these platforms, it is seductive (though not obligatory) for information providers to both track and commodify that activity in a variety of ways (Gillespie and Postigo 2012). Moreover, users may be unaware that their activity across the web is being tracked by the biggest online advertisers, and they have little or no means to challenge this arrangement even if they do (Turow 2012).

Yet privacy is not the only politically relevant concern. In these cycles of anticipation, it is the bits of information that are most legible to the algorithm, and thus tend to stand in for those users. What Facebook knows about its users is a great deal; but still, it knows only what it is able to know. The most knowable information (geolocation, computing platform, profile information, friends, status updates, links followed on the site, time on the site, activity on other sites that host "like" buttons or cookies) is a rendering of that user, a "digital dossier" (Solove 2004) or "algorithmic identity" (Cheney-Lippold 2011) that is imperfect but sufficient. What is less legible or cannot be known about users falls away or is bluntly approximated. As Balka (2011) described it, information systems produce "shadow bodies" by emphasizing some aspects of their subjects and overlooking others. These shadow bodies persist and proliferate through information systems, and the slippage between the anticipated user and the user herself that it represents can be either politically problematic, or politically productive.

But algorithms are not always about exhaustive prediction; sometimes they are about sufficient approximation. Perhaps just as important as the surveillance of users are the conclusions providers are willing to draw based on relatively little information about them. Hunch.com, a content recommendation service, boasted that they could know a user's preferences with 80–85 percent accuracy based on the answers to just five questions. While this radically boils down the complexity of a person to five points on a graph, what's important is that this is sufficient accuracy for their purposes.[1] Because such sites are comfortable catering to these user caricatures, the questions that appear to sort us most sufficiently, particularly around our consumer preferences, are likely to grow in significance as public measures. And to some degree, we are invited to formalize ourselves into these knowable categories. When we encounter these providers, we are encouraged to choose from the menus they offer, so as to be correctly anticipated by the system and provided the right information, the right recommendations, the right people.

Beyond knowing the personal and the demographic details about each user, information providers conduct a great deal of research trying to understand, and then operationalize, how humans habitually seek, engage with, and digest information. Most notably in the study of human–computer interaction (HCI), the understanding of human psychology and perception is brought to bear on the design of algorithms and the ways in which their results should be represented. Designers hope to anticipate users' psycho-physiological capabilities and tendencies, not just their preferences and habits. But in these anticipations, too, implicit and sometimes political valences can be inscribed in the technology (Sterne 2003): the perceptual or interpretive habits of some users are taken to be universal, contemporary habits are imagined to be timeless, particular computational goals are assumed to be self-evident.

We are also witnessing a new kind of information power, gathered in these enormous databases of user activity and preference, which is itself reshaping the political landscape. Regardless of their techniques, information providers who amass this data, third-party industries who gather and purchase user data as a commodity for them, and those who traffic in user data for other reasons (that is, credit card companies), have a stronger voice because of it, in both the marketplace and in the halls of legislative power, and are increasingly involving themselves in political debates about consumer safeguards and digital rights. We are seeing the deployment of data mining in the arenas of political organizing (Howard 2005), journalism (Anderson 2011), and publishing (Striphas 2009), where the secrets drawn from massive amounts of user data are taken as compelling guidelines for future content production, be it the next microtargeted campaign ad or the next pop phenomenon.

The Evaluation of Relevance

When users click "Search," or load their Facebook News Feed, or ask for recommendations from Netflix, algorithms must instantly and automatically identify which of the trillions of bits of information best meets the criteria at hand, and will best satisfy a specific user and his presumed aims. While these calculations have never been simple, they have grown more complex as the public use of these services has matured. Search algorithms, for example, once based on simply tallying how often the actual search terms appear in the indexed web pages, now incorporate contextual information about the sites and their hosts, consider how often the site is linked to by others and in what ways, and enlist natural language processing techniques to better "understand" both the query and the resources that the algorithm might return in response. According to Google, its search algorithm examines over two hundred signals for every query.[2]

These signals are the means by which the algorithm approximates "relevance." But here is where sociologists of algorithms must firmly plant their feet: "relevant" is a fluid and loaded judgment, as open to interpretation as some of the evaluative terms media scholars have already unpacked, like "newsworthy" or "popular." As there is no independent metric for what *actually* are the most relevant search results for any given query, engineers must decide what results look "right" and tweak their algorithm to attain that result, or make changes based on evidence from their users, treating quick clicks and no follow-up searches as an approximation, not of relevance exactly, but of satisfaction. To accuse an algorithm of bias implies that there exists an unbiased judgment of relevance available, to which the tool is failing to hew. Since no such measure is available, disputes over algorithmic evaluations have no solid ground to fall back on.

Criteria

To be able to say that a particular algorithm makes evaluative assumptions, the kind that have consequences for human knowledge endeavors, might call for a critical analysis of the algorithm to interrogate its underlying criteria. But in nearly all cases, such evaluative criteria are hidden, and must remain so. Twitter's Trends algorithm, which reports to the user what terms are trending at that moment in their area, even leaves the definition of "trending" unspecified. The criteria they use to assess "trendiness" are only described in general terms: the velocity of a certain term's surge, whether it has appeared in Twitter's Trend list before, and whether it circulates within or spans across clusters of users. What is unstated is how these criteria are measured, how they are weighed against one another, what other criteria have also been incorporated, and when if ever these criteria are overridden. This leaves algorithms perennially open to user suspicion that their criteria skew to the provider's commercial or political benefit, or incorporate embedded, unexamined assumptions that act below the level of awareness, even that of the designers (Gillespie 2012).

An information provider like Twitter cannot be much more explicit or precise about its algorithms' workings. To do so would give competitors an easy means of duplicating and surpassing its service. It would also require a more technical explanation than most users are prepared for. It would hamper their ability to change their criteria as they need. But most of all, it would hand those who hope to "game the system" a road map for getting their sites to the top of the search results or their hashtags to appear on the Trends list. While some collaborative recommendation sites like Reddit have made public their algorithms for ranking stories and user comments, these sites must constantly seek out and correct instances of organized downvoting, and these tactics cannot be made public. With a few exceptions, the tendency is strongly toward being oblique.[3]

Commercial Aims

A second approach might entail a careful consideration of the economic and the cultural contexts from which the algorithm came. Any knowledge system emerges amid the economic and political aims of information provision, and will be shaped by the aims and strategies of those powerful institutions looking to capitalize on it (Hesmondhalgh 2006). The pressures faced by search engines, content platforms, and information providers can subtly shape the design of the algorithm itself and the presentation of its results (Vaidhyanathan 2011). As the algorithm comes to stand as a legitimate knowledge logic, new commercial endeavors are fitted to it (for instance, search engine optimization), reifying choices made and forcing additional ones.

For example, early critics worried that search engines would offer up advertisements in the form of links or featured content, presented as the product of algorithmic calculations. The rapid and clear public rejection of this ploy demonstrated how strong our trust in these algorithms is: users did not wish the content that providers wanted us to see for financial reasons to be intermingled with content that the provider had algorithmically selected. But the concern is now multidimensional: the landscape of the Facebook News Feed, for example, can no longer be described as two distinct territories, social and commercial; rather, it interweaves the results of algorithmic calculations (what status updates and other activities of friends should be listed in the feed, what links will be recommended to this user, which friends are actively on the site at the moment), structural elements (tools for contributing a status update, commenting on an information element, links to groups and pages), and elements placed there based on a sponsorship relationship (banner ads, apps from third-party sites). To map this complex terrain requires a deep understanding of the economic relationships and social assumptions it represents.

Epistemological Premises

Finally, we must consider if the evaluative criteria of the algorithm are structured by specific political or organizational principles that themselves have political ramifications. This is not just whether an algorithm might be partial to this or that provider or might favor its own commercial interests over others. It is a question of whether the philosophical presumptions about relevant knowledge on which the algorithm is founded matter. Some early scholarship looking at the biases of search engines (in order of publication, Introna and Nissenbaum 2000; Halavais 2008; Rogers 2009; Granka 2010) noted some structural tendencies toward what's already popular, toward English-language sites, and toward commercial information providers. Legal scholars debating what it would mean to require neutrality in search results (Grimmelmann 2010; Pasquale and Bracha 2008) have meant more than just the inability to tip results toward a commercial partner.

The criteria public information algorithms take into account are myriad; each is fitted with a threshold for what will push something up in the results, position one result above another, and so on. So evaluations performed by algorithms always depend on inscribed assumptions about what matters, and how what matters can be identified. When a primitive search engine counted the number of appearances of a search term on the web pages it had indexed, it reified a particular logic, one that assumed that pages that include the queried term were likely to be relevant to someone interested in that term. When Google developed PageRank, factoring in incoming links to a page as evidence of its value, it built in a different logic: a page with many incoming links, from high-quality sites, is seen as "ratified" by other users, and is more likely to be relevant to this user as well. By preferring incoming links from sites themselves perceived to be of high-quality, Finkelstein notes, Google had shifted from a more populist approach to a "shareholder democracy": "One link is not one vote, but it has influence proportional to the relative power (in terms of popularity) of the voter. Because blocks of common interests, or social factions, can affect the results of a search to a degree depending on their relative weight in the network, the results of the algorithmic calculation by a search engine come to reflect political struggles in society" (Finkelstein 2008, 107). When a news discussion site decides what ratio of negative complaints to number of views is sufficient to justify automatically hiding a comment thread, it represents their assessment of the proper volatility of public discourse, or at least the volatility they prefer, for the user community they think they have (Braun 2011). A great deal of expertise and judgment can be embedded in these cognitive artifacts (Hutchins 1995; Latour 1986), but it is judgment that is then submerged and automated.

Most users do not dwell on algorithmic criteria, tending to treat them as unproblematic tools in the service of a larger activity: finding an answer, solving a problem, being entertained. However, while the technology may be "blackboxed" (Latour 1987; Pinch and Bijker 1984) by designers and users alike, that should not lead us to believe that it remains stable. In fact, algorithms can be easily, instantly, radically, and invisibly changed. While major upgrades may happen only on occasion, algorithms are regularly being "tweaked." Changes can occur without the interface to the algorithm changing in the slightest: the Facebook news feed and search bar may look the same as they did yesterday, while the evaluations going on beneath them have been thoroughly remade. The blackbox metaphor fails us here, as the workings of the algorithm are both obscured *and* malleable, "likely so dynamic that a snapshot of them would give us little chance of assessing their biases" (Pasquale 2009). In fact, what we might refer to as an algorithm is often not one algorithm but many. Search engines like Google regularly engage in "A/B" testing,[4] presenting different rankings to different subsets of users to gain on-the-fly data on speed and customer satisfaction, then incorporating the adjustments preferred by users in a subsequent upgrade.

Each algorithm is premised on both an assumption about the proper assessment of relevance, and an instantiation of that assumption into a technique for (computational) evaluation. There may be implicit premises built into a site's idea of relevance, there may be shortcuts built into its technical instantiation of that idea, and there may be friction between the two.

The Promise of Algorithmic Objectivity

More than mere tools, algorithms are also stabilizers of trust, practical and symbolic assurances that their evaluations are fair and accurate, and free from subjectivity, error, or attempted influence. But, though algorithms may appear to be automatic and untarnished by the interventions of their providers, this is a carefully crafted fiction: "Search engines pride themselves on being automated, except when they aren't." (Grimmelmann 2008, 950) In fact, no information service can be completely hands-off in its delivery of information: though an algorithm may evaluate any site as most relevant to your query, that result will not appear if it is child pornography, it will not appear in China if it is dissident political speech, and it will not appear in France if it promotes Nazism. Yet it's very important for the providers of these algorithms that they seem hands-off. The legitimacy of these functioning mechanisms must be performed alongside the provision of information itself.

The *articulations* offered by the algorithm provider alongside its tool are meant to provide what Pfaffenberger (1992) calls "logonomic control," to define the tool within the practices of users, to bestow the tool with a legitimacy that then carries to the information provided and, by proxy, the provider. The careful articulation of an algorithm as impartial (even when that characterization is more obfuscation than explanation) certifies it as a reliable sociotechnical actor, lends its results relevance and credibility, and maintains the provider's apparent neutrality in the face of the millions of evaluations it makes. This articulation of the algorithm is just as crucial to its social life as its material design and its economic obligations.

It is largely up to the provider to describe its algorithm as being of a particular shape, having therefore a certain set of values, and thus conferring to it some kind of legitimacy. This includes carefully characterizing the tool and its value to a variety of audiences, sometimes in a variety of ways: an algorithm can be defended as a tool for impartial evaluation to those critical of its results, and at the same time be promised as a tool for selective promotion to potential advertisers (Gillespie 2010). As Mackenzie

(2005) observes, this process requires more than a single, full-throated description: it depends both on "repetition and citation" (81) and at the same time requires "the 'covering over' of the 'authoritative set of practices' that lend it force." (82) When an information provider finds itself criticized for the results it provides, the legitimacy of its algorithm must be repaired both discursively and technically. And users are complicit in this: "A society that obsesses over the top Google News results has made those results important, and we are ill-advised to assume the reverse (that the results are obsessed over because they are important) without some narrative account of why the algorithm is superior to, say, the 'news judgment' of editors at traditional media" (Pasquale 2009).

This articulation happens first in the presentation of the tool, in its deployment within a broader information service. Calling them "results" or "best" or "top stories" or "trends" speaks not only to what the algorithm is actually measuring, but also to what it should be understood as measuring. An equally important part of this discursive work comes in the form of describing how the algorithm works. What may seem like a clear explanation of a behind-the-scenes process may not actually be a glimpse of a real backstage process, but a "performed backstage" (Hilgartner 2000), carefully crafted to further legitimize the process and its results. The description of Google's PageRank system, the earliest component of its complex search algorithm, was published first as a technical paper (already a crafted rendition of its mathematical workings), but was subsequently mythologized— as the defining feature of the tool, as the central element that made Google stand out above its then competitors, and as a fundamentally democratic computational logic—even as the algorithm was being redesigned to take into account hundreds of other criteria.

Above all else, the providers of information algorithms must assert that their algorithms are impartial. The performance of *algorithmic objectivity* has become fundamental to the maintenance of these tools as legitimate brokers of relevant knowledge. No provider has been more adamant about the neutrality of its algorithm than Google, which regularly responds to requests to alter its search results with the assertion that the algorithm must not be tampered with. Google famously pulled out of China in 2010 entirely rather than censor its results, though Google had complied with China's rules before, and may have pulled out rather than admit it was losing to its Chinese competitors. Despite Google's stance, it did alter its search results when complaints arose about a racist Photoshopped image of Michelle Obama at the top of the Image search results; Google provides a SafeSearch mechanism for keeping profanity and sexual images from minors; and the provider refuses to autocomplete search queries that specify torrent file-trading services. Yet Google regularly claims that it does not alter its index or manipulate its results. Morozov (2011) believes that this is a way to deflect responsibility: "Google's spiritual deferral to 'algorithmic neutrality' betrays the company's growing unease with being the world's most important information gatekeeper. Its founders prefer to treat technology as an autonomous and fully objective force rather than spending sleepless nights worrying about inherent biases in how their systems—systems that have grown so complex that no Google engineer fully understands them—operate."

This assertion of algorithmic objectivity plays in many ways an equivalent role to the norm of objectivity in Western journalism. Like search engines, journalists have developed tactics for determining what is most relevant, how to report it, and how to assure its relevance—a set of practices that are relatively invisible to their audience, a goal that they admit is messier to pursue than it might appear, and a principle that helps set aside but does not eradicate value judgments and personal politics. These institutionalized practices are animated by a conceptual promise that, in the discourse of journalism, is regularly articulated (or overstated) as a kind of totem. Journalists use the norm of objectivity as a "strategic ritual" (Tuchman 1972), to lend public legitimacy to knowledge production tactics that are inherently precarious. "Establishing jurisdiction over the ability to objectively parse reality is a claim to a special kind of authority" (Schudson and Anderson 2009, 96).

Journalist and algorithmic objectivities are by no means the same. Journalistic objectivity depends on an institutional promise of due diligence, built into and conveyed via a set of norms journalists learned in training and on the job; their choices represent a careful expertise backed by a deeply infused, philosophical and professional commitment to set aside their own biases and political beliefs. The promise of the algorithm leans much less on institutional norms and trained expertise, and more on a technologically inflected promise of mechanical neutrality. Whatever choices are made are presented both as distant from the intervention of human hands, and as submerged inside of the cold workings of the machine.

But in both, legitimacy depends on accumulated guidelines for the *proceduralization* of information selection. The discourses and practices of objectivity have come to serve as a constitutive rule of journalism (Ryfe 2006). Objectivity is part of how journalists understand themselves and what it means to be a journalist. It is part of how their work is evaluated, by editors, colleagues, and their readers. It is a defining signal by which journalists even recognize what counts as journalism. The promise of algorithmic objectivity, too, has been palpably incorporated into the working practices of algorithm providers, constitutively defining the function and purpose of the information service. When Google includes in its "Ten Things We Know to Be True" manifesto that "Our users trust our objectivity and no short-term gain could ever justify breaching that trust," this is neither spin nor corporate Kool-Aid. It is a deeply ingrained understanding of the public character of Google's information service, one that both influences and legitimizes many of its technical and commercial undertakings, and helps obscure the messier reality of the service it provides.

Still, these claims must compete in the public dialogue with other articulations, which may or may not be so friendly to the economic and ideological aims of the stakeholders. Bijker (1997) calls these competing "technological frames," the discursive characterizations of a technology made by groups of actors who also have a stake in that technology's operation, meaning, and social value. What users of an information algorithm take it to be, and whether they are astute or ignorant, matters. How the press portrays such tools will strengthen or undermine the providers' careful discursive efforts. This means that, while the algorithm itself may seem to possess an aura of technological neutrality, or to embody populist, meritocratic ideals, how it comes to appear that way depends not just on its design but also on the mundane realities of news cycles, press releases, tech blogs, fan discussion, user rebellion, and the machinations of the algorithm provider's competitors.

There is a fundamental paradox in the articulation of algorithms. Algorithmic objectivity is an important claim for a provider, particularly for algorithms that serve up vital and volatile information for public consumption. Articulating the algorithm as a distinctly technical intervention helps an information provider answer charges of bias, error, and manipulation. At the same time, as can be seen with Google's PageRank, there is a sociopolitical value in highlighting the populism of the criteria the algorithm uses. To claim that an algorithm is a democratic proxy for the web-wide collective opinion of a particular website lends it authority. And there is commercial value in claiming that the algorithm returns "better" results than its provider's competitors, which posits customer satisfaction over some notion of accuracy (van Couvering 2007). In examining the articulation of an algorithm, we should pay particular attention to how this tension between technically assured neutrality and the social flavor of the assessment being made is managed—and, sometimes, where it breaks down.

Entanglement with Practice

Though they could be studied as abstract computational tools, algorithms are built to be embedded into practice in the lived world that produces the information they process, and in the lived world of their users (Couldry 2012). This is especially true when the algorithm is the instrument of a business for which the information it delivers (or the advertisements it pairs with it) is the commodity. If users fail or refuse to fit that tool into their practices, to make it meaningful, that algorithm will fail. This means we must consider not their "effect" on people, but a multidimensional "entanglement" between algorithms put into practice and the social tactics of users who take them up. This relationship is, of course, a moving target, because algorithms change, and the user populations and activities they encounter change as well. Still, this should not imply that there is no relationship. As these algorithms nestle into people's daily lives and mundane information practices, users shape and rearticulate the algorithms they encounter; and algorithms impinge on how people seek information, how they perceive and think about the contours of knowledge, and how they understand themselves in and through public discourse.

It is important that we conceive of this entanglement not as a one-directional influence, but as a recursive loop between the calculations of the algorithm and the "calculations" of people. The algorithm that helps users navigate Flickr's photo archive is built on the archive of photos posted, which means it is designed to apprehend and reflect back the choices made by photographers. What people do and do not photograph is already a kind of calculation, though one that is historical, multivalent, contingent, and sociologically informed. But these were not Flickr's only design impulses; sensitivity to photographic practices had to compete with cost, technical efficiency, legal obligation, and business imperatives. And the population of Flickr users and the types of photos they post changed as the site grew in popularity, was forced to compete with Facebook, introduced tiered pricing, was bought by Yahoo, and so forth.

Many Flickr users post photos with the express purpose of having them be seen: some are professional photographers looking for employment, some are seeking communities of like-minded hobbyists, some are simply proud of their work. So just as the algorithm must be sensitive to photographers, photographers have an interest in being sensitive to the algorithm, aware that being delivered in response to the right search might put their photo in front of the right people. Just as Hollywood's emphasis on specific genres invites screenwriters to write in generic ways,[5] the Flickr algorithm may induce subtle reorientations of photographers' practices toward its own constructed logic, that is, toward aspiring to photograph in ways adherent to certain emergent categories, or orienting their choice of subject and composition toward those things the algorithm appears to privilege. "What we leave traces of is not the way we were, but a tacit negotiation between ourselves and our imagined auditors" (Bowker 2006, 6–7).

Algorithmically Recognizable

This tacit negotiation consists first and foremost of the mundane, strategic reorientation of practices many users undertake, toward a tool that they know could amplify their efforts. There is a powerful and understandable impulse for producers of information to make their content, and themselves, recognizable to an algorithm. A whole industry, search engine optimization (SEO), promises to boost websites to the top of search results. But we might think of optimization (deliberate, professional) as just the leading edge of a much more varied, organic, and complex process by which content producers of all sorts orient themselves toward algorithms. When we use hashtags in our tweets—a user innovation that was embraced later by Twitter—we are not just joining a conversation or hoping to be read by others, we are redesigning our expression so as to be better recognized and distributed by Twitter's search algorithm. Some may work to be noticed by the algorithm: teens have been known to tag their status updates with unrelated brand names, in the hopes that Facebook will privilege those updates in their friends' feeds.[6] Others may work to evade an algorithm: Napster and P2P users sharing infringing copyrighted music were known to slightly misspell the artists' names, so users might find "Britny Speers" recordings but the record industry software would not.[7]

Is this gaming the system? Or is it a fundamental way we, to some degree, orient ourselves toward the means of distribution through which we hope to speak? Based on the criteria of the algorithm in question (or by our best estimate of its workings), we make ourselves *already algorithmically recognizable* in all sorts of ways. This is not so different than newsmakers orienting their efforts to fit the routines of the news industry: timing a press release to make the evening broadcast, or providing packaged video to a cable outlet hungry for gripping footage, are techniques for turning to face the medium that may amplify them. Now, for all of us, social networks and the web offer some analogous kind of "mediated visibility" (Thompson 2005, 49), and we gain similar benefit by turning to face these algorithms.

Backstage Access

But who is best positioned to understand and operate the public algorithms that matter so much to the public circulation of knowledge? Insight into the workings of information algorithms is a form of power: vital to participating in public discourse, essential to achieving visibility online, constitutive of credibility and the opportunities that follow. As mentioned before, the criteria and code of algorithms are generally obscured—but not equally or from everyone. For most users, their understanding of these algorithms may be vague, simplistic, sometimes mistaken; they may attempt to nudge the algorithm in ways that are either simply considered best practices (hashtags, metadata) or that fundamentally misunderstand the algorithm's criteria (as with repeatedly retweeting the same message in the hopes of trending on Twitter). Search engine optimizers and spammers have just as little access, but have developed a great deal of technical skill in divining the criteria beneath the algorithm through testing and reverse-engineering. Communities of technology enthusiasts and critics engage in similar attempts to uncover the workings of these systems, whether for fun, insight, personal advantage, or determined disruption. Legislators, who have only just begun to ask questions about the implications of algorithms for fair commerce or political discourse, have thus far been given only the most general of explanations: information providers often contend that their algorithms are trade secrets that must not be divulged in a public venue.

Furthermore, some stakeholders are in fact granted access to the algorithm, though under controlled conditions. Advertisers are offered one kind of access to the backstage workings of that system, for bidding on preferred placement. Information providers that offer Application Programming Interfaces (APIs) to their commercial partners and third-party developers give them a glimpse under the hood, but bind them with contracts and nondisclosure agreements in the very same moment. Access to, understanding of, and rights regarding the algorithms that play a crucial role in public discourse and knowledge will likely change, for different stakeholders and under specific circumstances—changing also the power to build for, navigate through, and regulate these algorithms available to these stakeholders and those they represent.

Domestication

As much as these tools may urge us to make ourselves legible to them, we also take them into our practices, shifting their meaning and sometimes even their design along the way. Silverstone (1994) has suggested that once technologies are offered to the public, they undergo a process of "domestication": literally, these technologies enter the home, but also figuratively, users make them their own, embedding them in their routines, imbuing them with additional meanings that the technology provider could not have anticipated. Public information algorithms certainly matter for the way users find information, communicate with others, and know the world around them. But more than that, users express preferences for their favorite search engines, opine about a site's recommendations as being buggy or intuitive or spot on. Some users put great stock in a particular tool, while others come to distrust it, using it warily or not at all. Apple iPhone users swap tips on how to make its Siri search agent speak its repertoire of amusing retorts,[8] then share in the outrage about its answers on hot-button political issues.[9] Satisfied Facebook users today become critics tomorrow when the algorithm behind their news feed is altered in a way that feels economically motivated—while through and after the uprising, they continue to post status updates. Users, faced with the power asymmetries of data collection and online surveillance, have developed an array of tactics of "obfuscation" to evade or pollute the algorithmic attempts to know them (Brunton and Nissenbaum 2011). While it is crucial to consider the ways algorithmic tools shape our encounters with information, we should not imply that users are under the sway of these tools. The reality is more complicated, and more intimate.

Users can also turn to these algorithms for a data-inflected reflection; many sites allow us to present ourselves to others and back to ourselves, including our public profile, the performance of our friendships, the expression of our preferences, or a record of our recent activity. Facebook's Timeline feature curates users' activities into chronological remembrances of them; the pleasure of seeing what it algorithmically selects offers a kind of delight, a delight beyond composing the photos and news posts in the first place. But algorithms can also function as a particularly compelling "technology of the self" (Foucault 1988) when they seem to independently ratify one's public visibility. It is now common practice to Google oneself: seeing me appear as the top result in a search for my name offers a kind of assurance of my tenuous public existence. There is a sense of validation when your pet topic trends on Twitter, when Amazon recommends a book you already love, or when Apple iTunes' "Genius" function composes an appealing playlist from your library of songs. Whether we actually tailor our Amazon purchases so as to appear well read (just as Nielsen ratings families used to over-report watching PBS and C-Span) or we simply enjoy when the algorithm confirms our sense of self, algorithms are a powerful invitation to understand ourselves through the independent lens they promise to provide.

Algorithms are not just what their designers make of them, or what they make of the information they process. They are also what we make of them day in and day out—but with this caveat: because the logic, maintenance, and redesign of these algorithms remain in the hands of the information providers, they are in a distinctly privileged position to rewrite our understanding of them, or to engender a lingering uncertainty about their criteria that makes it difficult for us to treat the algorithms as truly our own.

Knowledge Logics

It is easy to theorize, but substantially more difficult to document, how users may shift their worldviews to accommodate the underlying logics and implicit presumptions of the algorithms they use regularly. There is a case to be made that the working logics of these algorithms not only shape user practices, but also lead users to internalize their norms and priorities: Bucher (2012) argues that the EdgeRank algorithm, used by Facebook to determine which status updates get prominently displayed on a users' news feed, encourages a "participatory subjectivity" in users, who recognize that gestures of affinity (such as commenting on a friends' photo) are a key criteria in Facebook's algorithm. Longford (2005) argues that the code of commercial platform "habituates" us, through incessant requests and carefully designed default settings, toward giving over more of our personal information. Mager (2012) and van Couvering (2010) both propose that the principles of capitalism are embedded in the workings of search engines.

But we need not resort to such muscular theories of ideological domination to suggest that algorithms designed to offer relevant knowledge also offer ways of knowing—and that as they become more pervasive and trusted, their logics are self-affirming. Google's search engine, amid its 200 signals, does presume that relevant knowledge is assured largely by public ratification, adjusted to weigh heavily the opinions of those who are themselves publicly ratified. This blend of the wisdom of crowds and collectively certified authorities is Google's solution to the longstanding tension between expertise and common sense, in the enduring problem of how to know. It is not without precedent, and it is not a fundamentally flawed way to know, but it is a specific one, with its own emphases and myopias. Now, Google's solution is operationalized into a tool that billions of people use every day, most of whom experience it as something that simply, and unproblematically, "works." To some degree, Google and its algorithm help assert and normalize this knowledge logic as "right," as right as its results appear to be.

The Production of Calculated Publics

Ito, boyd, and others have recently introduced the term "networked publics" (boyd 2010; Ito 2008; Varnelis 2008) to highlight both the communities of users that can assemble through social media, and the way the technologies structure how these publics can form, interact, and sometimes fall apart. "While networked publics share much in common with other types of publics, the ways in which technology structures them introduces distinct affordances that shape how people engage with these environments" (boyd 2010, 39). To the extent that algorithms are a key technological component of these mediated environments, they too help structure the publics that can emerge using digital technology.

Some concerns have been raised about how the workings of information algorithms, and the ways we choose to navigate them, could undermine our efforts to be involved citizens. The ability to personalize search results and online news was the first and perhaps best articulated of these concerns. With contemporary search engines, the results two users get to the same query can be quite different; in a news service or social network, the information offerings can be precisely tailored to the user's preferences (by the user, or the provider) such that, in practice, the stories presented as most newsworthy may be so dissimilar from user to user that no common object of public dialogue is even available. Sunstein (2001) and, more recently, Pariser (2011) have argued that, when algorithmic information services can be personalized to this degree, the diversity of public knowledge and political dialogue may be undermined. We are led—by algorithms and our own preference for the like-minded—into "filter bubbles" (ibid.), where we find only the news we expect and the political perspectives we already hold dear.

But algorithms not only structure our interactions with others as members of networked publics, they also traffic in *calculated publics* that they themselves produce. When Amazon recommends a book that "customers like you" bought, it is invoking and claiming to know a public with which we are invited to feel an affinity—though the population on which it bases these recommendations is not transparent, and is certainly not coterminous with its entire customer base. When Facebook offers as a privacy setting that a user's information be seen by "friends, and friends of friends," it transforms a discrete set of users into an audience—it is a group that did not exist until that moment, and only Facebook knows its precise membership. These algorithmically generated groups may overlap with, be an inexact approximation of, or have nothing whatsoever to do with the publics that the user sought out.

Some algorithms go further, making claims about the public they purport to know, and the users' place amid them. I have argued elsewhere that Twitter's Trends algorithm promises users a glimpse of what a particular public (national or regional) is talking about at that moment, but that it is a constructed public, shaped by Twitter's specific, and largely unspecified criteria (Gillespie 2012). Klout, an online service that tracks users' activity and reputation on Facebook, Twitter, and elsewhere, promises to calculate users' influence across these various social media platforms. Their measures are intuitive in their definition, but completely opaque in their mechanisms. The friction between the "networked publics" forged by users and the "calculated publics" offered by algorithms further complicates the dynamics of networked sociality.

With other measures of public opinion, such as polling or surveys, the central problem is extrapolation, where a subset is presumed to stand for the entire population. With algorithms, the population can be the entire user base, sometimes hundreds of millions of people (but only that user base the algorithm provider has access to). Instead, the central problem here is that the intention behind these calculated representations of the public is by no means actuarial. Algorithms that purport to identify what is "hot" engage in a calculated approximation of a public through its participants' traceable activity, then report back to them what they have talked about most. But behind this, we can ask, What is the gain for providers in making such characterizations, and how does that shape what they're measuring? Who is being chosen to be measured in order to produce this representation, and who is left out of the calculation? And perhaps most important, how do these technologies, now not just technologies of evaluation but of representation, help to constitute and codify the publics they claim to measure, publics that would not otherwise exist except that the algorithm called them into existence?

These questions matter a great deal, and will matter more, to the extent that the representations of the public produced by information algorithms get taken up, by users or by authorities, as legitimate, and incorporated into the broader modernist project of reflexivity (Giddens 1990). "Society is engaged in monitoring itself, scrutinizing itself, portraying itself in a variety of ways, and feeding the resulting understandings back into organizing its activities" (Boyer and Hannerz 2006, 9). What Twitter claims matters to "Americans" or what Amazon says teens read are forms of authoritative knowledge that can and will be invoked by institutions whose aim is to regulate such populations.

The belief that such algorithms, combined with massive user data, are better at telling us things about the nature of the public or the constitution of society, has proven alluring for scholars as well. Social science has turned eagerly toward computational techniques, or the study of human sociality through "big data" (Lazer et al. 2009; for a critique, see boyd and Crawford 2012), in the hopes of enjoying the kind of insights that the biological sciences have achieved, by algorithmically looking for needles in the digital haystacks of all this data. The approach is seductive: having millions of data points lends a great deal of legitimacy, and the way algorithms seem to spot patterns that researchers couldn't see otherwise is exciting. "For a certain sort of social scientist, the traffic patterns of millions of e-mails look like manna from heaven" (*Nature* 2007). But this methodological approach should heed the complexities described so far, particularly when a researcher's data has been generated by commercial algorithms. Computational research techniques are not barometers of the social. They produce hieroglyphs: shaped by the tool by which they are carved, requiring of priestly interpretation, they tell powerful but often mythological stories—usually in the service of the gods.

Finally, when the data is us, what should we make of the associations that algorithms claim to identify about us as a society—that we do not know, or perhaps do not want to know? In Ananny's (2011) uncanny example, he noticed the Android Market recommending a sex-offender location app to users who downloaded Grindr, a location-based social networking tool for gay men. He speculates how the Android Market algorithms could have made this association—one even the operators of the Android Market could not easily explain. Did the algorithm make an error? Did the algorithm make too blunt an association, simply pairing apps with "sex" in the description? Or did the Android recommendation engine in fact identify a subtle association that, though we may not wish it so, is regularly made in our culture, between homosexuality and predatory behavior? Zimmer (2007) notes a similar case: a search for the phrase "she invented" would return the query, "did you mean 'he invented'?" That is, it did so until Google changed the results. While unsettling in its gender politics, Google's response was completely "correct," explained by the sorry fact that, over the entire corpus of the web, the word "invented" is preceded by "he" much more often than "she." Google's algorithm recognized this— and mistakenly presumed it meant the search query "she invented" was merely a typographical error. Google, here, proves much less sexist than we are. In a response to Ananny's example, Gray has suggested that, just as we must examine algorithms that make associations such as these, we might also inquire into the "cultural algorithms" that these associations represent, (that is, systematically associating homosexuality with sexual predation) across a massive, distributed set of "data points"—us.

Conclusion

Understanding algorithms and their impact on public discourse, then, requires thinking not simply about how they work, where they are deployed, or what animates them financially. This is not simply a call to unveil their inner workings and spotlight their implicit criteria. It is a socio-logical inquiry that does not interest the providers of these algorithms, who are not always in the best position to even ask. It requires examining why algorithms are being looked to as a credible knowledge logic, how they fall apart and are repaired when they come in contact with the ebb and flow of public discourse, and where political assumptions might not only be etched into their design, but also constitutive of their widespread use and legitimacy.

I see the emergence of the algorithm as a trusted information tool as the latest response to a fundamental tension of public discourse. The means by which we produce, circulate, and consume information in a complex society must necessarily be handled through the division of labor: some produce and select information, and the rest of us, at least in that moment, can only take it for what it's worth. Every public medium previous to this has faced this challenge, from town criers to newspapers to broadcasting. In each, when we turn over the provision of knowledge to others, we are left vulnerable to their choices, methods, and subjectivities. Sometimes this is a positive, providing expertise, editorial acumen, refined taste. But we are also wary of the intervention, of human failings and vested interests, and find ourselves with only secondary mechanisms of social trust by which to vouch for what is true and relevant (Shapin 1995). Their procedures are largely unavailable to us. Their procedures are unavoidably selective, emphasizing some information and discarding others, and the choices may be consequential. There is the distinct possibility of error, bias, manipula-tion, laziness, commercial or political influence, or systemic failures. The selection process can always be an opportunity to curate for reasons other than relevance: for propriety, for commercial or institutional self-interest, or for political gain. Together this represents a fundamental vulnerability, one that we can never fully resolve; we can merely build assurances as best we can.

From this perspective, we might see algorithms not just as codes with consequences, but as the latest, socially constructed and institutionally managed mechanism for assuring public acumen: a new knowledge logic. We might consider the algorithmic as posed against, and perhaps supplanting, the *editorial* as a competing logic. The editorial logic depends on the subjective choices of experts, who are themselves made and authorized through institutional processes of training and certification, or validated by the public through the mechanisms of the market. The algorithmic logic, by contrast, depends on the proceduralized choices of a machine, designed by human operators to automate some proxy of human judgment or unearth patterns across collected social traces. Both struggle with, and claim to resolve, the fundamental problem of human knowledge: how to identify relevant information crucial to the public, through unavoidably human means, in such a way as to be free from human error, bias, or manipulation. Both the algorithmic and editorial approaches to knowledge are deeply important and deeply problematic; much of the scholarship on communication, media, technology, and publics grapples with one or both techniques and their pitfalls.

A sociological inquiry into algorithms should aspire to reveal the complex workings of this knowledge machine, both the process by which it chooses information for users and the social process by which it is made into a legitimate system. But there may be something, in the end, impenetrable about algorithms. They are designed to work without human intervention, they are deliberately obfuscated, and they work with information on a scale that is hard to comprehend (at least without other algorithmic tools). And perhaps more than that, we want relief from the duty of being skeptical about information we cannot ever assure for certain. These mechanisms by which we settle (if not resolve) this problem, then, are solutions we cannot merely rely on, but *must* believe in. But this kind of faith (Vaidhyanathan 2011) renders it difficult to soberly recognize their flaws and fragilities.

So in many ways, algorithms remain outside our grasp, and they are designed to be. This is not to say that we should not aspire to illuminate their workings and impact. We should. But we may also need to prepare ourselves for more and more encounters with the unexpected and ineffable associations they will sometimes draw for us, the fundamental uncertainty about who we are speaking to or hearing, and the palpable but opaque undercurrents that move quietly beneath knowledge when it is managed by algorithms.

Acknowledgments

I want to thank my colleagues at Culture Digitally for their help and advice on this essay, and the generous support of the Collegium de Lyon and The European Institutes for Advanced Study (EURIAS) Fellowship Programme.

Notes

1. Ethan Zuckerman, "Eli Pariser talks about the filter bubble." *The Boston Phoenix*, May 26, 2011. http://thePhoenix.com/Boston/arts/121405-eli-pariser-talks-about-the-filter-bubble/, accessed April 22, 2013.

2. Google, "Facts about Google and competition," http://www.google.com/competition/howgooglesearchworks.html, accessed April 22, 2013. Google and Bing have since engaged in a little competitive "signals" war, first when Bing announced that it uses 1,000 signals, and Google following that its 200 signals have as many as 50 variations, bringing their total nearer to 10,000. See Danny Sullivan, "Dear Bing, we have 10,000 ranking signals to your 1,000. Love, Google," http://searchengineland.com/bing-10000-ranking-signals-google-55473, accessed April 22, 2013.

3. Foregoing the possibility of a perfectly transparent algorithm, there is a range of choices open to a developer as to how straightforward to be. This can be as simple as being more forthright in the characterization of the tool, or by providing an explanation for why certain ads were served up with a page, or it could be providing more careful site documentation.

4. Brian Christian, "The A/B Test: Inside the technology that's changing the rules of business." *Wired.com*, April 25, 2012. http://www.wired.com/business/2012/04/ff_abtesting/, accessed April 22, 2013.

5. Christian Sandvig, personal communication.

6. danah boyd, personal communication.

7. ABC News, "Napster faced with big list, trick names," March 5, 2001. http://abcnews.go.com/Entertainment/story?id=108389, accessed April 22, 2013.

8. http://siri-sayings.tumblr.com/, accessed April 22, 2013.

9. Jenna Wortham, "Apple says Siri's abortion answers are a glitch." *New York Times*, November 30, 2011. http://bits.blogs.nytimes.com/2011/11/30/apple-says-siris-abortion-answers-are-a-glitch/, accessed April 22, 2013.

10   The Fog of Freedom

Christopher M. Kelty

Talk of freedom and liberty pervade the past and present of the digital computer and the Internet, from everyday "academic freedom" to the more specific notion of a "freedom to tinker"; from the prestigious Computers, Freedom and Privacy conference to "net neutrality"; from "Internet Freedom" in North Africa and the Middle East and the Occupy movement in the United States to the famous case of Free Software, which has articulated precise freedoms as well as a legally constituted commons in reusable technologies; from the "FreedomBox" to the Freedom Fone to "Liberté Linux (see figure 10.1).[1]

What kind of talk is this? Idle chatter? A rhetorical flourish? Serious business? Or perhaps it is more than talk? Freedom is associated with the digital computer and the Internet to a greater extent than it is to most other technologies. And the digital computer and the Internet are associated with freedom much more than with other ideals, like justice, well-being, health, or happiness. Further, arguments are made just as often that digital computers and the Internet restrict rather than enhance freedom, leading to a morass of claims about the powers—good and evil—of these new technologies that drape the globe and permeate our consciousness.

There are many ways to dismiss this association as ideology or marketing hype, but there are fewer ways to take it seriously. Careful attention to the history and development of the digital computer and the Internet should be balanced with careful attention to the political theories of freedom and liberty if we want to make sense of the inflated claims associating freedom and computers.

In this chapter I explore the relationship between the concept of freedom and the historical path that the design of computer technology has taken; to do this convincingly requires bringing the approaches of science and technology studies (STS) and media and communication studies (MCS) into closer dialogue with political theory. In particular, I will revisit here

the story of the invention of the personal computer out of the world of batch-processing and mainframe computing in the 1960s, and the roles of people such as JCR Licklider and Douglas Engelbart (Bardini 2000; Campbell-Kelly 1996; Ceruzzi 2003; Markoff 2005; Streeter 2011; Turner 2006; Waldrop 2001). Alongside this story I offer an analysis of the conceptual distinction in political theory between positive and negative liberty, most famously, but not exclusively, associated with Isaiah Berlin. Both parts of this story have been told many times, but never together.

Most contemporary accounts of the birth of the personal computer tend to critically diagnose one particular kind of freedom: libertarianism. What I will demonstrate here is that even a very remedial attention to the conceptual distinctions available in political theory can yield a much richer story about how freedom is related to the design and innovation of computer technology. The distinction between positive and negative freedom, as an example, can be used to articulate and explain different aspects of the invention of the personal computer; it helps specify the meaning of "freedom to" and "freedom from," how the computer was first imagined to restrict human thought, and then enhance it, and how this relates to assumptions about the capacities and limitations of the human organism.

Scholarship in STS, history of science, and MCS tends to leave the concept of freedom relatively untroubled, whereas work in political theory tends to trouble the concepts of freedom without worrying too much about the details of technology. Neither approach clearly investigates how new technologies change the meaning of freedom itself. My intuition is that the invention of the personal computer clearly represents a transformation of the "powers of freedom" (Rose 1999) at our disposal—both how we practice

Figure 10.1
Diverse expressions of the link between freedom and computers. Collage by C. Kelty. 1. Net Neutrality meets Norman Rockell (http://www.flickr.com/photos/doctabu/3659665238/). 2. A proposed logo for the Freedom Box by Joshua Spodek and John Emerson (http://joshuaspodek.com/freedombox-logo-designs). 3. Internet freedom t-shirt. 4. Trademarked UNIX "Live Free or Die" license plate (http://www.unix.org/license-plate.html). 5. "Internet Freedom Speech," Secretary of State Hilary Clinton, January 2010. 6. Computers, Freedom and Privacy Conference banner, 2011 (http://www.cfp.org/). 7. Freedom Computer Service, Phoenix, AZ (http://www.freedomcomputerservice.com/). 8. France 24 advertisement for "The Tweets," June 2011 (Ad agency: Marcel Paris). 9. Freedom Fone Logo (http://freedomfone.org/). 10. "Document Freedom Day" from the Open Document Foundation (http://www.documentfreedom.org/). 11. Liberté Linux Distribution Logo (http://dee.su/liberte). 12. "Microsoft Is Trashing Your Freedom" sticker (http://windows7sins.org/).

freedom, and how we restrict it. But we have neither a descriptive nor a normative theory of this transformation.

The concept of freedom is not only something lived and loved, but also an analytical tool for exploring the implications of the design of new technologies. For instance, the concepts of individual and collective liberty can help make sense of the design of networks—and specifically of the case of the design of the ARPAnet protocols in the 1970s. In that case one sees the classic problems of constitutional design, including issues of contract, neutrality, and justice articulated at the same time in John Rawls's work (1971). By the 1980s, the IT industry was embroiled in debates about "vendor lock-in" and network standardization. The concept of civic-republican liberty or "freedom as non-domination" (Pettit 1997) provides a sophisticated way to understand these debates—and these debates themselves set the terms of debate for what "free software" would come to mean and how a distinctive kind of copyright license was necessitated (Kelty 2008). Although this chapter is restricted to one slice of the story, and one kind of conceptual specification, it is and should be read as part of a much larger field of possibilities.

The association of freedom with information technology, therefore, is not just talk. The intuition that these technologies are directly and materially related to our freedom is predictable. After all, these tools engage our individual capacities to think, create, and manipulate the world, and they transform the collective relationships we have with others. Anything that is both so intimate and so political a technology concerns more than discourse or hype—it is also about design, construction, maintenance, and repair, and about money and power as well.

A notable feature of this constant association is that *new information technologies are seen as a cause both of freedom and of control and coercion.* This polarization is visible not just in the present but in particular moments in the past as well, when new technologies were created in order to respond to or correct perceived encroachments on freedom created by a previous generation of technologies. The personal computer was perceived as a liberation from the constraints of the mainframe; free software has been understood as a liberation from the constraints of proprietary software; "open systems" were seen as a way to liberate the computer industry from "vendor lock-in"; the Internet was designed with the capacity to free organizations from the constraints of bounded, hierarchically controlled local networks, and later understood as an inherently "liberating" tool of personal, political, and innovative expression. In each case, slightly different aspects of the concept of freedom are at work (such as negative, positive, neutral, or nondomination). And in each case, the question is raised as to how these concepts are *built into, designed into, or made durable in* the creation, innovation, and dissemination of new information technologies. Only by looking at both the detailed history of these technologies and the theoretical refinements of the concept of freedom can we hope to make sense of these intuitions.

Freedom, Thought in Three Domains

The aim of this book is to articulate the intersections between scholarly work in science and technology studies and media and communications studies. I would like to do that by reference to a third domain: that of political philosophy. Both STS and MCS have developed their own peculiar concept of politics based in understanding the empirical realities of technology and media. Frequently, however, this version of politics is a *terminus*: it is the end of the line of analysis. Technology is political; media industries distort politics; new technologies should support freedom, not restrict it.

STS, especially when dealing with the material aspects of scientific and technological culture, has developed a now-standard technique of displaying the ways that technologies are political. From Langdon Winner's account of Robert Moses' Long Island bridges to Bruno Latour's sleeping policemen and Berlin keys, to Shapin and Shaffer's account of political order in seventeenth-century science, to the politics of expertise and the "participatory turn"—in all these cases, the goal is to demonstrate that science and technology are political (see, respectively, Winner 1980; Latour and Venn 2002; Shapin and Schaffer 1985; see also Epstein 1995; Jasanoff 2003; and Nowotny, Scott, and Gibbons 2001). But as Marres and Lezaun (2011) point out, this approach often designates these things as "sub-political": politics are embedded in, designed into, lurk within the things and ideas of science and technology, and it is the analyst's prerogative to reveal this subterranean political action to readers. This "sub-politics" is distinguished from politics *proper* as a kind of hidden order of politics. Whether or not politics *proper* functions in a healthy and orderly form, the "sub-political" domain of technology necessarily haunts it. Only when scholars turn their attention to the governance of science and technology, or the politics of science policy, does the proper domain of politics become an explicit object of analysis. However, in these cases it is not analyzed *in the same way* as the objects of science and technology, though recent work emerging out of science studies has begun to do just that (Barry 2001; Latour 2010; Marres 2009; Marres and Lezaun 2011).

MCS has a different relationship to political theory. Communication studies has always been about the relationship of democracy, freedom, and the medium of communication, but like work in STS, it is reticent to put the communications horse in front of the democracy cart. For instance, in the august tradition of what is now called "media reform" work in communications, there is an explicit connection made between the material and economic configuration of the media and telecommunications industries, and the possibility for a healthy politics—especially democratic politics of free speech in the (mediated) public sphere. The focus on free speech has allowed scholars and policymakers alike to focus on the details of new technologies. From Robert McChesney and Ithiel de Sola Pool to Paul Starr and Michael Schudson, there is a rich tradition of interrogating how free speech is challenged by new technologies, and how it warps, distorts, defends, or enlarges a public sphere or the possibilities for deliberative and participatory engagement in the life of a democracy (de Sola Pool 1983; Klinenberg 2007; McChesney 1999; Schudson 1978, 1998; Starr 2004). These approaches retain the public sphere as a kind of ideal type that communication regimes can fall short of, instead of something that emerges or is co-constituted by the communications media. To be fair, the work of people like Michael Warner (2002) and William Warner (2005) push in this direction, enough so that there are now openings for the pursuit of a different theory of freedom (and free speech, as in Coleman 2009).

There are also ongoing debates in MCS about the nature of engagement by or participation of citizens via different technologies—whether the classic critiques of national broadcast culture, or the current concerns about the intersection of new media, citizen journalism, and politics. Arguably this approach has the same "sub-political" orientation as STS in that the structure of media industries, the patterns of use, or the design of specific affordances are revealed as being political without questioning the proper domain of politics itself. If these theories are normative, they are so (for better or for worse) with respect to relatively unquestioned formulations of free speech and democratic participation.

STS has shown more interest in free speech recently, and MCS has turned more toward an understanding of the heterogeneity and complexity of technical systems, or the "distributed cognition" they might enable (Boczkowski 2010; Coleman 2009, Gillespie 2007; Lievrouw 2011). Nonetheless, both steer well clear of any direct transformation of the concepts of political theory. By contrast, in the places where political theory is contested—that is, in mainstream history, philosophy, political science, and sociology—it is by no means required that a dispute about political theory will involve questions of science, technology, or communications media at all.[2] As a result, the proper "technologies" of political theory remain those of face-to-face speech and deliberation, rational and affective relationships, and certain highly circumscribed forms of action like voting, protesting, canvassing, funding, or donating, all of which leave the proper domain of technology or communications media as untouched as in the reverse case.

The great virtue of bringing in more political theory is that freedom comes in many flavors. It apparently has to if it is to support the impressive array of its uses and abuses.[3] As Isaiah Berlin said, freedom is a word "so porous that there is little interpretation that it seems able to resist." (Berlin 1958, 6) This has, however, not stopped anyone who cares deeply about the concept from carefully proposing an array of distinctions and refinements that form a considerably well tricked-out workshop from which one might draw. Understanding this diversity is preliminary to making any progress in understanding how new technologies might encode, incorporate, address, or transform freedom in actual practice.

To begin with, there are the classic distinctions between negative and positive liberty, and between individual or collective liberty (Berlin 1958; Christman 1991; Miller 1983; Steiner 1994; Taylor 1979; von Hayek 1960).[4] There are debates about whether there are "two concepts of liberty," "three concepts of liberty" or only one (MacCallum 1967; Nelson 2005; Skinner 2002). There is a large, robust, and very precise analytical concern with the compatibility of free will and determinism (Fischer 1999). There is a general division of labor in the literature between political and individual liberty, as well as attempts to integrate them (Pettit 2001). There is the longstanding tradition of "republican" liberty, recently revived (Pettit 1997, 2001; Skinner 1998). There are debates about the existence of collective subjects, about the multiplicity of the individual (May 1992; May and Hoffman 1991); and so on. All this is no doubt remedial for the political theorist. What is not remedial is the question of how these different concepts relate to innovation, and in particular to the innovation of the digital computer and the Internet.

A rapprochement among STS, MCS, and political theory would be welcome, and there is some evidence of one (Bennett 2010; Braun and Whatmore 2010; Marres and Lezaun 2011). The history of computing technology is a useful case because it nicely interweaves objects and problems central to both STS and MCS. The digital computer and the Internet were conceived as communications devices long before they were consumer goods; they blur the lines between industries (telecommunications, computing, entertainment, and, recently, advertising) and create novel challenges for policy and regulators. They are evolved in an ecology of "convergence" with other devices, and engineers, designers, and analysts have long treated them as something that provides, enhances, or ensures *freedom* of some kind.

But triangulating STS and MCS with political theory requires two adjustments. First, from the direction of political theory, the range of refinements concerning freedom is rich enough that those of us in STS or MCS should begin to challenge some of the stories and claims that are routinely made in our fields, specifically concerning the relationship between freedom and the design of technologies. Second, scholars in STS or MCS should begin to articulate how "designing freedom into" technologies *changes the concept and practice of freedom itself.*

How can freedom inhere in technologies? Is freedom something more or less real than software, or electrons, or solder? We might approach freedom as having simply a discursive reality: one can ask how particular actors talk (or talked) about freedom as part of the design of particular technologies (the most obvious case would be that of Ted Nelson's 1974 *Computer Lib/ Dream Machines*; see figure 10.2). Or freedom can be approached as being a set of rules for or definitions of action: one can ask how freedom was defined in a particular historical moment and a particular place as evidence for how it might have been used in the design of information technology (an example would be Rawls's [1971] theory of neutrality, and how it has structured debates about the Internet). Freedom can also be approached as an ethical or moral framework of some kind, and one therefore might settle on a particular normative definition of freedom and then critique various actors or entities for falling short of it in the design of a technology (this is often the approach of free software advocates and analysts).

But to say that freedom can inhere in a technology is to suggest that it has a material existence of some kind—and by implication, that we build, repair, and maintain freedom in particular ways. Engineers, designers, or hackers—just as much as philosophers, jurists, or legislators—repeatedly subject the concept to distinctions and reconstructions that respond to the creation of new institutions, changed conditions (such as movements for liberty and revolutions), and changed understandings of humans and non-humans (McKeon 1957). Freedom cannot be unaffected by our attempts to bring it into being, to enhance it, or to restrict it—explicitly or not. This is all the more so when such attempts result in arrangements of life that make particular aspects of the concept *durable.*

A separate, and related, question is whether engineers and designers— just as much as philosophers, jurists, or legislators—must *intend* to design freedom into a technology for the concept to play a role. What designers

Figure 10.2

Front Cover of Ted Nelson's 1974 classic *Computer Lib/Dream Machines*. Autographed copy inscribed "For Chris Kelty, with best wishes. 11.11.09."

say or intend does not simply map on to the technologies that result. It is too hard a case to make that most or all designers, engineers, or marketers are driven by some particular ideal of freedom to make things one way or another—and that they have the power to do so. Many other motivations crowd the field from simple self-interest to a concern with beauty to a nationalist concern with productivity to egoism, and so on. And many other interests determine the configuration of any given technology. At best, we can point to the kinds of problems that designers and firms think exist and need solutions, and how they attempt to solve them. In doing so, they transform the capacities for and practices of freedom for a subsequent generation, and it is possible to observe this process in action.

What follows thus has an avowedly pragmatic character: it requires identifying the reconstruction of a concept as a result of its testing, use, and rectification by actors in the world (Dewey 2006). The computer has literally transformed the concept of freedom in the last thirty years. It is this claim that I think neither STS nor MCS has taken seriously, instead leaving it implicit in the general conclusion that "technology is political." What might be the consequences of this transformation, for STS and MCS, to be sure, but also for our *theory and practice of freedom* more generally?

Are Computers Libertarians?

In the social and cultural studies of the history of the digital computer to date, the kind of freedom most often attributed to innovators and their problem-solving activities has been that of libertarianism. This is not an unreasonable association. It is easy to find clear and sometimes disturbingly powerful examples, such as Peter Thiel, cofounder of PayPal, venture capitalist, and early investor in Facebook. He is a frequent supporter of libertarian causes, from the predictable (Ron Paul's campaign) to the absurd (a $1.25 million donation to the Seasteading Institute, a group seeking to build sovereign nations on artificial islands in international waters).[5] Whether Thiel is at all representative of Silicon Valley capitalists, engineers, developers, or designers is a harder claim to make, and one for which there is little other than anecdotal evidence. Nonetheless, the idea of a distinctive brand of Silicon Valley libertarianism has become a kind of mythos of its own.

In 1995 Richard Barbrook and Andrew Cameron inaugurated the Silicon Valley libertarian mythos, dubbing it "The Californian Ideology" (Barbrook and Cameron 1996). The critical nuance that Barbrook and Cameron offered was that Silicon Valley libertarianism combined elements of both the traditional left and the traditional right; it brought together ostensible lefties like Stewart Brand with ostensible conservatives like Newt Gingrich and George Gilder, combining "the free-wheeling spirit of the hippies and the entrepreneurial zeal of the yuppies (44)." In 2000, journalist Paulina Borsook published *Cyberselfish: A Critical Romp through the Terribly Libertarian Culture of High Tech,* in which she savaged the feral "technolibertarians" of high tech culture, specifically those she perceived to be dominating Silicon Valley and its politics. In both of these cases, "cyberculture" is represented by cyberpunk fiction, *Wired* magazine, *Mondo 2000*, Silicon Valley entrepreneurs and engineers, and libertarianism associated with free markets, deregulation, and radical individualism. Whether or not these specifics should stand in for either the place or the ideology is unclear, and sometimes the proposed connections between Silicon Valley and libertarianism verge on conspiracy.[6]

It is only recently that scholars such as Fred Turner (2006) and Thomas Streeter (2011) have started to put together richer, more convincing accounts of the specific kinds of associations that have permeated information technology and its innovations since the 1960s. Fred Turner's *From Counterculture to Cyberculture* has made perhaps the most sustained contribution to the cultural understanding of "cyberculture" by charting the detailed ways in which the network of folks including Stewart Brand, Peter Schwartz, and Kevin Kelly helped give a particular cultural meaning to some of the most celebrated moments of the history of computing— from Douglas Engelbart's famous 1968 demonstration of what a personal computer could be (where Brand manned the camera) to the 1984 Hacker's conference (which Brand co-organized) to one of the earliest and most celebrated "virtual communities": the Whole Earth 'Lectric Link or WELL (of which Brand was naturally a member).

Turner makes the distinction between the New Left and the New Communalists, the latter of which Turner suggests "turned away from political action and toward technology and the transformation of consciousness as the primary sources of social change (2006, 4)." His interest is not precisely in the design of technology, however, or in the specific association of technology with freedom, but in the association of technology and consciousness. It was the works of Theodore Roszak (*The Making of a Counterculture,* 1969) and Charles Reich (*The Greening of America,* 1970) that provided the templates for a new kind of social change, beyond, outside, or perhaps within, the failed systems of contemporary governance and political action. What seems to make the story surprising is the countercultural *embrace* of technology—Norbert Wiener and cybernetics, Buckminster Fuller, the personal computer, to name a few examples of this embrace—and not the conventional association of communalist hippies with Luddism or pre-technological naturalism. On the contrary, it is a story of the wresting of technology from the maws of bureaucracy, hierarchy, and the "organiza-tion man"—and the association of technology with *consciousness*. Turner writes: "If the mind was the first site of social change, then information would have to become a key part of a countercultural politics. And if those politics rejected hierarchy, then the circles within circles of information and systems theory might somehow make sense not only as ideas about information but also as evidence from the natural world for the rightness of collective polity" (2006, 38).

What followed was cyberculture, hacker culture, Silicon Valley, the cult of the personal computer, the rise of the "virtual community." These slowly became associated with libertarianism through this complicated associa-tion of individual politics with consciousness. It was, as Thomas Streeter fleshes out, a romantic conception of self-mastery and actualization, an Emersonian American individualism of long and high repute melded with real and focused design and engineering work, in the context of a Califor-nia still studded with utopian hopes all up and down the coast. This story makes good cultural sense of a large part of what has come to pass in the information technology ecology of the last forty years. But the concept of liberty implied by the association of technology and libertarianism is mostly a derivative one, drawn from the political beliefs and interests of certain individuals who either identify themselves as libertarians, or who are identified as such by those who suspect them of something.

However, the diversity of political associations, and the sophistication with which people in the high tech industry think about freedom (and other values) far outweighs this vocal minority's simplistic utopias (or their critics' anxieties). There are conservatives who value strong social bonds and strong government enforcement, and there are liberals who want to make technologies serve communities over individuals; there are hackers with vigorous, anarchist schemes of mutual aid and education, and there are entrepreneurs with visions of human-scale technology projects; there are crusaders for personal privacy, and there are well-intentioned engineers working against consumerism, imperialism, and so on.

The question then remains: are the technologies that have emerged from Silicon Valley in the last forty years (the personal computer chief among them) recognizably "libertarian" in design? The question is poorly posed, in part because the definition of libertarianism routinely goes unques-tioned. Even if libertarianism designates a precise understanding of liberty (and it is not clear that it does), it may not be the most appropriate tool for the job, as it were. The rush to critique the practices of those involved may in fact obscure the ways in which freedom has both been understood and transformed as the technology of the computer has evolved. In the following section, I ask instead how we might make better sense of this story by thinking about a different conceptual analysis of freedom—that of negative and positive liberty.

Negative and Positive Liberty

Isaiah Berlin's *Two Concepts of Liberty*, delivered in 1958, rehearsed a distinction that is possible to find in nearly every canonical meditation on freedom—that between negative and positive liberty. The text is useful in part because of the care with which Berlin disentangled the various approaches to freedom as a concept. It is primarily a work of analytic philosophy, and is clearly designed to make a definitive case for how we should think about freedom generally, even if it has subsequently been subjected to significant critique.

Berlin begins by suggesting that negative and positive versions of liberty answer different questions: "the 'negative' sense [of liberty] is involved in the answer to the question 'What is the area within which the subject—a person or group of persons—is or should be left to do or be what he wants to do or be without interference by other persons? . . . the positive sense is involved in the answer to the question 'What, or who, is the source of control or interference, that can determine someone to do or be one thing rather than another?'" (Berlin 1958, 6–7).

These two questions—about the zone of control and the source of control—have very different implications, often summed up in the difference between a "freedom from" and a "freedom to," where the former usually signals a notion of freedom defined negatively (via the absence of something), while the latter signals a notion having positive content (and requiring support, legislation, or enforcement of some kind). Liberty as an absence of coercion is a definition in terms of a lack (ergo, the *negative* part): "coercion implies the deliberate interference of other human beings within the area in which I wish to act. You lack political liberty or freedom only if you are prevented from attaining your goal by human beings" (Berlin 1958, 7).

In Berlin's version of the distinction, certain things are clearly specified, such as the fact that it is *other humans* who coerce, that they do so *deliberately*, and that they interfere with *the goals of those being coerced*. By this definition any form of unintentional or serendipitous constraint is excluded.

The fact that I cannot fly, though I very much want to, is not a constraint on my freedom by this definition.[7]

However, there are a number—and it is probably a large number—of real-world cases for which this definition is not precise. The famous case of Robert Moses' design of bridges too low to allow public buses to pass into wealthy Long Island neighborhoods, for instance, raises issues: Is this interference deliberate? Is it a bridge that interferes, or is it *other people* interfering, mediated by a bridge? Is there an identifiable goal that people on a public bus had in going to Long Island (Winner 1980)? Although the facts of the case support a general sense of injustice, it is not clear that freedom, defined in this negative sense, was restricted; or to put it more precisely, it is not clear what exactly constitutes "the area within which the subject . . . should be left to do or be what he wants to be or do." Is it the bus, or Long Island, or New York, or a parkway, or something abstract like "choice of destination" or "ability to move?" Negative liberty has the enviable characteristic of being an incredibly simple definition of liberty, combined with the unfortunate disadvantage of rarely helping make sense of real-world cases.

Positive liberty, by contrast, is about the source of control, and as Berlin eloquently puts it, has a much wider remit:

The "positive" sense of the word "liberty" derives from the wish on the part of the individual to be his own master. I wish my life and decisions to depend on myself, not on external forces of whatever kind. I wish to be the instrument of my own, not of other men's, acts of will. I wish to be a subject, not an object; to be moved by reasons, by conscious purposes which are my own, not by causes which affect me, as it were, from outside. I wish to be somebody, not nobody; a doer-deciding, not being decided for, self-directed and not acted upon by external nature or by other men as if I were a thing, or an animal, or a slave capable of playing a human role, that is, of conceiving goals and policies of my own and realizing them. (Berlin 1958, 16–17)

For such a stirring and seemingly intuitive definition of liberty, it may come as a surprise that Berlin suggests positive liberty is "no better than a specious disguise for brutal tyranny." But positive liberty is dangerous not for its visions of autonomy or self-actualization per se, but because of the attempt by a person or persons to impose that vision on others. This violates the simpler and more primal definition of negative liberty: it is evil to restrict freedom in the name of freedom, however certain we are of its rightness. This is a point John Stuart Mill made forcefully in *On Liberty*.[8]

The notion of negative liberty has recently—and perhaps wrongly—come to be associated with libertarianism. Both libertarianism and negative liberty are often accused of implying the absence of government, or the removal and deregulation of markets, or the radical reliance on individual responsibility (frequently encoded today as "neoliberalism"). But this is to rush beyond the relatively narrow zone that theories of negative liberty seek to make precise: the zone of individual coercion, and more specifically, its absence. The myth promulgated about a libertarian Silicon Valley stumbles on this distinction. Libertarians are fierce partisans of negative liberty in many cases, protesting any and all attempts to enforce ideas of the good, of welfare, or of individual success. But on the contrary, they are seen (by their critics) as pushing a particular kind of positive liberty—a vision of well-being that is resolutely individualist and radically divorced from any sense of communal or collective organization or obligation, a belief they seek to enshrine in the dismantling of the state, deregulation of markets, and ever-stronger legal protections of property. What makes libertarians scary (to those who denounce them) is not that they want to be let alone, but precisely the fact that they seem to want to legislate a particularly loathsome vision of radically individual freedom on everyone. Libertarians see themselves as defending liberty; their critics see them as forcing a particular kind of liberty on others.

The association of Silicon Valley with libertarianism—even the modified libertarianism of Barbrook and Cameron's Californian Ideology or the digital utopians described by Turner—would seem to struggle with the distinction between positive and negative liberty. Or to put it differently, if there is something to be concerned about in Silicon Valley's approach to liberty, it is not that it is overly libertarian, but that it is a kind of positive liberty imposed not through government action, but through the creation and dissemination of *technologies that coerce us* and that *interfere with our goals*. In this case, it is a set of technologies that has been designed to liberate (or coerce) the individual into being a freer, and more individual, individual.

As Berlin notes, distinguishing between negative and positive liberty has the function of making a logical distinction between the area of control and the source of control. Insofar as we are talking about political liberty, that source has always been considered the government, and only secondarily the church, society, corporations, or technology. The distinction allows us to differentiate the source of control (here presumably the *designed and implemented technology*), and the area of control (what it enables or prevents us from doing, our goals). If it is the case that new technologies do coerce in this sense, then they are precisely something to which libertarians should *object*. But they rarely object, and even when they do, for instance when the area of control is defined as "personal privacy," they tend to do so by *building more technologies* to preserve privacy. Often the accusation (as well as the assertion) of libertarianism seems to confuse the source and area of control. What goals are being restricted, by what people—or by what technologies? With Berlin's text in hand, it is possible to tell the story of the development of the personal computer differently than with the blunt criticism of libertarianism. The following section explores the classic distinction of positive and negative liberty, as well as Berlin's understanding of how and why positive liberty is tied to particular understandings of human nature.

Batch Processing, Mainframes, and Freedom of (Augmented) Thought

The personal computer was once identified with bureaucratic, centralized, and standardized corporations, as Turner (2006) and Streeter (2011) remind us. Computers exemplified "instrumental reason" and the separation of means and ends; they were associated with the organization man, with the military-industrial complex, and with the "closed world" of destructive military power in Vietnam and the Cold War (Edwards 1996). They served as emblems for protestors in the 1960s decrying the psychological inauthenticity of mainstream American life. "These computers were not celebrated as fun; they were imagined as powerful . . . [The computer reached] its fullest cultural expression in HAL, the murderously intelligent computer in Stanley Kubrick's film *2001*" (Streeter 2011, 28). Similarly, Turner's book begins with the Free Speech activist Mario Savio at Berkeley in the 1960s proclaiming: "'At Cal you're little more than an IBM card'" (Savio, in Turner 2006, 12). Significant in Savio's words is the choice of IBM, one of the largest monopolies in American history, and the punch card, the emblem of so-called "batch processing" by which means and ends were effectively separated into problems and calculations.

The perception of computers as cold, impersonal symbols of control was shared just as much by people *within* the industry as those outside it sporting "I am a human being—do not fold, spindle, or mutilate" buttons. Streeter, along with Mitchell Waldrop and others, single out J. C. R. Licklider as one example (Waldrop 2001). Though he was one of the first program directors at the storied Information Processing Techniques Office at the Advanced Research Projects Agency, Licklider's vision of the potential of future computers was radical by the expectations of the day. As one of the few individuals in the early 1960s who would have had more or less unrestricted time in front of a computer, Licklider constantly sang the praises of interactivity and the power of the computer to *augment*, not to replace, human thought (Waldrop 2001, 147–149; Licklider 1960). His famous 1960 paper, "Man-Computer Symbiosis," suggested a crypto-cyborgian path toward a new humanity, an augmented intelligence greater than anything humans alone could achieve.

Licklider was far from alone in his frustrations with inaccessible mainframes locked behind closed doors, hierarchical and inefficient batch processing of computing tasks, and the guardianship of "high priests" of the machine. Innovations like Grace Hopper's early prototype of a software compiler, John Backus's FORTRAN programming language, John McCarthy's LISP programming language, and the various "time-sharing" schemes for computers were often presented as liberations from hierarchy, bureaucracy, and *constraint* (Wexelblat 1981). They enabled freedom by allowing people to work as individuals in relationship to the machine and to pursue *individual* goals, not those of an organization. Each innovation in interaction was figured as liberation from the decisions of the past. To program, compile, run, and see the output of a program—all in one sitting—was routinely represented as a kind of revelation for people, almost from the very beginning.

The concept of negative liberty helps make sense of these stories, in part. As an individual engineer or programmer in the 1950s and 1960s, you were routinely "prevented from attaining your goal by human beings" (Berlin 1958, 7) who possessed the keys to the computer room and who decided which tasks to process and when to return the results. It was a kind of power that was resented by engineers, and often described in terms of dependency and frustration—if not quite as enslavement. Most often, the language used was that of "high priests" or of the inner sanctum, a language of protestant and catholic reformation that is endemic to the cultural world of information technology (Kelty 2008, 66–76). Note that this is also a more precise sense of coercion than the diffuse public sentiment that computers contain one's essential information or control one's destiny in ways that are inaccessible or mysterious; here the constraint was directly identified with the people, processes, and corporations that interfered with a goal.

But what was that goal? In a mundane sense, it was often a problem circumscribed by other needs: solve this problem, design that system, keep track of this payroll, and so on. But in the sense given it by Licklider, the goal was something grander: *thinking*. The goal was expanding human intellect in ways that allow the exploration of problems, not just "to solve preformulated problems or to process data according to predetermined procedures" (Licklider 1960, 5). Citing Poincaré, Licklider says: "The question is not, 'What is the answer?' The question is, 'What is the question?' One of the main aims of man–computer symbiosis is to bring the computing machine effectively into the formulative parts of technical problems" (ibid., 5).

Insofar as this kind of coercion was confined to the control of a corporation over its employee, it does not violate negative freedom per se, but raises a different problem, that of the employment contract. Whether individuals freely enter into an employment relation, or are coerced, is complicated by the introduction of machinery of any kind into the workplace. Such machinery arguably impacts freedom in various modes, and the system of batch processing with mainframes computers is no different.

However, what Licklider pointed to was something else, something related to the very *development and innovation* of these machines, not just their integration into industrial or postindustrial capitalism. Licklider's vision was not about breaking down the hierarchical restraints of bureaucracy, and it was not quite the liberation from the "psychological inauthenticity" that 1960s protesters associated with corporations and the military-industrial complex. Rather Licklider was talking about what the computer would become, how it would evolve, in whose interests, and for what purposes. That he associated computing with thinking was also not new—but that he identified a restriction on thinking related to freedom was significant. Computers may replicate one kind of thought (logic and calculation, problem solving) but in their present form, they restrict another: interpretive, uncertain, problem-seeking thought. It is not "What is the answer?" but "What is the question?" Licklider forged a deep association between the *design* of future computers and *freedom of thought*. One can sense how this freedom was positive in a sense: it was not so much about how humans coerce other humans via machines, but about how machines *fail* to liberate us. If the computer of the future would liberate us, it must do so by *design*.

Although Licklider inspired a generation with visions of a "dream machine" of interactive displays, computer graphics, and "the computer as a communications medium," it was one of his star grantees, Douglas Engelbart at Stanford Research Institute, who forged the most precise association between computers and freedom of thought.[9] Engelbart's vision, as Bardini (2000) has shown, was far richer and more radical than Licklider's. Licklider was more impresario than engineer, more psychologist of "human factors" than visionary philosopher-engineer. Engelbart by contrast had a vision of the augmentation of human intelligence that was broad, evolutionary in orientation, and crafted in response to a sense of a disjunction between the complexity of the changing world and the ability of humans to control it.

In the opening to his famous 1962 report *Augmenting Human Intellect*, Engelbart specifies the kind of problem solving he wants to pursue: "We do not speak of isolated clever tricks that help in particular situations. We refer to a way of life in an integrated domain where hunches, cut-and-try, intangibles, and the human 'feel for a situation' usefully co-exist with powerful concepts, streamlined terminology and notation, sophisticated methods, and high-powered electronic aids" (1).

Engelbart's report does not directly address liberty, but it does address something crucial to any concept of liberty: the view taken of what constitutes a person, a human, a self, or human nature. Berlin's understanding of positive liberty was concerned with the ways in which those who would impose it must posit a "man divided against himself . . . the transcendent, dominant controller and the empirical bundle of desires and passions to be disciplined and brought to heel" (Berlin 1958, 19). Positive liberty is anathema when it imposes freedom on someone "for their own good," where that good is not determined by the individual. A whole range of critiques follow from this claim, but it is important to realize that at the core of Berlin's definition is the idea that humans understand and know themselves, that they are not victims of some external or internal manipulation, ideology, or desire.

There is much to say about how Engelbart constructs his vision of human nature (relying on Benjamin Lee Whorf among others) in order to speculate about the kind of machine necessary to truly act as a partner in intelligence. Engelbart insists that human potential is limited physically and evolutionarily—that is, that our capacity to face and solve complex problems is not figured as a social, political, or cultural problem of the organization of knowledge, but as a physical and evolutionary one (which includes here the evolution of language, technology, and machinery), which has been outpaced by our collective life in modernity. By constructing the limitation of human potential in this way, the design of technology becomes a liberation of a particular sort: liberation from the evolved limits of the human body itself. The true self is not so much submerged beneath the passions as latent in the technology we have yet to design.

Engelbart is nowhere explicitly concerned in the report with the problem of liberty or coercion. Rather, the language of the report tends to discuss the envisioned computer of the future in terms of slavery: The computer will be a servant to the human, "a fast and agile helper" that can serve many masters without keeping any of them waiting, but one so intimately connected to the activity of thinking that, like language, it might become indistinguishable from that activity (Engelbart 1962, 70). In a kind of technological Hegelian moment of recognition, our servant-machines will confront us, augment us, and lead us into a domain of human thought impossible in the bodies we have been given by nature.

This is, to be sure, not a question of negative liberty at all. In Berlin's terms other humans must prevent one from achieving a goal, and that is not the case here; just as the inability to fly is not a restriction on freedom, neither is the inability to think. But it might be a case of positive liberty. Berlin, recall, associates positive liberty with autonomy and self-actualization ("I wish to be a subject, not an object; to be, moved by reasons, by conscious purposes which are my own, not by causes which affect me, as it were, from outside.") But the idea of a positive liberty dependent on the existence of external technologies and "augmented thought" would seem to contradict Berlin's notion. Berlin's definition is one of an authentic liberty fully immanent to the autonomous rational thinking human. But as he points out, it is an immediate step in theories of positive liberty to raise the question, "May I not be a slave to nature? Or to my own 'unbridled' passions?" As soon as this internal division of the self is allowed, and an outside force admitted that shapes who we are, it becomes possible to order them, to claim that the "higher self" is the result of civilization, education, and social order, while the lower self is a creature of passion, unreasonable, addicted, and enslaved by nature—*evolved* to be a certain way, perhaps.

It is not so very different, therefore, to see Engelbart's work as introducing a similar distinction: the lower self is that unaugmented intelligence which is the result of nature, of evolution, and which is incapable of facing the tasks and problems thrown at it by our complex world, and only through augmentation will we achieve the state of a "higher self" capable of responding. It is an easy step to suggest that others be coerced in their own interests, that we know what they need better than they do themselves, and what they need is augmented intelligence. The *problem* we face is that the world is too complex for humans (in their current form) to understand; the solution is to augment humanity with tools that can understand it—and to do it before we destroy ourselves.[10]

Engelbart does not make this argument explicitly. Nor does anyone necessarily read him this way. But asking about the concept of positive and negative liberty allows us to make sense of what Engelbart proposed for the future design of computing, and explains why freedom is in an uncertain and perhaps difficult tension with that design.

Augmenting Human Intellect is not the only form Engelbart's influence has taken. Engelbart is remembered much more widely for the 1968 demonstration of the oN-Line System. This demonstration of a computing system (or more accurately, a *simulation* of a proposed computer system) took place simultaneously at the Stanford Research Institute in Stanford (where Engelbart sat) and an auditorium in San Francisco (where the audience sat) via a rudimentary, experimental network link. The demonstration included almost every now-familiar aspect of a personal computer: an early prototype of the mouse, remote network access, word processing, files, desktops, cut and paste, and a host of other techniques that would only slowly be brought into existence over the ensuing decade (most visibly by the engineers at Xerox PARC and the young founders of Apple Computer). The demonstration had a galvanizing effect on a generation of young engineers primed to see a kind of liberation in the demonstration. Whatever the computer had been up until that point, it was now poised to become something radically different—a true augmentation of human cognitive possibility. All that was needed was for it to be correctly designed and brought to the people (see figure 10.3).

Engelbart's liberation was about the freedom to think and to do more than humans could by themselves—incomplete and fragile beings that we are. Only through augmentation could our true selves emerge and come to grips with our dangerously complex world. It was of a piece with the critiques of Reich and Roszak; the constriction and psychological inauthenticity of the 1950s must be replaced by the expanded consciousness of the 1970s. It was of a piece with certain visions of the New Left as well, especially the focus on participatory democracy and the critique of the military-industrial complex (if not quite the large bureaucratic corporation itself). Computers could lead the way, if they were designed to augment rather than restrict human development.

Engelbart's vision had obvious appeal to young designers, engineers, and entrepreneurs in the late 1960s and early 1970s. Chief among them were folks like Seymour Papert, Alan Kay, and Ted Nelson. Papert, an MIT mathematician and disciple of Jean Piaget, created a tool for teaching programming to children; Kay created a prototype iPad called the Dynabook in the early 1970s. Both clearly associated personal freedom with education and childhood and a desire to bring computers to kids as early as possible— to augment thought from the get-go. Papert and Kay sought to make it possible for all humans to augment their intelligence and their freedom (and here is the objection) whether they wanted to or not. Nelson, for his part, sought to bring these innovations and augmentations to people as broadly as possible, and in the very idiom of liberation (see figure 10.2).

What Licklider and Engelbart had understood early on—that it was the design of computers that was the proper locus of intervention if one wanted to bring a different future into the present—Kay and Papert took to heart. They designed software systems and programming languages, not just individual devices, that instantiated a particular vision of positive

Freedom.

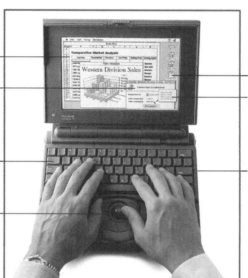

liberty: creativity, constructive learning, expressive communication, the ability to think unconstrained, like an artist or a scientist. Kay's work at Xerox PARC led directly to the design of the Alto, and through that to the Lisa and the Apple Macintosh. Not only this, but many were also involved in the debates about the computer and human freedom conducted among scholars like Hubert and Stuart Dreyfus, Joseph Weizenbaum, Sherry Turkle, and others. Not only did a new device, a new mode of thinking enabled by machines, emerge, but so too a reconstructed concept (or concepts) of human freedom.

Conclusion

The story I have told here is just one part of a much larger story, but even here it is clear that the practice of freedom was transformed. Prior to the innovations of the personal computer, freedom was a practice confined to an autonomous human subject in dialogue with other human subjects. The theory of positive and negative liberty in Berlin explicitly privileges the human capacity to coerce or escape coercion, and worries over the idea of a "man divided against himself." Large-scale bureaucratically controlled, batch-processing mainframes are not just emblems of this view of freedom; they literally encode it in their structure and use. It is the reaction against this design—and toward the individualized, interactive devices that lead to the personal computer—from which a new practice of freedom takes shape, an "augmented thought" perceived as something that will enable humans to think in ways not presently possible, and perhaps enable them to protect themselves. The justification for these innovations, however, makes more sense as a kind of positive liberty: these innovations will liberate us, by their designs, from our incapacity or failure as thinking beings, whether we want to be freed or not. Innovation in the name of freedom leads to a form of coercion—and it will only be with more innovation, also in the name of freedom, that we will be freed from that coercion.

One critique would be simply to point out that our capacity for freedom is not contained in our tools and technologies, but is rather expanded by them. Arguably what Licklider or Engelbart wanted (and what Apple

Figure 10.3
A 1991 advertisement for the Apple PowerBook 100/140/170. Part of a four-part advertisement about the "modest requests" consumers expressed for the next generation of computers. The other images in the series are boldly titled Power; Simplicity; and Humanity.

among others delivered) was not a particular substantive definition of freedom built into our technologies, but a new capacity for *any kind* of freedom. This may be so, but even if it is, it requires a reconstruction of the idea of freedom. Whatever freedom *used to be*, we didn't have it until we had smartphones (note the focus on augmented intelligence in the very name) and iPads and Facebook accounts—and what's more, we (or at least Isaiah Berlin) did not know we needed these things in order to achieve freedom. The essential tension between the historical design of computer technologies and the freedom we possess is not resolved by insisting on a static distinction between positive and negative liberty, a distinction that maintains a stable concept progressively enlarged by the technological innovations of human beings. Instead we now occupy a world in which our very ability to become free depends on our ability to design it into our technologies—and yet we don't have a theory, positive or normative, that would guide us in this endeavor.

Acknowledgments

Thanks to Tarleton Gillespie, Pablo Boczkowski, and Kirsten Foot for inviting me to participate in this project; to Greg Downey, Steven Jackson, Tarleton Gillespie, Luis Felipe Rosado Murillo, and Hannah Landecker for their careful readings of this article; and to the Science Studies Program at UC San Diego, the Center for Science, Technology, Medicine and Society Program at UC Berkeley, and the Interdisciplinary Humanities Center at UC Santa Barbara for invitations to present this work and for providing fantastic feedback. Thanks also to Zoe Borovsky of UCLA Library and Glen Worthey and Polly Armstrong of Stanford Special Collections for helping try to track down the Apple Ad. And thanks to Nancy Bixler and MIT Press for excellent editorial help.

Notes

1. The *Freedom to Tinker* blog run by Edward Felten is at https://freedom-to-tinker.com/, accessed April 1, 2013. The Association for Computing Machinery and the Computer Professionals for Social Responsibility run the conference each year; see http://www.cfp.org/, accessed April 1, 2013. Net neutrality is primarily associated with issues of *equality*, and in particular *equality of access* (or in legal terminology, *nondiscrimination*; see Wu 2003, 2004). A neutral net is one that separates content from conduit and gives every individual or firm equal access to the network and the ability to innovate (Gillespie 2006).

The definition of Free Software is available at the Free Software Foundation website, http://www.gnu.org/philosophy/free-sw.html, accessed April 1, 2013. The FreedomBox was initiated by Eben Moglen's analysis of the dangers of cloud computing; see http://freedomboxfoundation.org/, accessed April 1, 2013. The Freedom Fone is an open-source telephony system in use in parts of Africa; see http://www.freedomfone.org/, accessed April 1, 2013. Other examples include Diaspora, a free software-inspired replacement for Facebook and other social media (see http://diasporaproject.org/, accessed April 1, 2013) and Tor, or "The Onion Router," a longstanding privacy protection system (see https://www.torproject.org/, accessed April 1, 2013). Among the many different distributions of Linux, Liberté Linux is perhaps the most appropriate example; see http://dee.su/liberte, accessed April 1, 2013.

2. In a recent review of "The consequences of the Internet for politics," Farrell (2012) makes this explicit, arguing that once political scientists can disentangle the relevant causal factors at play, it will no longer be necessary to study the Internet as such. The Internet will either be assimilated into political theory without harm, or retreat into the background of everyday life along with other irrelevant invisible material infrastructures.

3. I use the terms "liberty" and "freedom" more or less interchangeably. There are some arguments against this indifference, such as Pitkin (1988) makes, but I am in reasonably respectable company in asserting that there is little distinction.

4. Berlin's work is not the origin of the distinction, but it is the first to label it as such. The distinction is clearly laid out in the work of Hobbes, Rousseau, Mill, and many others.

5. See http://www.seasteading.org/about/, accessed April 1, 2013.

6. The six-hour-long 2010 Adam Curtis documentary called *All Watched over by Machines of Loving Grace*, for instance, not only associates Ayn Rand with Silicon Valley, but in the process implicates 1960s systems theory in ecology, Richard Dawkins's theory of the selfish gene, civil war in the Democratic Republic of the Congo, the Rwandan genocide, and the Chinese Politburo, all as causes of the 2007–2008 financial crisis. A clever send-up of Curtis provides a nice critique in a succinct three-minute film called *A Loving Trap*, http://www.youtube.com/watch?v=x1bX3F7uTrg, accessed April 1, 2013.

7. An oblique but effective critique of this notion comes from the field of disability studies; see, e.g., Richard Hull (2009).

8. "The Object of this essay is to assert one very simple principle . . . that the sole end for which mankind are warranted, individually or collectively, in interfering with the liberty of action of any of their number, is self-protection" (Mill 1989, 13).

9. Engelbart's work at the Stanford Research Institute was funded in small part by Licklider's program at ARPA (though at the time of that funding in 1967, ARPA was under the direction of Robert Taylor).

10. As an aside, it should also be possible to see clearly in this approach the origins of "transhumanism" or "singulatarian" arguments about the fate of humanity that have become similarly strongly associated with Silicon Valley, especially in the last decade.

11 Rethinking Repair

Steven J. Jackson

"There is a crack in everything. That's how the light gets in."
—Leonard Cohen, *Anthem*[1]

What world does contemporary information technology inhabit? Is it the imaginary nineteenth-century world of progress and advance, novelty and invention, open frontiers and endless development? Or the twenty-first-century world of risk and uncertainty, growth and decay, and fragmentation, dissolution, and breakdown?

This chapter is an exercise in broken world thinking. It asks what happens when we take erosion, breakdown, and decay, rather than novelty, growth, and progress, as our starting points in thinking through the nature, use, and effects of information technology and new media. Broken world thinking is both normative and ontological, in the sense that it makes claims about the nature of technology and its relationship to broader social worlds, some of which may differ from deep-rooted cultural assumptions. But it is also empirical and methodological, an argument and provocation toward doing new and different kinds of research, and new and different kinds of politics, in media and technology studies today.

There are two basic components of the approach advocated here. The first is an appreciation of the real limits and fragility of the worlds we inhabit—natural, social, and technological—and a recognition that many of the stories and orders of modernity (or whatever else we choose to call the past two-hundred-odd years of euro-centered human history) are in process of coming apart, perhaps to be replaced by new and better stories and orders, but perhaps not. We know, now irrefutably, that the natural systems we have long lived within and relied on have been altered beyond return (though not necessarily beyond repair, in the sense articulated here); by any reasonable expectation, we are now living, as Bill McKibben (2010) has argued, on a sort of Earth 2.0 in which many of the old socionatural bets are off. The instabilities of the postwar economic order and the social relations attendant upon it have recently come home to roost (as many of us are reminded as we watch friends, neighbors, and family members fall out of the hopes, comforts, and securities of the middle class). The form and possibility of the "modern infrastructural ideal" (Graham and Marvin 2001) is increasingly under threat, as cracks (sometimes literal ones) show up in our bridges, our highways, our airports, and the nets of our social welfare systems. For these and other reasons, broken world thinking asserts that breakdown, dissolution, and change, rather than innovation, development, or design as conventionally practiced and thought about are the key themes and problems facing new media and technology scholarship today.

Attached to this, however, comes a second and more hopeful approach: namely, a deep wonder and appreciation for the ongoing activities by which stability (such as it is) is maintained, the subtle arts of repair by which rich and robust lives are sustained against the weight of centrifugal odds, and how sociotechnical forms and infrastructures, large and small, get not only broken but *restored*, one not-so-metaphoric brick at a time. On this road we travel the path from despair to admiration, even reverence, and are confronted above all by the remarkable resilience, creativity, and sheer magnitude of the work represented in the ongoing maintenance and reproduction of established order.

Here, then, are two radically different forces and realities. On one hand, a fractal world, a centrifugal world, an always-almost-falling-apart world. On the other, a world in constant process of fixing and reinvention, reconfiguring and reassembling into new combinations and new possibilities—a topic of both hope and concern. It is a world of pain and possibility, creativity and destruction, innovation and the worst excesses of leftover habit and power.

The fulcrum of these two worlds is *repair*: the subtle acts of care by which order and meaning in complex sociotechnical systems are maintained and transformed, human value is preserved and extended, and the complicated work of fitting to the varied circumstances of organizations, systems, and lives is accomplished. Repair in this connotation has a literal and material dimension, filled with immediate questions: Who fixes the devices and systems we "seamlessly" use? Who maintains the infrastructures within and against which our lives unfold? But it also speaks directly to "the social," if we still choose to cut the world in this way: how are *human* orders broken and restored (and again, who does this work)?

Some of these effects are captured in the language of "articulation work" so usefully described by Susan Leigh Star and Anselm Strauss (1999). Articulation is about fit, or more precisely, the art of fitting, the myriad (often invisible) activities that enable and sustain even the most seemingly natural or automatic forms of order in the world. Articulation supports the smooth interaction of parts within complex sociotechnical wholes, adjusting and calibrating each to each. In building connections, it builds meaning and identity, sorting out ontologies on the fly rather than mixing and matching between fixed and stable entities. Articulation lives first and foremost in practice, not representation; as its proper etymology suggests, it's a creature of bones, not words. When articulation fails, systems seize up, and our sociotechnical worlds become stiff, arthritic, unworkable.

The same broad features characterize the work of repair—itself a facet or form of articulation work (and vice versa). Repair is about space and function—the extension or safeguarding of capabilities in danger of decay. But it is also an inescapably timely phenomenon, bridging past and future in distinctive and sometimes surprising ways. Repair inherits an old and layered world, making history but not in the circumstances of its choosing. It accounts for the durability of the old, but also the appearance of the new (a different way of approaching the problem of innovation, as will be discussed: behind and prior to the origin stands the fix). Above all, repair occupies and constitutes an *aftermath*, growing at the margins, breakpoints, and interstices of complex sociotechnical systems as they creak, flex, and bend their way through time. It fills in the moment of hope and fear in which bridges from old worlds to new worlds are built, and the continuity of order, value, and meaning gets woven, one tenuous thread at a time. And it does all this quietly, humbly, and all the time.

So the world is always breaking; it's in its nature to break. That breaking is generative and productive, in ways that will be sketched later in this chapter. It is also consequential, and many of the things we care about as media and technology scholars turn out to be implicated in precisely such moments. And it is always being recuperated and reconstituted through repair. The question then becomes what we make of these facts, and what we do next.

Shipbreaking

One place to begin is the following:

Figure 11.1
Edward Burtynsky, *Shipbreaking #4*.[2]

The image, *Shipbreaking #4*, comes from photographer Edward Burtynsky's beautiful and evocative series on the shipbreaking industry of Bangladesh. As the series proceeds, we follow Burtynsky's lens through the amazing process by which aging ocean vessels (the bone and sinew of globalization) are beached, stripped, and dismantled; a parallel series, *Ship Recycling*, follows the ghostly afterlife of these ships, as their fragments get dispersed and repurposed through a variety of local markets. Or if the work of the shipbreakers seems too exotic or obscure, consider any of the following: the e-waste scavengers who reclaim precious metals, often under horrendous and unregulated conditions, from processors, monitors, printers, and cell phones in landfills around the world (Burrell 2012); the ubiquitous cell-phone repair stands that now show up (alongside food stalls, bicycle repair, and jerry-can gas operations) as regular features of roadside commerce in sub-Saharan Africa and other developing countries (Jackson, Pompe, and Krieshok 2011, 2012); or the work of the Wikipedia editors, crafting, honing, and maintaining entries against error, ambiguity, and vandalism.

Burtynsky's photos and the additional examples given earlier tell us important things about the themes of breakdown, maintenance, and repair raised here. The first is the extent to which such work is rendered invisible under our normal modes of picturing and theorizing technology. Burtynsky's photos share, in exquisite detail, a side or moment of technological life that goes for the most part unrecognized. On one level, these activities are entirely routine, a normal and inevitable feature of technology's course in the world. Things are made, and things fall apart. Objects are produced, and objects are discarded. Technologies are developed, and technologies fade into history, leaving rarely more than a trace behind. But our modes of academic and popular representation around these two moments of technological life are deeply unbalanced. If we are to understand maintenance, repair, and technology more broadly, scenes such as Burtynsky's must be made empirically and conceptually familiar, even normal. This may require some effort of the analytic imagination, trained as we have been in technology and the social sciences by the primacy of production and design. It may help then to be reminded of the sheer weight and value that such activities represent. By some estimates, 80 percent of the world's commercial ocean fleets end up on the beaches of Bangladesh or in neighboring India in this way. And 80 percent of the domestic steel industry in Bangladesh (which has no naturally occurring ore deposits) is sourced in this way. However far from a Western and productivist imagination, these activities are anything but marginal.

Burtynsky also reminds us of the consequences and distributions of breakdown and repair—a point of significance for the discussions of power and knowledge that follow. These are not, in almost every case, Bangladeshi ships coming home to a final resting spot, nor are the workers on these beaches attached or supported (save by this one connection) to the wider worlds of trade and commerce that these ships have come from. (That, indeed, is why the ships come *here*: to be disassembled and repurposed free of the responsibilities and entanglements that would necessarily follow in other places.) Because we don't see it, it is easy to forget that the forms of breakdown and repair practiced on the beaches of Bangladesh come at the end of a complex and consequential distribution, with deep and troubled ties to global economic flows and structures; as Doreen Massey (1994) reminds and Burtynsky affirms, some are more on the receiving end of globalization than others.

Finally, the beautiful ebb and flow of Burtynsky's images remind us that while their modern flavor and intensities may vary, activities such as this are ancient, even timeless ones, and have always been part of the story of technology, humans, and the sea. Activities such as this form part of the secret history of breakdown, maintenance, and repair that has always sustained (but invisibly) the higher profile stories of exploration, empire, and globalization that shipping, quite literally, has carried. This is a point with deep and surprisingly invisible roots. Ask yourself this: for all the representations of great ships in history you've encountered, at what times and in what forms have you seen such vessels? In almost every instance it will be at moments of birth, or at the heights of strength and glory: the christening before the maiden voyage, rounding the cape, facing down the Spanish fleet, and so on. But what happens (or *happened*) to these ships? Save for the special cases of hostile sinking, shipwreck, or honorable retirement and preservation, it was this: they were disassembled, repurposed, stripped, and turned into other things, in sites and locations like the shipbreaking beaches of Bangladesh that have dropped out of history and imagination.

This chapter argues that breakdown, maintenance, and repair constitute crucial but vastly understudied sites or moments within the worlds of new media and technology today. It argues that much of what we care about as media and technology scholars is implicated or enacted in exactly such moments, and that the productivist bias of the field obscures this fact. It asks how we might begin to think differently around the phenomena of breakdown, maintenance, and repair, and how we might use this difference to launch other and more hopeful programs of research. And it argues for the contributions that broken world thinking and a repair-centered ethics might make to the project of defining an appropriate moral and practical stance vis-à-vis the world of media and technology today.

Repair and Innovation

At first glance, nothing could seem farther apart than the apparently separate questions of innovation and repair. Innovation, in the dominant coding, comes first: at the start of the technology chain, in moments of quasi-mythical origination, a creature of garage-turned-corporate engineers, operating with or without the benefits of market research and user experience operations. Repair comes later, when screens and buttons fail, firmware is corrupted, and the iPhone gets shipped back to wherever iPhones come from. (We generally prefer to think not at all of what happens *after* such moments, in the piles of e-junk accumulated in attics and landfills or shipped overseas to Africa or Asia.) In scientific computation and collaboration, the language of innovation is generally reserved for new and computationally intensive "bright and shiny tools," while repair tends to disappear altogether, or at best is relegated to the mostly neglected story of people (researchers, information managers, beleaguered field technicians) working to fit such artifacts to the sticky realities of field-level practices and needs. In both cases, dominant productivist imaginings of technology locate innovation, with its unassailable standing, cultural cachet, and valorized economic value, at the top of some change or process, while repair lies somewhere else: lower, later, or after innovation in process and worth.

But this is a false and partial representation of how worlds of technology actually work, when they work. In practice, there's nothing unassailable about the contribution that innovation (in this narrow sense) makes. Against fans and critics of design alike, innovation rarely if ever inheres in moments of origination, passing unproblematically into the bodies of the objects and practices such work informs. For this reason, the *efficacy* of innovation in the world is limited—until extended, sustained, and completed in repair. The remarkable qualities and energies that innovation names and unleashes—creativity, invention, imagination, and artfulness—are therefore distributed more broadly in the technology landscape than our dominant discourses of innovation and the systems of economic, professional, and social value built around them are keen to acknowledge. They also often depend, as the standpoint discussion to follow will explore, on precisely the kinds of breakdowns charted here. From this perspective, worlds of maintenance and repair and the instances of breakdown that occasion them are not separate or alternative to innovation, but sites for some of its most interesting and consequential operations.

For the same basic reasons, repair—perhaps especially under conditions of modern industrial production—may constitute one of our most significant sites and sources of sociotechnical difference. Whether at the level of national "technological styles" (Hughes 1987) that shape and differentiate the nature of "same" technologies in different national contexts, or the simple but consequential variations by which industrial commodities are brought into, enlivened, and sustained within the circumstances of individual homes and lives, repair may constitute an important engine by which technological difference is produced and fit is accomplished. It may also be the case that breakdown and repair are very often the aspects or portions of broader technological systems that show the most variation across national, cultural, or other comparative contexts, as a growing body of work on the distinctive repair ecologies of the developing world has begun to demonstrate (see, for example, Jackson, Pompe, and Krieshok 2012; Burrell 2012). To repurpose Tolstoy, "All working technologies are alike. All broken technologies are broken in their own way."[3]

How might we begin to reverse this dominant view, and reimagine or better recognize the forms of innovation, difference, and creativity embedded in repair? Burtynsky once again gets us started. One of the more impressive features of Burtynsky's series and the cultural practices it references is the apparent technological simplicity with which Bangladeshi shipbreaking is conducted. Confronted with the bewildering size and array of a modern ocean freighter (and in sharp contrast to the technological conditions surrounding its production), teams of workers armed with nothing more sophisticated than a blowtorch are able to separate, dismantle, and repurpose a ship and its constituent parts in a matter of weeks. Under anything other than the most stubborn of productivist imaginations, this activity can only appear as a remarkable feat of innovation, and the site of a remarkable and distributed expertise.

Or, to take an example closer to home, consider the Internet. As explored by historians like Janet Abbate (1999). the incredible development of the network form and capacity of the early Internet—surely one of the central innovation stories of our day—did not follow anything like the smooth or automatic curve that production-driven or law-like representations of IT growth have suggested (think here of the various "laws"—Moore's, Kryder's, Butter's, and so on—that have been offered to explain the explosive growth of computational processing, storage, and network transmission capacities). Instead, as Abbate documents, the Internet grew by *breaking*, bumping up against the limits of existing protocols and practices and working around them, leaving behind almost by accident some of the properties that we now enumerate as key and distinctive virtues of the Internet as an infrastructural form. Far from being a generalized cultural tendency or a property of individual minds, innovation in the technology space, as in culture more generally, is therefore organized around problems. This makes innovation simultaneously specific and in some measure collective in nature. And its engine is breakdown and repair.

Such starting points might lead us toward new and alternative programs of empirical research in the technology and innovation space, with special attention to the existence, dynamics, and tensions of innovation beyond moments of ideation, design, and up-front adoption. For example, it is telling that some of the most consequential work emerging from early ethnographic work in the IT design and human–computer interaction fields—some of it conducted in industrial research labs—has centered on repair (Suchman 1987, Orr 1996). The same broad interest has begun to show in other fields ranging from sociology (Henke 2000, Graham and Thrift 2007) and architecture (Brand 1994), to environmental planning (Hetherington 2004) and engineering (Petroski 2006). My own work with collaborators in this space (Jackson, Pompe, and Krieshok 2011, 2012) has explored the distinctively different landscapes of technology repair that characterize the extension of information technology infrastructure in sub-Saharan Africa. If the broad sense of this chapter is correct, such early empirical forays only begin to scratch the surface of the possibilities and forms of creativity, innovation, and difference to be found in the work of repair.

Knowledge/Power and Repair

Thorny questions of knowledge and power have, since Foucault (1980) at least, formed a crucial strand in our thinking about the nature and status of technology in social life. We know, from experience and long traditions of work in the social sciences, that questions of visibility and invisibility may be intimately linked to power. The ability to limit or manage external visibility of our lives and work, or conversely to exert the force of our gaze on others, has long been recognized as a crucial site for the operation of power in institutions, in workplaces, and in culture in general. At the same time, visibility may be tied crucially to systems of reward and recognition: think only of the differential visibility of faculty and nighttime cleaning staff on American university campuses and its relation to the highly skewed distributions of income that follow.

But a second set of links among visibility, power, and knowledge in the context of maintenance and repair needs to be considered, one with perhaps special relevance to the analytic and methodological interests that frame this volume. The question is this: can repair sites and repair actors claim special insight or knowledge, by virtue of their positioning vis-à-vis the worlds of technology they engage? Can breakdown, maintenance, and repair confer special epistemic advantage in our thinking about technology? Can the fixer know and see different things—indeed, different worlds—than the better-known figures of "designer" or "user"? Following on the claims of Hegelian, Marxian, and feminist theorists, can we identify anything like a standpoint epistemology of repair?

The question has deep and suggestive roots. Social theorists of multiple stripes have acknowledged the special place of breakdown in the opening to thought of heretofore hidden dynamics, processes, and powers. Take

Heidegger's notion of "tool-being," built around the central distinction between tools that are "ready-to-hand" versus "present-at-hand" (Heidegger [1977] 2008b; see also Harman 2002). In the former state, technologies function as anticipated, do and stay where they're supposed to, and therefore sink below the level of conscious reflection. In the latter, the material world resists, obstructs, or frustrates action, and therefore calls attention to itself (precisely because we must now work to figure out and overcome barriers in our no-longer seamless world). The same basic insight informs American pragmatist theories of mind and consciousness. For theorists like James ([1907] 2000) and Dewey (1896, 1922), the possibility of consciousness begins where habit and routine fail and thought is called on to take over for rote or reflexive action. Broadly parallel insights by Vygotsky (1962) and subsequent generations of activity theorists position breakdowns or gaps (for example, the crucial distance between learner and teacher that constitutes a generative "zone of proximal development") not as barriers or irreducible divides, but rather dynamic resources and engines for change. It is therefore precisely in moments of breakdown that we learn to see and engage our technologies in new and sometimes surprising ways. The same broad principle has been taken up in more recent work in new media and technology studies, for example, Bowker and Star's (1999) observation that technologies and practices which rise (or sink) to the level of infrastructure are frequently invisible until breakdown, and that special acts and moments of "infrastructural inversion" may be required to call these phenomena and their associated politics back to the center of thought and action.

Such insights call attention to the world-disclosing properties of breakdown, and the distinct epistemic advantages that can follow from moving repair (and repair workers) to the center of our thinking about new media and technology today. Breakdown disturbs and sets in motion worlds of possibility that disappear under the stable or accomplished form of the artifact. Thus a standpoint epistemology of repair may offer a different response to the longstanding problem of commodity fetishism, by which the meaning and politics of technology are obscured, stripped, and neutered, and the fiction of separate "social" and "technological" worlds is produced. If Marxism seeks to disrupt the commodity fiction of the object by connecting it backward to moments of origin, discovering the congealed forms of human labor, power and interests that are built into objects at their moment of production, broken world thinking draws our attention around the sociality of objects forward, into the ongoing forms of labor, power, and interest—neither dead nor congealed—that underpin the ongoing survival of things as objects in the world. In doing so, it may hold up a clear and revealing light to relations of value and order that are sometimes made invisible under the smooth functioning of complex sociotechnical systems.

Repair, Maintenance, and the Ethics of Care

Finally, foregrounding maintenance and repair as an aspect of technological work invites not only new functional but also *moral* relations to the world of technology. It references what is in fact a very old but routinely forgotten relationship of humans to things in the world: namely, an ethics of mutual care and responsibility.

An important source for this thinking comes from the world of feminist scholarship, in particular an interrelated body of work emerging from the 1970s through the 1990s across the fields of ethics, sociology, and political theory. Against deontological theories of truth and ethics and the virtues of impartiality and universalism such theories upheld (think Rawls's [1971]) "veil of ignorance" and the theory of justice that was built on it), this body of work sought its grounding in the strength, variance, and responsibility of interhuman relations. From this perspective, to be human is to bear certain burdens of ethical dependence and responsibility vis-à-vis a world of other ethical actors. Those burdens are shaped and discharged in specific rather than categorical relations. Running through and beneath the whole system is an "ethics of care," predicated on a baseline moral relationship that linked, bound, and shaped ethical responsibility in chains of mutual entanglement and dependency. This ethics constitutes the basis of political claims making, and the condition of possibility for a collective moral life (Gilligan 1982). It also establishes the moral baseline or starting point from which we might begin to recognize and discharge our moral responsibilities in the world—vis-à-vis other ethical actors, but also an expansionary world of things that we, individually and collectively, are increasingly implicated in producing and consuming.

But why should we care about care? For the purposes of understanding media and technology—how it's produced, what it does, what powers and freedoms it opens up and forecloses—the language of care does double work. As elaborated here, it speaks to the ongoing work of maintaining media artifacts, systems, and technologies; it is itself a form of tailoring, appropriation, and resistance (to use language more commonly appearing in media and technology scholarship). But it also opens up an important moral and political terrain. To care for something (an animal, a child, a sick relative, or a technological system) is to bear and affirm a moral relation to it. For material artifacts, this goes beyond the instrumental or functional relations that usually characterize the attachments between people and things. Care brings the worlds of action and meaning back together, and reconnects the necessary work of maintenance with the forms of attachment that so often (but invisibly, at least to analysts) sustain it. We care because we care.

Thus, the ethics of repair admits of a possibility denied or forgotten by both the crude functionalism of the technology field and a more traditionally humanist ethics (which has mostly ignored technology anyway). What if we care about our technologies, and do so in more than a trivial way? This feature or property has sometimes been extended to technologies in the past, but usually only ones that come out of deep folk or craft traditions, and rarely the products of a modern industrial culture. Heidegger's writings, for example, are full of such distinctions between modern and premodern technologies (centered on such canonical figures as bridges and jugs), which confront and engage the world in radically different ways: for modern technologies, after the manner of "testing" ([1977] 2008b); for folk and craft devices, under a gentler and more supple form of "gathering" ([1977] 2008a). Richard Sennett (2009) has written beautifully of traditions of craft and the special relationship between worker and the object of labor this has historically produced. The decline of craft traditions—which Sennett extends in principle to modern pursuits as varied as medicine and computer programming, parenting and citizenship—constitutes a significant weakening of our connection to the worlds of goods and work we inhabit today.

Some of the best and most intriguing work in new media and technology studies today has begun to challenge and question this assumption, for example Sherry Turkle's (2007) insistence on the deep and meaningful relations between humans and "evocative objects;" Lucy Suchman's (2006) attention to "affiliative objects" and the work of human–machine reconfiguration at the heart of much information research and technology today; N. Katherine Hayles's (1999) posthumanist exploration of the deep and growing entanglements between the worlds of people and of things in robotics and artificial intelligence; and Bruno Latour's (2004) and Donna Haraway's (1991) alternative treatments of cyborg or collectivist ontologies, presenting ways of thinking that *don't* rest on the presumption of a bright red line between people and things running through our lives and politics.

The tricky proposition for media and technology studies posed by broken world thinking and other posthumanist approaches is this: is it possible to love, and love deeply, a world of things? Can we bear a substantive ethical, even moral, relationship to categories of objects long consigned to a realm of thin functionalism (a mistake that many of the dominant languages of technology research and design—"usability," "affordances," and so on—tends to reify)? What if we can build new and different forms of solidarity with our objects (and they with us)? And what if, beneath the nose of scholarship, this is what we do every day?

How to Fix Technology Studies

These three themes—innovation, knowledge/power, and the ethics of care—constitute missing elements or dimensions of the way we in new media and technology studies typically think about breakdown, maintenance, and repair (when we think about it at all). But they also raise new challenges and opportunities in the study of technology more generally, some of which connect to the very old problem of how to frame a more humane and progressive politics of technology.

We should begin by guarding against the twin analytic dangers of nostalgia and heroism, two properties that have often challenged left-leaning and progressive thinking about technology in the past. To begin, while broken world thinking calls special attention to the work by which technologies and practices are sustained in the world, it has no automatic preference for stasis over change—another good reason for putting innovation (rather than preservation or conservation) front and center in our discussions of maintenance and repair. Nor does it hearken back to a lost age of harmony and balance in our relationships with technology. While it's true that different technologies emerge from and instantiate different regimes of maintenance and repair, the form of broken world thinking advocated here rejects the idea of making this the basis for large-scale distinctions between, for example, modern and premodern technologies (one of the places where the broken world thinking advocated here departs from Heidegger [1977] [2008b] and later-twentieth-century critical theorists of technology, from Marcuse [1964] to Ellul [1964]). By the same token, repair is not always heroic or directed toward noble ends, and may function as much in defense as in resistance to antidemocratic and antihumanist projects. One thinks here of the remarkable recuperative routines and strategies by which the atrocities of Nazi ambition and the Nazi war machine were normalized and sustained within the production systems and civil society of war-time Germany (Arendt 1963, Goldhagen 1996).

Such cautionary notes aside, broken world thinking offers fresh potential to both longstanding and emergent approaches in media and technology studies today. First, and if nothing else, it can help us think beyond the remarkably restricted and usually binary sets of actors that have dominated media and technology studies to date: senders and receivers, producers and consumers, designers and users. The world of technology is more complex and less orderly than that, full of dynamics, tensions, and powers that neat binary distinctions—and the systems of explanation built on them—struggle to explain. Modes of thought that expand our cast of characters, including but certainly not limited to the breakers, fixers, and maintainers highlighted here, are therefore necessary and promising additions to the field.

Second, attention to maintenance and repair may help to redirect our gaze from moments of production to moments of sustainability and the myriad forms of activity by which the shape, standing, and meaning of objects in the world is produced and sustained—a feature especially valuable in a field too often occupied with the shock of the new. More robust theoretical and empirical engagement with maintenance and repair can help remedy the productivist bias that persists in some of the field's central approaches: the social construction of technology, for example, with its emphasis on up-front moments of stabilization and path dependency (Bijker 1997, Hughes 1987); studies of technology or network diffusion (Rogers [1962] 2003), with their emphasis on the spread of technology or messages with arguably less regard for local variations and staying power in the sites they travel to; or concerns with media or technological appropriation (Silverstone 1994) which still tend to emphasize early moments of encounter and domestication in the encounter between technology and social groups. Robust attention to maintenance and repair work may complement and extend the core research interests of any and all of these programs, and is certainly not opposed in spirit or principle to any; indeed, insofar as broken world thinking adds weight to the argument against technology's autonomy and self-sufficiency, it extends the core move toward the socialization of knowledge and technology shared by each.

Third, maintenance and repair may have particular contributions to make to our thinking around the *timeliness* of technology—something we have, as a field, been remarkably bad at to date. Some of the reasons for this are obvious and already referenced: the privileging of design and production, emphasis on moments of initial encounter, and general predilections for the new. Some are more subtle and perhaps difficult to address: the differential pull factor of student, colleague, and sometimes funder interest as exerted on new as opposed to old technologies ("That's so 2009!"); the frequent obscurity and ephemerality of maintenance and repair work, which leaves few of the documentary or statistical traces that systems of production do; and the deep methodological challenges of conceptualizing and studying time in general. Setting aside such challenges, bringing maintenance and repair work to the fore in our thinking about technology may help to extend and fill out this temporal story, offering new insights and approaches to the understanding of technology as a timely or rhythmic phenomenon (Jackson et al. 2011).

Fourth, recentering maintenance and repair may help with the necessary project of building bridges to new and adjacent fields whose methods, insights, and modes of work hold great promise to complement and enrich our own (and vice versa). This includes growing or prospective interfaces with fields like material culture (Miller 2005); craft studies (Sennett 2009; McCullough 1998); technology for development; and the diffuse body of work around sustainability studies. It may also help build new analytic connections to cultural phenomena—maker and DIY communities, craft and slow food movements, and cultural forms from fan fiction to the steampunk movement—that feature breaking, maintenance, and repair as central sites of activity and meaning.

Finally, moving maintenance and repair back to the center of thinking around media and technology may help to develop deeper and richer stories of relationality to the technological artifacts and systems that surround us, positioning the world of things as an active component and partner in the ongoing project of building more humane, just, and sustainable collectives. In June 2012 controversy erupted around the design of the retina display on Apple's newly redesigned MacBook Pro computer. As early reviews enthused and critics conceded, the new MacBook Pro was a functionally and aesthetically elegant machine, continuing recent trends in Apple design toward simple, compact, and seamless functionality predicated on the tight control and integration of hardware and software elements. It was also, as Kyle Wiens of iFixit.org[4] reported in a review for *Wired* magazine, "the least repairable laptop we've ever taken apart":

Unlike the previous model, the display is fused to the glass, which means replacing the LCD requires buying an expensive display assembly. The RAM is now soldered to the logic board—making future memory upgrades impossible. And the battery is glued to the case, requiring customers to mail their laptop to Apple every so often for a $200 replacement. The design may well be comprised of "highly recyclable aluminum and glass"—but my friends in the electronics recycling industry tell me they have no way of recycling aluminum that has glass glued to it like Apple did with both this machine and the recent iPad.

Defenders of the new machine and broadly similar design choices in Apple's MacBook Air series, the iPad, and a host of industry competitors quickly responded. Some argued that repairability was an increasingly outmoded virtue in electronics and in any case a necessary victim of the trend toward ever more compact and mobile design. Others noted that electronics repair was irrelevant to the vast majority of consumers anyway, who were more inclined to throw away than repair even the older and more fixable generation of personal computers. Still others argued that the debate about repair was moot, since consumers had effectively voted with their feet and wallets, consistently opting for size and functionality over more upgradable and fixable designs.

But the controversy did not end here. Over the long July 4th weekend of 2012, Apple quietly announced its intention to withdraw thirty-nine of its products from the Electronic Product Environmental Assessment Tool (EPEAT), a green ratings system supported by the U.S. Environmental Protection Agency and leading firms in the electronics industry (including Apple itself), arguing that "[Apple's] design direction was no longer consistent with EPEAT requirements," including the ratings system's "easy to disassemble using common tools" requirement. Reaction was swift. Users on Apple fan sites registered their dismay, noting Apple's past record of green-friendly innovations and the perceived inconsistency between the company's brand image and the decision to withdraw from EPEAT. Municipal governments, universities, and other institutional buyers that had incorporated EPEAT standards into their procurement process announced their decision to review all Apple purchases. Bloggers and technology news sites like ArsTechnica and Slashdot covered the story extensively, fanning and amplifying the initial controversy. On July 13, 2012, Apple rescinded its decision, announcing its intention to rejoin and renew its relationship with EPEAT. In an open letter on the Apple website, Senior Vice-President of Hardware Manufacturing Bob Mansfield reaffirmed Apple's past and continuing accomplishments in energy efficiency and the move away from toxic chemicals like brominated flame retardants (BFRs) and polyvinyl chloride (PVC), and vowed to work with EPEAT to update and extend green standards and practices in the electronics and computing industries.

Conclusion: Learning from Benjamin

One of the inspirations and patron saints for this project is the great German literary critic and social theorist, Walter Benjamin. Living through the dying days of the Weimar Republic and the rise of fascism (a force that would eventually destroy him), Benjamin nevertheless produced some of the gentlest, most inspiring, and most deeply humanistic criticism of a period not known for those virtues. In his peculiar, fragmentary, archival, and recuperative mode of working (best exemplified in the fragments of his brilliant but unfinished "Arcades" project [Benjamin 1999]), Benjamin also provides one possible example of a broken world methodology, or what scholarly work predicated on the assumptions and conditions of broken world thinking might look like. This sensibility is further reflected in his choice of historical subjects: not princes, leaders, and the products of high culture, but the detritus of nineteenth-century commercialism, the layabouts and ragpickers with whom Benjamin periodically aligns his own work.[5]

Finally, Benjamin leaves us some of modernity's most arresting images. My favorite, and the one which best captures the heart of broken world thinking, starts with a reflection on the 1920 Paul Klee painting *Angelus Novus* (see figure 11.2). Here, from a piece titled "Theses on the Philosophy of History," is Benjamin's commentary on the work:

A Klee painting named "Angelus Novus" shows an angel looking as though he is about to move away from something he is fixedly contemplating. His eyes are staring, his mouth is open, his wings are spread. This is how one pictures the angel of history. His face is turned toward the past. Where we perceive a chain of events, he sees one single catastrophe which keeps piling wreckage upon wreckage and hurls it in front of his feet. The angel would like to stay, awaken the dead, and make whole what has been smashed. But a storm is blowing from Paradise; it has got caught in his wings with such violence that the angel can no longer close them. This storm irresistibly propels him into the future to which his back is turned, while the pile of debris before him grows skyward. This storm is what we call progress. (1969, 257–258)

This remains one of our most vivid and shocking indictments of a progressivist history. In place of a grand historical march toward freedom or salvation, or the forward and certain momentum of Marxian dialectics, we are left with this: a catastrophe, blowing blindly backward into the future, an image made all the more horrific by the poignancy of the angel's frustrated desire "to stay, awaken the dead, and make whole what has been smashed."

But this is not where Benjamin concludes. In the end, Benjamin winds up in the arcades of nineteenth-century Paris, studying poets and ragpickers, and finding grounds for resilience and hope. In the aftermath of history and its lineage of wreckage and debris, he quietly goes about the business of collecting and recuperating the world around him.

So: do we live in late modernity, postmodernity, alternative modernity, or liquid modernity? Knowledge societies, information societies, network

Figure 11.2
Paul Klee's painting *Angelus Novus*.[6]

societies, or risk societies? New media, old media, dead media, or hypermedia? The world of information, the world of search, the world of networks, or the world of big data?

The answer is simple: like every generation before, we live in the aftermath.

Acknowledgments

I wish to thank Geof Bowker, Matthew Stahl, Tarleton Gillespie, Chris Kelty, Greg Downey, John King, Jonathan Grudin, and the participants in Bonnie Nardi's Spring 2012 Collapse Computing class at the University of California, Irvine, for their helpful comments on earlier drafts of this work.

Notes

1. *Anthem.* Written by: Leonard Cohen ©1992 Stranger Music Inc. All rights administered by Sony/ATV Music Publishing LLC, 8 Music Square West, Nashville, TN, 37203. All rights reserved. Used by permission.

2. Photo © Edward Burtynsky, represented by Nicholas Metivier, Toronto / Howard Greenberg and Bryce Wolkowitz, New York. Images from the *Shipbreaking* and *Ship Recycling* series are available at http://www.edwardburtynsky.com/.

3. See Tolstoy's opening lines to *Anna Karenina* (1886): "All happy families are alike. All unhappy families are unhappy in their own way."

4. This is a nonprofit organization dedicated to technology repair, recycling, and consumer education whose activities include Consumer Reports®-style "teardowns" of leading products in the computing and consumer electronics sectors. See http://ifixit.org, accessed April 22, 2013.

5. Quoting the French edition of Baudelaire's *Oeuvres*, volume 1, Benjamin writes, "'Here we have a man whose job it is to gather the day's refuse in the capital. Everything that the big city has thrown away, everything it has lost, everything it has scorned, everything it has crushed underfoot he catalogues and collects. He collates the annals of intemperance, the capharnaum of waste. He sorts things out and selects judiciously: he collects like a miser guarding a treasure, refuse which will assume the shape of useful or gratifying objects between the jaws of the goddess of Industry.' This description is one extended metaphor for the poetic method, as Baudelaire practiced it. Ragpicker and poet: both are concerned with refuse" (Benjamin 2003, 48).

6. © *Angelus Novus*, 1920 (Indian ink, color chalk, and brown wash on paper), Paul Klee (1879–1940)/The Israel Museum, Jerusalem, Israel/Carole and Ronald Lauder, New York/The Bridgeman Art Library.

12 Identifying the Interests of Digital Users as Audiences, Consumers, Workers, and Publics

Sonia Livingstone

Introduction—Why Consider Users?

I was asked to act as discussant on the essays by Greg Downey, Tarleton Gillespie, Chris Kelty, and Steven Jackson as if we were all together at a conference. Conference delegates—like most audiences—listen for a purpose, relating what they hear to their prior standpoint. You, too, as my reader, start from somewhere particular, doubtless wondering what I have to say. While all the papers—now, essays in this volume—are concerned with the shifting relations among communication technologies, social practices, and institutions of power—put simply, with how to imagine what the Internet could and should be (Mansell 2012)—I shall contrast their various conceptions of the ordinary person whose interests are so vitally at stake in the digital era. Should you be used to regarding the producer as more important than the consumer, the text more subtle than its various actualizations by readers, or the technology more fascinating than its uses, then I hope to persuade you that the study of media, communication, and information technologies should always address the activities of users in context. Only thus can we uncover the social shaping and social consequences of the digital (Lievrouw and Livingstone 2006).

My degree of linguistic artifice—encoded by the nineteenth-century novelist through a direct address to the "dear reader"—signals that, as a reader of these four essays, addressing the reader of this text, I hope to illuminate the reader or user of digital technologies more generally. In my own work, I have examined the interpretative agency of television *audiences* (Livingstone 1998), their contested relations with *publics* (Livingstone 2005), and the fraught ways they are framed as *citizens* or *consumers* in policy discourses (Lunt and Livingstone 2012). Given this horizon of expectations (Jauss 1982), you will not be surprised that I am interested in how these conceptions of the ordinary person (itself no simple idea [Thumim

2012]) resonate or contrast across the four essays, implicitly or explicitly, in ways that are important for our analysis of the communication process.

But where, you may ask, are the readers or users in the essay? Surely Downey is concerned with the too-often invisible information laborers, Gillespie with complex algorithms of which the users have never even heard, Kelty with grand questions of freedom and coercion, and Jackson with those who repair broken technologies and technological infrastructures. I suggest that although their starting points lie with the sociotechnical systems that modern globalized societies are so vigorously building, the authors are each, in different ways, concerned with the messy realities of everyday life, with what is visible or invisible, transparent or opaque in the emerging domain of digital infrastructures. Most important, each has a vision of the user (reader) in the digital era, as I shall unpack here. Moreover, each fears that the implied reader (user) of their own text risks underestimating how the interests of digital users are losing out in the unequal struggle that they—and we—are engaged in. The collective noun each essay chooses to foreground this struggle is, I suggest, productive for future analysis.

User as Proletariat

Digital communication relies on the essential yet routinely underestimated work of "human 'information labor,'" argues Downey, in chapter 8 of this volume. We google a question and the answer "comes up." We check Amazon for something to buy and helpful recommendations are instantly at our service. We tell our students to research a new topic and the task seems effortless. But as Downey rightly observes, this apparent cornucopia is only possible because of an invisible army of coders, selectors, translators, and other new intermediaries. And because we can't see them, we naively acknowledge that neither their efforts (thereby colluding in their exploitation) nor their motivations—or, more accurately, the motivations of their employers—are available to our critical scrutiny (thereby undermining our media literacy). What are these workers doing? Downey offers three case studies that reveal the ordinary lives of these hidden laborers who do what he calls "jumping context"—ensuring the efficient distribution of meanings from producer to consumer that is essential to the exercise of power. Calling for wider recognition of this work, Downey appeals to the media-literate teacher and the cultural critic who worry first about the students who, being "digital natives" beguiled by the ease of modern interfaces that "free" them from the effort of finding information, lack the critical literacy to evaluate what they find, and worry second about those who find themselves co-opted to the invisible workforce of the information laborer (via crowdsourcing, produsage, or other forms of "free labor," as Tiziana Terranova [2000] has termed it). Somewhat contentiously, Downey includes both his students and those scholars excited by the potential for amateur, playful, alternative, or flexible uses of the digital environment not only in the former but also in the latter category.

Presumably following Adorno and Horkheimer's (1977) post-Marxist analysis of "the culture industry," Downey implies that the two are linked—the user as consumer is served by the user as worker; indeed, the user as consumer by night is, precisely, the user as worker by day. "We" either fall into this trap too or we must stand sternly apart and, indeed, seek their rescue. In the face of hidden exploitation and imminent struggle, as critics, we must promote resistance (Downey gives the example of the Occupy movement as a possible direction, though history will judge whether this is a sufficient or effective form of resistance). As teachers, we must make the task of interpretation harder, not easier, for our students, deconstructing the interface and revealing its illegibility behind its apparent legibility; here Downey mobilizes a particular version of media literacy, aligned with those for whom the media represent all-powerful, profit-driven, ideologically exploitative institutions that promote pernicious values to their audiences. Other conceptions of media literacy, which see no going back from today's thorough-going and ubiquitous mediated environment, aim less to teach people to defend against the media and more to engage with and productively harness whatever media power they can appropriate for themselves and those they may speak for (Frau-Meigs and Torrent 2009; Hobbs 2010). The irony is that, for the first conception of media, raising individuals' media literacy has proven to be a weak (though worthy) tool. Possibly, there is more political potential for the second conception, insofar as its focus is not to counter the power of media owners, but rather to harness the power of the media so as to reach the ears of the national or international state and regulatory bodies that have power over them (as in media reform or digital rights movements).

Users as Publics

Readers and users can be more or less obscured by theory, although they are omnipresent come what may. Of the four essays, I had the least work to do in discerning their role in Gillespie's essay for, although hardly signaled by a title about algorithms, users are at the center of his concern with relevance. Algorithms, he argues, represent a new "knowledge logic," one that is displacing the editorial logic of the print era (and, perhaps, the call for much of the exploited labor which worries Downey). To whom or what is this new logic relevant? To "our participation in public life" (see chapter 9). In other words, to us as democratic citizens, now divided less (or not only) by inequalities in the labor market or new stratifications introduced by globalization, but rather by all the matters that divide citizens—opinions, perspectives, visions of the good society. Thus, Gillespie asks, how are the criteria by which we analyze and judge public participation changed in the digital era? In the print era, where arguably Jürgen Habermas's ([1962] 1989) theory of the public sphere best captured the ideals of public participation, critics concerned themselves with questions of inclusion, trust, deliberation, rationality, and the public good. But in the digital era, we are faced with vast and largely inaccessible databases built on unaccountable practices of selection, encoding, "cleaning," "the promise of objectivity," and, perhaps most fascinating, the recursive re-presentation of a "calculated" public back to itself (it being no longer the *Times* letters page but personally tailored Facebook "likes" that tell us whether others think as we do).

Gillespie addresses "us" as citizen-users, as publics (and this is my preferred approach; see Livingstone 2005, and Lunt and Livingstone 2012). But his fear is that we have already been sold, over our heads, for calculated publics that are far from organic (see networked publics, Ito 2008); rather, they are the means by which users are transformed into a commodity and sold to advertisers. The parallel with Ien Ang's (1990) analysis of the television ratings industry is strong and, like Ang, in chapter 9 Gillespie points to "the slippage between the anticipated user and the user themselves." But while Ang was deeply pessimistic about the television and marketing industry, she had more faith that the complexities of everyday life escape the raters' scrutiny—and thus their data, and inferences drawn from it, are flawed. Like Ang, Gillespie is guided by the findings of media ethnographies, a welcome inclusion in a volume on science and technology studies; but his concern is, rightly, greater. For while he agrees that everyday complexities undermine the validity of the "big data" so excitedly being captured by the industry (boyd and Crawford 2012), by contrast with television, the Internet industry feeds its "findings" back to us as users immediately, relentlessly, and persuasively. How can I not fall for the conceit that my weekly Facebook update reveals my popularity? And how far can we, as citizens, be properly skeptical of the ubiquitous yet insidious re-presentation of public discourse and political interests presented to us by Web 2.0?

Users and Humanity

Where Downey and Gillespie debate the politics of workers, users, and publics in the digital age, Kelty frames his concerns in ethical terms, attempting to move beyond the familiar polarization of freedom versus control (or exploitation) in order to examine "how new technologies change the meaning of freedom itself" (chapter 10, this volume). Kelty elegantly complicates Isaiah Berlin's (1958) familiar distinction between negative freedom ("freedom from" interference) and positive freedom ("freedom to" be a self-directed agent) by observing that negative freedom, commonly associated with libertarian ideas of the Internet, conveys a particular vision of liberty whose hostility to state intervention in the private sphere (including markets and the lifeworld) ends up "forcing a particular kind of liberty on others." In other words, the protection of negative freedoms becomes, necessarily, the promotion of positive freedoms also: as Kelty notes, having advocated for freedoms from intervention or control, "it is an easy step to suggest that others be coerced in their own interests, that we know what they need better than they do themselves." In relation to the Internet, this paradox is often overlooked because, while government interventions are often noticeable and therefore contested, "the creation and dissemination of technologies that coerce us and that interfere with our goals" tends to operate under the radar of critical scrutiny. Yet, as ever more aspects of our civic, personal, and intellectual lives become digitally mediated (Hepp 2012), these questions of design and implementation become all the more important, the point being not to push back against imposing forces but rather to recognize the subtleties of coercion "by design" (recall Gillespie's concern about the obscurity of algorithms).

You may ask, my dear reader, where is the user in all of this? By contrast with Downey's user-as-laborer or Gillespie's user-as-public, Kelty's user is the most elevated, for it is all humanity: the user who has the right to be free, the user who desires to dictate the freedoms of others, the user who, in Berlin's terms, wishes "to be a subject, not an object; to be moved by reasons, by conscious purposes which are my own" (quoted in Kelty, chapter 10)—and, now, to do so on the Internet. Yet paradoxically, by underestimating the power of technological design, it is precisely this user who, in the digital era, risks falling for "a specious disguise for brutal tyranny" (Berlin, quoted in chapter 10). Yet as scholars we do believe that we know better what is in the interests of users (indeed, of humanity): Kelty's history of the personal computer reveals a driving belief in human emancipation—that technology can deliver "a particular vision of positive liberty: creativity, constructive learning, expressive communication, the ability to think unconstrained, like an artist or a scientist." Unsurprisingly, then, where Downey calls for media literacy, perhaps enabling technologically mediated protest, and where Gillespie calls for transparency in the workings of algorithms, Kelty asks users to become designers, for "our very ability to become free depends on our ability to design it into our technologies."

Users as Carers: Ethical Users

Jackson's vision—combining politics and ethics—is one of entropy (Arnheim 1971), of a world relentlessly falling apart, notwithstanding the incessant but only temporarily successful efforts of another invisible army of workers to rebuild and repair. Elegantly illustrating his argument with an image of a once-glamorous ocean liner being dismantled and stripped by Bangladeshi shipbreakers, Jackson's argument takes a step beyond Downey's emphasis on what is now called the problem of "the last mile" (which, as broadband providers worry today, is the most troublesome and expensive). For while Downey's messenger boys were essential to completing the communicative process, Jackson's shipbreakers, who not only strip but also repurpose the salvageable parts of the ship, play a necessary (if not-very-powerful, and certainly unsung) role. Their literal acts of recycling illustrate the cyclic (rather than linear) relation between producer and user in digital communication. Still, though the energy lies in the workers who power the process, its direction and influence is determined by the producers.

Jackson draws on Star and Strauss's (1999) analysis of the role of articulation in sustaining sociotechnical infrastructures (by supporting "the smooth interaction of parts" within the whole), but his emphasis on repair is devoted to sustaining not altering the communication process. His Bangladeshi shipbreakers seem not to deviate or cheat on their task, nor do they strike. Similarly, I first thought Downey's "jumping context" to be akin to what anthropologists call the "re-appropriation" of meaning from one context to the next (Miller 1987), or what cultural studies analyses call the "circuit of culture," linking political economy and lived culture (Hall 1999; Johnson 1986). But, more Frankfurt School than cultural or consumption studies, Downey's messenger boys appear to have no agency in the process that absorbs them. Yet Stuart Hall's analysis of articulation (for example, between encoding and decoding; Hall 1980) posits a far from smooth interaction, instead pointing to a site of struggle over the determination of meaning. Thus a focus on the (re)production and circulation of meanings (rather than just their distribution) would ask not only how the messenger boys fit into the system of communication that relied on them but also whether their labor shaped or altered, to some degree, the nature and outcome of the communicative flow, indeed, of the circuit of culture. Just as one wonders further about the lives of Jackson's shipbreakers, one might also ask not only what the messengers were paid (not enough!) or where they put their hat and coat, but also whether they ever lost or altered or even destroyed the messages they were entrusted to carry. One might also ask who could not afford to send a message, whether there were places they couldn't or wouldn't deliver to, and whether they organized any protest against their treatment.

How shall we value the work of these unsung workers and users? Where Downey offers a political vision of an exploitative labor market underpinning our ubiquitously enjoyed communication apps, Jackson is more humanistic, arguing that repair "fills in the moment of hope and fear in which bridges from old worlds to new worlds are built, and the continuity of order, value, and meaning gets woven, one tenuous thread at a time" (chapter 11, this volume). Just as Daniel Miller (1998) argues that shopping—profitable to be sure for the supermarkets—is also an act of love by those taking food home to their families, Jackson analyzes everyday activities of recycling and repair (which are certainly commonplace in any domestic setting for digital media use; Livingstone 2002) as "the subtle acts of care by which order and meaning . . . are maintained and transformed." The last mile may pose the greatest challenge for the provider, but to any domestic user, that's when the invisible tasks really begin. Siting, installing, connecting, updating, customizing, and repairing are all everyday tasks associated with digital technologies, and in completing these, the circuit is not neatly completed but, rather, significantly reshaped: manufacturers' instructions are not followed, manuals are discarded, complex functionality is underused, and workarounds, hacks, and other fixes are endemic (Bakardjieva 2005).

Research on everyday uses and abuses of technology has long sought to counter the "productivist bias" of the field that worries Jackson. To advance his "repair-centered ethics," even "a standpoint epistemology of repair," why not start at home, adding users to his list of "neglected" people in the social history of technology? Complementing the dominant focus on innovation and distribution, Jackson in chapter 11 usefully invites consideration of other dimensions of the social life of objects, including unnoticed forms of labor, alternative relations of power and, his main focus, an ethics of care surrounding the embedding of technological objects in our lives. Yet these can only come into focus if we transcend linear conceptions of technological innovation, and binary contrasts between producers and consumers—hence the value of cyclic thinking. However, can an ethic of care suffice to counter the forces of entropy by which all that we humans create continuously degrades, decays, and disappears? And what of the capitalist effort to profit even from these acts of repair (consider the repair shops springing up on every high street, the profits now discovered in "green" businesses, and, of course, the motivations of the Bangladeshi shipbreakers' employers)? I think this might be Downey's reply to Jackson.

Conclusion

In his brilliant dissection of literature, Umberto Eco (1984) showed there is always an implied reader, conceived by Eco as the combination of textual (or design) features that hail, inscribe, and presume familiarity with the knowledge and interests of the reader. In this short commentary, I have sought to reveal both the reader of this volume (including myself), in order to highlight the differences of position that we are, together, debating, but also, more important, the user (today's reader) of digital technologies (as conceived, or implied, by our four authors). From my perspective, it is crucial to recognize that, as first audience reception and then media ethnography have shown, implied readers do not always map precisely onto empirical readers; preferred readings encoded into a text are not always decoded as anticipated; and media products can be surprisingly, even resistantly appropriated by "ordinary people" with, sometimes, problematic consequences for their authors, designers, and producers (Bakardjieva 2005; Silverstone 2006). Undoubtedly, even acting collectively the public generally lacks the power to counter the meanings imposed by global media corporations. Nor, typically, is it aware of the conservative meanings embedded in the texts and technologies that surround its members. Yet communication is inherently co-constructed, often unpredictable, and thoroughly embedded in the particular contexts that, in turn, help shape its direction and outcome. As reception theorist Wolfgang Iser elegantly explains, "as the reader passes through the various perspectives offered by the text, and relates the different views and patterns to one another, he sets the work in motion, and so sets himself in motion too" (1980, 106).

So, readers and viewers, audiences and publics, users and consumers—call them what you will—are not dutifully positioned at the end of a well-planned chain of control, from innovation to production to marketing and diffusion and, finally, obedient receipt of the goods or meanings on offer. In this commentary, I have built on the text-reader metaphor of cultural studies, social semiotics, and reception aesthetics (Hall 1980; Hodge and Kress 1988; and Iser 1980, respectively) as extended to theorize the user of new media technologies (Livingstone 2004; Woolgar 1996). The concepts of reader and user permit recognition of agency, but they tend to underplay the significance of collectivities. When positioning agents, individual or aggregated, within a larger frame, the choice of collective noun matters, for different terms mobilize different discourses, point to different opportunity structures, prioritize different interests.

Faced with encroaching world domination by the major technology companies, our four authors are all rather pessimistic. Yet in an endorsement of user agency, each in his different way also issues a call to action—to users in general, and to us as critical scholars in particular. So how pessimistic should we be? We might retort to Gillespie that, just as readers in the print era dominated by the editorial logic could still differentiate Fox News from *The New York Times*, and viewers generally trust public service news on television more than commercial services, so too are Internet users striving to upgrade their digital literacy, while also finding that longstanding forms of critical literacy still stand them in good stead. Consider the example of Jackson's consumer revolt against Apple's abandonment of green recycling or, more modestly, the common view that Wikipedia is good for uncontentious facts but not for an election campaign update. Yet no simple overthrow of power, no straightforward celebration of user agency is plausible. Returning us to the circuit of culture, ever more complexly renegotiated at each site of articulation, Gillespie observes the "recursive loop" by which, "as these algorithms have nestled into people's daily lives . . . , users shape and rearticulate the algorithms they encounter . . . [and then, in turn] algorithms impinge on how people seek information, how they perceive and think about the contours of knowledge, and how they understand themselves in and through public discourse" (chapter 9). So, although the circuit depends on users for its completion, and although their agency (or, as some would have it, the social contexts that condition their actions) render the circuit unpredictable, open to a measure of resistance even, this does not mean the circuit is led by—or works primarily in the interests of—the users.

Indeed, as Roger Silverstone (2006) stressed, drawing on Michel de Certeau (1984), it is not often that the tactics of everyday life (what Gillespie calls the tactics of "obfuscation") succeed in circumventing or redirecting the strategies of established power. And the more media-literate the users become (as Downey hopes), the more those who stand to gain by "reading" the user will strive to stay ahead (Jenkins 2003). Yet, significantly, any optimism about countering the power of the major corporations (conceived in terms of labor management, algorithms, or design) calls on users as publics to demand what matters to the public sphere—inclusion, transparency, accountability, redress, fair representation, and so on. All of these were fought for in previous eras, through public discourse, and through legislative struggles, the establishment of regulators, and even the courts. For the most part, these are fights yet to be held in the digital era, though early instances are already mounting. Inevitably they will pitch the nation-state, speaking for its citizens, against globalized corporations, in a complex and compromised negotiation of interests as part of a new and increasingly transnational struggle over the determination of knowledge. Within this struggle, the user as worker, citizen, and ethical human being has a vital part to play.

13 The World Outside and the Pictures in Our Networks

Fred Turner

Walter Lippmann must be rolling in his grave. In the 1920s, Lippmann marveled as the commercial ambitions of the industrial age married the new technologies of mass media. Since the turn of the century, radio had transformed the living rooms of American homes into listening posts, where families gathered to hear distant, disembodied voices and to imagine the places they spoke from. New printing technologies had turned the pages of magazines from black-and-white blocks of text into multicolored extravaganzas of photographic delight. And perhaps most amazingly of all, the cinema drew new crowds to stare at moving pictures projected on the wall. To Lippmann, the rise of mass media required a new and critical outlook on public life. Never a fan of hoi polloi, Lippmann argued that the mass media fundamentally deceived their audiences. Media, he explained, put "pictures in our heads" (Lippmann 1922). These pictures set the terms by which audiences decided how to act in the world, but they did not necessarily represent the world as it was. On the contrary, they represented the interests of those who made the pictures in the first place. To study the power of media, he implied, was to study the power of special interests to control our view of the world.

Lippmann's argument has echoed down through media theory for almost a hundred years. Until the advent of digital media technologies at least, scholars largely agreed: media—which was almost always assumed to be *mass* media—had power because of their ability to create and distribute representations and so to shape audience's perceptions of reality. Media technologies in turn did the work of industrial technologies. That is, they made sure that the same representations reached as many people as possible. The most powerful media were often assumed to be precisely those that could broadcast the most complex combinations of sound and picture to the widest array of audiences. Audiences might be dupes (as in the panic literatures of the 1930s and the 1950s) or they might be active makers of meaning (as in the cultural studies work of the 1980s and 1990s). Either way, it was the ability of media technologies to deliver pictures into their heads with which they had to wrestle.

Imagine how surprised Walter Lippmann might be then, to read the four essays to be discussed here. Not a single one deals with representation. Nor do any of the four treat media technologies primarily as systems for the delivery of a worldview. On the contrary, in these essays media and the technologies on which they depend have melted into the infrastructure of everyday life. The fear of broadcasting has given way to critical wonder at the power of networking. The power of mass-produced sounds and images to shape reality has disappeared from discussion. Power itself has been redistributed, into interactivity, collaboration, and the co-production of meaning in real time. The old industrial order has not disappeared entirely. As Greg Downey and Steven Jackson point out, its disrespect for the natural environment and for the human life cycle persists, alongside the hierarchies of class on which it depends. But the terms of media power have shifted. As Tarleton Gillespie and Chris Kelty suggest, a new information-industrial complex has begun to form and with it, a new set of challenges to public life.

Consider the case of the lowly algorithm. As Gillespie points out, algorithms are the building blocks of the new media-technology order. Not bits—algorithms. The distinction is important and worth dwelling on. To date, scholars who have emphasized the utopian possibilities of digital media tend to have built their cases around the properties of bits. Lev Manovich (2001), Henry Jenkins (2006), Lawrence Lessig (2008), and many others have pointed out that because bits can be copied infinitely without loss to the original, because they can be circulated almost instantly and sampled just as fast, they have made it possible for ordinary people to become producers of media. According to Lessig, the properties of bits have dramatically amplified the fecundity of culture. As he explains in his 2008 book *Remix*, digital media make it technically possible for all users to remix all content and so to create new artworks of their own (Lessig 2008). Henry Jenkins likewise argues that when texts are digitized and when fans can interact with authors and producers over digital systems, the power of audiences and of media makers will converge (Jenkins 2006). In Jenkins' view, each will serve the other in a benevolent feedback loop. In each case, it is the power of bits to be copied, transported, and manipulated with ease that underlies their claims for the cultural impact of digital systems.

In Gillespie's contribution to this book, however, it is not bits but the instruction sets that manipulate them that matter. In chapter 9 Gillespie has provided a handy taxonomy of six ways that algorithms shape public life. His categories can be broken into two broad groups: the work algorithms do and the kinds of publics they produce by doing it. As Gillespie explains, algorithms seek and make patterns in data. In that sense, they do the sort of work media analysts used to ascribe to human producers of things like movies and record albums. They select and curate. And perhaps even more influentially, they encode the terms by which a given cultural production can even be recognized by the social and technical systems that have deployed the algorithms. People who produce texts must aim to produce them in forms that the algorithm will acknowledge if they hope to find an audience. Audiences in turn must approach digital texts through institutionalized algorithms of access—that is, search engines—that will shape what those audiences can see and hear. The algorithm, in other words, is a new and powerful middleman.

The algorithm is also a stand-in for real people. That is, as Gillespie acknowledges, and as both he and Alexander Galloway have argued at length (Gillespie 2007; Galloway 2004, 2006; Galloway and Thacker 2007), algorithms are tools made by people to serve discrete ends. At the same time, embedded as they are deep within complex machines and written in a code that few users will ever understand, algorithms render their creators invisible. Finally, as if that weren't enough, Gillespie points out that scholars, pundits, and everyday users tend to take a certain pleasure in the fact that algorithms act on their own, as pieces of science and technology, and so seem to stand outside and even beyond ordinary politics.

In that sense, algorithms can be tools for accomplishing both practical and ideological tasks simultaneously. This is where they require us to ask the question that we have traditionally put to mass media: Who benefits? In the mass media era, answering this question meant mapping the corporations that produced our movies, music, and news. In the digital era, as Gillespie shows, it involves interrogating algorithms—first, by denying that they are apolitical and second, by seeking out the ideals they encode and the communities that benefit from those ideals. As Mark Andrejevic (2007) has demonstrated, digital media shape our pictures of reality by drawing us into interactive relationships with our devices, and through them, with various institutions. To fully come to grips with the process, though, Gillespie demonstrates that we need to take apart the algorithms themselves and to analyze the social relations they encode.

Though I very much agree with Gillespie on this point, I also think we need to continue to interrogate representations. This time, though, we need to explore the ways in which databases create pictures of our worlds and circulate them among themselves. To the extent that digital communication technologies shape our possibilities for political action (think voting, or your credit score, or the mailing lists you are and are not on), their ability to generate pictures of the world and act on the basis of those pictures—without any direct input from us and often without our knowledge—ought to terrify us. In the mass media era, representations drew their power from their visibility. But in the digital era, representations of the world live in databases too, invisible to most human beings, though transparent to algorithms. In the past, it may have been the pictures in our heads that shaped our actions; now, it is also the pictures of our actions made of bits, stored in databases, available to algorithms. Most of us will be able to neither read the algorithms themselves, nor identify their makers. What's more, algorithms may outlive their makers and may interact with one another in ways their makers never predicted. In the mass media era, we struggled to theorize the agency of authors and audiences in relation to highly visible representations; today, as Gillespie shows, we need to begin to theorize both actors and images that circulate invisibly.

When we do, Chris Kelty suggests, we will begin to develop a new understanding of our contemporary political condition. For Kelty, as for Gillespie, digital media technologies are both tools to do things with and emblems of a potential political order. As he shows in his brief history of the personal computer in chapter 10, these two dimensions of computing shape one another. That is, the ability of computers to solicit interactivity and to extend our abilities to acquire and manipulate knowledge has helped us to imagine a more collaborative, intellectually expansive society. The texture of our imaginings has changed with the times: from augmentation in the 1950s to liberation in the 1970s to libertarian individualism in the 1990s. But the imaginings themselves have persisted.

How then, Kelty wonders, should we ask computers to help us imagine our polis today? What might freedom mean in a society becoming ever more densely interlinked, not only by computers but by cars and ships and airplanes as well? And how can we design computers to encourage freedom both practically and symbolically?

These questions would have delighted Walter Lippmann. In his day, too, media technologies seemed to model modes of governance. Particularly as World War II got under way, the one-to-many structure of mass media seemed to many critics to be tailor-made for fascist domination (Turner 2012). After all, how better might a dictator reach the masses than through radio and film? As Kelty notes, these questions have hovered alongside the rise of personal computing and the Internet. Even the notion that a computer could be a "personal" technology reflected a highly individualis-tic political ideal (Turner 2006; Streeter 2011).

These questions have become new again, however, because of the degree to which computers have been integrated into everyday life. If Gillespie reveals an invisible network of computers, each hosting databased repre-sentations of the world and semi-autonomous algorithms speaking in code to one another, Kelty makes the case that we need to create a theory of free-dom that can accommodate this new media infrastructure. As he explains, "we now occupy a world in which our very ability to become free depends on our ability to design [freedom] into our technologies—and yet we don't have a theory, positive or normative, that would guide us in this endeavor" (chapter 10).

Kelty himself takes several first steps toward developing such a theory. As he does, the computer itself, together with the writings of figures such as J. C. R. Licklider and Ted Nelson, exerts a powerful gravitational pull on his thinking. Early on, for instance, he distinguishes between "positive" and "negative" freedom—that is, between "freedom to" and "freedom from." At one level, this distinction allows us to imagine computers as tools that permit us to take certain actions in the world and so to become more able to express our choices in the world. The distinction is practical and helpful. As Kelty notes, it also takes advantage of the growing understanding that tech-nologies both embody political choices and solicit them from their users.

Yet the distinction tends to underplay the symbolic side of the politics of computing. Donna Haraway's canonical essay "A Cyborg Manifesto" in *Simians, Cyborgs, and Women* (1991) offers an interesting counterpoint to Kelty's approach. In contrast to Kelty's empirically grounded, hands-on approach to the problem, Haraway hardly addresses the question of how bodies and machines might physically intersect. Rather, she simply adopts the *figure* of their intersection, the cyborg, and then transforms it into an emblem of hybrid identities, transgendered being, and a new mode of machine-linked female strength. She draws these images from the feminist movement in which she has long taken an active part. And the essay in turn reimagines the liberating possibilities of information technologies on behalf of that movement.

Haraway's example reminds us that Kelty is right: we absolutely need a fully fleshed-out theory of freedom that takes account of technology. We need to find ways in turn to build machines that incorporate that freedom to the extent that we can. But Haraway's essay also illustrates the ways in which social rather than engineering movements have tended to be the pri-mary incubators of new visions of liberty. Technologists have often reached out to those movements—as Ted Nelson did to the counterculture of the 1960s, or as the leaders of Google do to Burning Man today—and imported their visions into the professional imaginaries of engineers and into the design and marketing of devices. Likewise, groups ranging from the German Bauhaus to the American technocrat movement of the early twentieth century have sought to blend the pursuit of political and technological innovation. Each of these cases suggests the importance of Kelty's fundamental insight: we need to theorize freedom in a new and more contemporary way. They also suggest that on the ground, that theory is likely to be born in the communities that bridge social movements and engineering worlds.

Set against the other essays in this quartet, Kelty's work seems to call for a third kind of freedom—not so much "freedom from" or "freedom to" as "freedom with." As he notes, theorists and technologists have long posited freedom as an output of activity, an endpoint. But as I read his essay, now chapter 10, I found myself wondering, what if freedom consisted of being an equal part of an activity, of being integrated into a community, of being a valued member of a process? What if freedom began not with the design of the machine or the outcome of its use, but within the social networks it enabled? And for that matter, how might media machines be used to generate chains of human–machine interaction that boost the agency of the individuals involved?

These questions thread their way throughout Greg Downey's analysis of information labor as well. By turning to telegraph boys and librarians and stenographers, Downey in chapter 8 instantly gives the lie to the claim that the network society emerged only after the arrival of digital technologies. On the contrary, looking at the nineteenth century, Downey reminds us that modern societies have always already been networked. What's more, human beings have always been integral components in information systems. These facts have two implications. The first, which Downey explores at length, involves reassigning to people the work theorists have traditionally assigned to communication technologies. As Downey points out, individual human beings have long done the work of transcoding information, causing it to leap across time and space, in keeping with the protocols set by the institutions in which they work. The second implication, which Downey urges his readers to take up, is that in analyzing the politics of information systems we need to do more than study authors and audiences, as so many did in the mass media era, and we need to do more than study the digital networks through which bits and their instructions flow. We need to continue to study the people and institutions that comprise key elements of our communication networks and key sources of their power.

Such an insight might sound banal to Walter Lippmann. But in our own time, it's critical. Over the last twenty years, as microcomputers and the World Wide Web have become ubiquitous, analysts and pundits alike have been dazzled by the new machinery. Or rather, by their dreams of the new machinery. How many of those who laud the egalitarian promise of computers have actually visited a server farm? Attended a meeting of the Internet Corporation for Assigned Names and Numbers? Visited a clean room in a silicon chip manufacturing plant? As powerful as bits and algorithms are, and as dramatically as new media technologies call for new theories of the public sphere, new media technologies retain a material dimension. Though their networking effects may be postindustrial, their material workings depend on industrial production and on workers embedded in industrial-style bureaucratic roles. For some time now, scholars focused on information labor have turned toward the rise of freelancing and peer production (Benkler 2007; Deuze 2007; Neff 2012; Terranova 2000; Weber 2004). But as Downey reminds us, these new regimes of production have been built and continue to function on the backs of an industrial infrastructure—an infrastructure that continues to depend on and replicate the class hierarchies of the industrial era.

In chapter 8 Downey also suggests some of the ways that the methods associated with the political economy of mass media might be repurposed for the study of information systems. Since at least the 1980s, for instance, questions of class have animated investigations across the analysis of film and television. Since the 1990s and the advent of the public Internet, however, class has taken little hold as an analytical lens outside the literature on the digital divide. Likewise, with the important exception of a handful of anthropologists and sociologists (Aneesh 2006; Boczkowski 2010; Helmreich 2000; Malaby 2009; Saxenian 2006), and of Downey himself (2008), relatively few analysts have explored the everyday lives of contemporary information workers who labor inside institutions, particularly toward the bottom of the status ladder. In film and television studies, on the other hand, scholars have for some time examined "below the line" labor—that is, work deemed within the industry to be noncreative (Mayer 2011). Such work includes everything from holding a microphone to keeping a film's accounts. To study it is to see an entirely new Hollywood, a Hollywood peopled not so much by stars and agents as by the kind of people who work on assembly lines everywhere.

Toward the end of his essay, Downey asks what we might learn if we sought to understand the lives of the many, many invisible laborers entwined in our digital networks. In part, he answers, we would gain a new appreciation for the spaces and times in which work is now done and for the communities linked by that work. For my own part, I think that such work could go a long way to finally putting to rest the utopian visions that, as Kelty notes, continue to haunt computing. How can we imagine that digital networks are bringing about an egalitarian utopia when we glimpse the actual lives of Chinese gold farmers? Or the clickworkers of Amazon's Mechanical Turk? Or for that matter, the lives of the many of us who work within information-driven organizations? How can we believe that a new, postindustrial age is upon us when so few of us live the lives of information entrepreneurs and when even many of those who do suffer the kind of precariousness long associated with migrant manual labor?

In short, Downey reminds us that despite two decades of claims to the contrary, information technology does not free us from the politics of labor as we knew them in the nineteenth century. They shift them, reconfigure them a bit, but they hardly do away with class, with the overworking of some bodies for the profit of others, and with the fact that factories, social or mechanical, never run without workers.

Such insights form the starting point for Steve Jackson's moving meditation of chapter 11, "Rethinking Repair." Despite its modest title, Jackson's essay reveals a Lippmannesque ambition—and eloquence. In the first decades of the twentieth century, Lippmann tried to identify what he believed to be the single most prominent threat to social order posed by the combination of mass production and mass media: the rise of a voracious, unthinking mass society. Just shy of a hundred years later, Jackson has undertaken a similar task under new technological, intellectual, and ecological conditions. Jackson writes from within the shadow cast by global warming and from within an academic field largely preoccupied with studying the creation and dissemination of media technologies that have had, at best, complex environmental effects. Where Lippmann feared the consequences of progress, Jackson can see them all too clearly. And like Lippmann, he urges us to analyze emerging media not simply in terms of the kinds of messages they carry or even of the publics they help form, but of the kind of world they are making, as well.

That world includes the natural environment and ourselves as natural organisms. Technologies, like individual lives and like communities of all kinds, grow, flourish, and decay. As Jackson notes, all of us have lately turned our eyes to the first stage of this process when it comes to information technology. Watching first microcomputers and then cell phones and Wi-Fi become ubiquitous, scholars have marveled at the early stages of technological innovation. Sometimes it seems as if we are all standing on the shore in Florida watching a rocket launch from Cape Canaveral. Once the rocket has left our sight, we stop thinking about it. This way of thinking has some uncomfortable antecedents, as Tom Lehrer's famous song points out: "'Once the rockets are up, who cares where they come down? That's not my department,' says Wernher von Braun" (Lehrer 1965). In the case of computers, the arc of innovation that begins in, say, Apple Computer's tinted-glass headquarters in Cupertino, California, ends in a mud brick village in China, with the smashing apart of toxic monitors and the stripping of wire casings and the slow but steady poisoning of the men, women, and children whose hands do the work. As Jackson implies, scholars who study digital media have a moral obligation to study the communities in which the rockets of innovation come down.

They also have an intellectual duty. Jackson points out that by concentrating on the development and dissemination of new media technologies, scholars are in fact overlooking one of the central sites of innovation itself: breakdown. In open source software development, for instance, programmers famously help write new code in order to "scratch an itch" (Weber 2004). Often they hope to create a tool that doesn't exist yet, but other times, they simply repair elements of systems that no longer work. Their repairs generate new innovations, which in turn, either don't function perfectly or break down in the end, and so lead to more innovations down the line. By pointing to this sort of process, Jackson reminds us that technological developments do not simply move in a single upward motion, with one generation of devices shooting out of sight, to be magically replaced by another. Rather, technology, like nature itself, moves in cycles.

In part, Jackson is acting on an impulse that informs all four of these essays. Like Gillespie, Kelty, and Downey, he points to the people and processes that disappear when we think of technology as a special category of being, outside nature and beyond politics. But Jackson goes farther too by invoking the larger technological and environmental conditions of our historical moment. As chapter 11 makes explicit, we are no longer witnessing the rise of mass society so feared by Walter Lippmann. We are instead witnessing the rise of global temperatures, the deterritorialization of manufacturing, the birth of a new world system that is hyper-interconnected by the very technologies of communication we study—and potentially, alongside it, the slow death of the planet's ecosphere, at least as far as humans are concerned.

In the face of these facts, Jackson advocates that we adopt what he calls "broken world thinking." In terms of media technology scholarship, this means following the entire life cycles of our machines. If we want to celebrate innovation and progress, fine—so long as we follow the rocket down and see where it lands. In the landing there will be another beginning, or at least so we can hope. In terms of our intellectual citizenship more broadly, it means studying media technology not only in the terms set for it by producers, distributors, and users, but also within the increasingly visible limits set for all of us by the natural environment within which we live and by our bodies, which are a part of it. In Walter Lippmann's time, media technology threatened the massification of society. In our time, communication technologies, coupled with the fossil-fueled power plants on which they depend and the transportation technologies that bring them to market, are threatening to end society as we know it. As Jackson argues, we need a mode of scholarship that studies media technology in relation to shifts not only in patterns of production and use, but also in the ecosphere.

The appeal of such an approach and its importance should be clear. As Gillespie, Kelty, and Downey all suggest, a new media-technological era has arrived. Elements of the old remain—mass media continue to flourish, as does industrial labor—but they do so under a steady rain of claims that digital technologies have finally freed us from the natural world and a steady stream of efforts by manufacturers and pundits to mask the fact that they haven't. The mass society that Lippmann feared has not only flourished, but so accelerated its workings as to begin to eat at its own foundations. Here and there, we are just beginning to see the ruins poking through. If Jackson is right, and I hope he is, we still have the chance to pay attention to the crumbling and so, in the end, to build something better.

References

Abbate, Janet. 1999. *Inventing the Internet*. Cambridge, MA: MIT Press.

Adorno, Theodore, and Max Horkheimer. 1977. The culture industry: Enlightenment as mass deception. In *Mass Communication and Society*, ed. James Curran, Michael Gurevitch, and Janet Woollacott, 349–383. London: Edward Arnold.

Akrich, Madeleine. 1992. The de-scription of technical objects. In *Shaping Technology/Building Society: Studies in Sociotechnical Change*, ed. Wiebe E. Bijker and John Law, 205–224. Cambridge, MA: MIT Press.

Akrich, Madeleine. 1995. User representations: Practices, methods and sociology. In *Managing Technology in Society*, ed. Arie Rip, Thomas J. Misa, and Johan Schot, 167–184. London: Pinter.

Althaus, Scott, and David Tewksbury. 2000. Patterns of Internet and traditional media use in a networked community. *Political Communication* 17:21–45.

Ananny, Mike. 2011. The curious connection between apps for gay men and sex offenders. *The Atlantic*, April 14. http://www.theatlantic.com/technology/archive/2011/04/the-curious-connection-between-apps-for-gay-men-and-sex-offenders/237340/, accessed April 22, 2013

Anderson, C. W. 2011. Deliberative, agonistic, and algorithmic audiences: Journalism's vision of its public in an age of audience. *Journal of Communication* 5:529–547.

Andrejevic, Mark. 2007. *iSpy: Surveillance and Power in the Interactive Era*. Lawrence: University Press of Kansas.

Aneesh, Aneesh. 2006. *Virtual Migration: The Programming of Globalization*. Durham, NC: Duke University Press.

Ang, Ien. 1990. *Desperately Seeking the Audience*. London: Routledge.

Arendt, Hannah. 1963. *Eichmann in Jerusalem: A Report on the Banality of Evil*. New York: Viking.

Arnheim, Rudolph. 1971. *Entropy and Art: An Essay on Disorder and Order*. Berkeley: University of California Press.

Auletta, Ken. 2010. Publish or perish. *New Yorker* 86 (10) (April):24–31.

Babbage, Charles. 1837. *The Ninth Bridgewater Treatise: A Fragment*. London: J. Murray.

Bacon, Francis. [1620] 1902. *Novum Organum*. American Home Library Company, New York. http://www.constitution.org/bacon/nov_org.htm, accessed April 22, 2013.

Bagdikian, Ben. 2004. *The New Media Monopoly*. Boston: Beacon Press.

Bakardjieva, Maria. 2005. Conceptualizing user agency. In *Internet Society: The Internet in Everyday Life*: 9–36. London: Sage.

Baldwin-Philippi, Jesse. 2011. Bringing science and technology studies to bear in communication studies research. *Communication Research Trends* 30 (2):4–20.

Baldwin-Philippi, Jesse. 2011. "Political pass-along in a digital era: How political campaigns encourage the re-circulation of their messages." Paper presented at the annual meeting of the National Communication Association, New Orleans.

Balka, Ellen. 2011. "Mapping the body across diverse information systems: Shadow bodies and how they make us human." Paper presented at the annual meeting for the Society for Social Studies of Science, Cleveland, OH.

Balsamo, Anne. 1996. *Technologies of the Gendered Body: Reading Cyborg Women*. Durham, NC: Duke University Press.

Balsamo, Anne. 2011. *Designing Culture: The Technocultural Imagination at Work*. Durham, NC: Duke University Press.

Barad, Karen. 2007. *Meeting the Universe Halfway: Quantum Physics and the Entanglement of Matter and Meaning*. Durham, NC: Duke University Press.

Barbrook, Richard, and Andy Cameron. 1996. The Californian ideology. *Science as Culture* 6 (1):44–72.

Bardini, Thierry. 2000. *Bootstrapping: Douglas Engelbart, Coevolution, and the Origins of Personal Computing*. Stanford, CA: Stanford University Press.

Barnhurst, Kevin G., and John C. Nerone. 2001. *The Form of News: A History*. New York: Guilford Press.

Barry, Andrew. 2001. *Political Machines: Governing a Technological Society*. New York: Athlone Press.

Barry, Andrew, Georgina Born, and Gisa Weszkalnys. 2008. Logics of interdisciplinarity. *Economy and Society* 37 (1):20–49.

Basen, Ira. 2011. "Age of the algorithm." *Maisonneuve*, May 9.

Battelle, John. 2005. *The Search: How Google and Its Rivals Rewrote the Rules of Business and Transformed Our Culture*. New York: Portfolio.

Battles, Matthew. 2003. *Library: An Unquiet History*. New York: W. W. Norton.

Baughman, James L. 1992. *The Republic of Mass Culture: Journalism, Filmmaking, and Broadcasting in America Since 1941*. Baltimore, MD: Johns Hopkins University Press.

Baym, Nancy. 2000. *Tune in, Log on: Soaps, Fandom, and Online Community*. Thousand Oaks, CA: Sage.

Baym, Nancy, and Robert Burnett. 2009. Amateur experts: International fan labour in Swedish independent music. *International Journal of Cultural Studies* 12 (5):433–449.

Beck, Ulrich. 2000. The cosmopolitan perspective: Sociology of the second age of modernity. *British Journal of Sociology* 51 (1):79–105.

Beck, Ulrich. 2002. The cosmopolitan society and its enemies. *Theory, Culture & Society* 19 (1–2):17–44.

Beck, Ulrich. 2006. *Cosmopolitan Vision*. Cambridge, UK: Polity Press.

Beck, Ulrich, and Natan Sznaider. 2006. Unpacking cosmopolitanism for the social sciences: A research agenda. *British Journal of Sociology* 57 (1):1–23.

Beer, David. 2009. Power through the algorithm? Participatory web cultures and the technological unconscious. *New Media & Society* 11 (6):985–1002.

Bell, Daniel. 1976. *The Coming of Post-Industrial Society: A Venture in Social Forecasting*. New York: Basic Books.

Benjamin, Walter. 1969. *Illuminations: Essays and Reflections*, ed. Hannah Arendt; trans. Harry Zohn. New York: Schocken.

Benjamin, Walter. 1999. *The Arcades Project*, trans. Howard Eiland and Kevin McLaughlin. Cambridge, MA: Harvard University Press.

Benjamin, Walter. 2003. *Selected Writings*. Vol. 4, ed. Howard Eiland and Michael Jennings, 1938–1940. Cambridge, MA: Harvard University Press.

Beniger, James. 1986. *The Control Revolution: Technological and Economic Origins of the Information Society*. Cambridge, MA: Harvard University Press.

Benkler, Yochai. 2007. *The Wealth of Networks: How Social Production Transforms Markets and Freedom*. New Haven, CT: Yale University Press.

Benner, Chris. 2002. *Work in the New Economy: Flexible Labor Markets in Silicon Valley*. Oxford: Blackwell Press.

Bennett, Jane. 2010. *Vibrant Matter: A Political Ecology of Things*. Durham, NC: Duke University Press.

Berger, Peter L., and Thomas Luckmann. 1966. *The Social Construction of Reality: A Treatise in the Sociology of Knowledge*. Garden City, NY: Doubleday.

Berland, Jody. 2009. *North of Empire: Essays on the Cultural Technologies of Space*. Durham, NC: Duke University Press.

Berlin, Isaiah. 1958. *Two Concepts of Liberty: An Inaugural Lecture Delivered before the University of Oxford on 31 October, 1958*. London: Clarendon Press.

Berlo, David K. 1960. *The Process of Communication: An Introduction to Theory and Practice*. New York: Holt.

Bermejo, Fernando. 2009. Audience manufacture in historical perspective: From broadcasting to Google. *New Media & Society* 11 (1&2):133–154.

Bernays, Edward L. 1928. *Propaganda*. New York: Liveright.

Berry, David. 2011. The computational turn: Thinking about the digital humanities. *Culture Machine* 12:1–22. http://www.culturemachine.net/index.php/cm/article/viewDownloadInterstitial/440/470, accessed April 22, 2013.

Berry, David. 2012. Introduction. In *Life in Code and Software: Mediated Life in a Complex Computational Ecology*, ed. David Berry. London: Open Humanities Press. http://www.livingbooksaboutlife.org/books/Life_in_Code_and_Software/Introduction, accessed April 22, 2013.

Bijker, Wiebe E. 1997. *Of Bicycles, Bakelites, and Bulbs: Toward a Theory of Sociotechnical Change*. Cambridge, MA: MIT Press.

Bijker, Wiebe E. 2001. The need for public intellectuals: A space for STS. *Science, Technology & Human Values* 28 (4):443–450.

Bijker, Wiebe E. 2010. How is technology made? That is the question! *Cambridge Journal of Economics* 34 (1):63–76.

Bijker, Wiebe E., Thomas P. Hughes, and Trevor Pinch. 1987. Introduction. In *The Social Construction of Technological Systems: New Directions in the Sociology and History of Technology*, ed. Wiebe E. Bijker, Thomas P. Hughes, and Trevor Pinch, 9–15. Cambridge, MA: MIT Press.

Bijker, Wiebe E., Thomas P. Hughes, and Trevor Pinch. 1987. *The Social Construction of Technological Systems: New Directions in the Sociology and History of Technology*. Cambridge, MA: MIT Press.

Bijker, Wiebe E., and John Law. 1992. General introduction. In *Shaping Technology/Building Society: Studies in Sociotechnical Change*, ed. Wiebe E. Bijker and John Law, 1–16. Cambridge, MA: MIT Press.

Bijsterveld, Karin. 2008. *Mechanical Sound: Technology, Culture, and Public Problems of Noise in the Twentieth Century*. Cambridge, MA: MIT Press.

Bird, S. Elizabeth. 2003. *The Audience in Everyday Life: Living in a Media World*. London: Routledge.

Blair, Ann, and Peter Stallybrass. 2010. Mediating information, 1450–1800. In *This Is Enlightenment*, ed. C. Siskin and W. Warner, 139–163. Chicago: University of Chicago Press.

Blondheim, Menahem. 2007. "The significance of communication" according to Harold Adams Innis. In *The Toronto School of Communication Theory: Interpretations, Extensions, Applications*, ed. Rita Watson and Menahem Blondheim, 53–81. Toronto: University of Toronto Press; Jerusalem: Hebrew University Magnes Press.

Bloor, David. 1976. *Knowledge and Social Imagery*. Chicago: University of Chicago Press.

Blumer, Herbert. 1933. *The Movies and Conduct*. New York: Macmillan.

Boczkowski, Pablo J. 1999. Understanding the development of online newspapers: Using computer-mediated communication theorizing to study Internet publishing. *New Media & Society* 1 (1):101–126.

Boczkowski, Pablo J. 2004. *Digitizing the News: Innovation in Online Newspapers*. Cambridge, MA: MIT Press.

Boczkowski, Pablo J. 2010. *News at Work: Imitation in an Age of Information Abundance*. Chicago: University of Chicago Press.

Boczkowski, Pablo J., and Leah A. Lievrouw. 2007. Bridging STS and Communication Studies: Scholarship on media and information technologies. In *The Handbook of Science and Technology Studies*, ed. Edward J. Hackett, Olga Amsterdamska, Michael Lynch, and Judy Wajcman, 949–977. Cambridge, MA: MIT Press.

Bogost, Ian. 2012. *Alien Phenomenology, or What It's Like to Be a Thing*. Minneapolis: University of Minnesota Press.

Bok, Derek. 2007. *Our Underachieving Colleges: A Candid Look at How Much Students Learn and Why They Should Be Learning More*. Princeton, NJ: Princeton University Press.

Bolter, J. David, and Richard Grusin. 1999. *Remediation: Understanding New Media*. Cambridge, MA: MIT Press.

Booth, Wayne, Gregory G. Colomb, and Joseph M. Williams. 2008. *The Craft of Research*. 3rd ed. Chicago: University of Chicago Press.

Borgman, Christine. 2000. *From Gutenberg to the Global Information Infrastructure: Access to Information in the Networked World*. Cambridge, MA: MIT Press.

Borsook, Paulina. 2000. *Cyberselfish: A Critical Romp through the Terribly Libertarian Culture of High Tech.* 1st ed. New York: PublicAffairs.

Bourdieu, Pierre. 1984. *Distinction.* London: Routledge.

Bourdieu, Pierre, and Loic J. D. Wacquant. 1992. *An Invitation to Reflexive Sociology.* Chicago: University of Chicago Press.

Bowker, Geoffrey. 1993. How to be universal: Some cybernetic strategies, 1945–1970. *Social Studies of Science* 23 (1):107–127.

Bowker, Geoffrey. 1994. *Science on the Run: Information Management and Industrial Geophysics at Schlumberger, 1920–1940.* Cambridge, MA: MIT Press.

Bowker, Geoffrey. 2006. *Memory Practices in the Sciences.* Cambridge, MA: MIT Press.

Bowker, Geoffrey C., and Susan Leigh Star. 1999. *Sorting Things Out: Classification and Its Consequences.* Cambridge, MA: MIT Press.

boyd, danah. 2010. Social network sites as networked publics: Affordances, dynamics, and implications. In *Networked Self: Identity, Community, and Culture on Social Network Sites,* ed. Zizi Papacharissi, 39–58. New York: Routledge.

boyd, danah, and Kate Crawford. 2012. Critical questions for big data. *Information, Communication, and Society* 15 (5):662–679.

Boyer, Dominic, and Ulf Hannerz. 2006. Introduction: Worlds of journalism. *Ethnography* 7 (1):5–17.

Brand, Stuart. 1994. *How Buildings Learn: What Happens after They're Built.* New York: Penguin.

Braudel, Fernand. 1973. *Capitalism and Material Life, 1400–1800.* London: Weidenfeld and Nicolson.

Braun, Bruce, and Sarah Whatmore, eds. 2010. *Political Matter: Technoscience, Democracy, and Public Life.* Minneapolis: University of Minnesota Press.

Braun, Josh. 2011. "Electronic components and human interventions: Distributing television news online." PhD diss., Cornell University.

Braverman, Harry. 1974. *Labor and Monopoly Capital: The Degradation of Work in the Twentieth Century.* New York: Monthly Review Press.

Briggs, Asa. 1965. *The Age of Improvement.* London: Longmans.

Brook, James, and Iain Boal. 1995. *Resisting the Virtual Life: The Culture and Politics of Information.* San Francisco: City Lights Books.

Bruns, Axel. 2008. *Blogs, Wikipedia, Second Life, and Beyond: From Production to Produsage.* New York: Peter Lang.

Brunton, Finn. 2011. "After WikiLeaks, us." *The New Everyday: A Media Commons Project*, April 6. http://mediacommons.futureofthebook.org/tne/pieces/after-wikileaks-us, accessed April 22, 2013.

Brunton, Finn, and Helen Nissenbaum. 2011. Vernacular resistance to data collection and analysis: A political theory of obfuscation. *First Monday* 16 (5). http://first-monday.org/htbin/cgiwrap/bin/ojs/index.php/fm/article/viewArticle/3493/2955, accessed April 22, 2013.

Bucher, Taina. 2012. Want to be on the top? Algorithmic power and the threat of invisibility on Facebook. *New Media & Society* 14 (7):1164–1180.

Buffon, George-Louis Leclerc, comte de. 1770. *Histoire Naturelle, Générale et Particulière*. Paris: Imprimerie royale.

Burrell, Jenna. 2008. Problematic empowerment: West African Internet scams as strategic misrepresentation. *Information Technology and International Development* 4 (4):15–30.

Burrell, Jenna. 2012. *Invisible Users: Youth in the Internet Cafes of Urban Ghana*. Cambridge, MA: MIT Press.

Burt, Ronald. 1982. *Toward a Structural Theory of Action: Network Models of Social Structure, Perception and Action*. New York: Academic Press.

Buschman, John E., and Gloria J. Leckie, eds. 2007. *The Library as Place: History, Community, and Culture*. Westport, CT: Libraries Unlimited.

Butler, Judith. 1993. *Bodies That Matter: On the Discursive Limits of "Sex."* New York: Routledge.

Callon, Michel. 1986. Some elements of a sociology of translation: Domestication of the scallops and the fishermen of St. Brieuc Bay. In *Power, Action and Belief*, ed. John Law, 196–233. London: Routledge and Kegan Paul.

Callon, Michel. 1999. Actor-network theory: The market test. In *Actor Network Theory and After*, ed. John Law and John Hassard, 191–195. Oxford: Blackwell.

Callon, Michel. 2004. The role of hybrid communities and socio-technical arrangements in the participatory design. *Journal of the Center for Information Studies* 5 (3):3–10.

Campbell-Kelly, Martin. 1996. *Computer: A History of the Information Machine*. 1st ed. New York: Basic Books.

Canales, Jimena. 2009. *A Tenth of a Second: A History*. Chicago: University of Chicago Press.

Candea, Matei, ed. 2010. *The Social after Gabriel Tarde: Debates and Assessments*. London: Routledge.

Canguilhem, Georges. 1978. *The Normal and the Pathological*. Hingham, MA: D. Reidel Publishing.

Caplan, Karen. 2012. "Bomb sight: The visual realism of aerial reconnaissance." *Society and Space: Environment and Planning D*. http://societyandspace.com/2012/09/05/bomb-sight-the-visual-realism-of-aerial-reconnaissance/, accessed April 22, 2013.

Carey, James W. [1983] 1989. Technology and ideology: The case of the telegraph. In *Communication as Culture*, ed. James Carey, 201–230. Winchester, MA: Unwin Hyman. (Orig. publ. in *Prospects: The Annual of the American Studies Association* 8.)

Carey, James W. 1989. *Communication as Culture*. Boston: Unwin Hyman.

Carey, James, and Lawrence Grossberg. 2006. Configurations of culture, history and politics. In *Thinking with James Carey*, ed. Jeremy Packer and Craig Robertson, 199–221. New York: Peter Lang.

Carpignano, Paolo. 1999. The shape of the sphere: The public sphere and the materiality of communication. *Constellations (Oxford, England)* 6 (2):177–189.

Cartwright, Lisa, and Brian Goldfarb. 2006. On the subject of neural and sensory prostheses. In *The Prosthetic Impulse: From a Posthuman Present to a Biocultural Future*, ed. Marquard Smith and Joanne Mora, 125–154. Cambridge, MA: MIT Press.

Castells, Manuel. 1996. *The Rise of the Network Society*. Malden, MA: Blackwell Publishers.

Ceruzzi, Paul. 2003. *A History of Modern Computing*. 2nd ed. Cambridge, MA: MIT Press.

Chaffee, Steven H., and Miriam J. Metzger. 2001. The end of mass communication? *Communication* 4 (4):365–379.

Chandler, Jr. Alfred D. 1977. *The Visible Hand: The Managerial Revolution in American Business*. Cambridge, MA: Belknap Press.

Chandler, Jr. Alfred D., and James W. Cortada, eds. 2000. *A Nation Transformed by Information: How Information has Shaped the United States from Colonial Times to the Present*. New York: Oxford University Press.

Chartier, Roger. 2005. *Inscrire et Effacer: Culture Ecrite et Littérature, XIᵉ–MVIIIᵉ Siècle*. Paris: Gallimard Seuil.

Cheney-Lippold, John. 2011. A new algorithmic identity: Soft biopolitics and the modulation of control. *Theory, Culture & Society* 28 (6):164–181.

Christensen, Kathleen, and Kathleen Barker, eds. 1998. *Contingent Work: American Employment Relations in Transition*. Ithaca, NY: ILR Press.

Christman, John. 1991. Liberalism and individual positive freedom. *Ethics* 101 (2):343–359.

Cmiel, Kenneth. 2009. Libraries, books, and the Information Age. In *The Enduring Book: Print Culture in Postwar America*, ed. Joan Shelley Rubin, David Paul Nord, and Michael Schudson, 325–346. A History of the Book in America 5. Chapel Hill: University of North Carolina Press.

Cohen, Julie. 2012. *Configuring the Networked Self: Law, Code, and the Play of Everyday Practice*. New Haven, CT: Yale University Press.

Coleman, Gabriella. 2009. Code is speech: Legal tinkering, expertise, and protest among free and open source software developers. *Cultural Anthropology* 24 (3):420–454.

Coleman, Gabriella. 2012. "Am I Anonymous?" *Limn* 2 (March). http://limn.it/am-i-anonymous/, accessed May 17, 2012.

Coleman, Gabriella. 2013. Anonymous and the Politics of Leaking. In *Beyond WikiLeaks: Implications for the Future of Communications, Journalism and Society*, ed. Bendetta Brevini, Arne Hintz, and Patrick McCurdy. London: Palgrave Macmillan.

Collins, Harry M. 1985. *Changing Order: Replication and Induction in Scientific Practice*. London: Sage Publications.

Comte, August. [1830–1845] 1975. *Philosophie Première; Cours de Philosophie Positive, Leçons 1 à 45*. Paris: Hermann.

Constant, Edward W. II. 1987. The social locus of technological practice: Community, system, or organization? In *The Social Construction of Technological Systems: New Directions in the Sociology and History of Technology*, ed. Wiebe E. Bijker, Thomas P. Hughes, and Trevor Pinch, 223–242. Cambridge, MA: MIT Press.

Coole, Diana, and Samantha Frost, eds. 2010. *New Materialisms: Ontology, Agency, and Politics*. Durham, NC: Duke University Press.

Cooper, Alan. 1999. *The Inmates Are Running the Asylum*. Indianapolis, IN: Macmillan.

Couldry, Nick. 2004. Theorising media as practice. *Social Semiotics* 14 Ay(2):115–132.

Couldry, Nick. 2008. Mediatization or mediation? Alternative understandings of the emergent space of digital storytelling. *New Media & Society* 10 (3):373–391.

Couldry, Nick. 2012. *Media, Society, World: Social Theory and Digital Media Practice*. Cambridge, UK: Polity Press.

Cowan, Ruth Schwartz. 1987. The consumption junction: A proposal for research strategies in the sociology of technology. In *The Social Construction of Technological Systems: New Directions in the Sociology and History of Technology*, ed. Wiebe E. Bijker, Thomas Parke Hughes, and Trevor Pinch, 261–280. Cambridge, MA: MIT Press.

Craig, Robert T. 1999. Communication theory as a field. *Communication Theory* 9 (2):119–161.

Crompton, Andrew. 2008. Three doors to other worlds. *Journal of Architectural Education* 62 (2):24–29.

Cronon, William. 1991. *Nature's Metropolis: Chicago and the Great West.* New York: W. W. Norton.

Cussins, Adrian. 1992. Content, embodiment and objectivity: The theory of cognitive trails. *Mind* 101 (404):651–688.

Czitrom, Daniel. 1982. *Media and the American Mind: From Morse to McLuhan.* Chapel Hill: University of North Carolina Press.

Dahlberg, Lincoln. 2004. Internet research tracings: Towards non-reductionist methodology. *Journal of Computer-Mediated Communication* 9 (3). http://onlinelibrary .wiley.com/doi/10.1111/j.1083-6101.2004.tb00289.x/full, accessed April 22, 2013.

Darnton, Robert. 2009. "Google and the new digital future." *New York Review of Books,* December 17.

Dayan, Daniel. 2001. The peculiar public of television. *Media Culture & Society* 23 (6):743–765.

Dear, Michael, and Steven Flusty, eds. 2002. *The Spaces of Postmodernity: Readings in Human Geography.* Oxford: Blackwell Publishers.

de Bergerac, Cyrano. [1657] 1995. *L'autre Monde, ou, Les Empires et Estats de la Lune: Édition Diplomatique d'un Manuscrit Inédit (Bibliothèque Fisher, University of Sydney, RB Add. Ms. 68),* trans. M. Sankey. Paris: Lettres Modernes.

de Certeau, Michel. 1984. *The Practices of Everyday Life.* Berkeley: University of California Press.

Deleuze, Gilles, and Félix Guattari. 1987. *A Thousand Plateaus: Capitalism and Schizophrenia.* vol. 2., trans. Brian Massumi. Minneapolis: University of Minnesota Press.

der Derian, James. 2009. *Virtuous War: Mapping the Military-Industrial-Media-Entertainment Network.* 2nd ed. New York: Routledge.

De Sola Pool, Ithiel. 1983. *Technologies of Freedom.* Cambridge, MA: Belknap Press.

Deuze, Mark. 2007. *Media Work.* Cambridge, UK: Polity Press.

Dewey, John. 1896. The reflex arc concept in psychology. *Psychological Review* 3:357–370.

Dewey, John. 1922. *Human Nature and Conduct: An Introduction to Social Psychology.* New York: Henry Holt and Company.

Dewey, John. [1916] 2006. *Essays in Experimental Logic.* Carbondale: Southern Illinois University Press.

Dillman, Don A. 2007. *Mail and Internet Surveys: The Tailored Design Method.* 2nd ed. New York: Wiley.

Dostal, Major Brad C. 2001. *Enhancing Situational Understanding through the Employment of Unmanned Aerial Vehicles.* Center for Army Lessons Learned. http://www.globalsecurity.org/military/library/report/call/call_01-18_ch6.htm, accessed April 22, 2013.

Douglas, Mary. 2007. *Thinking in Circles: An Essay on Ring Composition.* New Haven, CT: Yale University Press.

Douglas, Susan. 1987. *Inventing American Broadcasting, 1899–1922.* Baltimore, MD: Johns Hopkins University Press.

Dourish, Paul. 2004. What we talk about when we talk about context. *Personal and Ubiquitous Computing* 8 (1):19–30.

Dourish, Paul. 2006. "Implications for Design." In CHI '06. *Proceedings of the SIGCHI Conference on Human Factors in Computing Systems*: 541–560.

Downey, Gregory J. 2000. Running somewhere between men and women: Gender and the construction of the telegraph messenger boy. In *Research in Science and Technology Studies: Gender and Work*, ed. Shirley Gorenstein, 129–152. Knowledge and Society 12. Stamford, CT: JAI Press.

Downey, Gregory J. 2001. Virtual webs, physical technologies, and hidden workers: The spaces of labor in information internetworks. *Technology and Culture* 42:209–235.

Downey, Gregory J. 2002. *Telegraph Messenger Boys: Labor, Technology, and Geography, 1850–1950.* New York: Routledge.

Downey, Gregory J. 2003. Telegraph messenger boys: Crossing the borders between history of technology and human geography. *Professional Geographer* 55:134–145.

Downey, Gregory J. 2004. Jumping contexts of space and time. *IEEE Annals of the History of Computing* 26 (2):94–96.

Downey, Gregory J. 2004. The place of labor in the history of information technology revolutions. In *Uncovering Labor in Information Revolutions, 1750–2000*, ed. Aad Blok and Greg Downey, 225–261. Cambridge, UK: Cambridge University Press.

Downey, Gregory J. 2006. Constructing "computer-compatible" stenographers: The transition to realtime transcription in courtroom reporting. *Technology and Culture* 47:1–26.

Downey, Gregory J. 2007. Constructing closed-captioning in the public interest: From minority media accessibility to mainstream educational technology. *Info* 9 (2/3).

Downey, Gregory J. 2007. Human geography and information studies. In *Annual Review of Information Science and Technology*, vol. 41, ed. Blaise Cronon, 683–727. Medford, NJ: Information Today, Inc.

Downey, Gregory J. 2007. The librarian and the Univac: Automation and labor at the 1962 Seattle World's Fair. In *Knowledge Workers in the Information Society*, ed. Catherine McKercher and Vincent Mosco, 37–52. Lanham, MD: Lexington Books.

Downey, Gregory J. 2008. *Closed Captioning: Subtitling, Stenography, and the Digital Convergence of Text with Television*. Baltimore, MD: Johns Hopkins University Press.

Downey, Gregory J. 2009. Cyberspace and the geography of information. In *Encyclopedia of Library and Information Sciences*. 3rd ed., ed. M. Bates and M. N. Maack, 1402–1411. New York: Taylor and Francis.

Downey, Gregory J. 2010. Gender and computing in the push-button library: From cataloging to metadata. In *Gender Codes: Women and Men in the Computing Professions*, ed. Thomas Misa, 143–161. Minneapolis, MN: Charles Babbage Institute.

Downey, Gregory J. 2010. Teaching reading with television: Constructing closed captioning using the rhetoric of literacy. In *Education and the Culture of Print in Modern America*, ed. Andrew R. Nelson and John L. Rudolph, 191–214. Madison: University of Wisconsin Press.

Downey, Gregory J. 2011. *Technology and Communication in American History. SHOT/AHA Historical Perspectives on Technology, Society, and Culture*. Washington, DC: American Historical Association.

Drucker, Johanna. 2003. "The Virtual Codex from page space to e-space." Paper presented at the Syracuse University History of the Book Seminar, Syracuse, NY. Published by Book Web Arts, http://www.philobiblon.com/drucker/, accessed April 22, 2013.

Drucker, Johanna. 2012. Beyond conceptualisms: Poetics after critique and the end of the individual voice. *The Poetry Project Newsletter* (April/May): 6–9.

Druckrey, Timothy, ed. 1996. *Electronic Culture: Technology and Visual Representation*. Preface by Allucquere R. Stone. New York: Aperture.

Du Gay, Paul, Stuart Hall, Linda Jones, Hugh Mackay, and Keith Negus. 1997. *Doing Cultural Studies: The Story of the Sony Walkman*. Thousand Oaks, CA: Sage.

Dyer-Witheford, Nick. 1999. *Cyber-Marx: Cycles and Circuits of Struggle in High-Technology Capitalism*. Urbana: University of Illinois Press.

Eco, Umberto. 1984. *The Role of the Reader: Explorations in the Semiotics of Texts*, 3–43. Bloomington: Indiana University Press.

Edwards, Paul. 1996. *The Closed World: Computers and the Politics of Discourse in Cold War America*. Cambridge, MA: MIT Press.

Edwards, Paul. 2003. Infrastructure and modernity: Force, time, and social organization in the history of sociotechnical systems. In *Modernity and Technology*, ed. Thomas J. Misa, Phillip Brey, and Andrew Feenberg, 185–225. Cambridge, MA: MIT Press.

Edwards, Paul. 2010. *A Vast Machine*. Cambridge, MA: MIT Press.

Eisenstein, Elizabeth L. 1979. *The Printing Press as an Agent of Change*. Cambridge: Cambridge University Press.

Elk, Mike. 2011. "Huffington's bogus defense of unpaid bloggers." *In These Times*, August 2.

Ellul, Jacques. 1964. *The Technological Society*, trans. John Wilkinson. New York: Vintage Books.

Ellul, Jacques. 1980. *The Technological System*, trans. Joachim Neugroschel. New York: Continuum.

Elmer, Greg. 2009. Exclusionary rules? The politics of protocols. In *Routledge Handbook of Internet Politics*, ed. Andrew Chadwick and Philip N. Howard, 376–383. London: Routledge.

Engelbart, Douglas. 1962. *Augmenting Human Intellect: A Conceptual Framework*. Summary report prepared for the Director of Information Sciences, Air Force Office of Scientific Research, Washington, DC. Stanford, CA: Stanford Research Institute. http://www.dougengelbart.org/pubs/augment-3906.html, accessed April 1, 2013.

Ensmenger, Nathan. 2010. *The Computer Boys Take Over: Computers, Programmers, and the Politics of Technical Expertise*. Cambridge, MA: MIT Press.

Epstein, Steven. 1995. The construction of lay expertise: AIDS activism and the forging of credibility in the reform of clinical trials. *Science, Technology & Human Values* 20 (4):408–437.

Epstein, William M. 1990. Confirmational response bias among social work journals. *Science, Technology, and Human Values* 15 (9):9–38.

Eschenfelder, Kristin R., Anuj C. Desai, and Greg Downey. 2011. The Pre-Internet downloading controversy: The evolution of use rights for digital intellectual and cultural Works. *Information Society* 27:69–91.

Eubanks, Virginia. 2011. *Digital Dead End: Fighting for Social Justice in the Information Age*. Cambridge, MA: MIT Press.

Fallows, James. 2011. "Learning to love the (shallow, divisive, unreliable) new media." *The Atlantic*, April.

Farrell, Henry. 2012. The consequences of the Internet for politics. *Annual Review of Political Science* 15 (1):35–52.

Feenberg, Andrew. 1991. *Critical Theory of Technology*. New York: Oxford University Press.

Feenberg, Andrew. 1999. *Questioning Technology*. New York: Routledge.

Fine, Robert. 2007. *Cosmopolitanism*. New York: Routledge.

Fine, Robert, and Vivienne Boon. 2007. Introduction. Cosmopolitanism: Between past and future. *European Journal of Social Theory* 10 (1):5–16.

Finkelstein, Seth. 2008. Google, links, and popularity versus authority. In *The Hyperlinked Society: Questioning Connections in the Digital Age*, ed. Joseph Turow and Lokman Tsui, 104–120. Ann Arbor: University of Michigan Press.

Fischer, Claude. 1992. *America Calling: A Social History of the Telephone to 1940*. Berkeley: University of California Press.

Fischer, John Martin. 1999. Recent work on moral responsibility. *Ethics* 110 (1):93–139.

Fiske, John. 1992. Audiencing: A cultural studies approach to watching television. *Poetics* 21:345–359.

Flayhan, Donna. 2005. Early medium theory, or roots of technological determinism in communication theory. In *The Legacy of McLuhan*, ed. Lance Strate and Edward Wachtel, 237–246. Cresskill, NJ: Hampton Press.

Flichy, Patrice. 2007. *Understanding Technological Innovation: A Socio-Technical Approach*. Cheltenham, UK: Edward Elgar.

Florida, Richard L. 2002. *The Rise of the Creative Class: And How It's Transforming Work, Leisure, Community and Everyday Life*. New York: Basic Books.

Forster, E. M. 1927. *Aspects of the Novel*. New York: Harcourt.

Foucault, Michel. 1977. *Discipline and Punish: The Birth of the Prison*, trans. Alan Sheridan. New York: Vintage Books.

Foucault, Michel. 1980. *Power/Knowledge: Selected Interviews and Other Writings, 1972–1977*, ed. Colin Gordon. New York: Knopf Doubleday.

Foucault, Michel. 1988. Technologies of the self. In *Technologies of the Self: A Seminar with Michel Foucault*, ed. Luther Martin, Huck Gutman, and Patrick Hutton, 16–49. London: Tavistock.

Foucault, Michel. 1991. Governmentality. In *The Foucault Effect: Studies in Governmentality*, ed. G. Churchill, C. Gordon, and P. Miller, 87–104. Chicago: University of Chicago Press.

Foucault, Michel. 1991. Questions of method. In *The Foucault Effect: Studies in Governmentality*, ed. Graham Burchell, Colin Gordon, and Peter Miller, 73–86. Chicago: University of Chicago Press.

Frau-Meigs, Divina, and Jordi Torrent, eds. 2009. *Mapping Media Education Policies in the World: Visions, Programmes and Challenges*. New York: The United Nations-Alliance of Civilizations and Grupo Comunicar.

Fuller, Matthew. 2005. *Media Ecologies: Materialist Energies in Art and Technoculture*. Cambridge, MA: MIT Press.

Gabler, Edwin. 1988. *The American Telegrapher: A Social History, 1860–1900*. New Brunswick, NJ: Rutgers University Press.

Galambos, Louis. 1988. Looking for the boundaries of technological determinism: A brief history of the U.S. telephone system. In *The Development of Large Technical Systems*, ed. Renate Mayntz and Thomas P. Hughes, 135–153. Boulder, CO: Westview Press.

Galison, Peter. 1994. The ontology of the enemy: Norbert Wiener and the cybernetic vision. *Critical Inquiry* 21 (2):228–266.

Galison, Peter. 2003. *Einstein's Clocks and Poincaré's Maps: Empires of Time*. 1st ed. New York: W. W. Norton.

Galloway, Alexander. 2004. *Protocol: How Control Exists after Decentralization*. Cambridge, MA: MIT Press.

Galloway, Alexander. 2006. *Gaming: Essays on Algorithmic Culture*. Minneapolis: University of Minnesota Press.

Galloway, Alexander R., and Eugene Thacker. 2007. *The Exploit: A Theory of Networks*. Minneapolis: University of Minnesota Press.

Gamson, Joshua. 1994. *Claims to Fame: Celebrity in Contemporary America*. Berkeley: University of California Press.

Gane, Nicholas, and David Beer. 2008. *New Media: The Key Concepts*. Oxford: Berg Publishers.

Gans, Herbert J. 1979. *Deciding What's News: A Study of CBS Evening News, NBC Nightly News, Newsweek, and Time*. New York: Pantheon Books.

Garrett, Jesse James. 2002. *The Elements of User Experience: User-Centered Design for the Web*. Indianapolis, IN: New Riders.

Gates, Kelly A. 2011. *Our Biometric Future: Facial Recognition Technology and the Culture of Surveillance.* New York: New York University Press.

Gibbons, Michael, Camille Limoges, Helga Nowotny, Simon Schwartzman, Peter Scott, and Martin Trow. 1994. *The New Production of Knowledge: The Dynamics of Science and Research in Contemporary Societies.* London: Sage.

Gibson, James J. 1977. The theory of affordances. In *Perceiving, Acting, and Knowing: Toward an Ecological Psychology,* ed. Robert Shaw and John Bransford, 67–82. Hillsdale, NJ: Lawrence Erlbaum.

Gibson, James J. 1979. *The Ecological Approach to Visual Perception.* Boston: Houghton Mifflin.

Gibson, James J. 1982. Notes on affordances. In *Reasons for Realism: Selected Essays of James J. Gibson,* ed. Edward S. Reed and Rebecca Jones, 401–418. Hillsdale, NJ: Lawrence Erlbaum Associates.

Giddens, Anthony. 1986. *The Constitution of Society: Outline of the Theory of Structuration.* Berkeley: University of California Press.

Giddens, Anthony. 1990. *The Consequences of Modernity.* Stanford, CA: Stanford University Press.

Gillespie, Tarleton. 2006. Engineering a principle: "End-to-end" in the design of the Internet. *Social Studies of Science* 36 (3):427–457.

Gillespie, Tarleton. 2007. *Wired Shut: Copyright and the Shape of Digital Culture.* Cambridge, MA: MIT Press.

Gillespie, Tarleton. 2010. The politics of "platforms." *New Media & Society* 12 (3):1–18.

Gillespie, Tarleton. 2012. "Can an algorithm be wrong?" *Limn* 2. http://limn.it/can-an -algorithm-be-wrong/, accessed April 22, 2013.

Gillespie, Tarleton. Forthcoming. *Speaking from Platforms.* New Haven, CT: Yale University Press.

Gillespie, Tarleton, and Hector Postigo. 2012. "Five more points." *Culture Digitally,* May 4. http://culturedigitally.org/2012/05/five-more-points/, accessed April 22, 2013.

Gilligan, Carol. 1982. *In a Different Voice: Psychological Theory and Women's Development.* Cambridge, MA: Harvard University Press.

Gillmor, Dan. 2008. *Principles for a New Media Literacy.* Cambridge, MA: Berkman Center for Internet and Society.

Gilroy, Paul. 1994. *The Black Atlantic: Modernity and Double Consciousness.* Cambridge, MA: Harvard University Press.

Gitelman, Lisa. 1999. *Scripts, Grooves, and Writing Machines: Representing Technology in the Edison Era*. Stanford, CA: Stanford University Press.

Gitelman, Lisa. 2006. *Always Already New: Media, History and the Data of Culture*. Cambridge, MA: MIT Press.

Gitelman, Lisa. 2013. *"Raw Data" Is an Oxymoron*. Cambridge, MA: MIT Press.

Gitelman, Lisa, and Virginia Jackson. 2013. Introduction. In *"Raw Data" Is an Oxymoron*, ed. Lisa Gitelman, 1–14. Cambridge, MA: MIT Press.

Gitlin, Todd. 2000. *Inside Prime Time*. Berkeley: University of California Press.

Goffey, Andrew. 2008. Algorithm. In *Software Studies: A Lexicon*, ed. Matthew Fuller, 15–20. Cambridge, MA: MIT Press.

Goggin, Gerard, and Christopher Newell. 2006. Disabling cell phones. In *The Cell Phone Reader*, ed. Anandam Kavoori and Noah Arceneaux, 155–172. New York: Peter Lang.

Goldberg, David T., and Stefka Hristova. 2008. "Blue velvet: Re-dressing New Orleans in Katrina's Wake." *Vectors Journal*. http://vectors.usc.edu/issues/index.php?issue=5, accessed April 18, 2013.

Goldhagen, Daniel. 1996. *Hitler's Willing Executioners: Ordinary Germans and the Holocaust*. New York: Vintage.

Gorman, Michael. 2003. *The Enduring Library: Technology, Tradition, and the Quest for Balance*. Chicago: American Library Association.

Graham, Stephen, and Simon Marvin. 1996. *Telecommunications and the City: Electronic Spaces, Urban Places*. London: Routledge.

Graham, Stephen, and Simon Marvin. 2001. *Splintering Urbanism: Networked Infrastructures, Technological Mobilities and the Urban Condition*. New York: Routledge.

Graham, Stephen, and Nigel Thrift. 2007. Understanding repair and maintenance. *Theory, Culture & Society* 24 (3):1–25.

Granka, Laura. 2010. The politics of search: A decade retrospective. *Information Society* 26 (5):364–374.

Gray, Mary. 2009. *Out in the Country: Youth, Media, and Queer Visibility in Rural America*. New York: New York University Press.

Grimmelmann, James. 2008. The Google dilemma. *New York Law School Law Review*. 53:939–950.

Grimmelmann, James. 2010. Some skepticism about search neutrality. In *The Next Digital Decade: Essays on the Future of the Internet*, ed. Berin Szoka and Adam Marcus, 435–459. Washington, DC: TechFreedom.

Grindstaff, Laura. 2002. *The Money Shot: Trash, Class, and the Making of TV Talk Shows*. Chicago: University of Chicago Press.

Gross, Paul R., and Norman Levitt. 1998. *Higher Superstition: The Academic Left and Its Quarrels with Science*. Baltimore, MD: Johns Hopkins University Press.

Grossberg, Lawrence. 2010. *Cultural Studies in the Future Tense*. Durham, NC: Duke University Press.

Grosswiler, Paul. 2005. Retrieving McLuhan for cultural studies and postmodernism. In *The Legacy of McLuhan*, ed. Lance Strate and Edward Wachtel, 247–260. Cresskill, NJ: Hampton Press.

Grosz, Elizabeth A. 2011. *Becoming Undone: Darwinian Reflections on Life, Politics, and Art*. Durham, NC: Duke University Press.

Grudin, Jonathan. 2006. Why personas work: The psychological evidence. In *The Persona Lifecycle: Keeping People in Mind*, ed. John Pruitt and Tamara Adlin, 642–663. San Francisco: Morgan Kaufmann.

Grudin, Jonathan, and John Pruitt. 2002. "Personas, participatory design and product development: An infrastructure for engagement." Paper presented at the Participatory Design Conference, Malmo, Sweden.

Gumbrecht, Hans Ulrich, and K. Ludwig Pfeiffer. 1994. *Materialities of Communication*. Stanford, CA: Stanford University Press.

Gumpert, Gary. 2005. Marshall McLuhan meets Communication 101: McLuhan as exile. In *The Legacy of McLuhan*, ed. Lance Strate and Edward Wachtel, 227–236. Cresskill, NJ: Hampton Press.

Habermas, Jürgen. [1981] 1987. *The Theory of Communicative Action, vol. 2: Lifeworld and System; A Critique of Functionalist Reason*. Trans. Thomas McCarthy. Boston, MA: Beacon Press. (Orig. publ. as *Theorie des kommunikativen Handelns, Band 2: Zur Kritik der funktionalistischen Vernunft*, Suhrkamp Verlag, Frankfurt-am-Main.)

Habermas, Jürgen. [1962] 1989. *The Structural Transformation of the Public Sphere: An Inquiry into a Category of Bourgeois Society*. Cambridge, MA: MIT Press. First published 1962 by Darmstadt Neuwied: Hermann Luchterhand. Trans. Thomas Burger with the assistance of Frederick Lawrence.

Hackett, Edward J., Olga Amsterdamska, Michael Lynch, and Judy Wajcman. 2008. Introduction. In *The Handbook of Science and Technology Studies*. 3rd ed., ed. Edward J. Hackett, Olga Amsterdamska, Michael Lynch, and Judy Wajcman, 1–7. Cambridge, MA: MIT Press.

Hacking, Ian. 1999. *The Social Construction of What?* Cambridge, MA: Harvard University Press.

Haddon, Leslie. 2006. The contribution of domestication research to in-home computing and media consumption. *Information Society* 22 (4):195–204.

Hage, Ghassan. 2011. Dwelling in the reality of utopia. *Traditional Dwellings and Settlements Review* 23 (1):7–12.

Hage, Ghassan. 2012. Critical anthropological thought and the radical political imaginary. *Critique of Anthropology* 32 (3):285–308.

Halavais, Alexander. 2008. *Search Engine Society*. Cambridge, UK: Polity Press.

Hall, Stuart. 1980. Encoding/decoding. In *Culture, Media, Language*, ed. Stuart Hall, Dorothy Hobson, Andrew Lowe, and Paul Willis, 128–138. London: Unwin Hyman.

Hall, Stuart. 1997. *Representation: Cultural Representations and Signifying Practices*. London: Sage.

Hall, Stuart. 1999. *Representation: Cultural Representations and Signifying Practices*. London: Sage.

Hansen, Sean, Nicholas Berente, and Kalle Lyytinen. 2009. Wikipedia, critical social theory, and the possibility of rational discourse. *Information Society* 25:38–59.

Haraway, Donna. 1991. *Simians, Cyborgs, and Women: The Reinvention of Nature*. New York: Routledge.

Haraway, Donna. 1997. *Modest _Witness @Second_Millenium.FemaleMan_Meets_OncoMouse™: Feminism and Technoscience*. New York: Routledge.

Hardt, Michael, and Antonio Negri. 2000. *Empire*. Cambridge, MA: Harvard University Press.

Harman, Graham. 2002. *Tool-Being: Heidegger and the Metaphysics of Objects*. New York: Open Court.

Hartmann, Maren. 2005. The triple articulation of ICT: Media as technological objects, symbolic environments and individual texts. In *Domestication of Media and Technology*, ed. Thomas Berker, Maren Hartmann, Yves Punie, and Katie Ward, 80–102. Maidenhead, UK: Open University Press.

Harvey, David. 1982. *The Limits to Capital*. Oxford: Oxford University Press.

Harvey, David. 2001. *Spaces of Capital: Towards a Critical Geography*. New York: Routledge.

Harvey, David. 2010. *The Enigma of Capital*. New York: Oxford University Press.

Hawking, Stephen W. 1980. *Is the End in Sight for Theoretical Physics? An Inaugural Lecture*. Cambridge, UK: Cambridge University Press.

Hayles, N. Katherine. 1999. *How We Became Posthuman: Virtual Bodies in Cybernetics, Literature, and Informatics*. Chicago: University of Chicago Press.

Hayles, N. 2005. *My Mother Was a Computer: Digital Subjects and Literary Texts*. Chicago: University of Chicago Press.

Hecht, Jeff. 2011. "Light is not fast enough for high-speed training." *New Scientist* 2832 (October 1). http://www.newscientist.com/article/mg21128324.700-light-is-not-fast-enough-for-highspeed-stock-trading.html, accessed April 22, 2013.

Heidegger, Martin. [1977] 2008. Building dwelling thinking. In *Basic Writings*, ed. David Farrell Krell, 343–364. San Francisco: Harper.

Heidegger, Martin. [1977] 2008. The question concerning technology. In *Basic Writings*, ed. David Farrell Krell, 307–342. San Francisco, CA: Harper.

Heidegger, Martin. 1977. *The Question Concerning Technology and Other Essays*, trans. William Lovitt. New York: Harper and Row.

Helmreich, Stefan. 2000. *Silicon Second Nature: Culturing Artificial Life in a Digital World*. Berkeley: University of California Press.

Helmreich, Stefan. 2007. An anthropologist underwater: Immersive soundscapes, submarine cyborgs and transductive ethnography. *American Ethnologist* 34 (4):621–641.

Hénaff, Marcel. 2002. *Le Prix de la Vérité: Le Don, l'Argent, la Philosophie*. Paris: Editions du Seuil.

Henke, Christoper. 2000. The mechanics of workplace order: Toward a sociology of repair. *Berkeley Journal of Sociology* 43:55–81.

Hepp, Andreas. 2012. *Cultures of Mediatization*. Cambridge, UK: Polity Press.

Hesmondhalgh, David. 2006. Bourdieu, the media and cultural production. *Media Culture & Society* 28 (2):211–231.

Hess, David J. 2001. Ethnography and the development of science and technology studies. In *Handbook of Ethnography*, ed. Paul Atkinson, Amanda Coffey, Sara Delamont, Lyn Lofland, and John Lofland, 234–245. Thousand Oaks, CA: Sage.

Hetherington, Kevin. 2004. Second-handedness: Consumption, disposal and absent presence. *Environment and Planning. D: Society and Space* 22:157–173.

Hildebrand, Lucas. 2009. *Inherent Vice: Bootleg Histories of Videotape and Copyright*. Durham, NC: Duke University Press.

Hilgartner, Stephen. 2000. *Science on Stage: Expert Advice as Public Drama*. Stanford, CA: Stanford University Press.

Hillis, Ken. 1999. *Digital Sensations: Space, Identity, and Embodiment in Virtual Reality*. Minneapolis: University of Minnesota Press.

Hilmes, Michelle. 1997. *Radio Voices: America Broadcasting, 1922–1952*. Minneapolis: University of Minnesota Press.

Hjarvard, Stig. 2008. The mediatization of society. *Nordicom Review* 29 (2):105–134.

Hobbs, Renée. 2010. *Digital and Media Literacy: A Plan of Action*. Washington, DC: The Aspen Institute and the John S. and James L. Knight Foundation.

Hodge, Robert, and Gunther Kress. 1988. *Social Semiotics*. Cambridge, UK: Polity Press.

Howard, Philip N. 2005. *New Media Campaigns and the Managed Citizen*. Cambridge, UK: Cambridge University Press.

Hughes, Thomas P. 1983. *Networks of Power: Electrification in Western Society 1880–1930*. Baltimore, MD: Johns Hopkins University Press.

Hughes, Thomas P. 1987. The evolution of large technical systems. In *The Social Construction of Technological Systems: New Directions in the Sociology and History of Technology*, ed. Wiebe E. Bijker, Thomas P. Hughes, and Trevor Pinch, 51–82. Cambridge, MA: MIT Press.

Hughes, Thomas P. 1989. *American Genesis: A Century of Invention and Technological Enthusiasm, 1870–1970*. New York: Viking.

Hughes, Thomas P. 1994. Technological momentum. In *Does Technology Drive History? The Dilemma of Technological Determinism*, ed. Merritt R. Smith and Leo Marx, 101–114. Cambridge, MA: MIT Press.

Huhtamo, Erkki. 1997. From kaleidoscomaniac to cybernerd: Notes toward an archaeology of media. *Leonardo* 30 (3):221–224.

Huhtamo, Erkki, and Jussi Parikka. 2011. *Media Archaeology: Approaches, Applications and Implications*. Minneapolis: University of Minnesota Press.

Hull, Richard. 2009. Disability and freedom. In *Arguing about Disability: Philosophical Perspectives*, ed. Kristjana Kristiansen, 93–104. New York: Routledge.

Hutchby, Ian. 2001. Technologies, texts and affordances. *Sociology* 35 (2):441–456.

Hutchby, Ian. 2001. *Conversation and Technology: From the Telephone to the Internet*. Cambridge, UK: Polity Press.

Hutchby, Ian. 2003. Affordances and the analysis of technologically mediated interaction: A response to Brian Rappert. *Sociology* 37 (3):581–589.

Hutchins, Edwin. 1995. *Cognition in the Wild*. Cambridge, MA: MIT Press.

Hyysalo, Sampsa. 2010. *Health Technology Development and Use: From Practice Bound Imagination to Evolving Impacts*. London: Routledge.

Ingold, Tim. 2007. *Lines: A Brief History*. London; New York: Routledge.

Innis, Harold A. 1951. *The Bias of Communication*. Toronto: University of Toronto Press.

Innis, Harold A. 1972. *Empire and Communications*. Toronto: University of Toronto Press.

Introna, Lucas, and Helen Nissenbaum. 2000. Shaping the Web: Why the politics of search engines matters. *Information Society* 16 (3):169–185.

Irwin, Alan. 2008. STS perspectives in scientific governance. In *The Handbook of Science and Technology Studies*. 3rd ed., ed. Edward J. Hackett, Olga Amsterdamska, Michael Lynch, and Judy Wajcman, 583–608. Cambridge, MA: MIT Press.

Iser, Wolfgang. 1980. Interaction between text and reader. In *The Reader in the Text: Essays on Audience and Interpretation*, ed. Susan Suleiman and Inge Crosman, 106–121. Princeton, NJ: Princeton University Press.

Ito, Mizuko. 2008. Introduction. In *Networked Publics*, ed. Kazys Varnelis, 1–14. Cambridge, MA: MIT Press.

Ito, Mizuko, Sonja Baumer, Matteo Bittanti, danah boyd, Rachel Cody, Becky Herr-Stephenson, Heather A. Horst, Patricia G. Lange, Dilan Mahendran, Katynka Martinez, C. J. Pascoe, Dan Perkel, Laura Robinson, Christo Sims, and Lisa Tripp. 2009. *Hanging Out, Messing Around, and Geeking Out: Living and Learning with New Media*. Cambridge, MA: MIT Press.

Jackson, Michelle H., M. Scott Poole, and Timothy Kuhn. 2002. The social construction of technology in studies of the workplace. In *Handbook of New Media: Social Shaping and Consequences of ICTs*. 1st ed., ed. Leah A. Lievrouw and Sonia Livingstone, 236–253. London: Sage.

Jackson, Steven J., Alex Pompe, and Gabriel Krieshok. 2011. "Things fall apart: Maintenance and repair in ICT for education initiatives in rural Namibia." *Proceedings of the 2011 iConference,* Seattle, WA.

Jackson, Steven J., Alex Pompe, and Gabriel Krieshok. 2012. "Repair Worlds: Maintenance, Repair, and ICT for Development in Rural Namibia." *Proceedings of the 2012 Computer Supported Cooperative Work Conference,* Seattle, WA.

Jackson, Steven J., David Ribes, Ayse Buyuktur, and Geoffrey C. Bowker. 2011. "Collaborative rhythms: Temporal dissonance and alignment in collaborative scientific work." *Proceedings of the 2011 Computer Supported Cooperative Work Conference, Hangzhou, China*.

James, William. 1970. *Essays in Pragmatism*. New York: The Free Press.

James, William. [1907] 2000. *Pragmatism and Other Writings*. New York: Penguin Classics. First published by Longmans, Green and Company, New York.

Jamieson, Kathleen Hall, and Joseph N. Cappella. 2008. *Echo Chamber: Rush Limbaugh and the Conservative Media Establishment.* New York: Oxford University Press.

Jasanoff, Sheila. 2003. Technologies of humility: Citizen participation in governing science. *Minerva* 41 (3):223–244.

Jasanoff, Sheila, ed. 2004. *States of Knowledge: The Co-Production of Science and Social Order.* London: Routledge.

Jauss, Hans. 1982. *Towards an Aesthetic of Reception.* Minneapolis: University of Minnesota Press.

Jenkins, Henry. 2003. Quentin Tarantino's *Star Wars*? Digital cinema, media convergence, and participatory culture. In *Rethinking Media change: The Aesthetics of Transition,* ed. David Thorburn and Henry Jenkins, 281–312. Cambridge, MA: MIT Press.

Jenkins, Henry. 2006. *Confronting the Challenges of Participatory Culture: Media Education for the 21st Century. Building the Field for Digital Media and Learning.* Chicago: MacArthur Foundation.

Jenkins, Henry. 2006. *Convergence Culture: Where Old and New Media Collide.* New York: New York University Press.

Jensen, Klaus Bruhn. 1990. Television futures: A social action methodology for studying interpretive communities. *Critical Studies in Mass Communication* 7 (2):129–146.

Jensen, Klaus Bruhn. 2008. Meaning. In *The International Encyclopedia of Communication,* ed. Wolfgang Donsbach, 2803–2807. Oxford: Blackwell.

Jensen, Klaus Bruhn. 2010. *Media Convergence: The Three Degrees of Network, Mass and Interpersonal Communication.* New York: Routledge.

Jensen, Klaus B., and Karl E. Rosengren. 1990. Five traditions in search of the audience. *European Journal of Communication* 5 (2):207–238.

Joerges, Bernward. 1999. Do politics have artefacts? *Social Studies of Science* 29 (3):411–431.

John, Richard R. 1995. *Spreading the News: The American Postal System from Franklin to Morse.* Cambridge, MA: Harvard University Press.

John, Richard R. 2010. *Network Nation: Inventing American Telecommunications.* Cambridge, MA: Belknap Press.

Johnson, Bonnie McDaniel, and Ronald E. Rice. 1984. Reinvention in the innovation process: The case of word processing. In *The New Media: Communication, Research, and Technology,* ed. Ronald E. Rice, 157–183. Beverly Hills, CA: Sage.

Johnson, Richard. 1986. What is cultural studies anyway? *Social Text* 16:38–80.

Jones, Steve. 1999. *Cybersociety 2.0: Revisiting Computer-Mediated Community and Technology*. Thousand Oaks, CA: Sage.

Joyce, James. 1963. *Stephen Hero*. Norfolk, CT: New Directions.

Joyce, James. 1917. *A Portrait of the Artist as a Young Man*. London: The Egoist Ltd.

Kalman, Yoram, Gilad Ravid, Daphne Raban, and Sheizaf Rafaeli. 2006. Pauses and response latencies: A chronemic analysis of asynchronous CMC. *Journal of Computer-Mediated Communication* 12 (1). http://jcmc.indiana.edu/vol12/issue1/kalman.html, accessed April 22, 2013.

Kant, Immanuel. 1957. *Perpetual Peace*. New York: Liberal Arts Press.

Kaptelinin, Victor, and Bonnie Nardi. 2006. *Acting with Technology: Activity Theory and Interaction Design*. Cambridge, MA: MIT Press.

Katz, Elihu. 2007. The Toronto School and communication research. In *The Toronto School of Communication Theory: Interpretations, Extensions, Applications*, ed. Rita Watson and Menahem Blondheim, 1–5. Toronto: University of Toronto Press; Jerusalem: Hebrew University Magnes Press.

Katz, Elihu, and Paul F. Lazarsfeld. [1955] 2006. *Personal Influence: The Part Played by People in the Flow of Mass Communications*, 2nd ed. New Brunswick, NJ: Transaction. (Orig. publ. Free Press.)

Katz, James Everett, and Ronald E. Rice. 2002. *Social Consequences of Internet Use: Access, Involvement, and Interaction*. Cambridge, MA: MIT Press.

Keane, John. 1999. Public life in the era of communicative abundance. *Canadian Journal of Communication* 24:165–178.

Kelty, Chris. 2008. *Two Bits: The Cultural Significance of Free Software*. Durham, NC: Duke University Press.

Kelvin, Lord William T. 1900. Presidential Address to the British Association for the Advancement of Science. http://physics.info/news/?p=1406, accessed April 18, 2013.

Kink, Natalie, and Thomas Hess. 2008. Search engines as substitutes for traditional information sources? An investigation of media choice. *Information Society* 24:18–29.

Kirschenbaum, Matthew. 2008. *Mechanisms: New Media and the Forensic Imagination*. Cambridge, MA: MIT Press.

Kittler, Friedrich. 1999. *Gramophone, Film, Typewriter*, trans. Geoffrey Winthrop-Young and Michael Wutz. Stanford, CA: Stanford University Press.

Kittler, Friedrich. 2010. *Optical Media: Berlin Lectures, 1999*, trans. Anthony Enns. Malden, MA: Polity Press.

Kleege, Georgina. 2005. Blindness and visual culture: An eyewitness account. *Journal of Visual Culture* 4:179–190.

Kline, Ronald. 2000. *Consumers in the Country: Technology and Social Change in Rural America*. Baltimore, MD: Johns Hopkins University Press.

Kline, Stephen, Nick Dyer-Witheford, and Greig de Peuter. 2003. *Digital Play: The Interaction of Technology, Culture, and Marketing*. Montreal: McGill-Queen's University Press.

Klinenberg, Eric. 2007. *Fighting for Air: The Battle to Control America's Media*. 1st ed. New York: Metropolitan Books.

Kling, Rob, ed. 1996. *Computerization and Controversy: Value Conflicts and Social Choices*. San Diego, CA: Academic Press.

Knorr Cetina, Karin. 1999. *Epistemic Cultures: How the Sciences Make Knowledge*. Cambridge, MA: Harvard University Press.

Kollock, Peter. 1999. The economies of online cooperation: Gifts and public goods in cyberspace. In *Communities in Cyberspace*, ed. Marc A. Smith and Peter Kollock, 220–239. New York: Routledge.

Kovach, Bill, and Tom Rosenstiel. 2010. *Blur: How to Know What's True in the Age of Information Overload*. New York: Bloomsbury.

Kraut, Robert, Charles Steinfield, Alice Chan, Brian Butler, and Anne Hoag. 1998. Coordination and virtualization: The role of electronic networks and personal relationships. *Journal of Computer-Mediated Communication* 3 (4). http://jcmc.indiana.edu/vol3/issue4/kraut.html, accessed April 22, 2013.

Kreiss, Daniel, Megan Finn, and Fred Turner. 2011. The limits of peer production: Some reminders from Max Weber for the network society. *New Media & Society* 13 (2):243–259.

Krippendorff, Klaus. 2004. *Content Analysis: An Introduction to Its Methodology*. 2nd ed. Thousand Oaks, CA: Sage.

Langlois, Ganaele. 2013. Participatory culture and the new governance of communication: The paradox of participatory media. *Television & New Media*. 14 (2):91–105.

Lasswell, Harold D. 1927. *Propaganda Technique in the World War*. New York: Peter Smith.

Lasswell, Harold D. 1948. The structure and function of communication in society. In *The Communication of Ideas*, ed. Lyman Bryson, 37–51. New York: Harper.

Latour, Bruno. 1986. Visualization and cognition: Thinking with eyes and hands. *Knowledge in Society* 6:1–40.

Latour, Bruno. 1987. *Science in Action: How to Follow Scientists and Engineers through Society*. Cambridge, MA: Harvard University Press.

Latour, Bruno. 1991. Technology is society made durable. In *A Sociology of Monsters: Essays on Power, Technology and Domination*, ed. John Law, 103–131. London: Routledge.

Latour, Bruno. 1993. *We Have Never Been Modern*, trans. Catherine Porter. Cambridge, MA: Harvard University Press.

Latour, Bruno. 1996. *Aramis, or the Love of Technology*, trans. Catherine Porter. Cambridge, MA: Harvard University Press.

Latour, Bruno. 2004. *Politics of Nature: How to Bring the Sciences into Democracy*, trans. Catherine Porter. Cambridge, MA: Harvard University Press.

Latour, Bruno. 2004. Why has critique run out of steam? From matters of fact to matters of concern. *Critical Inquiry* 30:225–248.

Latour, Bruno. 2005. *Reassembling the Social: An Introduction to Actor-Network Theory*. Oxford: Oxford University Press.

Latour, Bruno. 2007. Can we get our materialism back, please? *Isis* 98 (1):138–142.

Latour, Bruno. 2010. *The Making of Law: An Ethnography of the Conseil d'Etat*. Malden, MA: Polity Press.

Latour, Bruno, and Couze Venn. 2002. Morality and technology: The end of the means. *Theory, Culture & Society* 19 (5–6):247–260.

Law, John. 1987. Technology and heterogeneous engineering: The case of Portuguese expansion. In *The Social Construction of Technological Systems: New Directions in the Sociology and History of Technology*, ed. Wiebe E. Bijker, Thomas P. Hughes, and Trevor Pinch, 111–134. Cambridge, MA: MIT Press.

Law, John. 1991. Introduction: Monsters, machines and sociotechnical relations. In *A Sociology of Monsters: Essays on Power, Technology and Domination*, ed. John Law, 1–23. London: Routledge.

Law, John. 2002. Objects and spaces. *Theory, Culture & Society* 19:91–105.

Law, John. 2004. *After Method: Mess in Social Science Research*. London: Routledge.

Law, John. 2008. On sociology and STS. *Sociological Review* 56 (4):623–649.

Law, John. 2010. The materials of STS. In *The Oxford Handbook of Material Culture Studies*, ed. Dan Hicks and Mary C. Beaudry, 173–188. Oxford: Oxford University Press.

Law, John, and John Hassard, eds. 1999. *Actor Network Theory and After*. Oxford: Blackwell.

Lazarsfeld, Paul F. 1941. Remarks on administrative and critical communication research. *Studies in Philosophy and Social Science* 9:2–16.

Lazarsfeld, Paul F., Bernard Berelson, and Hazel Gaudet. 1944. *The People's Choice: How the Voter Makes up His Mind in a Presidential Campaign*. New York: Columbia University Press.

Lazarsfeld, Paul F., and Robert K. Merton. 1948. Mass communication, popular taste, and organized social action. In *The Communication of Ideas*, ed. Lyman Bryson, 95–118. New York: Harper.

Lazer, David, Alex Pentland, Lada Adamic, Sinan Aral, Albert-Laszlo Barabasi, Devon Brewer, Nicholas Christakis, et al. 2009. Computational social science. *Science* 323:721–723.

Lazzarato, Maurizio. 1996. Immaterial labor. In *Radical Thought in Ital: A Potential Politics*, ed. Paulo Virno and Michael Hardt; trans. Paul Collili and Ed Emory, 133–147. Minneapolis: University of Minnesota Press.

League of Professional System Administrators. 2006. "The System Administrators' Code of Ethics." https://lopsa.org/CodeOfEthics, accessed May 10, 2012.

Lehrer, Tom. 1965. "Wernher von Braun." *That Was the Year That Was*. Original live album of satiric songs; now a compact disc. Shout! Factory, Los Angeles.

Leonardi, Paul M., and Stephen R. Barley. 2010. What's under construction here? Social action, materiality, and power in constructivist studies of technology and organizing. *Academy of Management Annals* 4 (1):1–51.

Lessig, Lawrence. 1999. *Code, and Other Laws of Cyberspace*. NewYork: Basic Books.

Lessig, Lawrence. 2008. *Remix: Making Art and Commerce Thrive in the Hybrid Economy*. New York: Penguin Press.

Lessig, Lawrence. 2010. "For the love of culture." *The New Republic*, January 26.

Levinson, Paul. 1997. *The Soft Edge: A Natural History and Future of the Information Revolution*. London: Routledge.

Levinson, Paul. 2009. *New New Media*. Boston: Allyn and Bacon.

Lévi-Strauss, Claude. 1969. *The Raw and the Cooked*. New York: Harper and Row.

Levy, Frank, and Richard J. Murnane. 2004. *The New Division of Labor: How Computers Are Creating the Next Job Market*. Princeton, NJ: Princeton University Press.

Licklider, Joseph Carl Robnett. 1960. Man-computer symbiosis. *IRE Transactions on Human Factors in Electronics* HFE1:4–11.

Liebes, Tamar, and Elihu Katz. 1993. *The Export of Meaning: Cross-Cultural Readings of Dallas*. Cambridge, UK: Polity Press.

Liestøl, Gunnar, Andrew Morrison, and Terje Rasmussen, eds. 2003. *Digital Media Revisited: Theoretical and Conceptual Innovations in Digital Domains*. Cambridge, MA: MIT Press.

Lievrouw, Leah A. 2009. New media, mediation, and communication study. *Information Communication and Society* 12 (3):303–325.

Lievrouw, Leah A. 2011. *Alternative and Activist New Media*. Cambridge, UK: Polity Press.

Lievrouw, Leah A. 2012. The next decade in Internet time: Ways ahead for new media studies. *Information Communication and Society* 15 (5):1–23.

Lievrouw, Leah, and Sonia Livingstone, eds. 2006. *Handbook of New Media*, updated student ed. London: Sage.

Lievrouw, Leah A., and Sonia Livingstone. 2006. Introduction to the updated student edition. *Handbook of New Media*, updated student ed., ed. Leah A. Lievrouw and Sonia Livingstone, 1–14. London: Sage.

Light, Jennifer. 1999. When computers were women. *Technology and Culture* 40 (3):455–483.

Lippmann, Walter. 1922. *Public Opinion*. New York: Macmillan.

Liu, Jie, Michel Goraczko, Sean James, Christian Belady, Jiakang Lu, and Kamin Whitehouse. 2011. "The data furnace: Heating up with cloud computing." Presented at the 3rd USENIX Workshop on Hot Topics in Cloud Computing, Portland, OR. http://research.microsoft.com/pubs/150265/heating.pdf, accessed May 11, 2012.

Liu, Lydia H. 2010. *The Freudian Robot: Digital Media and the Future of the Unconscious*. Chicago: University of Chicago Press.

Livingstone, Sonia. 1998. Audience research at the crossroads: The "implied audience" in media theory. *European Journal of Cultural Studies* 1 (2):193–217.

Livingstone, Sonia. 1998. *Making Sense of Television: The Psychology of Audience Interpretation*. 2nd ed. London: Routledge.

Livingstone, Sonia. 2002. *Young People and New Media: Childhood and the Changing Media Environment*. London: Sage.

Livingstone, Sonia. 2004. The challenge of changing audiences: Or, what is the audience researcher to do in the age of the Internet? *European Journal of Communication* 19 (1):75–86.

Livingstone, Sonia, ed. 2005. *Audiences and Publics: When Cultural Engagement Matters for the Public Sphere*. Portland, OR: Intellect.

Livingstone, Sonia. 2009. On the mediation of everything. *Journal of Communication* 59 (1):1–18.

Longford, Graham. 2005. Pedagogies of digital citizenship and the politics of code. *Techné: Research in Philosophy and Technology* 9 (1):68–96.

Lovink, Geert. 2008. *Zero Comments: Blogging and Critical Internet Culture*, 83–98. New York: Routledge.

Lundby, Knut, ed. 2009. *Mediatization: Concept, Changes, Consequences*. New York: Peter Lang.

Lunt, Peter, and Sonia Livingstone. 2012. *Media Regulation: Governance and the Interests of Citizens and Consumers*. London: Sage.

Lyell, Charles. 1832. *Principles of Geology*. Vol. 1. London: Murray.

Lyon, David. 2003. Surveillance technology and surveillance society. In *Modernity and Technology*, ed. Thomas J. Misa, Philip Brey, and Andrew Feenberg, 161–184. Cambridge, MA: MIT Press.

MacCallum, Gerald C., Jr. 1967. Negative and positive freedom. *Philosophical Review* 76 (3):312–334.

Mackenzie, Adrian. 2005. The performativity of code: Software and cultures of circulation. *Theory, Culture & Society* 22 (1):71–92.

MacKenzie, Donald. 1991. Notes toward a sociology of supercomputing. In *Social Responses to Large Technical Systems: Control or Anticipation*, ed. Todd R. LaPorte, 159–175. Dordrecht: Kluwer.

MacKenzie, Donald, and Judy Wajcman. 1999. Introductory essay: The social shaping of technology. In *The Social Shaping of Technology*. 2nd ed., ed. Donald MacKenzie and Judy Wajcman, 3–27. Buckingham, UK: Open University Press.

MacLeod, Roy. 1980. On visiting the "moving metropolis": Reflections on the architecture of imperial science. *Historical Records of Australian Science* 5 (3):1–16.

Mager, Astrid. 2012. Algorithmic ideology: How capitalist society shapes search engines. *Information, Communication and Society* 15 (5):769–787.

Malaby, Thomas. M. 2009. *Making Virtual Worlds: Linden Lab and Second Life*. Ithaca, NY: Cornell University Press.

Mangu-Ward, Katherine. 2007. "Wikipedia and beyond." *Reason*, June.

Manovich, Lev. 1999. Database as symbolic form. *Convergence: The International Journal of Research into New Media Technologies* 5 (2):80–99.

Manovich, Lev. 2001. *The Language of New Media*. Cambridge, MA: MIT Press.

Mansell, Robin. 2012. *Imagining the Internet: Communication, Innovation, and Governance*. Oxford: Oxford University Press.

Marcum, Deanna B., ed. 2001. *Development of Digital Libraries: An American Perspective*. Westport, CT: Greenwood Press.

Marcuse, Herbert. 1964. *One-Dimensional Man*. Boston: Beacon Books.

Markoff, John. 2005. *What the Dormouse Said: How the Sixties Counterculture Shaped the Personal Computer Industry*. New York: Viking.

Marres, Noortje. 2009. Testing powers of engagement: Green living experiments, the ontological turn, and the undoability of involvement. *European Journal of Social Theory* 12 (1):117–133.

Marres, Noortje, and Javier Lezaun. 2011. Materials and devices of the public: An introduction. *Economy and Society* 40 (4):489–509.

Martens, Hans. 2010. Evaluating media literacy education: Concepts, theories and future directions. *Journal of Media Literacy Education* 2 (1):1–22.

Marvin, Carolyn. 1988. *When Old Technologies Were New: Thinking about Electric Communication in the Late Nineteenth Century*. New York: Oxford University Press.

Marx, Karl, and Friedrich Engels. [1932] 1970. *The German Ideology, Parts I and III*, ed. C. J. Arthur. New York: Lawrence & Wishart. Originally published by the Marx-Engels Institute.

Marx, Leo. 1964. *The Machine in the Garden: Technology and the Pastoral Ideal in America*. New York: Oxford University Press.

Massey, Doreen. 1994. Power-geometry and a progressive sense of place. In *Mapping the Futures: Local Cultures, Global Change*, ed. Jon Bird, Barry Curtis, Tim Putnam, George Robertson, and Lisa Tickner, 59–69. London: Sage.

Massumi, Brian. 2002. *Parables for the Virtual: Movement, Affect, Sensation*. Durham, NC: Duke University Press.

May, Larry. 1992. *Sharing Responsibility*. Chicago: University of Chicago Press.

May, Larry, and Stacey Hoffman eds. 1991. *Collective Responsibility: Five Decades of Debate in Theoretical and Applied Ethics*. Savage, MD: Rowman and Littlefield.

Mayer, Vicki. 2011. *Below the Line Producers and Production Studies in the New Television Economy*. Durham, NC: Duke University Press.

Mayntz, Renate, and Volker Schneider. 1988. The dynamics of system development in a comparative perspective: Interactive videotex in Germany, France and Britain. In *The Development of Large Technical Systems*, ed. Renate Mayntz and Thomas P. Hughes, 263–298. Boulder, CO: Westview.

McChesney, Robert. 1999. *Rich Media, Poor Democracy: Communication Politics in Dubious Times*. Urbana: University of Illinois Press.

McChesney, Robert. 2004. *The Problem of the Media: U.S. Communication Politics in the 21st Century*. New York: Monthly Review Press.

McChesney, Robert. 2008. *The Political Economy of Media: Enduring Issues, Emerging Dilemmas*. New York: Monthly Review Press.

McCullough, Malcolm. 1998. *Abstracting Craft: The Practiced Digital Hand*. Cambridge, MA: MIT Press.

McKeon, Richard. 1957. The development and significance of the concept of responsibility. *Revue Internationale de Philosophie* 39 (1):3–32.

McKibben, Bill. 2010. *Earth: Making a Life on a Tough New Planet*. New York: St. Martin's Griffen.

McLuhan, Marshall. 1962. *The Gutenberg Galaxy: The Making of Typographic Man*. Toronto: University of Toronto Press.

McLuhan, Marshall. 1968. *Understanding Media: The Extensions of Man*. New York: McGraw-Hill.

McLuhan, Marshall, and Quentin Fiore. [1967] 1996. *The Medium Is the Massage: An Inventory of Effects*. San Francisco: HardWired. First published by Bantam Books.

McWilliams, Brian. 2005. *Spam Kings: The Real Story behind the High-Rolling Hucksters Pushing Porn, Pills, and %*@)# Enlargements*. Sebastopol, CA: O'Reilly.

Melody, William H., and Robin E. Mansell. 1983. The debate over critical vs. administrative research: Circularity or challenge. *Journal of Communication* 33 (3):103–116.

Messer-Davidow, Ellen, David Shumway, and David Sylvan. 1993. Disciplinary ways of knowing. In *Knowledges: Historical and Critical Studies in Disciplinarity*, ed. Ellen Messer-Davidow, David Shumway, and David Sylvan, 1–21. Charlottesville: University of Virginia Press.

Metzger, Miriam. 2009. Media effects in the era of Internet communication. In *The Sage Handbook of Media Processes and Effects*, ed. Robin Nabi and Mary Beth Oliver, 561–576. Thousand Oaks, CA: Sage.

Meyrowitz, Joshua. 1985. *No Sense of Place: The Impact of Electronic Media on Social Behavior*. Oxford: Oxford University Press.

Meyrowitz, Joshua. 1994. Medium theory. In *Communication Theory Today*, ed. David Crowley and David Mitchell, 50–77. Cambridge, UK: Polity Press, and Stanford, CA: Stanford University Press.

Mill, John Stuart. 1989. *On Liberty and Other Writings*, ed. Stefan Collini. Cambridge, UK: Cambridge University Press.

Miller, Daniel. 1987. *Material Culture and Mass Consumption*. Oxford: Blackwell.

Miller, Daniel. 1998. *A Theory of Shopping*. Cambridge, UK: Polity Press.

Miller, Daniel. 2005. *Materiality*. Durham, NC: Duke University Press.

Miller, David. 1983. Constraints on freedom. *Ethics* 94 (1):66–86.

Mills, Mara. 2011. Do signals have politics? Inscribing abilities in cochlear implants. In *Oxford Handbook of Sound Studies*, ed. Karin Bijsterveld and Trevor Pinch, 320–346. New York: Oxford University Press.

Mol, Annemarie. 2002. *The Body Multiple: Ontology in Medical Practice*. Durham, NC: Duke University Press.

Monfort, Nick, and Ian Bogost. 2009. *Racing the Beam: The Atari Video Computer System*. Cambridge, MA: MIT Press.

Morley, David. 1980. *The "Nationwide" Audience: Structure and Decoding*. London: British Film Institute.

Morley, David. 1993. Active audience theory: Pendulums and pitfalls. *Journal of Communication* 43 (4):13–19.

Morley, David. 2011. Decoding diaspora and disjuncture: Arjun Appadurai in dialogue with David Morley. *New Formations* 73:39–51.

Morozov, Evgeny. 2011. "Don't be evil." *The New Republic*, July 13. http://www.newrepublic.com/article/books/magazine/91916/google-schmidt-obama-gates-technocrats, accessed April 22, 2013.

Morris, Merrill, and Christine Ogan. 1996. The Internet as a mass medium. *Journal of Computer-Mediated Communication* 1 (4). http://jcmc.indiana.edu/vol1/issue4/morris.html, accessed April 22, 2013.

Mosco, Vincent. 1982. *Pushbutton Fantasies: Critical Perspectives on Videotex and Information Technology*. Norwood, NJ: Ablex.

Mosco, Vincent. 2009. *The Political Economy of Communication*. 2nd ed. London: Sage.

Mosco, Vincent, and Catherine McKercher. 2008. *The Laboring of Communication: Will Knowledge Workers of the World Unite?* Lanham, MD: Lexington Books.

Mumford, Lewis. 1934. *Technics and Civilization*. New York: Harcourt, Brace and Co.

Nakamura, Lisa. 2002. *Cybertypes: Race, Ethnicity, and Identity on the Internet*. New York: Routledge.

Nardi, Bonnie, ed. 1996. *Context and Consciousness: Activity Theory and Human-Computer Interaction*. Cambridge, MA: MIT Press.

Nature. 2007. "A matter of trust." *Nature* 449:637–638.

Neff, Gina. 2012. *Venture Labor: Work and the Burden of Risk in Innovative Industries*. Cambridge, MA: MIT Press.

Nelson, Eric. 2005. Liberty: One or two concepts / Liberty: One concept too many? *Political Theory* 33 (1):58–78.

Nelson, Alondra, and Thuy Linh N. Tu, and Alicia Headlam Hines, eds. 2001. *Technicolor: Race, Technology, and Everyday Life*. New York: New York University Press.

Netz, Reviel. 1999. *The Shaping of Deduction in Greek Mathematics: A Study in Cognitive History*. Cambridge: Cambridge University Press.

Newhagen, John E, and Sheizaf Rafaeli. 1996. Why communication researchers should study the Internet: A dialogue. *Journal of Communication* 46 (1):4–13.

Nichols, John. 2012. *Uprising: How Wisconsin Renewed the Politics of Protest, from Madison to Wall Street*. New York: Nation Books.

Niederer, Sabine, and José van Dijck. 2010. Wisdom of the crowd or technicity of content? Wikipedia as a sociotechnical system. *New Media & Society* 12 (8):1368–1387.

Nietzsche, Friedrich. [1887] 1967. *On the Genealogy of Morals and Ecce Homo*, trans. Walter Kaufmann. New York: Random House.

Nissenbaum, Helen. 2009. *Privacy in Context: Technology, Policy, and the Integrity of Social Life*. Palo Alto, CA: Stanford University Press.

Norman, Donald A. 1988. *The Design of Everyday Things*. New York: Basic Books.

Norman, Donald A. 1999. Affordance, conventions, and design. *Interaction* 6 (3):38–43.

Norris, Pippa. 2001. *Digital Divide: Civic Engagement, Information Poverty, and the Internet Worldwide*. New York: Cambridge University Press.

Nowotny, Helga, Peter Scott, and Michael Gibbons. 2001. *Re-Thinking Science: Knowledge and the Public in an Age of Uncertainty*. London: Polity Press.

Nye, David E. 1994. *American Technological Sublime*. Cambridge, MA: MIT Press.

Ohmann, Richard. 1996. *Selling Culture: Magazines, Markets, and Class at the Turn of the Century*. New York: Verso.

Orr, Julian E. 1996. *Talking about Machines: An Ethnography of a Modern Job*. Ithaca, NY: Cornell University Press.

Oudshoorn, Nelly, and Trevor Pinch, eds. 2003. *How Users Matter: The Co-Construction of Users and Technology*. Cambridge, MA: MIT Press.

Packer, Jeremy, and Stephen B. Crofts Wiley, eds. 2011. *Communication Matters: Materialist Approaches to Media, Mobility and Networks*. Cambridge, UK: Routledge.

Packer, Jeremy, and Stephen B. Crofts Wiley. 2012. Introduction: The materiality of communication. In *Communication Matters: Materialist Approaches to Media, Mobility and Networks*, ed. Jeremy Packer and Stephen B. Crofts Wiley, 3–16. London: Routledge.

Papacharissi, Zizi. 2009. The virtual geographies of social networks: A comparative analysis of Facebook, LinkedIn and ASmallWorld. *New Media & Society* 11 (1&2):199–220.

Papacharissi, Zizi. 2012. Without you, I'm nothing: Performances of the self on Twitter. *International Journal of Communication* 6:1989–2006.

Parikka, Jussi. 2010. *Insect Media: An Archaeology of Animals and Technology, Posthumanities*. Minneapolis: University of Minnesota Press.

Parikka, Jussi. 2012. New materialism as media theory: Medianatures and dirty matter. *Communication and Critical/Cultural Studies* 9 (1):95–100.

Parikka, Jussi. 2012. *What Is Media Archaeology?* Cambridge, UK and Malden, MA: Polity Press.

Pariser, Eli. 2011. *The Filter Bubble: What the Internet Is Hiding from You*. New York: Penguin Press.

Park, David W., and Jefferson Pooley. 2008. *The History of Media and Communication Research: Contested Memories*. New York: Peter Lang.

Parks, Malcolm, and Kory Floyd. 1996. Making friends in cyberspace. *Journal of Computer-Mediated Communication* 1 (4). http://jcmc.indiana.edu/vol1/issue4/parks.html, accessed April 22, 2013.

Parviainen, Jaana. 2002. Bodily knowledge: Epistemological reflections on dance. *Dance Research Journal* 34 (1):11–26.

Pasquale, Frank. 2009. "Assessing algorithmic authority." *Madisonian.net*, November 18. http://madisonian.net/2009/11/18/assessing-algorithmic-authority/, accessed April 22, 2013.

Pasquale, Frank, and Oren Bracha. 2008. Federal Search Commission? Access, fairness and accountability in the law of search. *Cornell Law Review* 93 (6):1149–1210. http://papers.ssrn.com/sol3/papers.cfm?abstract_id=1002453, accessed April 22, 2013.

Peck, Jamie. 1996. *Work-Place: The Social Regulation of Labor Markets*. New York: Guilford Press.

Peirce, Charles S. 1955. *Philosophical Writings of Peirce*. New York: Dover Publications.

Pentzold, Christian. 2010. Imagining the Wikipedia community: What do Wikipedia authors mean when they write about their "community"? *New Media & Society* 13 (5):704–721.

Peters, John Durham. 1999. *Speaking into the Air: A History of the Idea of Communication*. Chicago: University of Chicago Press.

Peters, John Durham. 2010. Introduction: Friedrich Kittler's light shows. In Friedrich Kittler, *Optical Media*, trans. Anthony Enns, 1–17. Cambridge, UK: Polity Press. (Orig. publ. as *Optische Medien / Berliner Vorlesung 1999*, Merve Verlag Berlin.)

Peters, John Durham. Forthcoming. *Two Cheers for Technological Determinism*.

Peterson, Ruth C., and Louis L. Thurstone. 1933. *Motion Pictures and the Social Attitudes of Children*. Oxford: Macmillan.

Petroski, Henry. 2006. *Success through Failure: The Paradox of Design*. Princeton, NJ: Princeton University Press.

Pettit, Philip. 1997. *Republicanism: A Theory of Freedom and Government*. Oxford: Oxford University Press.

Pettit, Philip. 2001. *A Theory of Freedom*. Cambridge, UK: Polity Press.

Pfaffenberger, Brian. 1992. Technological dramas. *Science, Technology & Human Values* 17 (3):282–312.

Pfaffenberger, Brian. 1996. "If I want it, it's okay": Usenet and the (outer) limits of free speech. *Information Society* 12 (4):365–386.

Piaget, Jean. 1969. *The Child's Conception of Time*. New York: Basic Books.

Piaget, Jean, and Barbel Inhelder. 1967. *The Child's Conception of Space*. New York: W. W. Norton.

Pinch, Trevor J. 1996. The social construction of technology: A review. In *Technological Change: Methods and Themes in the History of Technology*, ed. Robert Fox, 17–35. Amsterdam: Harwood.

Pinch, Trevor, and Wiebe Bijker. 1984. The social construction of facts and artefacts: Or how the sociology of science and the sociology of technology might benefit each other. *Social Studies of Science* 14 (3):399–411.

Pinch, Trevor, and Wiebe Bijker. 1987. The social construction of facts and artifacts: Or how the sociology of science and the sociology of technology might benefit each other. In *The Social Construction of Technological Systems: New Directions in the Sociology and History of Technology*, ed. Wiebe E. Bijker, Thomas P. Hughes, and Trevor Pinch, 17–50. Cambridge, MA: MIT Press.

Pinch, Trevor, and Richard Swedberg. 2008. *Living in a Material World: Economic Sociology Meets Science and Technology Studies*. Cambridge, MA: MIT Press.

Pinch, Trevor, and Frank Trocco. 2002. *Analog Days: The Invention and Impact of the Moog Synthesizer*. Cambridge, MA: Harvard University Press.

Pitkin, Hanna Fenichel. 1988. Are freedom and liberty twins? *Political Theory* 16 (4):523–552.

Plotnick, Rachel. 2012. At the interface: The case of the electric pushbutton, 1880–1923. *Technology and Culture* 53 (4):815–845.

Plotnick, Rachel. 2012. Predicting push-button warfare: U.S. print media and conflict from a distance, 1945–2010. *Media Culture & Society* 34 (6):655–672.

Plotnick, Rachel. 2013. "Touch of a button: Long-distance transmission, communication and control at World's Fairs." *Critical Studies in Media Communication*. 30 (1):52–68.

Poe, Marshall. 2006. "The hive." *Atlantic Monthly*, September.

Poincaré, Henri. 1908. *Science et Méthode*. Paris: E. Flammarion.

Porter, David, ed. 1997. *Internet Culture*. New York; London: Routledge.

Postman, Neil. 1985. *Amusing Ourselves to Death*. New York: Penguin.

Preda, Alex. 2006. Socio-technical agency in financial markets: The case of the stock ticker. *Social Studies of Science* 36 (5):753–782.

Pruitt, John, and Tamara Adlin, eds. 2006. *The Persona Lifecycle: Keeping People in Mind*. San Francisco: Morgan Kaufmann.

Rabelais, François. [1532] 1964. *Les Cinq Livres de Rabelais*, trans. R. Delbiausse. Paris: Éditions Magnard.

Radway, Janice. 1984. *Reading the Romance: Women, Patriarchy, and Popular Literature*. Chapel Hill: University of North Carolina Press.

Radway, Janice. 1988. Reception study: Ethnography and the problems of dispersed audiences and nomadic subjects. *Cultural Studies* 2 (3):359–376.

Rappert, Brian. 2003. Technologies, texts and possibilities: A reply to Hutchby. *Sociology* 37 (3):565–580.

Ravetz, Jerome. 1971. *Scientific Knowledge and Its Social Problems*. Oxford: Oxford University Press.

Rawls, John. 1971. *A Theory of Justice*. Cambridge, MA: Belknap Press of Harvard University Press.

Reich, Charles. 1970. *The Greening of America: How the Youth Revolution Is Trying to Make America Livable*. 1st ed. New York: Random House.

Reich, Robert. 1991. *The Work of Nations: Preparing Ourselves for 21st Century Capitalism*. New York: A. A. Knopf.

Rice, Ronald E., and Everett M. Rogers. 1980. Re-invention in the innovation process. *Knowledge* 1:449–514.

Rieder, Bernhard. 2012. "ORDER BY column_name: The relational database as pervasive cultural form." Presented at The Lived Logics of Database Machinery conference, London.

Rip, Arie, and Johan Schot. 2002. Identifying loci for influencing the dynamics of technological development. In *Shaping Technology, Guiding Policy*, ed. Robin Williams and Knut Sorensen, 155–172. Cheltenham, UK: Edward Elgar.

Robins, Kevin, and Frank Webster. 1989. *The Technical Fix: Education, Computers and Industry*. New York: St. Martin's Press.

Robins, Kevin, and Frank Webster. 1996. *Times of the Technoculture: From the Information Society to the Virtual Life*. New York: Routledge.

Robinson, Colin. 2010. "How Amazon kills books and makes us stupid." *The Nation*, July 19.

Robson, Gary. 2000. *Alternative Realtime Careers: A Guide to Closed Captioning and CART for Court Reporters*. Vienna, VA: National Court Reporters Association.

Rogers, Everett. 1997. *History of Communication Study*. New York: Free Press.

Rogers, Everett. [1962] 2003. *Diffusion of Innovations*. 5th ed. New York: Free Press.

Rogers, Everett M., and D. Lawrence Kincaid. 1981. *Communication Networks: Toward a New Paradigm for Research*. New York: Free Press.

Rogers, Jackie Krasas. 2000. *Temps: The Many Faces of the Changing Workplace*. Ithaca, NY: Cornell University Press.

Rogers, Richard A. 1998. Overcoming the objectification of nature in constitutive theories: Toward a transhuman, materialist theory of communication. *Western Journal of Communication* 62 (3):244–272.

Rogers, Richard A. 2009. The Googlization question, and the inculpable engine. In *Deep Search: The Politics of Search Engines beyond Google*, ed. Konrad Becker and Felix Stalder, 173–184. Edison, NJ: Transaction Publishers.

Rose, Nikolas. 1999. *Powers of Freedom: Reframing Political Thought*. Cambridge, UK: University of Cambridge Press.

Ross, Andrew. 1996. *Science Wars*. Durham, NC: Duke University Press.

Rossi, Paolo. 2000. *Logic and the Art of Memory: The Quest for a Universal Language*. Chicago: University of Chicago Press.

Rosenzweig, Roy. 2006. Can history be open source? Wikipedia and the future of the past. *Journal of American History* 93 (1):117–146.

Roszak, Theodore. 1969. *The Making of a Counter Culture: Reflections on the Technocratic Society and its Youthful Opposition*. Garden City, NY: Doubleday.

Roychoudhuri, Onnesha. 2010. "Books after Amazon." *Boston Review*, December.

Ryfe, David. 2006. The nature of news rules. *Political Communication* 23 (2):203–214.

Sagrans, Erica, ed. 2011. *We Are Wisconsin: The Wisconsin Uprising in the Words of the Activists, Writers, and Everyday Wisconsonites Who Made It Happen*. Minneapolis, MN: Tasora Books.

Saxenian, AnnaLee. 2006. *The New Argonauts: Regional Advantage in a Global Economy*. Cambridge, MA: Harvard University Press.

Schaffner, Ingrid, Matthias Winzen, Geoffrey Batchen, and Hubertus Gassner. 1998. *Deep Storage: Collecting, Storing, and Archiving in Art*. Munich: Prestel.

Schiller, Dan. 1999. *Digital Capitalism: Networking the Global Market System*. Cambridge, MA: MIT Press.

Schiller, Herbert. 1984. *Information and the Crisis Economy*. Oxford: Oxford University Press.

Schiller, Herbert. 1989. *Culture, Inc.: The Corporate Takeover of Public Expression*. Oxford: Oxford University Press.

Schneider, Volker. 1991. The governance of large technical systems: The case of telecommunications. In *Social Responses to Large Technical Systems: Control or Anticipation*, ed. Todd R. LaPorte, 19–42. Dordrecht: Kluwer.

Schot, Johan, and Adri Albert de la Bruhèze. 2003. The mediated design of products, consumption and consumers in the twentieth century. In *How Users Matter: The Co-Construction of Users and Technology*, ed. Nelly Oudshoorn and Trevor Pinch, 229–245. Cambridge, MA: MIT Press.

Schramm, Wilbur Lang. 1997. *The Beginnings of Communication Study in America: A Personal Memoir*. London: Sage.

Schudson, Michael. 1978. *Discovering the News: A Social History of American Newspapers*. New York: Basic Books.

Schudson, Michael. 1998. *The Good Citizen: A History of American Civic Life*. New York: Martin Kessler Books.

Schudson, Michael, and Chris Anderson. 2009. Objectivity, professionalism, and truth seeking in journalism. In *The Handbook of Journalism Studies*, ed. Karin Wahl-Jorgensen and Thomas Hanitzsch, 88–101. New York: Routledge.

Schuler, Douglas, and Aki Namioka. 1993. *Participatory Design: Principles and Practices*. London: Routledge.

Sconce, Jeffrey. 2000. *Haunted Media: Electronic Presence from Telegraphy to Television*. Durham, NC: Duke University Press.

Sennett, Richard. 2009. *The Craftsman*. New Haven, CT: Yale University Press.

Shah, Dhavan, Jack McLeod, and So-Hyang Yoon. 2001. Communication, context and community: An exploration of print, broadcast and Internet influences. *Communication Research* 28:464–506.

Shannon, Claude E., and Warren Weaver. [1949] 1963. *The Mathematical Theory of Communication*. Urbana: University of Illinois Press.

Shapin, Steven. 1995. Trust, honesty, and the authority of science. In *Society's Choices: Social and Ethical Decision Making in Biomedicine*, ed. Ruth Ellen Bulger, Elizabeth Meyer Bobby, and Harvey Fineberg, 388–408. Washington, DC: National Academies Press.

Shapin, Steven, and Simon Schaffer. 1985. *Leviathan and the Air-Pump: Hobbes, Boyle and the Experimental Life*. Princeton, NJ: Princeton University Press.

Shaw, Donald L., and Maxwell E. McCombs. 1977. *The Emergence of American Political Issues: The Agenda-Setting Function of the Press*. St. Paul, MN: West Publishing Company.

Shirky, Clay. 2008. *Here Comes Everybody: The Power of Organizing without Organizations*. New York: Penguin Press.

Siebers, Tobin. 2008. *Disability Theory, Corporealities*. Ann Arbor: University of Michigan Press.

Siegert, Bernhard. 2011. The map is the territory. *Radical Philosophy* 169:13–16.

Siles, Ignacio. 2011. From online filter to Web format: Articulating materiality and meaning in the early history of blogs. *Social Studies of Science* 41 (5):737–758.

Siles, Ignacio. 2012. The rise of blogging: Articulation as a dynamic of technological stabilization. *New Media & Society* 14 (5):781–797.

Siles, Ignacio. 2012. Web technologies of the self: The arising of the "blogger" identity. *Journal of Computer-Mediated Communication* 17 (4):408–421.

Siles, Ignacio, and Pablo J. Boczkowski. 2012. At the intersection of content and materiality: A texto-material perspective on agency in the use of media technologies. *Communication Theory* 22 (3):227–249.

Silver, David. 2000. Looking backwards, looking forward: Cyberculture studies 1990–2000. In *Web.Studies: Rewiring Media Studies for the Digital Age*, ed. David Gauntlett, 19–30. Oxford: Oxford University Press.

Silver, David, and Adrienne Massanari, eds. 2006. *Critical Cyberculture Studies*. New York: New York University Press.

Silverstone, Roger. 1994. *Television and Everyday Life*. London: Routledge.

Silverstone, Roger, ed. 2005. *Media, Technology and Everyday Life in Europe*. Aldershot, UK: Ashgate.

Silverstone, Roger. 2005. The sociology of mediation and communication. In *The Sage Handbook of Sociology*, ed. Craig Calhoun, Chris Rojek, and Bryan Turner, 188–207. London: Sage.

Silverstone, Roger. 2006. Domesticating domestication: Reflections on the life of a concept. In *The Domestication of Media and Technology*, ed. Thomas Berker, Maren Hartmann, Yves Punie, and Katie Ward, 229–248. Maidenhead, UK: Open University Press.

Silverstone, Roger, and Eric Hirsch. 1992. *Consuming Technologies: Media and Information in Domestic Spaces*. London: Routledge.

Simmel, Georg. 1906. The sociology of secrecy and of the secret societies. *American Journal of Sociology* 11:441–498.

Siskin, Clifford, and William Warner. 2010. *This Is Enlightenment*. Chicago: University of Chicago Press.

Sismondo, Sergio. 1993. Some social constructions. *Social Studies of Science* 23 (3):515–523.

Sismondo, Sergio. 2008. Science and technology studies and an engaged program. In *The Handbook of Science and Technology Studies*. 3rd ed., ed. Edward J. Hackett, Olga Amsterdamska, Michael Lynch, and Judy Wajcman, 13–31. Cambridge, MA: MIT Press.

Skinner, Quentin. 1998. *Liberty before Liberalism*. Cambridge, UK: Cambridge University Press.

Skinner, Quentin. 2002. A third concept of liberty. *Proceedings of the British Academy* 117:237–268.

Slack, Jennifer Daryl. 1984. *Communication Technologies and Society: Conceptions of Causality and the Politics of Technological Intervention*. Norwood, NJ: Ablex.

Slack, Jennifer Daryl, and J. Macgregor Wise. 2006. *Culture + Technology: A Primer*. New York: Peter Lang.

Slaughter, Mary M. 1982. *Universal Languages and Scientific Taxonomy in the Seventeenth Century*. Cambridge, UK: Cambridge University Press.

Smith, Daniel Jordan. 2007. *A Culture of Corruption: Everyday Deception and Popular Discontent in Nigeria*. Princeton, NJ: Princeton University Press.

Smith, Marc A., and Peter Kollock, eds. 1999. *Communities in Cyberspace*. New York: Routledge.

Smythe, Dallas. 2001. On the audience commodity and its work. In *Media and Cultural Studies: KeyWorks*, ed. Meenakshi Durham and Douglas Kellner, 253–279. Malden, MA: Blackwell Publishing.

Sokal, Alan D., and Jean Bricmont. 1999. *Fashionable Nonsense: Postmodern Intellectuals' Abuse of Science*. New York: Picador.

Solove, Daniel. 2004. *The Digital Person: Technology and Privacy in the Information Age*. New York: New York University Press.

Spigel, Lynn. 1992. *Make Room for TV: Television and the Family Ideal in Postwar America*. Chicago: University of Chicago Press.

Spigel, Lynn. 2010. Housing television: Architectures of the archive. *Communication Review* 13 (1):52–74.

Sproull, L., and Sara Kiesler. 1991. *Connections: New Ways of Working in the Networked Organization*. Cambridge, MA: MIT Press.

Stabile, Carol. 1994. *Feminism and the Technological Fix*. New York: Manchester University Press.

Stalder, Felix, and Christine Mayer. 2009. The second index: Search engines, personalization and surveillance. In *Deep Search: The Politics of Search beyond Google*, ed. Konrad Becker and Felix Stalder, 98–115. London: Transaction Publishers.

Standage, Tom. 1998. *The Victorian Internet: The Remarkable Story of the Telegraph and the Nineteenth Century's On-line Pioneers*. New York: Walker and Co.

Star, Susan Leigh. 1999. The ethnography of infrastructure. *American Behavioral Scientist* 43 (3):377–391.

Star, Susan Leigh, and Geoffrey C. Bowker. 2006. How to infrastructure. In *Handbook of New Media*, updated student ed., ed. Leah A. Lievrouw and Sonia Livingstone, 230–245. London: Sage.

Star, Susan Leigh, and James R. Griesemer. 1989. Institutional ecology, "translations" and boundary objects: Amateurs and professionals in Berkeley's Museum of Vertebrate Zoology, 1907–39. *Social Studies of Science* 19 (3):387–420.

Star, Susan Leigh, and Anslem Strauss. 1999. Layers of silence, arenas of voice: The ecology of visible and invisible work. *Computer Supported Cooperative Work* 8:9–30.

Starr, Paul. 2004. *The Creation of the Media: Political Origins of Modern Communications*. New York: Basic Books.

Steiner, Hillel. 1994. *An Essay on Rights*. Oxford: Blackwell.

Sterne, Jonathan. 2003. *The Audible Past: Cultural Origins of Sound Reproduction.* Durham, NC: Duke University Press.

Sterne, Jonathan. 2012. *MP3: The Meaning of a Format.* Durham, NC: Duke University Press.

Stone, Allucquere R. 1995. *The War of Desire and Technology at the Close of the Mechanical Age.* Cambridge, MA: MIT Press.

Strate, Lance. 2004. A media ecology review. *Communication Research Trends* 23 (2):1–48.

Streeter, Thomas. 2011. *The Net Effect: Romanticism, Capitalism, and the Internet.* New York: New York University Press.

Striphas, Theodore G. 2009. *The Late Age of Print: Everyday Book Culture from Consumerism to Control.* New York: Columbia University Press.

Striphas, Theodore G. 2010. "How to have culture in an algorithmic age." *Differences and Repetitions*, July 13. http://www.diffandrep.org/2010/07/13/how-to-have-culture-in-an-algorithmic-age/, accessed April 22, 2013.

Suchman, Lucy. 1987. *Plans and Situated Actions: The Problem of Machine-Human Communication.* Cambridge, UK: Cambridge University Press.

Suchman, Lucy. 2006. *Human-Machine Refigurations: Plans and Situated Actions.* Cambridge: Cambridge University Press.

Suchman, Lucy. 2011. Anthropological relocations and the limits of design. *Annual Review of Anthropology* 40:1–18.

Suchman, Lucy. 2012. Configuration. In *Inventive Methods: The Happening of the Social*, ed. C. Lury and N. Wakeford, 48–60. London: Routledge.

Suchman, Lucy. Forthcoming. Situational awareness: Deadly bioconvergence at the boudaries of bodies and machines. *Mediatropes.*

Suchman, Lucy, Randall Trigg, and Jeanette Blomberg. 2002. Working artefacts: Ethnomethods of the prototype. *British Journal of Sociology* 53:163–179.

Sunstein, Cass R. 2001. *Republic.com 2.0.* Princeton, NJ: Princeton University Press.

Swanson, Don R. 1986. Undiscovered public knowledge. *Library Quarterly* 56 (2):103–118.

Swiss, Thomas, and Andrew Herman. 2000. *The World Wide Web and Contemporary Cultural Theory.* New York: Routledge.

Taylor, Charles. 1979. What's wrong with negative liberty. In *The Idea of Freedom: Essays in Honor of Isaiah Berlin*, ed. Alan Ryan, 175–193. Oxford: Oxford University Press.

Taylor, T. L. 2006. *Play Between Worlds: Exploring Online Game Culture*. Cambridge, MA: MIT Press.

Terranova, Tiziana. 2000. Free labor: Producing culture for the digital economy. *Social Text* 18 (2):33–58.

Terranova, Tiziana. 2004. *Network Culture: Politics for the Information Age*. London: Pluto Press.

Thompson, Emily. 2002. *The Soundscape of Modernity: Architectural Acoustics and the Culture of Listening in America, 1900–1930*. Cambridge, MA: MIT Press.

Thompson, John. 2005. The new visibility. *Theory, Culture & Society* 22 (6):31–51.

Thumim, Nancy. 2012. *Self Representation and Digital Culture*. Basingstoke, UK: Palgrave Macmillan.

Thurlow, Crispin, Laura Lengel, and Alice Tomic. 2004. *Computer-Mediated Communication: Social Interaction and the Internet*. Thousand Oaks, CA: Sage.

Tolstoy, Leo. 1886. *Anna Karenina*, trans. Nathan Haskell Dole. New York: Thomas Y. Crowell and Co.

Tort, Patrick. 1989. *La Raison Classificatoire: Les Complexes Discursifs;—Quinze Etudes*. Paris: Aubier.

Tuchman, Gaye. 1972. Objectivity as strategic ritual: An examination of newsmen's notions of objectivity. *American Journal of Sociology* 77 (4):660–679.

Tufte, Edward R. 2006. *The Cognitive Style of PowerPoint: Pitching out Corrupts Within*. Cheshire, CT: Graphics Press.

Turkle, Sherry. 2007. *Evocative Objects: Things We Think With*. Cambridge, MA: MIT Press.

Turner, Fred. 2005. Where the counterculture met the new economy: The WELL and the origins of virtual community. *Technology and Culture* 46 (3):485–512.

Turner, Fred. 2006. *From Counterculture to Cyberculture: Stewart Brand, the Whole Earth Network, and the Rise of Digital Utopianism*. Chicago: University Of Chicago Press.

Turner, Fred. 2009. Burning Man at Google: A cultural infrastructure for new media production. *New Media & Society* 11 (1–2):73–94.

Turner, Fred. 2012. *The Family of Man* and the politics of attention in cold war America. *Public Culture* 24 (1):55–84.

Turow, Joseph. 2012. *The Daily You: How the New Advertising Industry Is Defining Your Identity and Your Worth*. New Haven, CT: Yale University Press.

Tushnet, Rebecca. 2008. Power without responsibility: Intermediaries and the First Amendment. *George Washington Law Review* 76 (4):986–1016.

Tykociner, Joseph T. 1971. *Outline of Zetetics*. Philadelphia: Dorrance.

Vaidhyanathan, Siva. 2001. *Copyrights and Copywrongs: The Rise of Intellectual Property and How It Threatens Creativity*. New York: New York University Press.

Vaidhyanathan, Siva. 2011. *The Googlization of Everything (And Why We Should Worry)*. Berkeley: University of California Press.

Valente, Thomas W., and Everett M. Rogers. 1995. The origins and development of the diffusion of innovations paradigm as an example of scientific growth. *Science Communication* 16 (3):242–273.

van Couvering, Elizabeth. 2007. Is relevance relevant? Market, science, and war: Discourses of search engine quality. *Journal of Computer-Mediated Communication* 12 (3). http://jcmc.indiana.edu/vol12/issue3/vancouvering.html, accessed April 22, 2013.

van Couvering, Elizabeth. 2010. "Search engine bias: The structuration of traffic on the World Wide Web." PhD diss., London School of Economics and Political Science.

van Dijck, José, and David Nieborg. 2009. Wikinomics and its discontents: A critical analysis of Web 2.0 business manifestos. *New Media & Society* 11 (5):855–874.

van Zoonen, Liesbet. 2002. Gendering the internet. *European Journal of Communication* 17 (1):5–23.

Varnelis, Kazys, ed. 2008. *Networked Publics*. Cambridge, MA: MIT Press.

Vaughan, Diane. 1997. *The Challenger Launch Decision: Risky Technology, Culture, and Deviance at NASA*. Chicago: University of Chicago Press.

Viveiros de Castro, Eduardo. 1992. *From the Enemy's Point of View: Humanity and Divinity in an Amazonian Society*. Chicago: University of Chicago Press.

Viveiros de Castro, Eduardo. 1998. Cosmological deixis and Amerindian perspectivalism. *Journal of the Royal Anthropological Institute* 4 (3):469–488.

Von Hayek, Friedrich. A. 1960. *The Constitution of Liberty*. London: Routledge and Kegan Paul.

VoxAnon. 2012. "Constitution of Voxanon @ irc.VoxAnon.net." http://anoninsiders.net/voxanon-constitution-707/, accessed April 16, 2013.

Vrba, Elisabeth S. 1994. An hypothesis of heterochrony in response to climatic cooling and its relevance to early hominid evolution. In *Integrative Paths to the Past: Paleoanthropological Advances in Honor of F. Clark Howell*, ed. R. L. Ciochon and R. S. Corruccini, 345–376. Englewood Cliffs, NJ: Prentice Hall.

Vygotsky, Lev. 1962. *Thought and Language*. Cambridge, MA: MIT Press.

Wajcman, Judy, and Paul Jones. 2012. Border communication: Media sociology and STS. *Media Culture & Society* 34 (6):673–690.

Waldrop, M. Mitchell. 2001. *The Dream Machine: J. C. R. Licklider and the Revolution That Made Computing Personal.* New York: Viking.

Walther, Joseph. 2011. Theories of computer-mediated communication and interpersonal relations. In *The Handbook of Interpersonal Communication.* 4th ed., ed. Mark Knapp and John Daly, 443–479. Thousand Oaks, CA: Sage.

Walther, Joseph, Geri Gay, and Jeffrey Hancock. 2005. How do communication and technology researchers study the Internet? *Journal of Communication* 55 (3):632–657.

Warner, Michael. 2002. Publics and counterpublics. *Public Culture* 14 (1):49–90.

Warner, William. 2005. Communicating liberty: The newspapers of the British Empire as a matrix for the American Revolution. [English Literary History] *ELH* 72 (2):339–361.

Warschauer, Mark. 2003. *Technology and Social Inclusion: Rethinking the Digital Divide.* Cambridge, MA: MIT Press.

Wasko, Janet. 1982. *Movies and Money: Financing the American Film Industry.* Norwood, NJ: Ablex.

Wasko, Janet. 2001. *Understanding Disney: The Manufacture of Fantasy.* Cambridge, UK: Polity Press.

Wasser, Frederick, and Harris Breslow. 2005. He didn't do it: Some cautions on the current McLuhan revival. In *The Legacy of McLuhan*, ed. Lance Strate and Edward Wachtel, 261–266. Cresskill, NJ: Hampton Press.

Watkins, S. Craig. 2009. *The Young and the Digital: What the Migration to Social-Network Sites, Games, and Anytime, Anywhere Media Means for Our Future.* Boston: Beacon Press.

Weber, Steven. 2004. *The Success of Open Source.* Cambridge, MA: Harvard University Press.

Wellman, Barry, and Stephen D. Berkowitz. 1988. *Social Structures: A Network Approach.* New York: Cambridge University Press.

Wexelblat, Richard. 1981. *History of Programming Languages.* New York: Academic Press.

Wheeler, James O., Yuko Aoyama, and Barney L. Warf, eds. 2000. *Cities in the Telecommunications Age: The Fracturing of Geographies.* New York: Routledge.

Williams, Raymond. 1974. *Television: Technology and Cultural Form.* London: Fontana.

Winner, Langdon. 1977. *Autonomous Technology: Technics-out-of-Control as a Theme in Political Thought*. Cambridge, MA: MIT Press.

Winner, Langdon. 1980. Do artifacts have politics? *Daedalus* 109 (1):121–136.

Winner, Langdon. 2001. Where technological determinism went. In *Visions of STS: Counterpoints in Science, Technology, and Society Studies*, ed. Stephen H. Cutcliffe and Carl Mitcham, 11–18. Albany: State University of New York Press.

Winthrop-Young, Geoffrey. 2011. *Kittler and the Media*. Cambridge, UK: Polity Press.

Woolgar, Steve. 1991. Configuring the user: The case of usability trials. In *A Sociology of Monsters: Essays on Power, Technology and Domination*, ed. John Law, 57–99. London: Routledge.

Woolgar, Steve. 1996. Technologies as cultural artifacts. In *Information and Communication Technologies: Visions and Realities*, ed. William H. Dutton, 87–102. Oxford: Oxford University Press.

Woolgar, Steve. 2002. *Virtual Society? Technology, Cyberbole, Reality*. Oxford: Oxford University Press.

Woolgar, Steve. 2004. What happened to provocation in science and technology studies? *History and Technology* 20 (4):339–349.

Woolgar, Steve, and Geoff Cooper. 1999. Do artefacts have ambivalence? Moses' bridges, Winner's bridges, and other urban legends in S&TS. *Social Studies of Science* 29 (3):433–449.

Wouters, Paul, Katie Vann, Andrea Scharnhorts, Matt Ratto, Ilina Hellsten, Jenny Fry, and Anne Beaulieu [The Virtual Knowledge Studio]. 2008. Messy shapes of knowledge: STS explores informatization, new media, and academic work. In *The Handbook of Science and Technology Studies*, 3rd ed., ed. Edward J. Hackett, Olga Amsterdamska, Michael Lynch, and Judy Wajcman, 319–351. Cambridge, MA: MIT Press.

Wright, Alex. 2007. *Glut: Mastering Information through the Ages*. Washington, DC: Joseph Henry Press.

Wu, Tim. 2003. Network neutrality, broadband discrimination. *Journal on Telecommunications & High Technology Law* 2:141–176.

Wu, Tim. 2004. The broadband debate: A user's guide. *Journal on Telecommunications & High Technology Law* 3:69–96.

Wyatt, Sally. 2008. Technological determinism is dead: long live technological determinism. In *The Handbook of Science and Technology Studies*. 3rd ed., ed. Edward J. Hackett, Olga Amsterdamska, Michael Lynch, and Judy Wajcman, 165–180. Cambridge, MA: MIT Press.

Yates, Frances. 1966. *The Art of Memory*. Chicago: University of Chicago Press.

Yates, JoAnne. 2005. *Structuring the Information Age: Life Insurance and Technology in the Twentieth Century*. Baltimore, MD: Johns Hopkins University Press.

Yates, Michael D. 2012. *Wisconsin Uprising: Labor Fights Back*. New York: Monthly Review Press.

Yau, Shing-Tung, and Steve J. Nadis. 2010. *The Shape of Inner Space: String Theory and the Geometry of the Universe's Hidden Dimensions*. New York: Basic Books.

Zielinski, Siegfried. 1996. "Media archaeology." *CTheory*. Special issue ga111. http://www.ctheory.net/articles.aspx?id=42, accessed April 22, 2013.

Zielinski, Siegfried. 2008. *Deep Time of the Media: Toward an Archaeology of Hearing and Seeing by Technical Means*, trans. Gloria Custance. Cambridge, MA: MIT Press.

Zimmer, Michael. May 9, 2007. "Google: 'Did you mean: "He invented"?'" http://www.michaelzimmer.org/2007/05/09/google-did-you-mean-he-invented/, accessed April 22, 2013.

Zimmer, Michael. 2008. The externalities of search 2.0: The emerging privacy threats when the drive for the perfect search engine meets Web 2.0. *First Monday* 13 (3). http://firstmonday.org/ojs/index.php/fm/article/view/2136/1944, accessed April 22, 2013.

Zittrain, Jonathan. 2008. *The Future of the Internet—And How to Stop It*. New Haven: Yale University Press.

Author Index

Note: italicized numbers refer to figures.

Subject Index

Note: italicized numbers refer to figures.